Is Latin America Turning Protestant?

Is Latin America Turning Protestant?

The Politics of Evangelical Growth

DAVID STOLL

UNIVERSITY OF CALIFORNIA PRESS
BERKELEY   LOS ANGELES   OXFORD

University of California Press
Berkeley and Los Angeles, California

University of California Press, Ltd.
Oxford, England

© 1990 by
The Regents of the University of California

Library of Congress Cataloging-in-Publication Data
Stoll, David.
    Is Latin America turning Protestant?:
the politics of Evangelical growth / David
Stoll.
    p. cm.
    Bibliography: p.
    ISBN 0-520-06499-2 (alk. paper)
    1. Evangelicalism—Latin America—
History—20th century. 2. Latin
America—Church history—20th century.
I. Title.
BR1642.L29S76 1990
280'.4'098—dc19   89-4790
                         CIP

Printed in the United States of America

1 2 3 4 5 6 7 8 9

Contents

List of Abbreviations

ABS	American Bible Society
AEG	Evangelical Alliance of Guatemala
AIBC	Association of Costa Rican Bible Churches
AIECH	Evangelical Indian Association of Chimborazo
AIET	Evangelical Indian Association of Tungurahua
ANPEN	National Association of Evangelical Pastors of Nicaragua
BLI	Bible Literature International
BPC	Brasil para Cristo
CAUSA	Confederation of Associations for the Unification of American Societies
CBN	Christian Broadcasting Network
CDS	Sandinista Defense Committee
CEDEN	National Evangelical Emergency Committee
CELADEC	American Evangelical Commission for Christian Education
CELEP	Latin American Center for Pastoral Studies
CEPAD	Evangelical Committee for Aid to Development
CEPRES	Evangelical Commission for the Promotion of Social Responsibility

CERT	Christian Emergency Relief Teams
CESA	Ecuadorian Agricultural Service Center
CEV	Evangelical Council of Venezuela
CLAI	Latin American Council of Churches
CLAME	Community of Latin American Evangelical Ministries
CMA	Christian and Missionary Alliance
CNPEN	National Council of Evangelical Pastors
COCIEG	Coordinating Commission of the Evangelical Church
CONELA	Latin American Evangelical Confederation
DAWN	Discipling A Whole Nation
EFMA	Evangelical Foreign Missions Association
EGP	Guerrilla Army of the Poor
FBU	Brethren and United Foundation
FDN	Nicaraguan Democratic Force
FEI	Federation of Ecuadorian Indians
FEINE	Indian Evangelical Federation of Ecuador
FSLN	Sandinista National Liberation Front
FTL	Latin American Theological Fraternity
FUNDAPI	Foundation for Aid to the Indian People
GMU	Gospel Missionary Union
IFMA	Interdenominational Foreign Mission Association
INDEPTH	Institute of In-Depth Evangelization
IRD	Institute on Religion and Democracy
ISAL	Church and Society in Latin America
LAM	Latin America Mission
LDS	Church of Jesus Christ of Latter-Day Saints
MAP	Medical Assistance Program
MARC	Missions Advanced Research Center

MCC	Mennonite Central Committee
MEC	Christian Student Movement
MICH	Indian Movement of Chimborazo
MIT	Tungurahua Indian Movement
MLN	National Liberation Movement
NACLA	North American Congress on Latin America
NAE	National Association of Evangelicals
NCC	National Council of Churches
NED	National Endowment for Democracy
NRB	National Religious Broadcasters
NTM	New Tribes Mission
O.C. Ministries	Overseas Crusades Ministries
PROCADES	Central America Socio-Religious Studies Project
PTL	"Praise the Lord"
PVO	private voluntary organization
SBC	Southern Baptist Convention
SEPAL	Servicio Evangelizador para América Latina
SIL	Summer Institute of Linguistics
TEE	Theological Education by Extension
ULAJE	Latin American Union of Evangelical Youth
UNELAM	Provisional Commission for Latin American Evangelical Unity
UNHCR	United Nations High Commissioner for Refugees
USAID	U.S. Agency for International Development
WCC	World Council of Churches
WEF	World Evangelical Fellowship
WLC	World Literature Crusade
WRC	World Relief Corporation
YWAM	Youth With A Mission

Preface

Latin America is a Catholic region, but there's no reason to assume
that this need always be so. It could become an evangelical region
at some point in time. I believe that if . . . Guatemala becomes the
first predominantly evangelical nation in Latin America, it will have
a domino effect.

Church growth planner, Overseas
Crusades Ministries, 1984[1]

Is Latin America turning Protestant? From Mexico to Argentina, forms of religion imposed by the Spanish Conquest are giving way in a far-reaching reformation. To date, attention has focused on the radical wing of the reformation, known as liberation theology. Because liberation theology is practiced mainly by Roman Catholics, it is often assumed that the reformation is being fought, by and large, within the Catholic Church. This may prove true. Despite the established church's often oppressive history in Latin America, recently it has shown a surprising capacity for reform. A large majority of Latin Americans still identify themselves as Catholic. Liberation theology seems to incarnate their hopes for a better life. In the Nicaraguan revolution, where liberation theology is so prominent, references to the impending kingdom of God crop up so often that Conor Cruise O'Brien has called it "a potential Geneva."[2]

But what about the churches descended from the old Geneva, of John Calvin and the Reformation in Europe? What about the evangelical Protestants of Latin America? Owing to the influence of North American missionaries, usually quite conservative politically, it is easier to see how Latin American evangelicals maintain the status quo than how they change it. In all but religion they seem dedicated less to protest than to conformity, less makers of revolutions than products of failed ones. In Latin America, it is easy to conclude, the role that Protestants played in the European Reformation has passed to radical Catholics.

As the Catholic Church counts its martyrs, however, Latin Americans are abandoning it at an accelerating rate. One bishop in Brazil has warned that Latin America is turning Protestant faster than Central Europe did in the sixteenth century.[3] A seemingly insignificant movement before World War II now includes 10 to 20 percent of the population in Brazil, Chile, and Central America, and is growing rapidly elsewhere as well.

Despite this success, evangelicals continue to be an anomaly in the interpretation of Latin American religious life. It is now widely accepted that religion is not just the opiate of the people but their hope for a better world, not just an impediment to social protest but a form of it. Yet in Latin America, this insight is rarely extended to evangelicals. It is easy to see why. In a traditionally Catholic region, evangelicals insist on breaking with Catholic mores. Downplaying the structural issues that Catholics raise, evangelicals insist that the only genuine revolution in Latin America will be spiritual. Despite their seeming indifference to oppression, they succeed in attracting millions of poor people from a Catholic Church which seems far more socially conscious. They also succeed in organizing vital, enduring local groups where Marxists have failed. Their churches flourish amidst the survivors of crushed radical movements, and they do so with generous support from the United States. As a result, they remain on the fringes in most assessments of the politics of religion in Latin America, ignored except to be denounced.

Lately those denunciations have been increasing. Alarm over evangelicals in Latin America is nothing new, but in the 1980s it spread, especially through the Catholic Church and the left. Numerous Latin Americans assume that North American money is responsible for the multiplication of evangelical churches. They further suspect that the U.S. government is using evangelicals to further its own interests. Only that kind of manipulation, opponents argue, can explain how evangelicals are able to disrupt the efforts of the left and the Catholic Church to organize the poor. Instead of an instance of popular struggle, according to this logic, religious movements incorporating tens of millions of Latin Americans become the negation of that struggle, a conspiracy designed to frustrate it.

I will argue that such explanations are inadequate. But the fears they reflect are well founded, especially now that the Reagan administration has remilitarized U.S. policy toward Latin America. Ironically, many evangelicals feel threatened by the same turn of events. Toward the end of the Vietnam War, as evangelical dissidents criticized the North American mission establishment, the latter put a certain distance between itself and U.S. foreign policy. But at home, the impulses behind global evangelism were also driving the religious right and Reaganism. Soon right-wing political activists were joining the missionary effort in Latin America, where they combined a burning desire to win the world for Christ with visions of enlarging North American hegemony.

These two very different challenges to evangelical Christianity, from partisans and opponents of North American expansion, inspired this work. For readers alarmed by evangelical growth, I want to provide a sense of its open-ended nature. For evangelicals, I wish to dramatize the danger of allowing their missions to be harnessed to U.S. militarism by the religious right. Although stressing that evangelical Protestantism must be understood from the ground up, as a popular movement, I want to emphasize the clear and present danger that it is being manipulated by the U. S. government.

Focusing on the politics of religion can create the impression that churches are a plaything for political forces. Certainly any spiritual claim can be interpreted in terms of functions such as legitimation, compensation, or protest.[4] Yet churches do not represent political interests in monolithic, unchanging ways; instead, they often serve as arenas for competing forces. As for religious experience, it has a dynamic of its own which can shape political loyalties as well as be shaped by them.* If religious commitments are dismissed as mere

*"There are no objective interests that a church is compelled to pursue," Scott Mainwaring has observed of the Catholic Church in Brazil. "Within the Church there are many conflicting views of the institution's true interests and how to pursue them. . . . Change within the Church results from the struggles of groups

reflections of political interests, we lose sight of the new and creative responses they produce.

I make these observations to underline a specific point. Just as religion should not be reduced to a playing field for contending political forces, evangelical Protestantism should not be reduced to a political instrument for dominant interests. This is important because, under the influence of Catholic and Marxist thinking, many observers have come to assume that evangelical religion has easily predictable political implications. Throughout what follows, I hope to provide a different picture of Latin American Protestantism, as a generator of social change whose direction is not predestined.

With this in mind, the first chapter looks at the dimensions of evangelical growth and the reactions to it. I argue that polemics against the "invasion of the sects" have tended to obscure a fact of great significance, the emergence of debates among evangelicals over how to respond to the social and economic crises swelling their congregations.

Catholic commentators tend to attribute evangelical gains to external agents, especially North American evangelists and money. But blaming evangelical growth on the United States suggests a deep distrust of the poor, an unwillingness to accept the possibility that they could turn an imported religion to their own purposes. In keeping with this realization, some Catholic observers stress how weaknesses in their own church have contributed to Protestantism.

Following the same line of thought, the second chapter explores how evangelical growth has been encouraged by Catholic clericalism. Owing to the centralized nature of authority in the Catholic Church, I argue, dissident members tend to leave the system. Dissident evangelicals, in contrast, can always join another congregation and remain evangelical. At a time when a paternalistic social order is breaking down, placing a new premium on individual initiative, it is not hard to see which system will be favored. What has

---

with different conceptions of faith, not from the institution's attempts to protect interests agreed on by the conflicting factions. In the Brazilian Church, the crucial debate is not how to further the Church's interests, but rather what its mission should be. . . . Religion can be a powerful force in determining political orientation, frequently even more powerful than class" (Mainwaring 1986: 5, 7, 12).

flung open Latin America to evangelical Protestantism, the second chapter suggests, is the Catholic Church's inability to decentralize its system of authority.

The third chapter turns to the United States and its support base for Protestant missions. To avoid generalizing about evangelicals, I differentiate them in terms of organization, theology, and politics. The chapter then focuses on the religious right and an ominous shift in rationales for missionary work. In contrast to the old fundamentalist warning that the end is near, the religious right is promising to "take dominion" over the earth, in a theocratic vision reviving confusion between Christian mission and North American empire.

Despite the resurgence of equations between God and the United States, some evangelicals have been challenging the way their missions operate. They accuse North American "mission multinationals" of pursuing their own agendas at the expense of Third World churches. The fourth chapter delves into this internal debate. All involved agree that Protestantism is not the cultural implant it once was, however. With few exceptions, Latin Americans now run their own churches.

That transformation is the subject of the fifth chapter, on the evangelical awakening in the region. As Protestant churches become more Latin American, unfortunately, many have become more authoritarian and mystical, with leaders who remain under the spell of ever more reactionary North American mentors. Meanwhile, most Latin American evangelicals continue to live in poverty. Unlike early converts who enjoyed the possibility of upward mobility, often improving their position within a single generation, these Christians face the mounting hardships of austerity and depression in debt-ridden, inflated economies. The two countervailing pulls, from North America's religious right and from Latin America's debt crisis, are encouraging unprecedented polarization among evangelicals.

The sixth chapter is dedicated to this struggle, between evangelicals who view their churches as a mighty fortress against upheaval, and those who hope to incorporate the social dimension of the Bible into the salvation their churches preach. By launching a reformation within the reformation, the latter group, theologically but not politically conservative, could show the way to a crucial meeting ground, one that is hard to visualize at present but could change two antagonists almost beyond recognition. I refer to an encounter between Latin America's most successful churches and its most innovative theologians, between evangelical Protestantism and liberation theology.

This work cannot predict the outcome of contests between different conceptions of the kingdom of God. Nor does it announce the Protestant conquest of Latin America. At present, it is clear only that evangelical Protestantism needs to be weighed side by side with the various currents in the Catholic Church. How the Latin American reformation will fare and which tendency will predominate are open questions. But to answer them I hope to take a first step. It is to raise the possibility that liberation theology has been overemphasized as the vanguard of religious reformation in Latin America. To suggest why, three case studies look at collisions between liberation theology and evangelical Protestantism.

The first, Chapter 7, takes up the 1982–1983 rule of an evangelical army general in Guatemala, Efraín Ríos Montt. Confronting a revolutionary movement supported by part of the Catholic Church, he waged a devastating counterinsurgency with Bible in hand. Since then, in parts of the western highlands, evangelical churches seem to have become the dominant religion.*

The second case, Chapter 8, looks at the conflict between liberation theology and conservative Protestantism in Sandinista Nicaragua. Nicaraguan evangelicals have paid dearly for the Sandinista-Contra war, caught between their revolutionary government and a U.S. administration using their religion to wage counterrevolution. Even if the Sandinistas remain in power, the hardships of defending the revolution from the United States suggest that conservatives who oppose the Sandinistas may have a brighter future than evangelicals who identify strongly with them.

The third case study, Chapter 9, looks at the controversies over the largest of the evangelical relief and development agencies, World Vision. As evangelicals display more interest in social issues, Catholic activists in Ecuador view World Vision's well-financed programs as an attempt to coopt their own efforts to organize Quichua Indians. Judging from the impact of World Vision on a Catholic dio-

*An abridged version of Chapter 7 appeared in *Harvest of Violence: The Maya Indians and the Guatemalan Crisis*, ed. Robert M. Carmack (Norman: University of Oklahoma Press, 1988).

cese famous for its social activism, a generous budget makes more of an impression on the poor than consciousness-raising.

These are pessimistic assessments of liberation theology, perhaps too pessimistic. But even if they are correct, many signs suggest that evangelical leaders are being forced to deal with some of the issues posed by their great ideological rival, issues that until recently they were able to ignore. The basic problem they face is the following: now that poor Latin Americans are flocking to evangelical churches for help in their struggle for survival, what will converts do if their income continues to deteriorate? As churches incorporate more and more of the poor, they may be forced to deal with the economic and social crisis fueling their growth. This is the challenge which makes Protestantism in Latin America an open-ended proposition. In the concluding chapter, therefore, I take a final look at the contest between evangelical Protestantism and liberation theology, as well as the still hazy prospects for a Protestant-based social reformation in Latin America.

This is an ambitious agenda, so perhaps I should confess how it originated, in front of a television set. The year was 1984: a paragon of the religious right was excoriating an evangelical mission for failing to join the Reagan administration's war on the Sandinistas. Ironically, while few Latin Americans knew of broadcaster Pat Robertson's support for the contras, many more Latin Americans suspected the agency he was attacking—World Vision—of being a CIA front. It occurred to me that important changes in Latin American Protestantism, such as the arrival of the religious right and the resistance to it by other evangelicals, were not being given the attention they deserved in the press or in scholarship. We were getting only pieces of the larger picture, usually in the form of polemics. With so many conflicting representations at work, I decided to play them against each other, in the hope of arriving at some kind of epiphany.

Three years earlier, I had completed a similar exercise on the subject of the Wycliffe Bible Translators, a U.S.-based mission which appears from time to time in the pages that follow. During visits to Guatemala, Nicaragua, and Ecuador from 1982 to 1984, I became acquainted with the various controversies—over a born-again dictator accused of genocide, a revolutionary government accused of persecuting Christians, and an evangelical relief agency accused of imperialism—which became the case studies. Following the decision to use the three for a wider look at evangelical gains, in May 1985, I undertook a four-month tour of Ecuador, Peru, Costa Rica, Nicaragua, Guatemala, and Mexico to interview evangelical leaders about the increasingly visible conflicts in their churches. What follows is based on those interviews, my previous experience with the mission scene, and a range of literature from sacred to profane.

What follows does not, it should be emphasized, provide encyclopedic coverage of the enormous number of evangelical bodies. Although I have tried to include the more well-known and controversial, readers may find groups of particular interest missing.[5] Nor does the book provide equal time for the various regions of Latin America. The three case studies were not chosen because the countries in which they occur—Guatemala, Nicaragua, and Ecuador—have the most evangelicals or are the most representative. They are the result of the author's attraction to religious uproars which, to his satisfaction, throw certain kinds of conflicts into high relief. For opportunistic reasons, therefore, Central America receives more attention than South America. But I do discuss the huge pentecostal churches of Brazil and Chile, as well as an instance of Catholic-Protestant competition in the least evangelical part of the continent, the Andes. I hope the cases resonate beyond their boundaries, to say something about the prospects for Protestantism all over Latin America.

A final omission stems from the impossibility of thanking everyone who helped me. You know who you are: soon you will know whether you regret coming to my rescue. But I wish to thank Brian O'Connell, Greg Starrett, Mary Crain, Lynel Horn, Barry Lyons, Viola Larson, John Stam, Dennis Smith, Thomas Scheetz, Robert Carmack, Sharon Philipps, Kamala Visweswaran, Andrés Fajardo, and Charlie Hale for commenting on parts of the manuscript. David Scotchmer, Santiago Tribout, and Gonzalo Hallo took special pains in this regard. Readers for various university presses, including Simon Collier, Richard N. Adams, Kent R. Hill and two anonymous readers for the University of California, were also very helpful. None should be held responsible for anything that follows because I did not always follow their advice. Thanks is also due the

Stanford Department of Anthropology, for looking the other way as I expended energies that might have been directed at my program.

Unfortunately, the political situation makes it advisable to protect the identity of most of the Latin Americans who helped me. Hence the unattributed sources in the notes, especially in the chapters on Guatemala and Nicaragua. But I wish to express my special gratitude to these people—Catholic and Protestant, leaders and dissenters, to the left and to the right. Some of them consented to be interviewed at a certain risk to themselves. Although they will no doubt disagree with positions taken in this book, it is dedicated to them and their struggle to love one another.

Chapter One

The Invasion of the Sects
in Latin America

From the house across the street, the rhythmic blows of tambour-
ines and the sound of hallelujahs. Shouts to the sky, the ecstasy of
a new Pentecost. On the bus, an itinerant vendor of eternal truths.
A fistful of incense or a pamphlet of revelations in exchange for
some coins. Next to a handsome new temple, a gringo and his local
colleague dressed in suits are in search of saints for the "latter
days." At the door, two preachers with a copy of Watchtower *and a*
chat if you have the time.

The radio in the hut high in the mountains, a Luis Palau crusade,
conquering the countryside in Christ's name. Laminated roofs on
the horizon, rural children with foreign godparents. Small air-
planes landing in a North American stronghold in the middle of the
Amazon Jungle. On the television, the seductive voices of Jimmy
Swaggart or Pat Robertson, electronic messages of salvation for a
lost modern world. Colorful tents, not of circuses but of evangelical
campaigns. A meeting of the redeemed in the Model Stadium, the
final showdown between Good and Evil.

The newspapers and magazines show signs of alarm: "invasion of
the sects," "cultural penetration," "evangelical explosion," "religious
contest in the nation," "new imperialist strategy." Worry. Confusion.
What is happening?

Thomas Bamat, 1986[1]

What if, after all the pain and hopelessness, there was a spiritual
solution to Latin America's problems? Luis Palau, the Argentine
evangelist, thought so. That was why he came to Guatemala in November 1982, to help evangelicals celebrate the hundredth anniversary of Protestantism there. The eyes of all Latin America were
on Guatemala, he told the huge crowd at a parade ground in the
capital. They could make it the first reformed nation in Latin America, a country where the word of God captivated so many military

officers and businessmen that it brought about a social and political transformation. The gospel could liberate Guatemalans from the chains of sin, Palau went on, and it could liberate them from the chains of poverty, misery, and oppression. Through the gospel of Jesus Christ, the evangelist promised, the new man could build a new Guatemala.

It was a sunny day, almost hot down on the crowded field, and the multitude cheered. The organizers had predicted that half a million people would show up. Afterward, they claimed that three quarters of a million did.[2] At the rear, soldiers in jungle fatigues lounged about the walls of a grim medieval-like structure, the old Polytechnic School for military officers, in the bowels of which "disappeared" political prisoners were said to be held in clandestine cells.[3]

But Luis Palau was not going to enter into debates about the current political situation: his message was spiritual. Besides, the president of the country was standing there beside him. "Here the one in charge is Jesus Christ," declared Efraín Ríos Montt, an army general who had seized power eight months before. The tone of his voice was harsh, almost belligerent, but hallelujahs rose from the crowd below. "We defend ourselves not by the army or its swords," he proclaimed, referring to the most successful counterinsurgency force in Central America, "but by the Holy Spirit."[4]

What Latin America lacked, the two men felt, was evangelical Protestantism. Only a mass conversion along these lines, a moral transformation at the popular level, Palau and Ríos Montt believed, could save Latin America from poverty and chaos.

"Some offer volunteer services," Palau was accustomed to state. "Others push Marxist revolutions. But the only way to truly change a nation for the better is to lead masses of people at the grass roots level to commit their lives to Jesus Christ.

"If we could eliminate infidelity and immorality in Latin America," Palau reasoned, "we could cut poverty by half in one generation. . . . If a man gives up immorality with women, gives up getting drunk and all the waste . . . that goes with it, and stops gambling, right there he is salvaging a big chunk of his salary. . . .

"The vast middle class now emerging [in Latin American Protestantism] was converted poor and rose through industry, honesty and justice to the educated, reasonable lifestyle that is commonly called the middle class. I think that's the biblical answer. . . .

"Consider the countries where you needn't fear secret police, where you can expect justice under the law, where the military is under the guidance of the people rather than oppressing them, where education is valued, where the press is relatively free," Palau said. "Almost all such nations have experienced spiritual awakenings touching society at the local level."[5]

Four months later, Pope John Paul II stood on the same spot and celebrated mass. He did not refer directly to the previous assembly, which his own organizers had vowed to surpass.[6] The crowd was indeed somewhat larger. But when the pope called upon the people to hew to their faith, one reason was that the Roman Catholic Church was losing ground to evangelical Protestants on many fronts. It could no longer claim Latin America as its own. The traditional religious monopoly was giving way. Part of that reformation was occurring within Catholic churches dating to the Spanish Conquest, but much of it was taking place outside.

Typologies, Growth Rates, and Variation by Country

Dealing with Protestantism on the level of all Latin America is an undertaking that secular scholars generally have avoided. In breaking with this tradition, I should acknowledge various difficulties of classification and quantification before going further. When scholars take on Roman Catholicism, they have the convenience of beginning with "the Church," even if this turns out to be something of a fiction. There is a single administrative hierarchy, in any case. My subject is not a church, in contrast, and those who refer to it as such are projecting considerable optimism into a confusing panorama. Instead, evangelical Protestantism is best defined as a tradition distinguished by three beliefs, including (1) the complete reliability and final authority of the Bible, (2) the need to be saved through a personal relation with Jesus Christ, often experienced in terms of being "born again," and (3) the importance of spreading this message of salvation to every nation and person, a duty often referred to as the Great Commission.

Another complication is that, although most of the vocabulary of Latin American Protestantism comes via the United States, it acquires different shades of meaning in its new home. Understanding the distinctions which have arisen is sufficiently important to be left to the third chapter. For now, let it suffice that, while in the United States "evangelical" connotes a theological conservative who emphasizes the Bible, personal salvation, and evangelism, in Latin America *evangélico* can refer to any non-Catholic Christian. The term includes the Mormons and Jehovah's Witnesses, whom most evangelicals regard as false sects, as well as Protestants whose exegesis is unsuitably liberal. In Latin American style, here "evangelical" will be an umbrella term referring to anyone who could conceivably be construed as such. In the same general way I will use the less common *protestante*, sometimes adding the qualifier "ecumenical" or "liberal" to refer to those Protestants, usually affiliated with the World Council of Churches, whose disinterest in saving souls places them outside the evangelical camp strictly defined.

"Fundamentalist," in contrast, seems to have translated without a hitch. As a term of opprobrium, it connotes doctrinal rigidity and is employed, somewhat promiscuously, against any Protestant inclined to quote Scripture as his or her final authority. When used with more precision, it refers to conservative Protestants who show more concern for defending the purity of their churches ("the fundamentals") than for enlarging them ("evangelizing," after the original Greek for "bringing good news"). As we shall see in the third chapter, an agile Christian can manipulate the terms "fundamentalist" and "evangelical" to present different faces to different constituencies, but the two also express deep conflicts within the evangelical tradition. The term "pentecostal" is another important dividing line: it refers to ecstatic forms of Protestantism defined in terms of special gifts bestowed by the Holy Spirit. Whereas only a minority of North American missionaries are pentecostal, most Latin American evangelicals are.

Typologies of the evangelical scene in Latin America carry agendas I would prefer to avoid. Perhaps the easiest to resort to, and also the most misleading, is by denomination. The well-known church traditions—Lutheran, Anglican, Reformed, Presbyterian, Baptist, Methodist, Moravian—emerged during the Reformation in Europe, its aftermath, or on the North American frontier. Although Protestants are still organized into denominations (or into sects resisting the slide into the established routines of denominational life), these entities have long since polarized along theological and political lines which crosscut their formal boundaries. Baptists tend to be stereotyped as fundamentalists, for example, but some of their churches have become quite liberal. Presbyterians have acquired a middle-of-the-road reputation, and some are flaming liberals; but it is less appreciated that much of the intellectual elite of fundamentalism has been Presbyterian.

Another way to characterize Latin American Protestantism is in terms of successive "waves" of arrival, including (1) the churches of European immigrants, such as German Lutherans in Brazil, (2) the "historical" or "mainline" denominations, (3) the fundamentalist "faith missions," and (4) the pentecostals. While a useful distinction, this too can quickly lead to misleading inferences. The Latin America Mission arrived as part of the fundamentalist wave, for example, but has come to encourage a more open and socially responsible theology. The Presbyterian Church of Brazil is a "historical" denomination which, in the 1960s, reacted sharply against the kind of thinking the Latin America Mission was starting to promote.

As for crosscutting political tendencies, these are constantly evolving. In the early 1970s, the Argentine theologian José Miguez Bonino identified three, including (1) evangelicals professing to turn their back on politics, (2) "liberals" working for reform within the capitalist system, and (3) "revolutionaries" calling for radical transformation.[7] Since then, parts of the "apolitical" camp have aligned with the North American religious right; many liberals have become distinctly less liberal; revolutionaries have lost most of whatever constituency they could claim; and a new current of theologically but not politically conservative evangelicals has emerged. Looking at Latin American Protestantism through a fifteen-year-old typology tends to inflate the importance of the left and minimize growing political differences among theological conservatives.

One of the most common terms used against evangelicals— sect—also has unsatisfactory implications. When journalists, politicians, and Catholic authorities issue warnings against the invasion of the sects, they tend to be accusing new groups of fanaticism, exonerating opponents from responsibility for the latest head-

bashing, and stigmatizing evangelicals across the board. Techni-
cally, according to the sociologist Bryan Wilson, sects are groups
that conceive of themselves as an elect, apply rigorous standards to
those seeking admission, and demand an overriding allegiance to a
higher truth. Although sects offend traditional religious authorities
and sometimes neighbors, their internal discipline often turns
members into model citizens. Within a generation or two, as converts become outnumbered by children and grandchildren born
into the sect, enthusiasm tends to cool, and the group takes on the
attributes of an established church.[8] Needless to say, Latin Americans who feel afflicted by a neighboring group of religious enthusiasts cannot be expected to take such a comfortable long-term view.

Even if a certain amount of classificatory imprecision can be for-
given, another inhibition to discussing Protestantism on the level
of Latin America is the lack of reliable quantification. According to
those who dare to make estimates, non-Catholic Christians have
grown to 10 percent or more of the Latin American population in
the 1980s, or upward of forty million people.[9] This may not sound
like an impressive percentage. But so many Latin Americans are
Catholic in name only that, except where unusually loyal to their
clergy, the majority of consistent churchgoers appear to be evangelicals. In Brazil, as long ago as 1973 the newspaper *Estado de São
Paulo* argued that there were more "real" Protestants in the country
(ten million) than "real" Catholics. The thirteen thousand Catholic
priests in Brazil were said to be outnumbered by seventeen thousand ordained Protestant pastors and thirteen thousand nonor-
dained ones.[10]

Most figures in circulation are the work of evangelical mission
strategists known collectively as the "church-growth movement."
Although not to be dismissed, they calculate rates of increase and
how to maximize them with the enthusiasm of investors pursuing
compound interest. Their work is also hedged about with the usual
uncertainties, of counting heads among ill-defined populations and
specifying religious loyalties. Estimates of the Protestant percentage of the population for each country are included in Appendix 1:
the sometimes wild differences between the three evangelical
sources should be considered a function of different methodologies,
not of growth from one year of data collection to the next.

The task of calculating evangelical growth, then comparing it

from country to country and period to period, is even more impres-
sionistic. If calibrated against the volume of complaint, evangelical
Protestantism is growing rapidly just about everywhere. A more
varied picture is suggested by evangelical missionaries, a compendium of whose reports has been published by Patrick Johnstone of
the Worldwide Evangelization Crusade.

Some of the lowest percentages of evangelical population continue to be in the Andean countries—Venezuela (in the 1 to 3 percent range), Colombia (1 to 4 percent), Ecuador (2 to 4 percent),
Peru (3 to 5 percent), and Bolivia (2 to 8 percent)—where Protestantism had a slow and difficult start. But since 1960 evangelical
churches have grown rapidly, at some of the highest rates in Latin
America, and the pleasure of evangelical prognosticators is
matched by the level of alarm from opponents, among the most
vociferous in the region. Expectations are also high in another
evangelical backwater, Paraguay (in the 2 to 4 percent range).

A suprisingly low percentage of evangelical population is in Mexico (in the 2 to 5 percent range), despite proximity to the United
States or perhaps because of it. One possible explanation is ease of
migration across the Rio Grande, as an alternative outlet for the
energies directed into Protestantism; another is national feeling
against North American influence. In any case, although evangelical growth has been dramatic in some parts of the country, such as
the northern border, Tabasco, and Chiapas, there are also prominent bare spots including the capital, and the country as a whole is
a bulwark of disinterest.

Argentina is another of the "big five" countries in terms of absolute Protestant population (see Appendix 2). Like Mexico, however, it is not a leader in terms of the percentage of total population.
Despite many an impressive revival, evangelicals number only in
the 3 to 7 percent range. Especially since the unfortunate Malvinas
War with Britain, certain evangelists have reported huge successes.
But historically, according to the Worldwide Evangelization Crusade, mass conversions have not resulted in as much church growth
as expected, owing to a high rate of backsliding. Uruguay (in the 2
to 5 percent range) is another country about which missionaries
express dissatisfaction: here the problem is described as spiritual
apathy.

The greatest embarrassment for evangelicals are former English and Dutch colonies of the Caribbean—Jamaica, the Bahamas, Belize, Barbados, Suriname, and Guyana—where nineteenth- and early twentieth-century revivals produced large Protestant populations, even majorities. But spiritual fires have dimmed in the established churches, whose members' declining commitment wipes out the gains being made by newer, more sectarian groups. Cuba is another disappointment: following the exodus of many pastors and believers to Florida after the 1959 revolution, recovery has been slow. But Caribbean evangelicals are growing rapidly in the other traditionally Catholic countries—the Dominican Republic (in the 2 to 7 percent range), Haiti (15 to 20 percent), and Puerto Rico (7 to 30 percent).

On the Latin American mainland, the two most evangelical countries until recently were Brazil, where Protestants claim as much as 18 percent of the population, and Chile, where they claim as much as 25 percent. Judging from the figures in Appendix 2, Brazil's twenty-two million evangelicals account for three of every five evangelicals in Latin America and the Caribbean. Together with their brethren in Chile, they add up to two of every three. Because the two countries account for 40 percent of the Latin American population, the rapid growth of their Protestants weighs a great deal in the aggregate. In Chile the rate of increase has slackened, but in Brazil, according to the Worldwide Evangelization Crusade, it is still "astonishing." From 1960 to 1970 evangelical growth was 77 percent; from 1970 to 1980 it was 155 percent.[11]

What makes evangelical gains noteworthy is not a mere increase in absolute terms. High Latin American birthrates could, after all, double the number of Protestants every twenty years without changing the proportion in the larger population. What is astonishing is the increasing presence of evangelicals as a percentage of total population, from the smallest of beginnings early in the century. According to the above-cited compendium of the Worldwide Evangelization Crusade (see Appendix 3), since 1960 evangelicals have approximately doubled their proportion of the population in the Southern Cone countries of Chile and Paraguay, Venezuela, and the Caribbean countries of Panama and Haiti. According to the same source, evangelicals have approximately tripled their proportion of the population since 1960 in Argentina, Nicaragua, and the Dominican Republic. In Brazil and Puerto Rico, the evangelical proportion has almost quadrupled since 1960. In two Central American countries, El Salvador and Costa Rica, as well as in two Andean countries, Peru and Bolivia, the evangelical proportion during the same period supposedly has quintupled. In two other Andean countries, Ecuador and Colombia, as well as in Honduras, it is supposed to have sextupled. And in Guatemala, the evangelical proportion of the population from 1960 to 1985 is supposed to have increased nearly seven times. If for rhetorical purposes we extrapolate the same growth rates from 1960 to 1985 for another twenty-five years, to 2010, Brazil becomes 57 percent, Puerto Rico 75 percent, and Guatemala 127 percent evangelical.[12]

In view of such spectacular numbers, it bears repeating that church growth estimates have to be approached with great caution. But if anything like these gains is occurring, as observers from different perspectives seem increasingly inclined to agree, then they have the potential to turn the religious landscape inside out. That was how it looked in Central America, anyway. By 1984, according to a spokesman for the most venerable evangelical mission to the region, 3.3 of the 21.9 million people from Guatemala to Costa Rica, or 15 percent of the population, considered themselves evangelical. If they continued to grow at the estimated rate of 13.4 percent per year, according to the same source, the figure could double to nearly one-third of the population by the late 1980s. In El Salvador, so many Catholics were converting to Protestantism that evangelicals could be a majority by 1994. In Guatemala, evangelical leaders claimed to represent nearly one-quarter of the country and hoped to have one-half by 1990.[13]

Wherever it occurs, evangelical growth varies according to rural/urban, regional, ethnic, and class factors which it is not my purpose to explore systematically.[14] What follows is not a synthesis of scholarship on the subject. It is not a sociology of Latin American Protestantism, a regional tour of church growth trends, or an attempt to sharpen up the numbers. Instead, I want to consider evangelical growth as given in order to put certain issues on the table.

In the first place, I focus on the efforts of the religious right to turn evangelical missions into an instrument for militaristic U.S. policies. For those who believe that evangelicals have always been an instrument of Washington, this may seem an unnecessary exercise. But I will argue that the religious right does in fact represent a departure, a new stage in the politicization of missionary work, which threatens not just Catholics and the godless but evangelicals themselves. Understanding that threat will underline the contradictory directions in which evangelicals are moving.

Second, I want to suggest that viewing liberation theology as the key to religious and social reformation in Latin America may be a mistake, that conversion to evangelical Protestantism may be the single most popular religious option in the region, and that continuation of this trend could fundamentally alter the religious landscape of Latin America. I further suggest the possibility, if only a dim one, that from this religious transformation could emerge a social vision with the potential to alter Latin America's cultural, moral, and political landscape as well.

Admittedly, this is a reckless argument. But in view of recent events, I think it should be laid out, if only to be refuted and laid to rest. The remainder of the first chapter is dedicated to a more modest task: to suggest how the polemics against evangelicals have obscured growing debates among them, over their future course.

Disaster Evangelism

Since the sixteenth century, Anglo Protestants and Latin Catholics have contended for political and cultural supremacy in the New World. To avoid perpetuating that struggle, in the early 1900s European Protestants refused to classify Latin America as a mission field. As a result, the North American contribution there has swelled to unusual proportions, to most of the Protestant mission force. With countries closing across Asia, more North American Protestant missionaries have located in Latin America—11,196 by 1985—than in any other part of the globe. One-third are concentrated among less than 10 percent of the world's population.[15]

Given such a preponderance, the wish of North American missionaries to transform Latin America can be hard to separate from the fact that their country dominates it. This is not the place to dwell upon the contemporary ruin: the debts to foreign banks driving entire countries into bankruptcy, the North American demand for cocaine keeping several economies afloat, the U.S.-trained militaries that dominate political life even under civilian administration. This is a Latin America without revolutions, at least economically successful ones, yet capitalism is changing it beyond recognition. The population streams into vast, dreary cities, where it burgeons with little hope of a better future. Behind those cities, in the hinterlands, brutal civil wars drag on year after year. Long lines of visa-seekers snake around U.S. embassies. Millions from all classes flee to the north, where so many destructive pressures on their countries originate.

When evangelists say that the secret of North American prosperity is its Protestant heritage, many Latin Americans are therefore willing to listen. The missions are well aware of the relation between social stress, the resources at their disposal to alleviate it, and interest in their religion. "We cannot fail to recognize the impact of this suffering," one missionary observed. "We pray that God will spare us from that kind of church growth strategy, but as the clouds gather on the horizon, we must prepare ourselves for a great harvest in times of acute suffering." [16] "One possible conclusion," a Brethren in Christ missionary summed up reluctantly, surveying the wreckage of Sandinista Nicaragua, "if you want church growth, pray for economic and political devastation." [17] "When there is any kind of trauma," an Overseas Crusades official stated, "that is when we need to rush resources in." [18]

Whether they like it or not, these groups are engaged in what can be called disaster evangelism. Drawn to wars and natural catastrophes, evangelists hand out food, set up medical clinics, help rebuild communities, and train leaders to start churches. The first occasion on which the modus operandi came to wide attention was the 1976 earthquake in Guatemala. When the earthquake tumbled the seemingly secure adobe walls of Mayan Indian towns, it took tens of thousands of lives and also shook the confidence of survivors in their old ways. Helping them pick their way out of the rubble was the now familiar legion of evangelists.

During that time, a graduate student named Sheldon Annis found himself traveling with a member of the Central American Mission. "In a remote, earthquake-ruined Guatemalan village," Annis wrote, "Edgardo Robinson [not his real name] is an imposing, even a commanding figure. He travels in a powerful new Bronco. He speaks robust and fluent Cakchiquel. He is eight or so inches taller than almost any village male. And he has the smouldering eyes—maybe the lunatic eyes—of a biblical prophet. In a land of earthquakes and violence, he is a man of the times.

"Politely but with no great interest, Edgardo listened to what I proposed to investigate. . . . I was especially interested in the semiotics of handweaving, and with considerable curiosity, asked how he would pursue such questions.

"'Look around you,' he said irritably, dismissing the abstract with the rubble around us. 'Do you want to talk to these people? Do you want to know how to get their attention? The way to get an Indian's attention is not these things you're asking, but to talk to him about God.'

"Edgardo knows how to talk to Indians about God. This is how he does it. First, he pulls into the marketplace, smiling at acquaintances and warmly greeting friends as he hops out of his vehicle. He strides to a spot—just the right spot—in front of the crumbled wreckage of the Catholic church. A circle gathers as he kneels in silent, personal prayer. . . .

"Slowly, then more visibly, the prophet's body starts to tremble. Clutching a worn bible, his hand raises skyward. His body struggles with itself. . . . He is on his feet, beginning to preach. His voice grows louder, the Bible slicing the air. 'Look at this earthquake, your lives, your sin; look at the destruction,' he cries. He rolls on and on, preaching of Christ's love and the war with Satan. Sweat rolls down his forehead. Finally, as his hoarse voice begins to calm, he leads the circle in song and prayer. Then he goes off to discuss the reconstruction of the two toppled evangelical churches."[19]

The Guatemalan quake seemed to confirm the advantages of relief and development work. Evangelical growth increased from 8 percent a year before the catastrophe to 14 percent after it.[20] Because relief work is so prominent in disaster evangelism, Latin Americans often complain that evangelicals are "buying" converts. When material benefits open a heart to the gospel, it stands to reason that they figure in the convert's motives. Ironically, no one is more displeased by the resulting beggar mentality than missionaries, who are soon agonizing over how to outwit it.

Even if North American money has been important at certain junctures, it is far from the complete explanation. If evangelical churches were really built on handouts, as opponents suggest, then they would be spiritless patronage structures, not the vital expressions that so many of them are. Where evangelical churches are successful, they proliferate far beyond the buying power of mission subsidies. With little or no training and without financial backing, people equipped with little more than Bibles are starting their own churches, beginning with their families and neighbors, then proselytizing vigorously for enough followers to make a living.

The two best known sociologists of Protestantism in Latin America, Christian Lalive d'Epinay and Emilio Willems, discovered that interest in evangelical Protestantism was related to how uprooted the population was. Recent migrants to cities and colonizers of frontier areas were the most receptive. The least receptive were those living under the old hacienda regime.[21] For people whose lives have been wrenched apart by war, capitalism, or ecological failure—those struggling to survive in the face of bureaucratic indifference, regrouping in shanty towns on the edge of cities, or colonizing marginal land—evangelical religion provides a new kind of social group.

Once understood what such groups can do for the poor, the appropriate question seems, not why many people convert, but why more do not. One of the most common effects of conversion is to put households on a more stable basis, by overcoming male addiction to alcohol, reining in male sexual license, and establishing church authorities as a sort of appellate court for aggrieved women.[22] For evangelicals moving from the countryside to the city, church networks serve as referral agencies and safety nets.[23] But born-again religion is not just a utilitarian exercise in which the disadvantaged adapt to capitalist development by organizing themselves into benefit societies. Evangelical churches are a new form of social organization with a powerful logic of their own. Something of that power is suggested by the prominence of a seemingly irrational and fruitless exercise—faith healing—as a path to conversion in Latin America. By appealing to the deepest needs of people, evangelical churches help them redefine themselves, reorganize their lives, and move in dramatic new directions.

So Close to God and the United States

Judging from the large numbers converting to evangelical churches, these were popular movements. Some of their leaders spoke of leading a reformation. But evangelicals were greeted with metaphors of infiltration and conquest.* Much of the money, planning, and organization behind their growth came from the behemoth to the north: even groups from other parts of the world, such as the Unification Church, the Hare Krishna, and Bahai, usually came by way of the United States.[24] Inevitably, the question arose of whether North American missionaries were serving their country rather than Christ.

In 1975, investigations by the U.S. Congress confirmed the Central Intelligence Agency's use of missionaries. During the early days of Overseas Crusades Ministries when it worked mainly in the Far East, a spokesman acknowledged, virtually all its personnel were debriefed by the CIA on returning home.[25] In Latin America, Catholic and Protestant missionaries also served as information sources, some wittingly and others not. In Chile a Belgian Jesuit named Roger Vekemans became a conduit for millions of dollars from the CIA, which also subsidized Catholic radio broadcasts to peasants in Colombia. By 1975, some evangelical missions already had rules against cooperating with intelligence agencies; others followed suit. But as the evangelical biweekly *Christianity Today* reported, restraining individual missionaries who felt a duty to serve their country was much harder.[26]

One U.S.-based religious group which definitely had a conspiratorial agenda was the Unification Church of Reverend Sun Myung Moon. Moon's disciples won a certain number of converts in Latin

---

* Having an outsize impact on public perceptions were a few extremely authoritarian movements that differed sharply from evangelical norms and were best described as cults. For some time, the most flagrant case was the Children of God. The group's founder and prophet, David Brandt Berg alias Moses David, had broken away from the Christian and Missionary Alliance, for which he worked as an evangelist, to minister to hippies and drug addicts in Huntington Beach, California. From that emerged his Children of God or Family of Love, which practiced "flirty fishing" or evangelism by sex, prompting indictments in various Latin America capitals for prostitution and corrupting minors (Consejo Episcopal Latinoamericano 1982:236–37; Silletta 1987:75–93; Albán Estrada and Muñoz 1987:134–41). Then there was the 1978 murder/suicide of the Reverend Jim Jones and nine hundred followers in Jonestown, Guyana. Jonestown was a North American expatriate community, not a mission, and had little to do with Latin American evangelicals. But it prompted numerous demands for expelling churches that had become Latin American in membership (e.g., *El Espectador* [Bogotá] November 30 to December 2, 1978; and *El Tiempo* [Bogotá] November 26–27 and December 3–5 and 10, 1978).

America, but their main vehicle was a free-spending political lobby named the Confederation of Associations for the Unification of American Societies (CAUSA). The acronym was the Spanish word for "cause": that of fighting communism in the Americas, to which end the group labored to improve the foreign image of military dictatorships and airlifted supplies to the Nicaraguan contras. CAUSA's head, David Woellner, was a retired U.S. Air Force general.[27]*

The Moon organization illustrated a recurring fear among Latin Americans forced to deal with the growing number of religious groups from the United States. What if, despite all the denials, North Americans persuaded converts to transfer their loyalties from their own country to the United States? "Invariably, a strong bond of mutual love and respect is built up between the missionaries and the convert," a Mormon social scientist among Mexican peasants in Puebla claimed. "Any hostile feelings which the [convert] may have harbored internally toward Americans are eliminated or at least reduced. . . . The [convert's] worldview is dramatically expanded as he comes to see himself as an important member of a growing, worldwide organization. His previous suspicion and distrust of outsiders is ameliorated for he now believes that at least some of them are genuinely concerned about him. This is just the start of the almost total transformation of his viewpoints, activities, and aspirations."[28]

Some of the sharpest trepidation over North American intentions was aroused by the evangelism of indigenous peoples, in Mex-

---

*In Uruguay Moon's disciples acquired one of the country's largest financial institutions, one of its largest newspapers, and a luxury hotel in the capital. The Moon organization also sold the government weapons from its armaments factory in Korea. In Bolivia it reportedly helped finance General García Meza's overthrow of an elected government in 1980—remembered as the "cocaine coup" for its other backers. After several years of courting the dictatorships of Brazil and the Southern Cone, the Moon organization turned to Central America. As in Bolivia, the rapid downfall of the generals so befriended did not suggest divine approval. In 1983, Moon's representative Colonel Bo Hi Pak, a retired South Korean army officer, helped organize a businessmen's group, the Association for the Development of Honduras, to support the ill-fated strongman General Gustavo Álvarez. That same year, Moon's people organized a conference in Guatemala City to improve the image of the soon-deposed President Ríos Montt (Jean François Boyer and Alejandro Alem, *Manchester Guardian Weekly,* February 24, 1985, pp. 12–13, and March 3, 1985, pp. 12, 14; Mariano Sotelo, *Latinamerica Press* September 29, 1983, pp. 5–6. For a list of Moon organizations, see Bromley 1985).

ico, Central America, the Andes, and the Amazon Jungle. Although the number of converts involved was often small, the conflicts over them dramatize how evangelism leads to competition with other religious and political groups.

Evangelical missionaries have long concentrated on American Indians: in Brazil not so long ago, 36.5 percent of the faith missions were to be found among the 0.5 percent of the population which was indigenous.[29] The concentration could be explained in ideological terms: these were the "last unreached peoples," presumed to be living in the deepest darkness, and so forth. But Latin Americans found it hard to distinguish between foreigners in search of adventure, natural resources, drugs, and souls. With their pervasive missions to Indians, moreover, evangelicals were occupying an especially sensitive position in Latin American affairs. It was not just that the majority of indigenous people lived in poorly integrated hinterlands rife with land grabbing and drug trafficking, gridded off into corporate concessions, and contested by troops and guerrillas; native people were not "national" in the integrationist, hispanicizing sense desired by their governments.

"Tribal peoples represent the most politically delicate of all mission fields," *Mission Frontiers* of Pasadena, California, explained. "They are virtually imprisoned in their own countries in most cases. National governments, run by majority peoples, at best are embarrassed or indifferent and at worst are even hostile to them. How can outsiders get past those officials who do not want anyone drawing attention to their tribal peoples? It is a wonder missions have been able to do it at all!"[30]

They did it by serving official plans to integrate native people, often with unfortunate results. But even if evangelical missions were problematic, they tended to treat native people with more respect than did national governments and fellow citizens. In effect, North American evangelicals were setting themselves up as mediators between native groups and the Latin societies that had colonized them. By serving both constituencies, the North Americans came to play a pivotal role in Indian affairs.

This was the crux of the periodic furors over evangelical missions to native people. Latin American nationalists feared that, by winning the loyalty of ethnic minorities, North Americans were setting up archipelagoes of influence. To illustrate the dangers of ethnic separatism, they needed only point to the mainly Protestant Miskito Indians of Nicaragua, whom the United States encouraged to revolt against the Sandinista government.

One of the two largest evangelical missions to native people was the New Tribes Mission (NTM). With 2,300 members in some two hundred language groups around the world, the fundamentalist NTM was accused of destroying the cultures of the still resisting nomadic bands in which it specialized. The other was the more flexible Wycliffe Bible Translators, whose 6,000 members had entered 1,100 language groups around the world. To avoid Catholic and anticlerical opposition, Wycliffe went to the field under the name of the Summer Institute of Linguistics (SIL). By claiming to be primarily a scientific research organization, it was able to obtain official contracts and cultivate government authorities, whose support usually protected it from expulsion, but also guaranteed a new controversy within a few years.

By the 1980s in Colombia, after successfully resisting several official recommendations to wind down its activities, the Summer Institute was said to receive almost daily threats against its members. One member was kidnapped and, when SIL refused to leave the country, executed in 1981. Five years later, another was knifed to death by a former employee from the poverty-stricken town next to the group's comfortable base.[31] That same month, SIL property in the capital was bombed along with the offices of other North American organizations.[32] Despite claims that SIL members were standing firm, a colleague in the Interamerican Mission reported that half left the country in the two years following the 1981 killing. As for the Interamerican Mission's own no-ransom policy, it was now spelled out on members' identification cards.[33]* Although vio-

---

*Just how complicated missionary life could get—and just how hard it could be to distinguish missionaries from other kinds of North Americans—was suggested by the saga of Russell Stendal, a young bush pilot on the Colombian frontier. The son of former Summer Institute translators, Stendal was admittedly something of a black sheep in the mission fraternity. A typically versatile missionary child, at age nineteen he was entrusted with starting a ranch in the eastern badlands. The profits were to support Colombian literacy workers and help local settlers improve their agriculture. But the young missionary was soon disillusioned by the ranch's Christian employees, who accused each other of smoking cigarettes and drinking alcohol, were lazy, and ended up suing Stendal for back

lence against North Americans received the most publicity, local evangelicals suffered the most. According to the president of the Colombian Evangelical Confederation, seven rural pastors were murdered in one year.[34]

In Mexico, a next-door neighbor became what U.S. mission planners regarded as a restricted field. There, as in Colombia, a major source of controversy was the Summer Institute, which for years had obfuscated its evangelical goals by claiming to be concentrating on linguistic research, then continued to move into new languages even after losing its government contract. Accusations against evangelicals as U.S. spies, legal restrictions, and expulsion of missionaries entering the country on tourist visas became regular occurrences. When the government banned religious broadcasting as a violation of the country's anticlerical constitution, evangelicals set up their stations on the U.S. side of the border.

In 1984, four Jehovah's Witnesses from the United States were kidnapped in Guadalajara while evangelizing door to door; they vanished without a trace. In the countryside, churches were occasionally burned and pastors killed. "We practice the Roman Catholic religion," signs in windows declared. "Evangelicals are not welcome here."[35] In Chihuahua, extremists naming themselves after

---

wages. Nearby pastors seemed to be interested chiefly in milking their congregations for money in order to imitate the living standard enjoyed by missionaries.

After several years of entrepreneurial heartbreak, Stendal decided to provide employment for local men, and also promote economic development by starting a fishing industry. That required taking out loans to build infrastructure, buy outboard motors for local men, and acquire a more expensive airplane for himself. Soon Stendal's fishermen turned to a more lucrative occupation—growing marijuana for smugglers to the United States—and forgot about paying back the money they owed him. Like everyone else in the area, the young evangelist found himself trapped in overlapping extortion rackets by drug traffickers, guerrillas, and the authorities.

Up to his ears in debt, to keep up the payments on his airplane and gather information for a strangely uninterested Drug Enforcement Agency at the U.S. embassy, Stendal agreed to do a flight for the drug runners himself. It was a fiasco. When the mafia found out about his contact with the embassy through their own people there, they threatened to kill him. Being kidnapped by guerrillas, in August 1983, was therefore not the worst predicament in which Stendal had found himself. At the start of his 142-day sojourn with the Revolutionary Armed Forces of Colombia (FARC), he happened to be armed with a concealed .38 revolver with which he tried to shoot himself free, seriously injuring a guard with dum-dum bullets. Despite all, Stendal succeeded in turning his actions into a book-length testimony to his evangelical faith (Stendal 1984).

the Knights Templar were demanding that the Catholic hierarchy expel Protestants, to the point of painting slogans on church walls such as "Cursed Huguenots, out of Chihuahua!"[36]

The Struggle within Protestantism

Latin Americans protesting against the invasion of the sects usually had little idea of the differentiation within Latin American Protestantism. They failed to discern the internal struggles emerging over how to respond to the world. Admittedly, such debates could be difficult to detect owing to the political conservatism of most evangelical leadership.

In contrast to liberal Protestants and much of the Catholic Church, prominent figures such as Luis Palau advised Latin Americans to concentrate on improving themselves rather than working for structural change. Such leaders claimed to be apolitical, but they customarily supported any regime in power. For a minority facing hostility from the Catholic Church in an unstable political milieu, aligning with a dictatorship might seem the only way to safeguard freedom of worship.[37] Then there was the belief, based on a fundamentalist interpretation of Romans 13:1, that any anticommunist government was divinely ordained. When much of the Catholic clergy turned against military regimes in the 1970s, evangelical leaders usually did not. Some energetically preached submission to dictatorships and defended the status quo as if it were God's handiwork.[38]

In exchange for freedom to evangelize, such evangelicals were allowing themselves to be used as a "parallel church," an alternate source of blessing for a regime which had alienated the traditional religious authorities.[39] When fearful that revolutionaries were about to take power, they could turn into apologists for inhuman policies. At a time when other Christians were challenging structures of oppression, they seemed to be propping the same structures up.

The conservatism of Latin American evangelicals was mainly passive, a policy of noninvolvement reinforced by experience as a minority religion. They might abstain from movements for social change, for fear of being manipulated by more powerful groups, but they also displayed a certain resistance to identification with the state. Except when polarized to the right by fear of revolutionary expropriations, evangelical support for the status quo was cautious. That attitude was encouraged by many of their missionaries, who were repelled by Latin American political culture.

These might seem like unimportant caveats. But in the 1980s they began to look significant with the increasing visibility of a new, more militant wave of evangelists from the religious right. Such evangelists were so politicized that previous conservatives looked moderate in comparison. Although some older evangelical missions were backing away from neocolonial postures, these soul winners were vowing, not only to win Latin America to Christ but also to save it from revolution. Soon their collisions with liberation theology were producing a new kind of holy war.

One such confrontation occurred in Guatemala, under Latin America's first evangelical dictator. Every Sunday on television, General Efraín Ríos Montt (1982–1983) preached to his countrymen on the importance of morality and good citizenship. Meanwhile, according to human rights groups, his army was putting down a communist insurgency by butchering thousands of Mayan Indians. Yet evangelicals in the United States leaped to Ríos Montt's defense, heaped him with praise, and offered to send large amounts of aid. One role his evangelical advisers played was denying that the Guatemalan army was committing massacres in its anti-guerrilla drives; another was serving as a humanitarian buffer for survivors, especially evangelicals, by recruiting them into the army's pacification effort.

Not long after Ríos Montt's fall, another confrontation between the religious right and liberation theology emerged, over the Reagan administration's war on the Sandinista revolution in Nicaragua. From the start, the religious right vouched for the operation as a defense of religious freedom. Then, after the U.S. Congress cut off aid to the Nicaraguan counter-revolutionaries in 1984, the religious right joined the campaign to come to their rescue. As the Iran/Contra scandal soon demonstrated, this supposedly private effort was coordinated by the Central Intelligence Agency, the National Security Council, and Lieutenant Colonel Oliver North from the basement of the White House. In fulfillment of many an anti-imperialist prophecy, evangelicals claiming to do missionary work were joining a CIA front.

Looming large in the demonology of right-wing missionaries was liberation theology, understood as a Moscow-inspired tactic to deceive the church into destroying itself. Usually we think of liberation theology as a Catholic phenomenon: ecumenical Protestants might have a part in it, but they were few in Latin America. As for the evangelical Protestants multiplying at such a rapid rate, the whole idea seemed antithetical: they scarcely seemed interested in revolutionizing faith and society. Virtually all evangelicals said they rejected liberation theology. Yet witch-hunts against suspected sympathizers in evangelical churches indicated that it was not just an external threat. Conservative leaders were alarmed that it was infiltrating their own churches. They feared a potential following, not least because most of their followers were poor and oppressed.

Evangelicals have usually made one or another form of the "prosperity gospel" part of their message. Believe on the Lord, evangelists promise, and he will reward you in this life as well as the next. Surveying the rise of many early converts into the middle class, mission theorists refer to such blessings as "redemption and lift."[40] But when the debt crisis hit Latin America in the 1980s and difficult times turned worse, evangelicals who had managed to improve their lot in earlier years found themselves getting poorer along with everyone else. What would happen if "redemption and lift" stopped working and evangelicals became open to new ideas about changing the social order?

"They're upset by liberation theology because it upsets their scheme totally," an evangelical theologian said of conservatives. "But their attacks have promoted it, because many people in the pews don't know what it is."[41] Liberation theology disturbed conservatives because, among other things, it raised issues they had ignored, issues they were now forced to confront even as they groped for different answers.

"I lived among poor people and saw what was going on around me," a staunch anticommunist missionary volunteered, "but it never got through to me. It's possible to isolate yourself from these things . . . to live in your own little world and never think about people around you who are dying of starvation. . . . I have had to come before the Lord in recent years and say I'm sorry. And the thing that has affected me is . . . liberation theology."[42]

Conservatives clearly had the upper hand in evangelical leadership, and most signs suggested that they would retain it. But impressed by the dedication of Christians practicing liberation theology, some evangelicals were trying to work out their own "biblical" equivalent. What might seem like minor differences among evangelicals, mere shadings of a common right-wing stance, were producing rather different positions. Leery of dramatic stands, the innovators concentrated on long-term tasks such as pastoral training. Under different conditions, their pupils could become a new, more socially responsive leadership.

Out in churches with dirt floors, where the congregation wailed away into the wee hours of the morning, waiting for the Holy Spirit to descend, it could be hard to tell exactly what was going on. Whatever religious professionals debated in their seminaries and publications, no matter how bitterly theological and political factions contended for supremacy, the believers in poverty-stricken barrios and provinces could not be counted upon to follow the total program of any rival tendency. Even the identity of the various factions could blur out there, with Catholics turning charismatic and then declaring themselves evangelicals, or evangelicals whose churches professed no interest in the things of this world suddenly joining peasant leagues. It was important to keep this kind of ambiguity in mind because Protestantism in Latin America continued to be a channel for dissent as well as North American influence.

Whatever is happening, scholars have been reluctant to call it a religious reformation. One reason is that the term evokes the Protestant Reformation in Europe, raising problems of comparison which will not be dealt with in this work. It also implies that religious change will have a profound impact on the social order. But I think the comparison is already being made. Implicitly, liberation theology is equated with the Protestant Reformation, while evangelical Protestantism is assigned the reactionary Catholic role of Counter-Reformation. This is an interesting inversion of European history, perhaps an appropriate one, but not one I will assume true in the pages that follow.

Instead, I will refer to the evangelical ferment in Latin America as an "awakening," even if this term can be used only in the most loose, suggestive, and perhaps misleading sense. In the United States, awakenings are the successive periods of evangelical revival which, since the 1700s, have changed the way North Americans understand themselves and their society. Looking backward, successive awakenings can be associated with the independence movement from Britain, the emergence of participatory democracy, and social reform. According to William McLoughlin, each North American awakening has redefined a millenarian core of beliefs that freedom and the Judeo-Christian ethic can perfect individuals, the nation, and the world.[43]

This is a far cry from how Latin Americans understand their history, let alone the pessimistic, otherworldly style of millennialism prevalent among evangelicals today. But if an awakening is understood as a period of religious ferment, in which masses of people arrive at a new sense of themselves and their society, then at least we pose a question for the future. As for reformation, it suggests that liberation theology and evangelical Protestantism are competing wings of a religious transformation that is broader than either and whose implications are far from clear.

Chapter Two

Reformation and
Counter-Reformation
in the Catholic Church

South America, a Methodist missionary named Thomas Wood wrote in 1900, provided "a most significant object lesson" in the comparative impact of Romanism and Protestantism on human welfare. Located at the bottom of the moral scale of Christendom, Wood argued, it provided the largest field in the world for disseminating the moral improvements peculiar to the United States. The main obstacle, in his opinion, was the priestcraft of the Catholic clergy, their idolatry and greed, plotting and misguidance which inspired incessant revolutions. But now the Latin race was being given a new chance to accept the gospel, through its passion to imitate the United States. Even if such efforts came to naught, Wood believed, this longing was acting like a divine yeast. It was preparing Latin Americans to receive what they really needed from the United States: the Bible. Through the Bible, Latin America would finally enter into North America's inheritance of blessings, in the form of great sweeping revivals.[1]

Wood was neither the first nor the last Protestant to blame the gap between the two Americas on the Catholic Church.[2] While the Protestant culture of North America had rewarded independence and innovation, the argument went, Latin America had been held back by a moral culture stressing obedience to authority. Even if such evaluations are simplistic, it is surely relevant that, as an administrative system, Catholicism dates to the Roman Empire, making it a candidate for the oldest bureaucracy in the world.

The contrast with evangelicals is striking. The first Protestant missions were modeled after commercial enterprises, Orlando Costas has pointed out, the overseas trading companies of mercantile capitalism.[3] As the world turned into a vast marketplace, the initiative passed to religious organizations which could extract the most advantage from an atmosphere of competition and free trade. The Catholic Church was not necessarily the loser: in sub-Saharan Africa it was growing much faster than Protestantism.[4] But in Latin America, it was the established church in a colonial order.

Even after Latin America gained independence from Spain in the early nineteenth century, the Catholic clergy enjoyed considerable political authority. When Protestant missionaries began to arrive, anticlericalism was already a potent force, particularly among an incipient bourgeoisie that resented the clergy's authority and hungered after its huge landholdings. With the liberal revolutions of the late nineteenth century, anticlerical factions took power, seized Catholic property, and declared religious liberty. In the hope of undermining the authority of the priests, anticlericals also welcomed the first Protestant missionaries.

Frontal assaults did not necessarily weaken Catholicism. Instead, they could strengthen it, in the way that persecution often has reinforced religious loyalties. As for Protestant missionaries, they usually failed to start large churches. What did debilitate the Catholic Church was the disintegration of Latin America's paternalistic social order, a society of mutual obligations between upper and lower classes in which the church served as spiritual guarantor. Such arrangements had protected much of the population against dislocation and impoverishment. As they crumbled under the impact of capitalist expansion, so did the Catholic Church's social foundations.

Donald Curry has described the process in a Brazilian town he calls Lusíada. At one time, the Catholic priests of Lusíada knit together large landowners and their laborers in a paternalistic order. But in the twentieth century, the wealthy switched from growing coffee to grazing cattle and threw their dependents off the land. In the new era of class strife, the Catholic Church adopted a helpless neutrality, trapping itself on the side of the rich. The erosion of

upper-class paternalism meant that clerics could no longer reproduce traditional notions of equity, isolating them from the poor.
Unsupported by the clergy, many dislocated peasants reorganized
into evangelical congregations.[5]

Although we can now trace these shifts to political economy, they
were fought out in the language of popular belief. Catholic peasantries believed that their welfare depended upon the correct observ-
ance of rituals by the entire community; priests were accustomed
to the role of intermediary with God. Neither was prepared to tolerate agitators fanning resentment against the order of things.

In rural Mexico and Colombia, the reaction against Protestantism reached a height in the 1940s and 1950s. In the vivid language
of the Inquisition, Catholic bishops accused Protestants of sowing
diabolical heresies, dividing and colonizing Latin America at the
behest of the United States. Sometimes incited by priests, mobs
burned Protestant meeting places, stoned, and occasionally killed
converts. In Colombia, during the civil war known as the *Violencia*,
the clerical party singled out evangelicals as suspected communists. From 1948 to 1958, Catholic mobs killed more than a hundred Protestants, destroyed fifty churches, and closed more than
two hundred schools.[6]

Eventually, reports of these events embarrassed Catholic authorities into discouraging violence. A new wave of Catholic missionaries from North America and Europe also dampened tempers.
The new arrivals were responding to Pope Pius XII's 1955 call to
reevangelize Latin America. Among other things, they hoped to
counteract the growing number of evangelical missionaries. But
many were from countries where Roman Catholicism was only the
largest of several denominations, not the state church. Culturally,
they could have more in common with Protestant competitors than
with their own brethren, whether Latin Americans or the Span-
iards and Italians who made up such a large percentage of the
clergy. Not only did the newcomers usually lack enthusiasm for
campaigning against Protestants: they were prone to imitate them.
After Fidel Castro took power in Cuba, the tribulations of the Catholic Church there seemed to confirm that communism was a far
greater threat.

At this point, with evangelicals still a small minority in most of
Latin America, the Catholic Church attempted to make peace with

them. From Rome, in the name of ecumenism, the Second Vatican Council (1962–1965) recognized Protestants as separated brethren. This and other Vatican II reforms were not just responses to competition from Protestants. But for present purposes, let us stress that aspect.

Besides neutralizing evangelicals as competitors, the Catholic Church wished to learn from them. It wanted to carry out a reformation from within, to fill the social and spiritual vacuums in which evangelicals flourished. In ways often neglected, such as promoting Bible reading and encouraging lay leadership, post-Vatican II reform in Latin America adopted Protestantism as a model. The most obvious example was charismatic renewal, the Catholic answer to pentecostal Protestantism; another was liberation theology. Both efforts at revitalization infused Catholicism with new ideas and energy. By providing restless Catholics with alternatives to Protestantism, they may have blocked evangelical growth at some points.

But liberation theology and charismatic renewal also proved divisive because they challenged authority as traditionally understood in the Catholic structure. Under some circumstances, furthermore, they seemed to encourage evangelical growth. When a new pope, John Paul II (1978–), tried to restore centralized authority, that too could easily encourage defections. Such was the interior drama behind Catholic polemics against evangelical growth, the quandary this chapter will explore.

The Catholic Reformation in Latin America

By the 1960s, many Catholic church workers were dissatisfied with the almost medieval structures they were supposed to administer. But how to modernize them was a matter of sharp debate. Another divisive issue was how to respond to oppressive governments. If the Catholic Church clung to the status quo, as it often had in the past, it would continue to alienate restless members of the lower classes. But if it turned against the power structure, its old allies would accuse it of subversion.

In response to such predicaments the Catholic clergy splintered in several directions, each trying to restore the church's authority in a different way. The most conservative clung to old sacramental and institutional forms; never accepting the Vatican II changes, they were still willing to consecrate military dictatorships to the Virgin. Then there were the reformers, more flexible, forward-looking institutionalists who displaced conservatives from church administration. They criticized capitalism and argued that the church needed to address Latin America's social inequities. The great stimulus behind their efforts was fear of social upheaval and bloodshed. Soon, the attempt to head off revolution with reform was splitting the Catholic clergy even further.

At first, Catholic activists expressed themselves in Christian Democratic trade unions, peasant leagues, and political parties. But as these organizations came up against the structure of power and privilege, they tended to be suppressed or coopted. Radicalized by their experiences, some Catholic activists joined revolutionary movements. Others held back from such commitments, fearing the human cost of overthrowing the old regime. They also distrusted the left, which they suspected would merely erect more powerful police states. The men who were supposed to be in charge, the bishops, wavered between talks of protest, mediation, and reconciliation.[7]

The question of whether to work within the established order or try to overturn it was accompanied by a second major question, whether to maintain the traditional chain of clerical authority. The Catholic hierarchy had long defended its prerogatives. The pope in Rome was, after all, the vicar of Christ on earth. Even though the hierarchy adapted to change by allowing a certain amount of independence at lower levels, how much to allow was always an issue.

In Latin America, the loss of popular influence was so obvious that, well before the Second Vatican Council, the church was experimenting with new ways to reincorporate the masses. In the 1960s and 1970s, the church exploded with new kinds of organizations intended to reach the poor and return them to the fold. One popular move was to start cooperatives, another to train lay catechists or "delegates of the Word." Still another was to organize "ecclesiastical base communities": ideally small, cohesive, and self-directed groups, for the most part of the poor, who studied the Bible and applied its teachings to their daily struggle for survival.

The most immediate stimulus for such efforts was the shortage of clergy. In one decade, according to Gary MacEoin, two of every five priests in Latin America left their holy office.[8] Fewer and fewer young men were going to seminary, and the vast majority of those who did were dropping out before they finished the lengthy course of study. Even when the decline in clerical vocations finally leveled off and began to reverse in the 1980s, training large numbers of lay leaders was the only way to restore the church's presence throughout the population.

Hovering about efforts to train lay leaders was the challenge of Protestantism. For Catholics dissatisfied with the top-heavy institutionalization of their church, it provided important arguments for empowering lay leaders and decentralizing authority. First, Protestants were fielding battalions of evangelists with which Catholics needed to compete. "The basic contrast is the priest versus the propagandist," a former priest in Costa Rica explained. "It's enough [for an evangelist] to have a Bible and know a few hymns. He may have taken a course, versus seven years of training for a Catholic priest."[9] Second, evangelicals were practicing more popular forms of worship than all but the base communities and charismatics. In the words of Thomas Bamat, they tended "to create more egalitarian and participatory relations. They allow even the poorest people to assume leadership roles, and they encourage emotional expression during liturgical services."[10]

Protestantism was an important model in another respect. With the blessing of Rome, Catholics of all classes were enthusiastically discovering one of the great attractions of Protestantism in Latin America, the Bible. What had once been merely a fixture in Catholic pulpits, even a proscribed text available only to the clergy and the persons they authorized, was now being exalted as a guide to faith. Because the Bible included many a thought-provoking message for the lower classes whom church workers were trying to organize, it was an important part of the "consciousness-raising" efforts of liberation theology.

Bible reading was also part of another Protestant-influenced movement, charismatic renewal. In contrast to liberation theology, which sought to revitalize the church by making it the vanguard of social change, the charismatic idea of renewal was baptism in the Holy Spirit. Charismatics were clearly heirs to the mystical tradition in Catholicism. But they acquired their particular "spiritual gifts" or *charismata*—faith healing, speaking in tongues—from pentecostalism, the most popular version of Protestantism in Latin America. As it turned out, such Catholics often traced their inspiration to charismatic Catholics and Protestants in the United States, not to Latin American pentecostals, who tended to be too prejudiced against the Catholic Church to work within it.[11] But charismaticism became a major opening for evangelical ideas. Because charismatic Catholics were embracing the essential triad of devotion to the Bible, the personal relation with Christ, and the priority of evangelism, some began to call themselves the evangelical wing of the Roman church.

Charismatics received less publicity than liberationists but, at least on the local level, sometimes surpassed their influence. Because charismatic renewal usually traveled with disinterest in politics, it became a reaction against liberation theology, attracting middle-class Catholics who shunned social issues and wished to concentrate on pastoral care. Although rivals, both movements competed with Protestantism by adopting some of its most appealing features: Bible reading, lay leadership, and close-knit fraternal groups.

In some situations, liberation theology and charismatic renewal may have succeeded as a hedge against further losses. In Brazil, Southern Baptists reported, grass-roots organizing and social programs were giving the Catholic Church new credibility among the masses of the poor. The estimated eighty thousand base communities, organized by Brazilian Catholics, were not just political action groups. They also represented a mass revitalization of the church at the popular level, one involving and activating previously nominal Catholics.[12] Sometimes evangelicals seemed awed and intimidated by the masses of people the Catholic Church could mobilize, especially when reinforced by the drawing power of papal visits. It could be argued that, by providing a competitive stimulus, Protestantism was strengthening Catholicism in important ways.

The Passing of Ecumenism

In North America and Europe, the ecumenical movement took great strides in bringing together Catholics and Protestants, but not in Latin America. Catholic authorities were particularly disappointed. As far as they could see, the most visible result of ecumenism was faster evangelical growth. Loyal Catholics who had never felt free to associate with evangelicals were now visiting their services and finding out what they believed; some became converts.[13] The Catholic Church wished to interpret ecumenism like a "comity" agreement between two missions, in which each confines itself to a certain sphere to avoid trespassing on the work of the others. In exchange for being tolerated, evangelicals were to refrain from further poaching.

A few Protestants in Latin America were cooperative enough—those who no longer hungered to convert the Catholic masses anyway. As for the more evangelically minded, some were willing to concede that parts of the Catholic Church were becoming more Bible- and Christ-centered. But they were also sure that ecumenism was a clerical ploy to coopt them, to stanch the flow of dissatisfied Catholics into their churches. They were not willing to accept Catholic claims to represent most of the population. The idea of reuniting Christians into one institutional body—the premise of ecumenism from the Catholic point of view—was preposterous. Even moderate evangelicals continued to believe that the best thing for the Catholic Church would be for a large percentage of its flock to turn Protestant.[14]

As a result, evangelicals showed little interest in negotiating. "We are very sincere, sometimes naive," the bishop of Ambato, Ecuador, told me plaintively, "but it is impossible to have ecumenism here because there is no one in a responsible position to deal with."[15] Even in revolutionary Nicaragua, where conservative Catholics and Protestants felt equally threatened by the Sandinista revolution, they did not join forces. "Here in Nicaragua you're either Catholic or Protestant," an evangelical leader declared in 1985. "We don't consider Catholics to be Christians and so we try to win them to our faith. They feel the same way about us. So anything calling itself ecumenical doesn't have much behind it."

For some fifteen years after Vatican II, nonetheless, Catholic authorities usually refrained from complaining about evangelicals in public. The informal gag rule seems to have originated in Rome, anxious to avoid further accusations of religious persecution. Local clergy trying to defend parishes against sectarian intruders resented their superiors' cool, distant attitude. But by the early 1980s, alarm over Protestant growth was once again respectable in the Catholic hierarchy. Besides the obvious gains evangelicals were making, another reason was their frank and hopeful talk about making the entire continent and a half Protestant.

"Latin America is a Catholic region," church-growth planner Jim Montgomery of O.C. (for Overseas Crusades) Ministries conceded, "but there's no reason to assume that this need always be so. It could become an evangelical region at some point in time. I believe that if . . . Guatemala becomes the first predominantly evangelical nation in Latin America, it will have a domino effect."

"Of course our emphasis is not political or to destroy the Catholic church," Montgomery continued, "but we have succeeded in gaining their attention. Many negative things are being written, and the evangelicals are accused of trying to take over the country. Unfortunately, the battle lines are drawn, although it's not our objective to be at war with the Catholic church." Montgomery was the author of Discipling A Whole Nation (DAWN or *Amanecer* in Spanish), a church growth scheme tested in the Philippines before being taken to Central America. The goal for Guatemala was "50 percent evangelical by 1990."[16]

Bishops, archbishops, even papal nuncios began to include "the sects" in their recitals of Latin America's woes. They did not abandon ecumenical bridge building to those Protestants willing to reciprocate, but now the emphasis was on defending the faith. As early as 1979, the conference of Catholic bishops at Puebla complained of an invasion of sects.[17] When Pope John Paul II toured Central America in March 1983, then went to Haiti to open the Latin American Bishops' Conference, the most compelling item on the agenda was the spread of fundamentalist Protestantism. In November 1984, the Vatican's apostolic delegate in Mexico declared that Latin American governments should move against the Summer Institute of Linguistics and other Protestant groups preying on Latin Americans.[18] Shortly thereafter, the Brazilian bishops sent the Vatican a report suggesting that behind sectarian infiltration in Latin America stood the Central Intelligence Agency.[19]

As for evangelicals, they began to suspect that the Catholic Church was responsible for their own difficulties, especially with governments. The Colombian Evangelical Confederation complained that, while Catholic clergy from abroad met with no obstacle, nearly all visa applications for Protestant missionaries were being turned down. Owing to their government's agreement with the Vatican, the confederation charged, evangelicals were barred from access to the media, prevented from serving as chaplains in the armed forces and, unlike Catholics, forced to pay taxes on their church properties.[20]

The Costa Rican Evangelical Alliance accused the Catholic Church of engineering a change in visa rules, to prevent more missionaries from relocating in Costa Rica to escape the fighting in neighboring countries. Faith healers and revivalists who had used a stadium in the capital were denied further access. The alliance also charged that the authorities were using building codes and public nuisance laws to prevent new church buildings. A legislative change had cost evangelicals their tax exemption (although not that of the Catholics), and they were fighting a new education law that could give the Catholic Church authority over their Bible institutes.[21]

Apparently in every country, and sometimes on the diocesan level, the Catholic hierarchy had entrusted a department of ecumenism or evangelization with the task of keeping an eye on evangelicals and suggesting how to counter them. "Either we save it now or we lose it completely," one such functionary told me, referring to the religious loyalties of all Ecuador. The Catholic Church was losing, not just nominal Catholics who only went to church to get baptized and buried, but committed believers and lay leaders. Until the 1970s, evangelical converts had usually been confined to the self-improving section of the lower classes. Now the idea of joining an evangelical church was reaching higher in the social scale.

Explaining Losses to Protestantism

Why were so many faithful defecting to Protestantism? Catholic thinkers came up with two reasons. The first was an internal critique of their church, pastoral in nature. Weaknesses in the spiritual care the Catholic Church provided its flocks had left them vulnerable to proselytism, the argument went. To compete with evangelicals the church needed to cut back bureaucracy, train more lay leaders, and make itself a more fraternal community. At the 1983 episcopal conference in Haiti, the Latin American bishops voted to imitate evangelical methods over the airwaves, encourage Bible reading, and make room for more lay participation.[22] Three years later, the Vatican released a report along the same lines.[23]

Unfortunately, such ideas were nothing new. Much of the church had been laboring to implement them for decades, a circumstance that helps explain why many Catholics felt they needed a second reason, political in nature, to account for the multiplication of evangelicals. Even conservatives believed that sectarian activity was a tactic of North American imperialism. Because Latin America bishops had been warning their flocks against U.S. designs since before the Bolshevik revolution, it was not hard to revive the theme of political conspiracy.

"What is going on in Guatemala may have grave consequences," Bishop Mario Enrique Ríos Montt, the brother of Guatemala's evangelical president, told a journalist in 1982. "It could well turn into a religious war more serious than our political war. . . . Don't forget the United States was founded by Protestants. The Catholic Church south of Texas is regarded as too large, too strong. Because we cannot be confronted or fought directly, we must be weakened and divided otherwise. . . . Protestants and Marxists are both against us—Protestantism as the arm of conservative capitalism; Marxism as the arm of atheistic Communism."[24]

Bishops such as Ríos Montt cited various grounds for suspicion. One was the 1969 report of the Rockefeller Commission, which had noted that the Catholic Church was "vulnerable to subversive penetration."[25] Although the report did not call for an evangelical campaign to undermine the Catholic Church, as frequently alleged, its language suggested that U.S. policymakers were losing faith in Catholicism as a bulwark against communism. With guerrilla priests popping up here and there, it would have been hard not to. This was why Washington was promoting the sects, the argument went, as an alternative to the Catholic Church, to counteract its stand for human dignity.

Another ground for suspicion was the timing of the evangelical boom. Hadn't the sects arrived and mushroomed at a strategic moment, at the most sensitive possible time, just as the Catholic Church was in the delicate task of reforming itself and the social order was about to explode? Finally, what about the evident generosity of evangelical financial backers? While the Catholic Church was struggling to maintain a huge infrastructure of parishes, convents, schools, and hospitals dating back centuries, the North Americans seemed to have the money to do whatever they pleased.

Some Catholics took conspiracy theory so far that they denied the sects were a religious phenomenon at all. Yet many evangelical groups had been on the scene and struggling along, with little success, for decades. Then, when capitalist development finally opened up the territory, they rushed in to take advantage of the situation at the same time that revolutionaries and Catholic reformers did. As for foreign funding, the Catholic Church also received substantial subsidies, from dioceses in North America and western Europe as well as from Catholic Relief Services, Adveniat, and Misereor. Part of the reason for the apparent disparity of resources was the Catholic Church's staggering load of institutional commitments. While the Catholics were holding down the territorial system of an established church, the evangelicals concentrated their resources on winning new members.[26] Wherever there was a field ripe unto harvest, evangelists swarmed there to blare at the people with loudspeakers, visit them door to door, and put up little cement block churches on every street.

After decades of imbibing sociological analysis, many Catholics were highly critical of their church. When you got down to details, however, their prescriptions for dealing with evangelical inroads were contradictory. Some attributed the losses to the conservatism of the Catholic hierarchy and called for delegating more authority to lay leaders. Meanwhile the conservatives blamed church radicals for alienating better-off Catholics and provoking government repression, thereby scattering their flocks; for conservatives, the solution was to recentralize church authority.

So divided was the Catholic Church that alarm over losses to evangelicals seemed one of the few things on which everyone could agree. Catholics of all stripes realized that evangelicals were profiting from their quarrels. Although some preferred to stress the role of North American money, others recognized that the problem reached deep into their own church, to its system of authority.[27] Clericalism was the key to understanding how the Catholic Church was, against its will, generating evangelical growth.

The Quandaries of
Clericalism and Activism

In a sense, charismatic renewal and liberation theology only brought Protestantism within the walls, where a series of dilemmas continued to drive Catholics into evangelical churches. One problem was the question of biblical versus clerical authority. While Catholics needed more instruction in the Bible to deepen their faith, Catholic pastoral experts cautioned, it had to be given by the church. "In one hand the Bible, in the other the catechism," Father Ernesto Bravo told me.[28] Otherwise, Bible reading could lead to the time bomb of free interpretation and sectarianism.

How much authority to grant lay leaders was a closely related problem. Some wearers of the Roman collar were skilled at encouraging lay initiative, such that the ventures they sponsored became independent and went their own way with little apparent conflict. But complaints of clerical domination were frequent, even against that wing of the church proclaiming liberation. The utopianism of Catholic social activists meant that, even as they criticized clericalism, their efforts to organize the poor could easily reproduce it.[29] When a lay leader bumped up against the low ceiling imposed by a priest insisting on his prerogatives, it was not unusual for the layman to defect to an evangelical group more appreciative of his abilities. Soon he was a pastor in his own right. "Individuals who didn't count for anything among ourselves," Bishop José Mario Ruiz Navas of Ecuador reported, "turn into leaders or preachers and exhibit qualities which they never had the chance to demonstrate among ourselves. At times they are thrust forward into considerable responsibility with little preparation, while we hardly trust them for anything."[30]

It was not that evangelical churches were necessarily democratic: the most rapidly growing, such as the Assemblies of God in Brazil, could be very authoritarian. Culture was often cited as an explanation: converts, especially from the lower classes, were said to be looking for a strong, paternalistic authority to replace the *patrón*-dominated order that had disintegrated around them. But evangelical Protestantism opened up a whole new ladder of leadership possibilities. Theoretically, any male could reach the top, even if married and without formal schooling. For dissidents, there was always the possibility of joining another evangelical church or starting their own. For dissident Catholics confronting a local priest, in contrast, there was often no place to go within the system.

Charismatic renewal was a major front in the contest over authority. Who was really in charge? The charismatic figures leading the renewal? Or a Rome-appointed bishop, whose talents were mainly bureaucratic?[31] The official answer was the bishop, of course, and where the renewal was led by priests in good standing with their superiors, it emphasized respect for the hierarchy.

In Costa Rica, evangelical missionaries told me that charismaticism had become a major source of defection to their own churches. Following a charismatic movement, they claimed, the Costa Rican hierarchy had suddenly clamped down at the end of the 1970s. "Whole groups of charismatics suddenly saw the contradiction between mystical experience, Bible reading for themselves, and the [Catholic] hierarchy," the Latin America Mission's Paul Pretiz told me.[32] "They went over to Protestantism en masse. So now the hierarchy always places a popular priest in charge, who is careful to include prayers to the Virgin and reinforce mother church."

Several features of charismatic renewal attracted evangelical fishers of men. First, renewed Catholics were eager to learn from revivalists and faith healers, who usually turned out to be Protestant. Second, the renewal's position as a sort of halfway house between Catholicism and Protestantism made it a useful stage for certain kinds of converts. Especially for middle- and upper-class Catholics, reluctant to injure their social status by joining a minority religion, a charismatic prayer group offered most of the advantages of turning evangelical without the need to admit it.* Third, if and when a priest attempted to rein in Catholic charismatics, the basis had been laid for a speedy exit into an evangelical church. As a result, Catholic charismatics were often said to be defecting to Protestantism wholesale. In any case, some evangelicals were using charismaticism to fill their tents. When Catholic authorities turned polemical, this was one of the reasons.[33]

Balancing traditional devotions with political activism was another predicament facing the Catholic Church. Some called it the

---

*One group parlaying a middle- and upper-class charismatic effervescence into a large evangelical congregation was the Word Church in Guatemala City, to which President Efraín Ríos Montt belonged.

problem of steering between "verticalism" and "horizontalism"— that is, avoiding excessive preoccupation with the spiritual or the material—each of which could leave unsatisfied expectations and a religious vacuum for evangelicals to occupy. Allan Figueroa Deck, a Jesuit laboring to preserve the Catholic loyalties of Hispanics in southern California, observed that: "Some want to 'sacramentalize' [Hispanics]; they are happy as long as the flow of baptisms, first Communions, confirmations and marriages is constant and copious. Others urge 'liberation'; they see conscientization, opening people's eyes to the sociopolitical and economic causes of oppression, as the goal par excellence.

"The fundamentalists have seen in this confusion an opportunity to make gains among Hispanics. Well-intentioned, progressive and liberation-minded priests, sisters and laity have sometimes moved too fast. They appear to be selling a 'this-worldly' Catholicism that many Hispanics cannot really identify with. On the other hand, some clergy seem stuck on a mechanistic sacramentalist approach that gives the impression that the last ecumenical council was Trent and not Vatican II.

"The Hispanic people sense that life in the real world requires change, intelligent adaptation and creative confrontation with actual problems. The old sacramentalist approach seems strangely out of place; the new fangled liberationist approach excessively 'mundane.' In recent years the conflict within the Catholic Church over pastoral goals . . . and political affairs has left many sincere Hispanics confused. Unintentionally, the ground is being prepared for fundamentalist proselytism.

"Hispanic immigrants . . . need stability and moderation, not more insecurity and extremes. The sects provide a peculiar combination of traditional religious conservatism (sure doctrines, simple or even simplistic morality . . .) with a kind of Americanization. . . . The fundamentalist sects offer the Hispanic an attractive, coherent package."[34]*

Liberation theology was certain to antagonize conservative Catholics in the middle and upper classes, the pillars of the church in former times, and especially military officers. Upset by social activ-

---

* From the mid-1970s to the mid-1980s, according to one estimate, Protestants have increased from 16 percent to 23 percent of the Hispanic population in the United States (Andrew M. Greeley, *America*, July 30, 1988, pp. 61–62).

ists, these previously impenetrable elites were often grateful for the consolation and uplift of a suitably conservative evangelist. "They view the [Catholic] church as an enemy because of its defense of human rights," stated a bishop and former police chaplain of his disillusioned flock. "In contrast, the evangelical churches are silent—a position more acceptable to them."[35]

Liberation theology also provided evangelicals with opportunities when military regimes showed no compunction about slaughtering opponents. The clearest examples were in Guatemala and El Salvador, where government repression drove Catholic activists into revolutionary movements. Then security forces went on the rampage against their defenseless families and neighbors. However much the Catholic Church hoped to regain the masses through social activism, that kind of commitment could carry a price which was too high for most.[36]

Paradoxically, as the Catholic Church tried to embrace the cause of the poor, it could undermine its function of protecting them. This was because, when religion appears to be an "opiate of the masses," it may well be functioning as what Christian Lalive d'Epinay calls a "haven of the masses." That is, under conditions of severe oppression, seemingly alienating forms of religion can provide a certain space in which the oppressed are allowed to express themselves, precisely because they do not threaten the established order. But consciousness-raising and other forms of activism undermined that sanctuary. As conflict escalated, those Christians who survived government reprisals were forced to choose between taking up arms, accepting consignment to a refugee camp, or going into exile—not a choice likely to attract more followers. Alternatively, hard-pressed Catholics could join an evangelical church.

Counter-Reformation

These were some of the contradictory results behind several decades of "reevangelizing" Latin America. However much liberation theology, charismatic renewal, and related developments had quickened the Catholic Church, they also had divided it. In the contest with evangelicals, the reforms had arguably left the Catholic Church more vulnerable than before. At the very least, revitalization had weakened centralized control. It was in response to this last, irrefutable result that, in the 1980s, Pope John Paul II tried to reunify the church on his own terms, by asserting the authority of Rome.

One way the pope tried to restore centralized authority, Dayton Roberts of the Latin America Mission pointed out, was by encouraging traditional Catholic piety, such as the cults of the Virgin Mary and the saints. The pope also stressed the role of the priest as essential intermediary between God and the faithful. To Protestants and Catholics who saw themselves in a personal, direct relationship with Jesus Christ, these were ominous steps backward. Since the Reformation in Europe, Protestants had regarded saint cults as idolatry. Reviving communal Catholic rituals, older evangelicals in Latin America feared, would revive the persecution they had suffered for refusing to join in.[37]

When asked to specify who he was denouncing as "false prophets" on a Latin American trip, John Paul II referred to the Seventh Day Adventists, Mormons, and Jehovah's Witnesses, not to more orthodox Protestants.[38] Evangelicals were not convinced, however. Accusations against such groups, they pointed out, were usually followed by indiscriminate blasts against "sects," which included their own churches. The messianic fervor greeting the pope on his 1983 Central American visit, William Taylor of the Central American Mission claimed, was producing a wave of old-fashioned Catholic polemicism.[39] Evangelicals were afraid that the pope's campaign to bring together the various factions in the Catholic church was at their expense, by making them the enemy to be rallied against. Like it or not, opposition to their inroads was a way to bring the different tendencies in the Catholic Church back together.

But the reassertion of hierarchical authority could become another opportunity for evangelicals. Since Catholic reformers had been influenced by the need to compete with Protestantism, both the base communities and charismatic renewal owed something to the religious vitality of evangelicals. Now when the pope went on tour in Latin America, Catholic authorities passed out large numbers of Bibles. In several countries, the United Bible Societies reported that it was selling more scripture through Catholic than Protestant churches.[40] But if the pope's pilgrimages to Latin America succeeded in reasserting central authority, still more Catholics might feel obliged to leave for churches where they could follow their own conscience.

"John Paul II defines the church in terms of *his* bishops," a former Jesuit explained. "The problem is, he generally names very mediocre men, then wonders what the difficulty is when they are incapable of any serious type of leadership charism. These men derive their power from above, and so they look there in times of challenge. The church as the 'people of God' (from Vatican II) is a threat to them. When they run into a dynamic group like the evangelicals, they are defenseless. Leadership has to be broadened out. And John Paul II knows that this is risky. He won't do it, and it's going to cost him. The pope's emphasis on obedience to hierarchy is actually destroying the church's future."[41]

This was the dilemma behind the polemics against sects. The Catholic Church would lose more people if it reasserted clerical authority, but it would also lose more if it did not. No matter what Catholics did, they were facing the pain of passing from spiritual shepherd of Latin America to the lesser role of the traditional church. It was as if Protestantism was an inevitable reformation growing out of Catholicism itself. Whether it happened inside or outside the church, it was going to happen.

Chapter Three

From Doomsday to Dominion in North American Evangelicalism

It no longer fits to picture us as redneck preachers pounding the pulpit. Evangelical Christianity has become the greatest show on earth. Twenty to forty years ago it was on the edge of things. Now it has moved to the center.

Dave Breese, television evangelist[1]

At first glance, Pat Robertson's "700 Club" might seem like an ordinary talk show. But this television host stressed the power of prayer to cure everything from headaches to revolutions; he also urged his viewers to take over the United States. For Robertson was adept at linking the everyday worries of his estimated fourteen million viewers—illness, debt, family quarrels—to the big issue, the campaign to save America. America was not just endangered by the external threat of communism, Robertson said. The gravest peril was unprecedented moral rot within. Behind the obvious sins such as pornography and abortion was a deeper evil, that of secular humanism. Presented as the modern way of doing things, secular humanism was the idea that man could solve his problems apart from God. It was the sum of all those philosophies—evolutionism, relativism, liberalism, social welfarism—which had taken America away from the Bible. It was high time for America to repent, Robertson warned. Nuclear war would break out in 1982, he predicted at one point, and Christ return to earth that same year.[2]

42

Four years after the date passed, Pat Robertson was running for president of the United States. Now he said that he wanted to continue the task Ronald Reagan had begun, of restoring the country to its biblical foundations. Along with other television evangelists such as Jimmy Swaggart of the Assemblies of God and Jerry Falwell, Robertson was a new power center in North American evangelicalism. Like the rest of fundamentalist television, in the 1970s he had harped on the impending end of the world. But by the mid-1980s, he and the rest of the religious right were telling their audience to set America straight for their children and grandchildren. Their destiny was, not the end of the world, but Christian dominion over it.

This might seem a puzzling shift. Yet it was only to be expected of premillennialism, the most popular theory about the end of the world in evangelical Protestantism. As mankind grows more sinful and evil increases, premillennialists hold, Christ will return to establish his thousand-year reign on earth. The sequence of events is laid down in the Bible, they believe. Approaching rapidly is the final battle between the forces of Good and Evil. It will take place in the Holy Land, to the east of Mount Carmel in the Valley of Armageddon, when Soviet, Islamic, European, African, and Chinese armies converge on Israel, only to be destroyed by Jesus Christ riding out of the east in clouds of glory.

The magnificent vision used to be associated with disinterest in politics. If the world's spiral downward into perdition was part of the Lord's plan, what was the point in trying to halt it? Only Jesus could usher in the kingdom, not the feeble efforts of men. Yet premillennialism may prove as dynamic and unsettling a doctrine as Calvinism in the sixteenth century. Just as a Calvinist could never know whether the Lord had numbered him among the elect, the chosen few to be saved from eternal punishment, premillennialists do not know when the Lord will return. It could be tonight or a generation hence. But he will return soon, and by reading themselves into pivotal roles in the divine plan, premillennialists can become activists with a tremendous sense of mission.[3]

For outsiders, it was easy to lump together all born-again Christians with an alarming manifestation like Pat Robertson. But the religious right did not go uncontested within evangelicalism, even among Christians who regarded themselves as conservatives. Such differences are of some importance to this work given the continued influence of North American evangelicals on their brethren in Latin America. This next chapter, therefore, looks at North American evangelicals in terms of their diverging forms of organization, theology, and politics. Then it examines several of the power struggles set off by the religious right's drive to take control of the evangelical movement. Understanding the disagreements among people who identify themselves as fundamentalists, evangelicals, or Bible Christians will, in later chapters, clarify how similar differences are manifesting themselves in Latin America, with the potential for different results.

The Decline of Liberal Protestantism

Before delving into evangelical Protestantism, we should distinguish it from the "mainline" denominations that, until recently, were considered the dominant wing of North American Protestantism. The contest between the two is usually dated to the early 1900s, when liberalizing tendencies in the mainline denominations set off a conservative revolt. Conservatives felt that new, historical interpretations of the Bible were destroying its authority as God's inspired word. To restore that authority, they insisted that the Bible was an infallible, inerrant guide to truth and stood on what they called the fundamentals of the faith.

Quarrels between fundamentalists and their adversaries, the so-called modernists, expressed wider disagreements, over how to understand the world and react to change. While fundamentalists insisted that anyone could arrive at the single, correct interpretation of reality (their own), modernists accepted the relativity of human cognition. Relaxing their view of religious truth, the latter found it hard to believe that God would, for example, send Hindus to hell just because a Christian missionary had failed to reach them. Consigning souls to eternal punishment on that basis seemed unfair and sadistic. Dissatisfied with the results of soul saving, then losing interest in it, modernists came to feel that only the "social gospel"—education, social reform, and the like—really addressed human needs.

For fundamentalists, this meant betraying the essence of the faith: personal salvation. But try as they might, they failed to recapture the mainline denominations. Modernists dismissed them as relics of a bygone age and went on to become pillars of American liberalism. As late as the 1960s, the mainly liberal-led denominations of the National Council of Churches (NCC) were the very picture of a confident religious establishment. From headquarters at 475 Riverside Drive in New York City and 120 Maryland Avenue in Washington, D.C., the NCC campaigned on behalf of human rights, nuclear arms control, and revolutionary movements. The same flame burned bright at the World Council of Churches (WCC) in Geneva, the United Nations of ecumenical Christianity.

But the leaders of major NCC-affiliated denominations were more liberal than their constituencies. As this and that cause alienated conservative members, church liberals seemed at a disadvantage in the show-the-flag atmosphere of American politics. According to Joseph Hough, the reason was a shift in the underlying appeal of liberal and fundamentalist religion. As late as the 1960s, Hough argued, liberal Protestants managed to stay optimistic about America. Despite many a disappointment, they kept the faith that Americans could make a better world for themselves and everyone else. But now liberals were turning against the heedless expansionism of their society, rejecting the projection of American power around the world and calling for painful new forms of equity at home.[4] Meanwhile, the hopes that ordinary Americans wished to have bolstered in church were to be found among fundamentalists, who had worked their way up to the motor-home stratum of the middle class and wished to enjoy it.

As for liberal religious life, it seemed to be running out of vitality and conviction. According to the standard evangelical indictment, the mainline clergy had replaced Bible study with pop psychology, evangelism with social services, religious faith with political causes, God with man. In the words of William Willimon, indiscriminate openness to new trends had led to a crisis of identity. Many mainline churches had lost the sense of being a distinct community with a distinct religious faith.[5]

There was no question but that much, though not all, leadership of the mainline denominations had abandoned evangelism, cutting off the flow of converts. The mainline groups also had difficulty holding onto their young people, either because the young were too disinterested to become steady churchgoers or because they were so interested that, in search of a firmer sense of religious authority, they joined evangelical groups. Mainline congregations aged and declined in size. In 1990 the median age of the NCC-affiliated American Baptists was expected to be sixty.[6]*

Owing to the many conservative stirrings even within liberal-led denominations, evangelicals were the new center of gravity in North American Protestantism. They populated broad expanses of lower- and middle-class American life, especially in the rapidly growing South and West. But they were far from a majority, numbering only 20 percent or so of the U.S. population.[7] They were also far from uniform. To understand the tensions within the evangelical camp, let us look first at how different tendencies competed for support among evangelicals, then at the contrasting ways in which they symbolized their Christian duties on this earth.

Several levels need to be distinguished. The first, that of organization, will help us make sense of the bewildering number of churches and agencies which evangelicals have started. The second, the theological, will clarify the differences between fundamentalists, neo-evangelicals, and pentecostals. The third, the political, addresses the contradictory positions which evangelicals have been taking, from cheering on the nuclear arms race to demonstrating against it.

Evangelical Organization

The idea that evangelicals were organized might seem a contradiction in terms. If ecumenical Protestantism was a bureaucracy without a constituency, a saying went, the evangelical movement was a constituency without a bureaucracy.[8] Many North American evangelicals did belong to conservative, non-NCC denominations, among them the Southern Baptists, who claimed 14.4 million

*NCC denominations included only 53 percent of U.S. Protestants by 1985, down from 76 percent in 1920 and 62 percent in 1960 (William Hutchison, quoted in *Sacramento Bee*, April 20, 1985, p. B7, and Hutcheson 1981). As a group, the NCC lost nearly five million members from the mid-1960s to the mid-1980s. During the 1970s alone, the United Presbyterians lost nearly three-quarters of a million, the Episcopalians nearly half a million, and the United Methodists almost a million (*Fundamentalist Journal*, November 1985, p. 14). The non-NCC Southern Baptists replaced the Methodists as the country's largest Protestant denomination.

members, and the Assemblies of God, who claimed 2.1 million. But they were best known for their thousands of independent churches and agencies, a system of "religious free enterprise" that can be traced to the vacuum of traditional authority on the North American frontier.[9]

The main religious figure on the frontier was the circuit-riding preacher, a man who, on the infrequent occasions when he was able to visit, specialized in reviving religious loyalties, hence the "revival." What counted was his ability to hold a crowd, not formal training or credentials; the main source of his authority was the Bible. The basis of success—appealing to a popular constituency rather than a hierarchy—led to a radical dispersion of authority and endless splits in ecclesiastical structures. Church-state combinations declined, driving the religious and political spheres apart and helping to secularize the state.[10]

By throwing open religious authority to anyone with the potential for leadership, revivalism led to organizing countless new enterprises for godly purposes. In the nineteenth century, some men started "faith missions" to evangelize parts of the world they felt were being neglected by denominational missions. Without denominational funding, they "lived on faith" by "looking to the Lord"—that is, to anyone who might be willing to help.

In the early 1900s, the faith missions and their supporters joined the fundamentalist revolt against liberal interpretations of the Bible. Because established seminaries were controlled by the adversary, fundamentalists started their own Bible institutes, whose graduates organized independent churches and specialized ministries, the so-called "parachurch agencies." Parachurch bodies—missions, radio stations, evangelistic associations—broke down denominational barriers by appealing to as wide an evangelical public as possible, regardless of affiliation. But that meant confronting churchgoers with a marketplace of worthy causes; competition between church and parachurch for evangelical dollars became keen.

Evangelical Theology

If fundamentalists were to be believed, they should have been able to agree on a single, correct interpretation of the Bible. Experience proved otherwise, leading to split after split in fundamentalist

ranks. Since most churchgoers were repelled by ecclesiastical ven-
dettas, fundamentalists found themselves in the byways of American life. The story of how some found their way back onto the high-
ways is usually dated to the formation of the National Association of
Evangelicals (NAE) in the early 1940s.

The NAE's leaders were determined to overcome sectarianism.
To express their wish to spread the gospel as well as to defend it,
they revived an older term as their appellation: evangelical. To
avoid confusing them with evangelicals in the widest sense, let
us refer to the NAE movement by another term they used, as
"neo-evangelicals." To appease suspicious fundamentalists, neo-
evangelicals continued to claim that they upheld the inerrancy of
scripture. But due to the incongruities of taking it entirely at face
value, they moved to more sophisticated methods of interpretation. Unlike fundamentalists, they came to terms with science and
dropped opposition to evolution as a test of faith. Finally, instead of
rejecting "the world" as fundamentalists were accustomed to, neo-
evangelical theologians began to talk about the need for "social concern." In the 1950s their spokesman emerged in the person of Billy
Graham, the most popular figure in North American religion.[11]

Remaining behind to man the battlements of Biblical inerrancy
were the fundamentalists. For the majority of fundamentalists,
their rock of ages was dispensationalism, a nineteenth-century
scheme to explain the many contradictions in scripture being exploited by sceptics. According to liberal scholarship, of course, the
contradictions grow out of the tangled human authorship of the
Bible. To refute that notion, dispensationalists came up with an
even more complicated system of distinctions, to show that apparent discrepancies were actually due to changes in the divine plan,
specifically, the stages or "dispensations" into which they divided
the biblical message. By emphasizing how divine requirements
changed during each age, dispensationalists not only resolved contradictions in the Bible but also were able to dismiss the scriptures
which contradicted their views. Thus verses about the kingdom—
often quoted to agitate for social improvements—could be deleted
from the present age and put into storage for the glorious period
following Christ's return.[12]

The Moody Bible Institute in Chicago and the Dallas Theological
Seminary were the leading exponents of dispensational thinking.

But while their graduates led many independent fundamentalist or "Bible" churches, they also managed to appeal to neo-evangelicals as well.[13] Playing both sides of the fence in this manner was not acceptable to a second, more separationist strain of fundamentalists, however: they denounced Moody, Dallas, and most other evangelical schools for "going soft" on the Bible. One of the best known champions of this second fundamentalist tendency was Bob Jones, whose Bob Jones University in Greenville, South Carolina, gave up a tax exemption rather than allow interracial dating. Another was Jerry Falwell, who founded the Moral Majority in 1979.

A third group of fundamentalists is of special interest, given the enormous success of their brethren in Latin America. They took their name from Pentecost, an occasion in the Book of Acts when the Holy Spirit descended on the apostles in tongues of fire and they preached in unknown languages. Pentecostal-like phenomena—faith healing, speaking in tongues, prophecy—have occurred in many times and places. But the contemporary movement is usually dated to the early 1900s, when such occurrences broke out in the United States among poor blacks and whites. Dispensationalists did not approve of the new manifestation: they had already relegated to a bygone age New Testament references to such practices. But many pentecostals took up dispensationalism anyway, reshaped it, and organized their own, more enthusiastic variant of fundamentalism.

The most notorious figures in pentecostalism were its faith healers. The more money you give to the Lord's work as represented by his humble servant here tonight, healers taught, the more the Lord will bless you in the form of restoring your health, reconciling your family, and bestowing you with wealth. Less flamboyant Christians were scandalized by the show-biz extravaganzas of faith healers, their claims to preside over miracles, collection of large sums of money, and rapid departure to the next engagement. "Our missionaries have to beat the bushes to get back to the field and they must render a strict account for every thin dime," an Assemblies of God official complained in 1956. "[But] we allow our churches to be 'cleaned out' periodically by men who are accountable to no one on earth or in heaven."[14]

From holding revivals in tents, churches, and auditoriums, the most successful healers went on to become radio and television evangelists. By the 1980s, they were known as the "faith confession" or "positive confession" movement. "Confession [of a need] brings possession," these men taught, or "name it and claim it." They implied that Christians who suffered affliction had only themselves to blame, for a lack of faith, and that true believers could turn God into a magic lantern to satisfy their desires. For guardians of orthodoxy, the glib promises and formulas of these men made them little better than idolaters.[15] But instead of being discredited, such teachers—like Oral Roberts and Kenneth Hagin in Tulsa, Oklahoma, and Kenneth Copeland in Fort Worth, Texas—attracted so many Christians that other leaders usually shied from confronting them, for fear of splitting the evangelical community down the middle. Pat Robertson of the Christian Broadcasting Network and Jim Bakker of the PTL ("Praise the Lord") Club picked up positive confession, and it dominated the evangelical airwaves.

This was a new kind of pentecostalism, reflecting the needs of Christians who had turned into consumers. It also had a wider social base, due partly to what was known as "charismatic renewal." Starting in the 1960s, numbers of North American Catholics and mainline Protestants began to have their own pentecostal experiences. Calling themselves neopentecostals or charismatics (again, after Greek for the pentecostal gifts or *charismata*), such Christians did not join pentecostal congregations. Instead, they vowed to remain in their old churches and renew them, hence the charismatic renewal. They did not care where you went to church: the important thing was fellowship in the Holy Spirit, turning charismaticism into a meeting ground for Catholics and Protestants.

The friendly, rhythmic worship services of charismatics could vibrate enough intimacy and warmth to make them feel like they were at heaven's gate. But their efforts to renew mainline churches usually failed. As a result, some joined pentecostal denominations such as the Assemblies of God. Others coalesced around their spiritual shepherds in new, distinctively charismatic churches. Still another outlet for their frustrations was the religious right. Charismatics cutting loose from established denominations were neither necessarily fundamentalists nor right-wing, but their inspirational leaders usually were. By the 1980s, many of the most energetic charismatic fellowships were being captured by right-wing visionaries.

But before moving into politics we need to ask, just how significant are the theological differences between fundamentalists and neo-evangelicals?[16] Historically, neo-evangelicalism grew out of fundamentalism. In practice, moreover, "fundamentalist" and "evangelical" have often functioned as alternate facades for the same operation. When the versatile Christian reaches out to the unsaved, he adopts an evangelical manner, to appeal to as wide an audience as possible. But when asking fundamentalist brethren for financial support, he claims to uphold the same "fundamentals" that they do. As he shepherds converts into new churches, fundamentalist doctrine comes to the fore. When an evangelical outreach draws on fundamentalist support, therefore, the two terms can refer to the phases of a cycle, from fundamentalist church to evangelism to consolidating a new fundamentalist church.

In this sense, the theological differences among the more conservative neo-evangelicals, the less separationist fundamentalists, and the more cautious pentecostals were not terribly significant. Members of the three categories accepted each other as different shadings of what they regarded as "mainstream evangelicalism" or the "evangelical establishment," roughly identifiable with the National Association of Evangelicals. But the unity the NAE establishment wished to maintain was under definite strain, owing to growing differences over how to view the world and change it.

In the first place, a growing number of neo-evangelicals no longer belonged in the fundamentalist camp: fundamentalists attacked them too often for going soft on the Bible. Although many neo-evangelicals still claimed to uphold an inerrant text, they conceded that their understanding of it might be flawed. The stricter fundamentalists, in contrast, tended to assert that not only the text but also their own understanding of it was inerrant.[17] Second, evangelicals and fundamentalists were dividing over what constituted legitimate "social involvement"[18]—that is, political commitment. Everyone claimed a "common Biblical norm," but they were coming to very different conclusions about its implications.[19]

Evangelical Politics

By the early 1970s, some neo-evangelicals were embarrassed by the failure of their churches to support the black civil rights move-

ment and oppose the Vietnam War. Here and there, signs of a critical social conscience emerged. Billy Graham was shaken by the fall
of his friend Richard Nixon in the Watergate scandal, repudiated
the crusading anticommunism of his youth, and spoke of nuclear
arms control as his "No. 1 social concern." [20]

One influence on Graham was what Richard Quebedeaux called
an "evangelical left." [21] Nurtured at the more open-minded seminaries and colleges, such as Fuller near Los Angeles and Wheaton
near Chicago, it drew inspiration from the "peace churches"—various Mennonite denominations and the United Brethren. The pacifist tradition of such bodies had been separationist and pietistic,
but these Christians were activists. Propagating their views from
educational lobbies and publications such as Evangelicals for Social
Action, *Sojourners,* and *The Other Side,* they claimed the right to
be heard in the National Association of Evangelicals. Although they
upheld the need for evangelism and rejected revolutionary violence, their mission in life was questioning North American militarism and convincing brethren of the need for social reform.

Peace and justice evangelicals reached their apogee during the
presidency of Jimmy Carter (1977–1981). A partisan's estimate that
they represented as many as one-quarter of white evangelicals
seems rather optimistic. [22] But millions of theologically conservative
black Protestants shared their concerns. Neo-evangelical heavy-
weights such as Billy Graham and *Christianity Today,* the biweekly
magazine he helped start in 1956, gave them a hearing. Through
the careers of people they influenced, their thinking filtered into
the leadership of many churches and agencies.

The landslide election of Ronald Reagan in 1980 was a rude
awakening. Left-of-center evangelicals had led the way in urging
brethren to get involved in social issues, but the religious right harvested the largest share of activists. It accused peace and justice
evangelicals of being liberal Protestants and criticized the neo-
evangelical establishment for tolerating them. The social issues that
well-educated neo-evangelicals from the eastern and northern
United States wished to raise—jobs for inner city blacks, world
hunger, the impending nuclear holocaust—did not capture the
imagination of most evangelicals.

What did catch their eye were fundamentalist warnings against
threats to the American way of life. The teaching of evolution, the
Supreme Court's 1962 decision to ban prayer from public schools,

its 1973 decision legalizing abortion, the Equal Rights Amendment for women, the gay rights movement—these were the issues preoccupying the majority of evangelicals. Stopping wars and helping the poor counted less than opposing the social changes which made them feel like strangers in their own country.

Some fundamentalists had tested the political waters in 1976, by supporting a Southern Baptist layman, Jimmy Carter, for president. Disappointed by Carter's policies once he was in office, they fell in with men reorganizing the right wing of the Republican party. These new allies were interested mainly in restoring laissez faire capitalism and fighting communism. But to recruit fundamentalists as foot soldiers for their wealthy financial backers, they were willing to exploit moral issues and signed up the television evangelists who became the prophets of the religious right.[23]

The Democratic incumbent, Jimmy Carter, was an elder in his local Southern Baptist congregation and taught Sunday school there. Few thought that he was an effective president, partly because he tried to comport himself in the manner of a Christian servant. That, in the eyes of the religious right, made him a wimp. They wanted a tough guy in the White House, and that is who they did much to elect. Ronald Reagan, a divorced movie actor who rarely bothered to go to church and gave little to charity, might not seem a very convincing born-again Christian. In contrast to Carter's talk about the need for humility, Reagan emphasized America's power and greatness. In contrast to Carter's attempts to promote human rights and negotiate peace in the Middle East, Reagan campaigned for new weapons systems and promoted wars. But to the religious right, he represented spiritual revival. He addressed the moral issues they cared about, especially opposition to abortion, which they regarded as murder. They never noticed that, in Guatemala and El Salvador, Reagan's election in 1980 was followed by a crescendo of official terror. The death squads of Central America thought that their man was in the White House. The religious right rejoiced in its new Christian president.

The Struggle for the NAE and the Southern Baptists

After Jerry Falwell announced that the religious right was going to "hijack" evangelicals from their moderate leaders, Billy Graham expressed his doubts. Why, Graham said, Falwell probably didn't represent more than 10 percent of evangelicals.[24] The most popular evangelist of them all did not support the religious right: he thought it had misused religion in the 1984 presidential campaign. Despite being a friend of Ronald Reagan for thirty years, Graham disagreed with "a lot" of the president's policies.[25] In Latin America, talk of keeping the church out of politics was used against the left. But when Billy Graham advised North Americans not to equate the gospel with a particular political system, he was warning them against the religious right.

A battle for North American evangelicalism was underway, between fundamentalists hitching their faith to Reaganism and evangelicals who wished to maintain the customary distance between church and state. One place to watch the contest was the National Association of Evangelicals (NAE). With forty-five denominations and more than two hundred agencies as members, the NAE was the most representative body on the evangelical scene. One front on which it was open to challenge was Biblical inerrancy. The concept was so divisive and brittle that, from the association's origin, its neo-evangelical founders had tried to downplay it. But as fundamentalists reacted against neo-evangelical innovations, they insisted that Biblical inerrancy was a necessary test of faith, a test that many NAE seminaries and colleges could no longer pass.

The other front on which the NAE had to defend itself was politics. Specifically, it had to fend off the new organizations which marched into Washington, D.C., every year with banners flying—Jerry Falwell's Moral Majority, Colonel Doner's Christian Voice, Ed McAteer's Religious Roundtable, Pat Robertson's Freedom Council, John Conlan's Faith America Foundation, Tim LaHaye's American Coalition for Traditional Values, Jay Grimstead's Coalition on Revival—each vowing to save America for God. Reflecting the wishes of constituents, the NAE joined certain religious right campaigns, against abortion, pornography, and the like. Its 1984 convention in Columbus, Ohio, was the kind of place where President Reagan could preach military intervention in Central America to loud applause.[26] But the NAE's leaders were not enthusiastic about the religious right; distrusting its crusades, they warned against reducing the church to a political program.[27]

As an illustration of the religious right's plans for their association, NAE officials could contemplate the spectacle of their most influential offspring, the National Religious Broadcasters (NRB). A product of the fundamentalist struggle to break into radio and television, the NRB defended the interests of broadcasters who, in some cases, were raising funds with methods worthy of a traveling medicine show. The losers were local churches, from whose members they were siphoning quantities of money. In 1981, the president of the Moody Bible Institute warned that such parachurch ministries were becoming the tail wagging the dog.[28]

The NRB's annual convention in Washington, D.C., was, meanwhile, becoming a three-ring circus for the religious right. Ronald Reagan was a regular participant. Invited speakers drummed up enthusiasm for CIA-subsidized "wars of liberation." In 1983, the convention gave President Efraín Ríos Montt of Guatemala an award for meritorious Christian service.[29] Not everyone was pleased by the NRB's transformation into a preconvention for the Republican party, however; according to members upset about the obvious politicization, it was becoming the National Republican Broadcasters.[30]

The religious right was also able to capture the helm of the country's largest Protestant denomination, the 14.4 million strong Southern Baptist Convention (SBC). Despite a conservative reputation, this "Catholic Church of the South" harbored a moderate as well as a fundamentalist theological tendency. In politics, Southern Baptists ran the gamut from the far right to cautious liberalism of the Jimmy Carter variety. When the religious right tried to use the denomination for its purposes, it was frustrated by moderates in charge of the institutional machinery.

One issue in the ensuing struggle was doctrinal integrity. Fundamentalists charged that the SBC's seminaries and missions were being taken over by liberals. Another debate was over the denomination's role in secular politics. More than any other Christian tradition, it is important to remember, Baptists pioneered the separation of church and state. In contrast to moderates who wished to maintain the principle of separation, fundamentalists wanted to turn the SBC into a power base for a new city of God.

Soon the confrontations at the SBC's annual conventions were the leading spectator sport in North American evangelicalism. As the moderates lost control, they accused their adversaries of unethical tactics such as packing delegations.[31] But by capturing the SBC's presidency year after year, the fundamentalists gained control of the appointments to its governing boards. Through the boards, by the late 1980s, they were starting to take control of the denomination's seminaries and agencies.

At stake was one of the largest evangelical missions, with 3,597 missionaries and 6,759 short termers in 1985. In Latin America, 1,276 missionaries worked with national denominations claiming 17,500 preaching points and 900,000 members.[32] Given the fundamentalist proclivity for sniffing out and purging suspected liberals, the mission board's president warned that imposing a rigid definition of Biblical inerrancy would undermine the SBC's effort to evangelize the world. Campaigns to make stands on foreign policy endangered the mission's policy of political neutrality.[33] That is, it would make Southern Baptist missionaries even more vulnerable to kidnappings and reprisals than they already were.

Despite talk of a possible schism in the SBC, there was little doubt which faction would carry the majority of the churches with it. The religious right seemed to be reflecting and reinforcing the dominant sentiments in white evangelical churches. According to a survey by James Guth, between 1981 and 1984 Southern Baptist ministers identifying themselves as Republicans increased from 29 to 66 percent.[34] At a 1986 NAE event in Washington, D.C., a poll of 110 evangelicals indicated that only 12 percent planned to vote for a Democratic candidate in the next presidential election.[35]

Nuclear Dispensationalism

Premillennialists have always looked to the end of the world with a certain eagerness. Not only will the last days be catastrophic, but really dedicated premillennialists are doing everything possible to hasten their arrival. In the 1980s more and more were becoming activists in this sense, as if the Lord needed their help to carry out his agenda. By personally fulfilling this or that prophecy, they hoped to tip the Lord's hand, so to speak. Perhaps the most popular and the least threatening of such efforts was completing the evangelism of the world, based on Matthew 24:14, that "good news of the Kingdom will be proclaimed to men all over the world. . . . And then the end will come."

Other attempts to fulfill prophecy were more alarming. Take the campaign to rebuild the Temple in Jerusalem. Because that would require demolishing a Muslim holy place on the same spot, it could set off the very holy war that premillennialists were predicting.[36] Then there was nuclear dispensationalism. Interpreting the Bible in terms of their geopolitical preoccupations, some premillennialists hailed nuclear weapons as divinely ordained instruments. Maybe the impending atomic flash was the dawn of the millennial kingdom. Whether to detonate the final action of history or simply defend the church against world atheism, nuclear dispensationalism captured the imagination of the religious right. "Developing nuclear weapons was a part of God's plan," exclaimed Ed McAteer, head of the Religious Roundtable. "Nuclear war may be the fulfillment of prophecy. We need to be prepared. Before we go, they go. I can do that in all good Christian conscience."[37]

As this kind of thinking suggests, premillennialism was an orthodox doctrine which, carried far enough, turned Christianity inside out. Belief in the Lord's return could degenerate into enthusiasm for new systems of mass murder, opposition to negotiations with the Soviet Union, even resignation to a nuclear holocaust. "Those who subscribe to this latter-day fatalism," wrote Tom Sine, "conclude that nothing can be done to alter the growing plight of the world's poor, change unjust economic structures, or advance the cause of God's kingdom here on earth. . . . Some even seem to derive satisfaction from global disasters that seem to confirm their end-time scenarios. . . . I am persuaded that the powers of darkness have pulled off an amazing coup."[38]

When Ronald Reagan's sympathy with nuclear dispensationalism became an issue in the 1984 election, moderate evangelicals disavowed it.[39] But even the religious right was having second thoughts about its enthusiastic prophecies of doom; maybe images of apocalyptic disaster were not the best way to get churchgoers into the political arena. Now that America was returning to greatness under the Reagan administration, talk of imminent national collapse seemed inappropriate. One thing was certain: the religious right was tired of the political backwardness of its brethren. "I trust you know that our destiny is to rule the nations," a pastor boomed out at a Sacramento, California, meeting. "Our great problem is that we can't find Christians to rule over their own neighborhood, let alone city, county, or state."[40]

Reconstruction and the Latter Rain

Based on biblical language about taking dominion over the earth, the religious right began to talk about "taking dominion" over American society and "reconstructing" it on biblical principles. Emblematic of their conquest outlook, some took the next logical step: that the Bible promised Christians political dominion over all the nations. "The command of our General is to bring the nations of the world under His dominion," one believer wrote. "We have been ordered to disciple them and promised that our Lord will be with us until the conquest is complete. The leaders and people of the nations that plot to throw off the rule of God are conspiring in vain. Individuals and nations must be told: the Kingdom of God has come and of its increase there will be no end."[41]

One inspiration for this kind of thinking was Reformed theology, descended from John Calvin and his experiment in Geneva. The religious right were not the only ones looking to the Reformed tradition for guidance on the church's role in society. Across the political spectrum, evangelicals were talking about the need, not just to wait passively for the second coming of Christ, but to realize the values of the kingdom here and now. Some neo-evangelicals used kingdom values such as social justice to distinguish between the cultural and the biblical, to separate the authentic gospel message from man-made distortions, and on that basis to issue radical critiques of North American evangelicalism.[42]

But in the view of right-wing Reformed thinkers, of the "Christian Reconstruction" movement, the idea was to return to God's rule as exemplified by the Puritans who colonized North America in the seventeenth century. Because these thinkers were also attracted to the survival-of-the-fittest ethics of the ultraright, their idea of making America a Christian nation was a ferocious combination of theocracy and social darwinism.[43] "The so-called underdeveloped societies," one luminary of reconstructionism wrote, "are underdeveloped because they are socialist, demonist and cursed."[44]

Another inspiration for taking dominion was an obscure pentecostal tradition known as the "latter rain." Conceived as an outpouring of the Holy Spirit, it watered the religious right and some of the most dynamic missions to Latin America. The tradition originated among evangelicals hungering to obtain the same kind of spiritual power bestowed by the Holy Spirit in New Testament times. That "former rain," they decided, would be followed by a "latter rain" of miracles at the end of the world. Historians have not given the latter rain a great deal of attention. Only recently has the influence of its teachings come into view.

But at least some of the present diffusion can be traced to a descent of the Holy Spirit during the revivals of the late 1940s, on the unlikely spot of North Battleford, Saskatchewan. The occasion was a local schism in the Canadian branch of the Assemblies of God. The leaders of the revolt prophesied a universal revival, a mighty move of the spirit that would sweep the globe in anticipation of Christ's return. Declaring their divine appointment, they announced the restoration of New Testament offices and appointed themselves apostles and prophets. Physical healing and other spiritual gifts they imparted through the laying on of hands. For their followers they pronounced detailed prophecies to obey. After arousing fears of taking over the Assemblies of God, the leaders were condemned as unbiblical and driven out of established churches.[45]

As the episode suggests, spiritual downpours of miracles and revelations were too disruptive for established pentecostal denominations. By this stage they were pursuing moderation and acceptance from the wider Christian world. Soon the latter rain seemed all but forgotten, leaving behind only fringe groups who regarded themselves as the "manifest sons of God" or "overcomers." Prior to Christ's return, they believed, they would take dominion over the earth and death itself.[46] But the ideas associated with the latter rain persisted as a sort of esoteric tradition running underground in the pentecostal movement. At the next great pentecostal revival, in the charismatic renewal of the 1960s, they percolated upward in the form of several related doctrines.

One such conviction was that, through "word power," elite

Christians could command events and rule the universe, a belief popularized in the "positive confession" or "name it and claim it" movement. Another latter rain doctrine stressed submission to pastoral authority: it manifested itself in the "shepherding" or "discipleship" movement. Like their latter rain mentors, shepherding leaders anointed themselves apostles and prophets, practiced the laying on of hands, and delivered prophecies for their disciples to follow to the letter.

An Argentine named Juan Carlos Ortiz—coincidentally, brother-in-law of the well-known evangelist Luis Palau—played a prominent role in formulating the shepherding doctrine. Although driven out of the Assemblies of God in his own country, Ortiz and his system were brought to the United States by a group called Christian Growth Ministries in Fort Lauderdale, Florida. As the Fort Lauderdale revivalists set up chains of submission to themselves around the country, they became too successful for the pentecostal establishment, which accused them of taking "unscriptural control" over the lives of followers and "sheepstealing" from the flocks of other men.[47]

During the resulting scandal, the shepherding movement is supposed to have mended its authoritarian ways. But under the name of the "restoration revival," the same leaders, along with many new ones, expanded their agenda for the 1980s.[48] Now that many charismatics had despaired of renewing established denominations, the restorationists urged them to defect to dynamic new charismatic fellowships that would "restore" the authentic New Testament church.[49] The restorationists also hoped for a mass revival to sweep the globe and usher in God's kingdom. On the foundation of the restored church, the world would be built anew. As for their own role, they saw themselves as corulers with Christ, spiritual lords of a new world order. Among them were the religious advisers surrounding Guatemala's evangelical dictator, Efraín Ríos Montt.

The Restoration Revival

The restoration movement had the support of some major television evangelists, including Pat Robertson. But at the grass roots it consisted of a multitude of charismatic ministries and churches. A number of leaders came out of the Assemblies of God, whose combination of fervor and supervision have produced many a spiritual empresario who decides to follow his own call. In Latin America, the restorationists were represented chiefly by small, new missions partaking of the tremendous pentecostal ferment. But their influence was also visible in two far-flung organizations. One was Youth With A Mission (YWAM), the largest of the agencies sending tens of thousands of young North Americans on brief evangelizing tours around the world. The other was the Full Gospel Businessmen's Fellowship, a network of men's clubs whose movers and shakers— generally Christian businessmen from the Sunbelt—were seeking to evangelize Latin America's business, political, and military elites.

This was the dynamic, expanding fringe of American evangelicalism. Restoration charismatics tended to be young, recently converted from lives of sin, and still undergoing spiritual crises. Some were disoriented products of the counterculture looking for a way to go straight. Certain leaders were formerly rock musicians. Occasionally, the personal magnetism of leaders, their claim to special relationships with God, and heavy demands on followers led to accusations that they were setting up cults. Without firm traditions or higher authorities except the Lord himself, these churches could have a "loose cannon" quality about them, as if anything might happen. At one moment, they seemed to be wallowing in the consumeristic self-gratification of the "name it and claim it" movement. Take another look, and they were shock troops for the religious right.

On biblical inerrancy and the need to confront evil, such Christians were as fundamentalist as they came. Some would say fanatical. There was no shade of gray in their moral universe, just black and white, good and evil. Their belief in spiritual warfare—battles with demons, miraculous deliverances, and the like—could become so strong that is seemed to overpower basic human decency. But restorationists did not preach separation from the world. By tolerating doctrinal differences that old-line fundamentalists did not, they avoided some of the dogmatism and feuding for which fundamentalists had become famous.

One reason restorationists attained a certain ecumenicity was their overriding commitment to right-wing politics. As a result, they helped knit together the religious right. In foreign affairs, their central tenet was identifying the United States as God's right hand in the struggle against communism. On the application of North American firepower around the world, they seemed to have no doubts. Whatever the cause was, it must be righteous.

Exemplifying the restorationist style was Maranatha Campus Ministries, one of the new charismatic groups moving into Latin America. At its best, Maranatha offered warm, enthusiastic worship and close-knit fellowship in its hundred college congregations. But its view of the world was extremely rigid; some would say superstitious. "Nothing is neutral in the Maranatha world," a former member reported. "Either it's God's will or it's the work of the devil, down to doing the laundry."[50]

Maranatha was the work of Bob Weiner, a youth minister who came across a bit like a football coach. At one of his rallies in 1981, the atmosphere was a bit like football practice the Monday after losing a game. Coach didn't think his team was trying hard enough. Some parents watching from the bleachers decided that Weiner was trying too hard. They complained that their kids were undergoing bizarre personality changes, flunking out of school, and giving Maranatha large sums of money intended for their education. When parents brought these concerns to Maranatha, one response was that they were being used by the devil.

Following incidents in which parents of Maranatha members kidnapped and "deprogrammed" their children, evangelical cult-watchers issued a report. They concluded that Maranatha was replacing the authority of the Bible with the authority of Bob Weiner. Among other things, the investigators were not impressed with the "words from the Lord"—prophecies or divine revelations—with which leaders kept their followers in line.[51] In Maranatha, the authoritarianism of the shepherding movement was alive and well.

Weiner was also known for what he referred to as "calling out the troops"—that is, directing his students to hold campus rallies for causes such as the Nicaraguan contras.[52] In the belief that the contras were Christian freedom fighters, members distributed a publication that offered contributors souvenir casings from bullets fired at Sandinistas.[53] Pointing to the danger of a Soviet amphibious assault along the Gulf Coast of the United States, Maranatha published an opinion poll reporting that a large majority of college males were willing to join the armed forces to fight in Central America.

North American Christians had a responsibility to be watchmen for liberty throughout the world, Maranatha's newspaper editorialized in 1984. Now that President Reagan was making crucial military decisions about Nicaragua, the newspaper urged its readers to bombard the entire situation with prayer. Whatever military measures might come into play in coming months, Maranatha observed, trust could not be placed in weapons. No, Christians would have to call on the Lord for supernatural intervention against the Sandinista revolution. No military action by the United States or anyone else would succeed, unless Christians first did battle in the spiritual realm.[54]

Dominion Theology

When enthusiasts talked about Christian dominion over the earth, they tended to be vague about whether this would occur before or after Christ's return. The precise chronology was a subject over which most evangelicals preferred not to quarrel. But fundamentalism owed much of its urgency to a sense of impending doom. Those who talked optimistically about restoring the church, reconstructing America on biblical foundations, and taking dominion over the earth were inviting controversy. They were contradicting a central tenet of premillennialism, that the world's slide into sin and disorder would be reversed only by Christ's physical return.

At the 1986 congress of the Coalition on Revival, an amalgam of restorationists and reconstructionists intent on galvanizing the church to take command of society, organizers felt that there was no point in debating millennial chronologies. This is part of the standard formula for evangelical unity, and the five hundred activists at the congress did not seem greatly concerned about their differences on the matter. But while most came out of premillennial backgrounds and reported to premillennial constituencies, quite a number seemed recent converts to postmillennialism. This is a very different picture of the end-times: Christ will return to earth, not in a terrible time of tribulation preceding the millennium as the

premillennial tendency has it, but only after his confident and victorious faithful have built the thousand-year kingdom.

Other participants at the Coalition on Revival were pushing a
new, politicized version of what is called "amillennialism." In the
pre- and postmillenial debate this is a third, intermediary position,
which usually has pictured God's reign on earth in rather spiritual
terms: the kingdom is said to have already arrived in the form of a
victorious church, for example. But now religious right activists
were giving amillennialism a militant new twist. They were concluding that, as the servants of a Christ present in spiritual form,
they would corule with him over the earth.[55]

Such distinctions may be hard to follow, but they represent theologies of power on the religious right. If premillennialists derived
their energy from the vision of an impending catastrophe, postmil-
lennialists and amillennialists inspired themselves with the thought
of building the kingdom. Each vision situated believers in the cock-
pit of the struggle between good and evil. Although the two contradicted each other, the religious right was so caught up in their emotional power that it was combining their images of apocalypse and
triumph in dramatic new ways.

"I'm panmillennial," ran a joke at the Coalition on Revival, "because I think it will all pan out in the end." Whether religious right
activists were pre-, post- or amillennial, they expected to take
charge. In a shift of eschatology becoming known as dominion or
kingdom theology, they were moving away from the long-held view
that Christ would return to a beleaguered Christian remnant. Instead, more now argued, Christ would return to a world occupied
and redeemed in anticipation of his coming. The Great Commission would be fulfilled only when the gospel held direct sway over
every government and the majority of earth's population had accepted Christ.

All over the world, dominion thinkers such as Pat Robertson believed, Christians would take power.[56] Nations floundering in debt
and corruption would be reconstructed along Christian lines. Their
rulers would look to God's Word for guidance on economics and
foreign affairs. Businessmen would become honorable. Ill-gotten
gains would pass into the hands of Christians, who would use them
to help the needy. Christian journalists would finally tell the world

the truth, about everything. In Latin America, bloodshed would be banished, and Cuba freed from tyranny.[57]

When religious right activists departed from premillennialism, they often tried to sound as if they were not doing any such thing. But despite lip service to the central hope of premillennialism, Christ's physical return, religious right activists were starting to criticize premillennialism as an "eschatology of defeat."[58] The key error, some argued, was the doctrine of "the rapture." This is the fundamentalist belief that, at a strategic moment just before the "great tribulation" preceding Christ's return, believers will be snatched away "to meet the Lord in the air" (I Thessalonians 4:16–17). According to the most popular version of the rapture, true Christians will therefore be saved the terror and pain experienced by the rest of humanity at world's end.

But for a growing number of religious right militants, such a belief was too convenient. "Rapture theology is laced with escapism," Dennis Peacocke told California activists in 1985. "It leaves earth to the highest bidder, which is Satan. . . . The Lord's prayer . . . says bring your kingdom to earth now. We've been waiting for the kingdom to come save us like a spaceship, but it's not going to. . . . We want God to solve our problems, like a welfarist God mentality, [as if] God is the great Washington, D.C., in the sky. We make welfare prayers instead of empowerment prayers to him. But the Bible says we're to be corulers with him."

Peacocke expected a real division in the church, and within the next few years. A lot of theology was going to have to be rewritten, he told the small audience. God was going to have to turn the church upside down, that is rightside up, to let the theology drain out and make room for what the Bible really said. There was going to be a lot of fallout. Bible Christians were going to be told that they were moving into the social gospel, that they were not teaching the gospel of Jesus Christ. But God was building up a new government in exile, and it would triumph.[59]

In the meantime there was the question of alliances: with whom could Christians make common cause? According to old-fashioned fundamentalists, partnership with the godless in any endeavor was "worldly." Yet now right-wing evangelicals were working with anyone who shared their convictions, including Catholics and Mormons. The most interesting of these new alliances was with the Reverend Sun Myung Moon.

Moon was from the north of Korea, where it used to be said that a messiah would be born. That tradition and his time in a communist labor camp shaped his aim in life: to defeat communism by unifying the world's religions around himself, hence the name of his Unification Church. In the early 1970s, Moon moved to the United States where he attracted thousands of young Americans around him in a personal cult. One factor working in his favor was an impressive series of bank accounts. The money apparently came from his business empire, estimated to control $1 billion in assets.[60] In 1978 a U.S. congressional panel concluded that another source of money was the Korean Central Intelligence Agency, for whom Moon appeared to be buying influence in Washington. As it turned out, Moon's ministry was directed above all to the power center of the Western world. His daily newspaper, *The Washington Times*, included former CIA officers on its staff, and it hewed faithfully to the agency's propaganda themes.[61] The paper was so influential that one activist called it the "newsletter" of the new right.[62]

Moon was also passing out money to his Christian allies. This might seem like normal promiscuity in politics, except for the nature of Moon's claims. Leading figures in the religious right, men who had made careers by denouncing liberals for worshipping man rather than God, were accepting money from a man who aimed to unify the world around himself as messiah, like antichrist in the book of Revelation.[63]

The Religious Right and World Mission

After the Vietnam War and the Watergate scandals, the evangelical missions began to distance themselves from Washington's foreign policy, at least rhetorically. Something similar had occurred toward the end of a previous era of military intervention, in the 1920s and 1930s, when evangelical missionaries criticized big-stick diplomacy in Mexico and the Caribbean.[64] By the 1970s, even conservatives were acknowledging that missionaries should not wrap the Bible in an American flag. But on the religious right, millennialist logic continued to produce enthusiastic equations between evangelizing the world and defending the United States.

If Christ would not return until his followers completed the Great Commission, such thinkers reasoned, it could hardly be accidental that such a high percentage of the world's Christians lived in the United States. Didn't 70 percent of the world's trained Christians and 80 percent of its Christian resources come from the United States? Didn't 90 percent of all the money spent on world evangelism?[65] Surely then, the United States had a special role in God's plan. Even though it was not the only country with the duty of completing the Great Commission, unto whom much had been given, much was required. If America had been more richly blessed than all other nations combined, then it was America's duty to bear an outsize share of the task.

Yet active efforts were being made to stop world evangelism. Wasn't door after door being slammed shut? Because the United States was the headquarters of world mission, numerous evangelicals believed, it must be a special target of the devil. Satan knew he had to destroy the United States as a bastion of godliness, as a missionary nation, before he could wreak havoc throughout the world.[66] The U.S. military machine was God's way of defending the peace so that his message of salvation could be made known.[67] Washington's adversaries around the world therefore continued to be God's adversaries, and evangelizing the world continued to hinge on U.S. power.

Not all North American evangelicals were governed by this logic. From the editorial pages of *Christianity Today*, intellectuals of the neo-evangelical establishment inveighed against it. Even the most well-known proponent of flag and Bible thinking in former decades, Billy Graham, repudiated it. Nor was the religious right the dominant force in the foreign missions. But with dominion theology, a loud reactionary wing was reviving potent equations between God and America. Out in the churches, chauvinistic thinking still had an enormous appeal. As a result, when revolution broke out close to home in Central America, few evangelical leaders were willing to object to enlisting missionary work in U.S. foreign policy.

Chapter Four

The Evangelical Mission
Movement

*One of the first things learned in mission work is that when you cast
your bread upon the water, it returns to you in the form of requests
for money. Most of the time the letters will beat you home! . . . The
majority of people I minister to around the world follow up our time
together with a letter requesting money.*

Monte Wilson[1]

Southern California might seem an unlikely center for the salvation
of the world. Yet this latter-day Babylon was headquarters for more
Christian missions than anywhere else on the globe.[2] Long before
southern California turned into a metropolis, its springlike climate
attracted seekers of salvation as well as good health and fortune.
Among the men who enriched themselves in the area's booms and
busts, some became preoccupied with the Lord's soon return. Two
of them, Union Oil Company founders Lyman and Milton Stewart,
sponsored the *Fundamentals* books which, in the early 1900s, gave
fundamentalism its name.[3] Lyman was also a financial backer of the
Bible Institute of Los Angeles. Through its Church of the Open
Door, next to the Los Angeles Public Library, passed the founders
of two groups, the Wycliffe Bible Translators and the New Tribes
Mission, whose nine thousand missionaries have worked in more
than eleven hundred languages around the world.

Southern California provided many an opportunity to start new
kinds of religious organizations. As the capital of the entertainment
industry, it gave evangelists new techniques for attracting the pub-

68

lic. Over the radio or through motion pictures, they could draw supporters from across the country. As millions of migrants arrived in southern California, those in the habit of going to church no longer felt obliged to continue attending the same denomination as their family back home. This enabled the most promotion-conscious pastors to attract huge congregations around themselves, creating the so-called "super churches."

Southern California was not an especially pious place. A 1984 survey showed that, on a Sunday morning, two of every three people in Orange County would rather be somewhere other than a worship service. Church attendance was below the national average.[4] But those who did go to church kept southern California a hotbed of religious experimentation, and their enthusiasm went in many directions.

One was thinking up new strategies to evangelize the planet. This was the main activity at the Fuller School of World Mission, the Missions Advanced Research Center at World Vision, and the U.S. Center for World Mission, all of which made southern California the capital of evangelical missions research. Another passion was the struggle against communism. There were demagogues dating to the McCarthy era, like Dr. Fred Schwarz of the Christian Anti-Communism Crusade; Bible smugglers like the Romanian refugee Richard Wurmbrand; even an organization called High Adventure Ministries which ran a radio station for Major Saad Haddad, the Lebanese Christian warlord.

In the 1970s, the world southern California evangelicals wished to save started coming to them. Millions of foreign immigrants speaking more than a hundred languages flooded into their area.[5] Many were refugees from the Asian and Central American wars pursued by two southern California politicians whom evangelicals helped vote into the White House, Richard Nixon and Ronald Reagan. But the massive immigration only seemed to intensify the determination to evangelize all nations and peoples. Fascinated by the approach of the year 2000, evangelicals were determined to confront every person on earth with the offer of salvation. From their churches, Bible colleges, and mission agencies, they were mustering for an unprecedented level of evangelism, to expound salvation on every city block, in every village, and on every radio band around the world.

The majority of men and women going abroad were specialists—pilots, church planters, linguists, teachers, broadcasters. They translated the Bible, produced native language records, tapes, and television programs, started Bible institutes and radio stations, administered correspondence courses, organized innumerable world conferences, and tried to saturate entire countries with their message. There were medical missions, missions to universities, even ships loaded with hundreds of young missionaries plowing the seas—the *Doulos* and *Logos* of Operation Mobilization, the *Anastasis* and *Good Samaritan* of Youth With A Mission. In remote mountains and jungles, bush airlines like the Missionary Aviation Fellowship maintained supply lines, evacuated medical patients, and provided help in disasters. Backing them up were relief and development organizations—World Vision, World Relief, World Concern, World Neighbors.[6]

This was not just a North American effort. It drew funds and volunteers from both Western Europe and the Third World. But more than half the world's evangelical missionaries came from the temples of a single, prosperous republic, which led the world in wealth, power, the export of weapons and religion. Amidst the arrogance of the new Rome, however, some evangelicals were asking interesting questions about their missions. Despite the obsession with numbers and growth rates, disagreements were in the air.

Accordingly, this chapter looks into the evangelical debates over missionary work, starting with a 1974 gathering known as the Lausanne Congress. Proclaimed as the dawn of a new era in missions, Lausanne sharpened differences between neo-evangelicals and fundamentalists. While some of the former were trying to "contextualize" the gospel in local, indigenous terms, the latter continued to insist on a single correct interpretation. Based on that same contextualization movement, evangelical dissenters also challenged the continuing missionary role in Latin America. As the most successful North American agencies swelled into "mission multinationals," critics accused them of placing Latin American churches in a new system of dependency.

Soldiers of Christ

Fifty years ago, as fundamentalists squabbled among themselves on the fringes of American life, it would have been hard to foresee their present strength on the mission field. But starting in the late 1940s, a generation of young fundamentalists trooped overseas to win the world for Christ. Many were military veterans, in a wave of mission interest that can be traced to the World War II revivals inspired by an organization called Youth for Christ. At a time of national catharsis, Joel Carpenter has pointed out, the evangelists of Youth for Christ borrowed techniques and images from consumer culture to make fundamentalist religion appeal to a wider audience.

Billy Graham came out of Youth for Christ, as did the founders of a number of leading missions. Symbolically, these men translated the war against fascism into the drive to evangelize the world.[7] One result was the paramilitary language—"beachheads," "invasions," "advances"—which many missions use to this day. Another was a defensive identification with the United States, in contrast to the questioning attitude that missionaries of the 1920s and 1930s displayed toward North American interests.[8] As evangelicals struggled to rejoin the mainstream, they embraced their country's new role as a world power.

Identifying with American power could attract converts, of course. But in an era of decolonization, it also made the missions more vulnerable to Third World nationalism. Toward the end of the Vietnam War, even conservatives began to sense that they were falling behind the times. A growing number of countries—sixty-seven according to a 1980 count—were keeping missionaries out or restricting their activities.[9] Even U.S. allies such as Taiwan and Israel were making life uncomfortable. But suspicious governments were often less a problem than restive converts. Many evangelical missionaries were ill-equipped to deal with decolonizing the church; they remained deeply involved in the administration of churches which, in their view, had yet to mature sufficiently for independence. Despite the avowed purpose of working themselves out of a job, they were not turning their functions over to the people they had trained. Of the resulting conflicts, the most frequent were over the huge gap in remuneration between missionaries and national pastors.[10] For missionaries who had idealized their work, quarrels over money were disillusioning in the extreme.

No less painful was the sterility of so many mission efforts. Failure to start thriving churches was the rule, not the exception. For every victory played up for the folks back home, there were several other assignments where little or nothing had been achieved. What spiritual harvests had occurred were full of weeds—unacceptably native interpretations of doctrine—because the people had assimilated bits and pieces of missionary teaching into their own belief system. Instead of conquering continents for Christ, missionaries had tied themselves down to servicing small enclaves of clients. Drives to evangelize the world had degenerated into two-bit patronage rackets. Where numbers of people were converting, usually it was under the auspices of national-led churches, which tended to be pentecostal, difficult for the majority of evangelical missionaries to accept theologically. Judging from where churches were growing rapidly, it seemed as if the recipe for success was for missionaries to leave.

Then there was the loss of interest in missionary work at home. Theological liberalism was to blame, evangelicals argued, but enthusiasm for mission careers was dwindling even among their own youth. At the 1970 convention of the Inter-Varsity Christian Fellowship, the traditional gathering for college students heading for the mission field, there was less enthusiasm for soulwinning than for social change.[11] At the convention, young activists denounced the racism of their churches and the militarism of their country.[12] The percentage of Inter-Varsity conventioneers pledging foreign service declined, at one point to 8 percent.[13] Even though the missionary force continued to grow in the late 1960s and early 1970s, support from key constituencies seemed to be stagnating.

The Lausanne Covenant

Maybe it was time for missionaries to go home. That was the conclusion reached by the mainline denominations of the National Council of Churches (NCC). From 1969 to 1979, the number of missionaries affiliated with the NCC declined from 8,279 to 4,817.[14] But their evangelical rivals hung on and, wherever possible, continued to expand. As far as evangelicals were concerned, the reasons were entirely biblical. While ecumenical Protestants were redefining Christian mission in terms of peacemaking and humanitarian service, evangelicals remained convinced of the need to save souls from hell. Many also believed that evangelizing the last unreached people would pave the way for Christ's return, bringing history to its triumphant conclusion. For these Christians, talk about a "moratorium" on missions demonstrated that liberals had turned their backs on the gospel. To suggest that the need for missionary work had ended was so false as to be diabolical.

Defending the priority of evangelism brought together the Lausanne Congress in 1974. Neo-evangelicals attribute great significance to this event: it was the most notable of two decades of world conferences organized by Billy Graham and his evangelistic association, in their customary role of integrating factionalized brethren into the neo-evangelical establishment. In the Lausanne Covenant, several thousand delegates affirmed the usual biblical imperatives. Underlining their disagreements with liberal Protestants, they radically expanded the definition of the need for missionary work, a point to which we will return. Just as significantly, however, they took certain positions that widened the differences between neo-evangelicals and fundamentalists.[15]

First, the Lausanne Congress acknowledged the distinction between Christianity and Western civilization. "When I go to preach the gospel," stated Billy Graham, repenting of his past, "I go as an ambassador for the Kingdom of God—not America."[16] This might seem an unremarkable concession. But it suggested that the gospel would have to be de-Westernized, which fundamentalists found hard to accept. Another innovation widening neo-evangelical differences vis-à-vis fundamentalists was Lausanne's declaration in favor of "social responsibility." This might seem like another unremarkable step, but some evangelicals saw it as a license for left-wing activism.

The Lausanne Covenant became the common denominator for the neo-evangelical missions movement. Along with European and Third World leaders, the major North American parachurch agencies set up an ongoing Lausanne Committee, to hold periodic consultations and keep the peace among the diverse groups which had been brought together.[17] Among fundamentalists, the whole process remained suspect.

Mission Think Tanks, Church Growth, Signs and Wonders

Figuring prominently in the Lausanne deliberations were research centers and the people who ran them. These were "missiologists"—

generally older missionaries who had returned from the field, acquired an advanced degree (often in anthropology), and now studied how to most efficiently and diplomatically evangelize the world. Instead of accepting faith or eschatology as an excuse for failure, missiologists made social science the framework for evaluating whether missionaries were effective or not.

The high mass and mecca of this applied discipline was in Pasadena, California, at the Fuller Theological Seminary and its School of World Mission. Named after a popular radio preacher, Fuller had been organized by neo-evangelical scholars in 1947. From the start, it pledged to uphold biblical inerrancy and other fundamentals of the faith. But since inerrancy was incompatible with critical scholarship, which the seminary also prized, in 1972 it adopted a doctrine of "limited inerrancy." Scandalized by Fuller's failure to hold the line on the Bible, fundamentalists tried, unsuccessfully, to strangle it financially.[18]

As for the School of World Mission, fundamentalists considered it the seminary's partner in subversion. One reason was that it specialized in "midcourse correction" of missionaries home on leave, battered by experience and in search of more rewarding approaches. When Fuller professors talked about culture change, they were referring not just to converting the natives but also to shaking up antiquated mission structures which, after all, were a subculture of their own. By 1985 Fuller had trained more than twenty-six hundred people in evangelical strategy, was enrolling around five hundred students each year and—although colleagues elsewhere might beg to differ—claimed to have produced half the missiological research in the world.

Avatar and sage of the School of World Mission was Donald McGavran. A wispy little ancient of a man with a career stretching back to 1923, McGavran managed to identify his name with most developments in missiology for two-thirds of a century. As a third generation Disciples of Christ missionary to India, he had found himself administering institutions such as schools and hospitals rather than evangelizing the lost. One of his first critiques was directed against the idea of the mission station as a beacon of light in pagan territory, around which a church is to be built. The approach was self-isolating, even anti-evangelical, McGavran argued, because it made the few initial converts dependent on mission patronage. The resulting mission-subsidized churches tended to become self-limiting patronage structures. Since existing converts did not wish to divide a fixed amount of mission largesse among more people, they failed to evangelize, defeating the purpose of the mission.

McGavran also had to decide whether to confront India's caste system. Did Hindus have to break with it to become Christians? Usually missionaries said yes, which meant converting individuals, plucking them out of their social group, and turning them into cultural misfits. But the only numerical successes which Christianity could boast were mass conversions from lower caste groups. From these popular movements, often beyond missionary control, McGavran concluded that people usually preferred to convert to the new religion, not as individuals, but as members of their social group. In the words of an admirer, Christianity usually did not "spread out indiscriminately, like ink in water, but along the lines of cultures and languages."[19] His core doctrine, derived from many a failure, was that missionaries should encourage "people movements" of entire tribes or other "homogenous units."

Eventually, after McGavran's mainline brethren rejected his insights, he shook the dust from his sandals and went over to the evangelicals. From the Fuller School of World Mission, where he became the first dean in 1965, he preached the need to research the most effective methods of evangelism through empirical, preferably quantitative testing.[20] The critical approach McGavran encouraged at Fuller led in a number of directions, including efforts to adapt evangelical Christianity to non-Western world views. But his first and most well-known product, one still attached closely to his own name and that of Fuller, was the church-growth movement. Church-growth reasoning was very simple and bound to be controversial in a religion predicated on universal brotherhood: if people preferred to become Christians as part of social groups, without having to cross racial, linguistic, or class barriers, then the most successful, fastest growing churches would be socially homogenous.

Church-growth experts were the sales and marketing specialists of evangelical world mission. Instead of going to the places with the fewest believers, those "unreached" by the gospel, they argued, missionaries should go where the most people were already converting. If there were only a few Christians in a place, maybe it was because the necessary conditions for success were lacking, in which case missionaries should find somewhere more rewarding to work. This was an interesting reversal of traditional wisdom, but it raised the possibility that trend-following missions would concentrate on taking credit for preexisting movements instead of starting new ones.

Theologians tended to look down on church growthers as philistines. There were frequent objections to their infatuation with statistics, graph paper, average annual growth rates, and resistance receptivity factors. When you got right down to it, the hundreds of theses and texts produced by the church-growth movement seemed to boil down to think positive, scratch where it itches, and encourage local leadership. It was an idolatry of quantitative success, critics argued, and potentially racist, too, because it could be used to justify segregation from the poor and nonwhite. That said, what church growthers called their "homogenous unit principle" was not so different from the premise behind nationalizing any mission church: that Peruvians, Sri Lankans, and so forth had the right to run their own affairs.[21]

If the goal was to attract the maximum number of people on Sunday morning, church-growth logic was hard to beat. Tailoring the church to the culture and using market techniques to offer an agreeable path to salvation definitely worked.[22] But as a result, church-growth advocates were not very interested in social and political issues. Controversial commitments were to be avoided, they advised, for fear of causing dissension and slowing growth. Their favorite pastime was lecturing mainline Protestants on why their memberships were falling. "Theological liberalism," McGavran's chief disciple and Fuller professor Peter Wagner admonished, "shows the highest negative correlation with growth."[23]

Soon devotion to growth rates was inspiring pilgrimages to the fastest growing temples in Latin America, those filled with pentecostals. For a time, Peter Wagner argued that what made pentecostal churches grow so rapidly was, not their distinctive religious inspiration in the Holy Spirit, but other characteristics which nonpentecostal churches could imitate, such as lay leadership and the expectation that each member evangelizes.[24] This was indeed a point where pentecostal churches were functioning more effectively than mission churches. Yet missionaries encouraging such changes continued to sense that they were out of touch with the masses of people they wanted to reach. As much was obvious when their own converts continued to fear evil spirits and return to traditional healers for cures.

Pentecostal churches dealt directly with beliefs in magic, and more generally with the complex, influential networks of sorcery and healing in Latin American society, through ecstatic forms of worship. Missionaries who derided such beliefs as superstitious and condemned pentecostal methods for dealing with them were not equipped to deal with Latin American religious life. If they wished to compete with pentecostals, they would have to help Latin Americans wrestle with evil spirits in a church context. They would have to make some allowance for faith healing, exorcism, and the like. Although they might not put it that way to antipentecostal supporters at home, they would have to develop pentecostal capabilities themselves. After all, had not Jesus announced his message with "signs and wonders"? What was needed to overawe the heathen, according to this school of thought, was the "power encounter" in which the new religion confronted and overwhelmed the old through its superior potency. Keeping up with the times, the Fuller School of World Mission offered a "Signs, Wonders and Church Growth" course, including a hands-on laboratory that reported miracles.[25]

Closed Countries

Looking out on the world to assess their chances for completing the Great Commission, evangelical prognosticators issued optimistic assessments of the latest revival in Argentina or Indonesia. Then they warned that the missions were falling behind the growth of population and anti-Americanism. According to *World Christian Encyclopedia* editor David Barrett, 34.4 percent of the world's population was Christian in 1900, but eighty years later the figure was only 32.8 percent.[26] Ironically, the slippage could be traced to Western Europe, where church attendance was thought to have fallen below that in Russia.[27] As far as North American evangelicals were concerned, Western Europe was now a mission field.

In buoyant moments, prognosticators derived considerable sat-

isfaction from Latin America, sub-Saharan Africa, and the eastern
rim of Asia, in each of which evangelical Christianity was growing
much faster than the population.[28] But they were most pleased by
reports from countries where they could hardly work at all: communist ones. Far from being liquidated, Christianity was making
headway in every communist country except Albania.[29] Official restrictions, persecution, and the apparent cooptation of established
churches had not prevented evangelical-style movements from
proliferating, sometimes underground. The same social forces that
North American fundamentalists feared as harbingers of the anti-
Christ—class and ethnic polarization, war, revolution, and ever
more awesome state power—appeared to be liberating social energy for a wave of conversion to Christianity.

The most exciting reports were from China. Until recently, the
missions had regarded their expulsion in 1949–1950 as one of history's great setbacks. But after Christians were suppressed during
the Cultural Revolution, they reemerged under Deng Xiaoping in
greater numbers than before. The reasons for this revival were a
matter of speculation. The Cultural Revolution apparently had
stirred up powerful reactions, especially among minority ethnic
groups where the Christian awakening was strongest.[30] When the
state tried to suppress religious traditions, Christianity could provide a way to reassert them in a new form. For people who dreamed
of establishing contact with the West, a church was perhaps the
only place to turn. Nor could it have hurt that, at a time when the
government was returning to private incentive and allowing entrepreneurs to flourish, Chinese were looking for new certitudes to
replace Maoism.

The size of the revival was also a matter of conjecture. According
to the association of officially recognized Protestant churches—
called the Three-Self Patriotic Movement after the missionary
goal of establishing self-governing, self-supporting, and self-
propagating local churches—there were three to four million Protestants and about the same number of Catholics in 1985. But according to partisans of the rapidly growing "house churches"—not
officially registered and prone to scrapes with the authorities—the
number of Christians had actually mushroomed to as many as fifty
million, almost 5 percent of the population.[31]

The difference in these figures reflected a bitter dispute over the attitude Westerners should take toward brethren in communist countries. On one side were the Bible smugglers, a regular industry specializing in helping Christians who claimed to be suffering from official persecution. According to the smugglers, the Three-Self Movement was a creature of the government's Religious Affairs Bureau, that is, a front for the identification, cooptation, and eventual suppression of genuine believers. Not to be taken in by the Chinese government's gestures, such as publishing Bibles and allowing renewed contacts with Western churches, the Bible smugglers engaged in bravado such as contrabanding scripture by the bargeload. But for older missions, who had spent nearly four decades meditating on their expulsion in 1949–1950, this kind of behavior could ruin everything. By reviving the Chinese government's fears of Western interference, the old hands felt, the new wave of anticommunist missionary work was inviting another round of closure.[32]

Christians were least successful at converting members of the other world religions—Buddhists, Hindus, and Muslims. In the 1970s, Islamic militancy and Arab bank accounts reminded evangelicals that they had been neglecting a strategic part of the globe. A "Koranic curtain" of distrustful governments and hostile religious authorities protected the majority of the Muslim population from Christian infiltration.[33] The few, struggling missions showed little promise. If the few converts were not already about to emigrate to the West, their neighbors were likely to force them to. But now that Islam was a geopolitical challenge, evangelical leaders started to harp on the subject, seminaries added courses, and missions were flooded with applications.[34]

Thanks to the availability of oil industry jobs, the Middle East was a favorite destination for missionaries in mufti. In evangelical parlance they were "tent-makers," who paid their own way by engaging in a trade like the tent-making Apostle Paul. They evaded restrictions by entering countries as technicians or language teachers, offered free English lessons to potential converts, and witnessed when the opportunity presented itself.* They hoped that

---

*U.S. diplomats have not always smiled on such ventures, for fear that they will provoke local religious authorities into retaliating against other North American interests. In the late 1940s, for example, an enterprising group of evangelicals from southern California organized an "Afghan Institute of Technology." Under

Islamic fundamentalism would become so fanatical and oppressive that it would drive westernized Muslims into their own, more tolerant arms.[35]

With much of the world's unevangelized masses living in closed or restricted countries, another way of getting at them was through shortwave radio. Two of the most powerful evangelical stations broadcast from relatively hospitable territory in Latin America: Radio HCJB or the "Voice of the Andes" in Quito, Ecuador, and Trans World Radio on the island of Bonaire in the Dutch Antilles. Although politically conservative and subject to vague accusations of imperialism, these evangelical broadcasters tried to be nonpolitical in their programming, to minimize jamming from suspicious governments, protect listeners from official retaliation, and open up more direct access, such as HCJB's correspondence courses in Cuba. In closed countries there was a great weakness to the approach, however: the inability to gather inexperienced new believers, isolated here and there next to their radio receivers, into churches.

To organize churches in new terrain there was no substitute for missionaries, prompting another solution fashionable by the 1980s: the recruitment of personnel from countries such as Korea and Brazil. Not only could some of these people slip past political barriers to North Americans but they could also leap certain cultural hurdles. In the words of one mission promoter, Western and Third World missions needed to "sit down . . . and plot the unreached people groups, tribe by tribe, language by language, social grouping by social grouping. Together they need to determine the unique prejudices and preferences of each unreached people group and match what they find with the mission agency most likely to be effective in penetrating that group."[36] Money was another factor: now that the career cost for a North American mission couple with children was reaching the million-dollar mark, Third World mis-

---

contract from the Kabul government, they used their technical school as an evangelical vehicle. But in the 1950s the U.S. State Department volunteered to finance the Institute—an offer the Afghan government gladly accepted—then contracted it out to the University of Wyoming, clamped down on the evangelists, and gradually pushed them out (J. C. Wilson 1979:48–57).

sionaries came a lot cheaper.[37] According to a survey, at least fifteen thousand such missionaries were in the field by the early 1980s.

The main barrier to sending more was financial. Evangelical students facing unemployment in depressed Third World economies were quick to volunteer for missionary work. But their own churches' ability to support religious professionals was very limited. Most money for mission careers continued to come from the United States: while various agencies such as the Christian Nationals Evangelism Commission (San Jose, California) and the Christian Aid Mission (Charlottesville, Virginia) channeled support to Third World missionaries, North American evangelicals generally preferred to support their own. Third World missions appeared weaker in Latin America than in other parts of the world: Latin Americans accounted for only 7 percent of the global total.[38]

Hidden Peoples

The Lausanne Congress had called for a fourfold increase in the number of missionaries from North America, to two hundred thousand by the year 2000.[39] But if missionaries were becoming less welcome in the Third World, if they were less effective than local citizens, and if a new generation of cheaper Third World missionaries was taking the field, then the question remained, why so many Western missionaries? Wasn't there already a church in every country? Wouldn't national churches be more adept at finishing the Great Commission? For years, mission boosters were helpless before the argument that there was already a national church in each country. Then they invented the "unreached people group."[40]

However infelicitous a term, the unreached people group fed off a formidable reservoir of evangelical legend, that surrounding the "unreached tribe." The expedition to savages lost in spiritual darkness had always been the most effective recruiter and fundraiser for the foreign missions. Missionaries killed attempting to reach hostile tribes were the great heroes of the mission movement. But now there were hardly any unreached tribes left. Moreover, as the tragic results of "saving" them for bulldozers and colonists dawned on evangelicals, the legend was fraying at the edges.

No, unreached people groups meant something bigger than missions to head-hunters. What if you looked at the great masses of the world's population—the Chinese, the Hindus, the Muslims—in microcultural terms? What if you applied Donald McGavran's idea of the "homogenous unit"—roughly a subculture—to these masses? If you did, it turned out that such hopelessly large, intimidating masses of population could be subdivided into hundreds and thousands of more digestible subunits. Because most did not have a Christian church, it could be argued that they had not been reached and needed missionaries.

The first to pursue this idea was the Missions Advanced Research Center (MARC), a Fuller spinoff that joined the relief and development agency World Vision. But the show was stolen by a Fuller professor named Ralph Winter who came up with a larger number of unreached groups, hence a more staggering definition of how much still had to be done, than anyone else. If Christianity really only grew along cultural lines, Winter declared at the Lausanne Congress in 1974, then cultural groups without a Christian nucleus would never be reached by normal church growth. The reason was that cultural barriers, often almost invisible to foreigners, prevented Christians in neighboring cultural groups from evangelizing them. If 75 to 85 percent of the world's non-Christians still had no church within their own cultural boundaries, as Winter calculated, then all those people would never be reached without a special effort.[41] Until now "hidden" from the view of mission planners, such "hidden peoples" ranged from the usual tribes in tropical jungles, to neglected castes in India, to seemingly idiosyncratic groupings such as Chinese restaurant workers in France; and Winter claimed to have counted 16,750 of them.

Even though a hidden people might live next door to Christians, Winter insisted, cultural prejudices were preventing effective evangelism. The existence of "prejudice barriers"—whether of class, ethnicity, or language—meant that each such group required a separate church-planting effort. What was needed was "cross-cultural evangelism," typically from someone outside the accumulated distrust and racism of the local system. In short, the Great Commission required missionaries, tens of thousands more of them. But evangelicals were not rising to the occasion, according to Winter. Playing to long-standing fears that missionaries were not accomplishing much, he claimed that only 9 percent were engaged in "frontier" evangelism, that is, working among groups with no established church. The rest were said to be servicing already established churches or doing social work.

Hence the need to reorient agencies to the hidden peoples and spark a revival at home, to support the final era of world evangelism. To this end, in 1976 Winter left Fuller and started his own research organization, the U.S. Center for World Mission. Housed in what used to be a Nazarene college in Pasadena, constantly battling to meet the next mortgage payment, the U.S. Center provided an organizational umbrella for three hundred workers, the majority of them young mission recruits taking courses and staffing forty or so shoestring agencies. While preparing to enter closed countries as "tent-makers," they compiled lists of unreached peoples and sent out bulletins full of prayer requests for them, in the hope of persuading others to make reaching the Nuristanis of Afghanistan or the Muslims of the Maldive Islands their personal objective.

Conveniently, looking at the world in terms of unreached people groups not only multiplied the need for missionaries but also made the task of finishing the Great Commission seem within reach. For each unreached group, there were probably several thousand evangelicals and ten or more congregations in the United States alone. If millions of Christians decided to work together, surely the entire world could be reached in a decade or two. Then, in keeping with Matthew 24:14, the way would be clear for the Lord's return. By the early 1980s, therefore, much of the missions movement was pushing the hidden peoples as a recruiting and fund-raising device.

The renovated imagery of the pioneer mission and the unreached tribe was credited with revitalizing the Inter-Varsity conference at Urbana and stimulating a wave of recruits in the 1980s.[42] But there were signs of weakness in the recruiting drive. While short-term missions, evangelical relief agencies, and charismatic groups were growing rapidly, along with a few giants such as the Wycliffe Bible Translators and the Campus Crusade for Christ, most of the more established missions were not. One factor was a significant resignation rate after the first term overseas: as many as half of new missionaries quit. In a survey of the more established agencies, 80 percent of the new recruits were replacing losses due to retirement or attrition.[43]

Anthropology and Ethnotheology

No matter what new direction evangelical missions went, from church growth to signs, wonders, and hidden peoples, it seemed like they needed cultural anthropology. For anyone pledged to uphold the fundamentals of the faith, this was a cruel fate. If the natives were all doomed to eternal torment unless they accepted your religion, you were not likely to approve of the anthropologist's more relaxed approach to the subject: that it was all relative. Instead of discouraging pagan rites, anthropologists were likely to join them. A century before, at the high noon of colonialism when it was still assumed that Christianity and civilization marched hand in hand, missionaries had helped anthropologists get their start by providing ethnographic reports. Even now, anthropologists customarily repaired to the nearest mission for local history, supper, and clean sheets. But relations had deteriorated, especially with fundamentalist missionaries, whom anthropologists now attacked for colonizing native people and undermining their cultures. Without so much as a thank-you, many missionaries felt, anthropologists had become enemies of the gospel.

Using anthropology was another story, however. Once missionaries grasped the full depth of misunderstanding between themselves and converts—often after investing entire careers—they had little choice. Among the first to suggest that the intelligent missionary was an applied anthropologist were Bible translation consultants of the American Bible Society (ABS). Headquartered in New York, the ABS was one of the few institutions to retain the respect of both evangelical and liberal Protestants. In visits to the field, its consultants were appalled by the ethnocentrism and futility of fundamentalist missionaries in cultures which they did not begin to understand.[44] One role ABS consultants played was editing *Practical Anthropology,* a journal started at the neo-evangelical Wheaton College in 1953. It published articles such as "Cultural Relativism for the Christian," "Mushroom Ritual versus Christianity," and "Minimizing Religious Syncretism Among the Chols."

Making fundamentalists aware of the cultural context of their work was not easy. Among other things, it required persuading them to look at their own background critically, in ways that contradicted cherished ideas. From the beginning, for example, evangelical anthropologists inveighed against the fundamentalist equation between Christianity, the United States, and Western civilization. Missionaries also had to be discouraged from satanizing features of other cultures which disgusted them. If missions were instruments of change, William and Marie Reyburn of the ABS argued, then they needed to understand the structure of what they were changing and the implications of those changes.

The kind of anthropology that the Reyburns and their colleagues urged missionaries to employ was functionalist. An approach dominating social anthropology at midcentury, functionalism was the study of how different features of a society operated together to create a stable, working system. Instead of attacking and destroying native cultures, the Reyburns said, missionaries should try to influence them in the right direction. As for unacceptable practices, they could be replaced with Christian substitutes, such as revivals for drunken fiestas or infant dedication ceremonies for Catholic baptismal rites.[45]

In this way, culture became the framework through which missionaries tried to stimulate the changes they desired. Yet functionalist engineering could easily become, in the words of another Bible society consultant, "downright manipulative."[46] So long as the standards employed were missionary rather than indigenous, outsiders would continue to impose their own criteria on local people.

To illustrate, let us turn to a supposed mission success story, among the Mayan peasant farmers of Chiapas, Mexico. Protestantism among one of the Mayan groups there, the Chol, can be traced to the anticlerical years of the Mexican Revolution, in the 1930s, when the government forced Catholic clergy to abandon Indian municipalities, killed Chol ritual leaders, and destroyed their "saints," wooden or plaster idols named after Christian figures.[47] As these events shook the confidence of the Chol in their traditions, revolutionary decrees and disorder helped them escape bondage on haciendas, only to fall into new forms of exploitation by saloon keepers and money lenders. In need of social cohesion, many Chol turned evangelical.

The Wycliffe Bible Translators hailed its work with the Chol Maya, as well as its equally spectacular results with the nearby Tzeltal Maya, as examples of how God's word could put idolatry and witchcraft to flight, free peasants from local exploiters, and transform previously alcoholic, homicidal communities into models of sobriety and progress. When we turn to critical assessments by some of the missionaries involved, a more complicated picture emerges. Contrary to Wycliffe's publicity for North American donors, Bible translation itself may not have had much to do with the mass conversions. Like a number of other Wycliffe translations, its Mayan New Testaments seem to have been only of passing interest to preliterate people unaccustomed to drawing inspiration from books. Several decades later, according to Wycliffe translator Wilbur Aulie, the Chol were not very interested in using their native language Bibles; neither were the Tzeltal according to another report.[48]

This was not the only shortcoming missionaries sensed. Besides lacking foundation in the scriptures, their Mayan converts also showed a distinct lack of Christian ethics. Most Tzeltal Protestants, a missionary concluded, had never gotten to know Jesus as their personal savior.[49] According to Wilbur Aulie, one sign of spiritual withering was the direction Chol pastors were taking. Operating under the auspices of the National Presbyterian Church of Mexico, the pastors were emulating their authoritarian Hispanic supervisors, abandoning their Indian identity, and conducting church services in Spanish rather than their own tongue. Their main interest seemed to be increasing their incomes.[50] According to other observers, Mayan pastors in Chiapas were frequently the wealthiest men in their communities, to the point of stepping into the shoes of the local tyrants they had helped overthrow.[51]

What had gone wrong with the effort to build an indigenous church? The reasons said something about the implications of mass conversion into evangelical Protestantism. Previously, many missionaries had accepted only converts who met their exacting standards. Now, however, it was becoming fashionable to encourage McGavran-style "people movements" like those among the Chol and Tzeltal. In Chiapas, Wycliffe missionaries leery of baptizing pagan practices into new churches had, by way of an alternative, encouraged "cultural substitutes." To heal the sick, for example, Mayan Protestants were supposed to call in church elders to pray rather than shamans to chant. Instead of conducting traditional planting and harvesting festivals, they were to devise Christian ones.

Although Mayan Protestants accepted such adjustments, their reading of the new religion seems to have remained very different from that of the missionaries. To begin with, the Tzeltal saw in the North Americans people of vastly greater wealth and power than themselves, people whom they wished to imitate. "Christ in their lives," a visiting anthropologist has suggested, was a Tzeltal explanation for North American wealth.[52] In converting, the Tzeltal converts were deciding to follow a new set of rules that achieved better results than the old ones. While the missionaries conceived of religious change in terms of internal transformation—the "born-again" experience—that seemed not to have translated into Tzeltal and Chol. Instead of a personal encounter with Christ, converts apparently saw themselves caught between conflicting powers at war over their souls, a war in which they decided to side with the stronger.

Antibiotics and literacy convinced many Maya of the superior efficacy of the new religion, at least for a while. In economic terms, Protestantism helped converts tighten up their household economies by eliminating wasteful vices. For a smaller number, it provided a way to accumulate property and capital. What it did not offer was a solution to the land and marketing monopolies, population growth, and ecological breakdown impoverishing the Mayan population of Chiapas. Although the missions tried to establish a new economic foundation by promoting colonization and agricultural improvement, such efforts were not enough.

The missionaries also failed to fully engage the spiritual energies of their converts, as demonstrated by the increasing number of Chol Protestants defecting to pentecostal churches. These splinter groups were more lively and participatory in style than the Presbyterian structure promoted by the mission. They also practiced a more indigenous and collective style of leadership.[53] But their most important attraction may have been healing. Here as in other parts, indigenous Protestants seemed more interested in faith healing than in western medicine, however important the latter had been for missionaries to demonstrate their power. In the face of staggering medical problems, typically stemming from loss of access to land, the magical rites of pentecostalism seemed more efficacious than the antibiotics which had given missionaries their entree.

This was the kind of failure forcing missionaries and their anthropological consultants to adopt a more sophisticated approach to communicating their message. Fundamentalists had assumed that they could dispel the fog of superstition about the heathen mind, then impress their statement of doctrine on it. But now evangelicals were being forced to make more complicated assumptions about the nature of truth and how it is perceived from culture to culture. In the words of Bible society consultant William Smalley, "man's heart is not a clean slate that the Gospel comes and writes upon for the first time. It is complex and has been scrawled upon and deeply engraved from birth to death."[54]

Missionaries had long struggled to prevent converts from misinterpreting the gospel in terms of their old beliefs. After cultural anthropology entered the picture, they continued to wage the battle in terms of fighting "syncretism" or "Christo-paganism." But now, at the Fuller School of World Mission and in the pages of the journal *Missiology*, which replaced *Practical Anthropology* after 1973, some evangelicals were making a significant concession to the relativity of cognitive systems. Influenced by Roman Catholic thinking on "inculturation" of the gospel, they were discussing how, as a step in spiritual development, converts from other cultures must be allowed to interpret Christianity in terms of their preexisting beliefs.

In a Papua New Guinea case, a Wycliffe translator observed that Samo converts had "accepted [Christianity] in terms of their own belief system . . . applying [the gospel message] to their needs . . . without altering their basic ideology." A Wycliffe bulletin for home supporters noted that a converted Mexican shaman retained "a worldview very different from ours."[55] Even if the ultimate goal was to Christianize the indigenous worldview in some universal, supracultural sense, members of the local culture would, for the time being, have to employ it in order to learn about the new religion.

Encouraged by anthropologists, the more flexible neo-evangelical missionaries were accepting the idea that a Brazilian Indian could legitimately interpret a scripture differently than they did. For evangelicals engaged in this kind of thinking, they were simply "contextualizing" the gospel in different cultures, a task they also referred to as "ethnotheology." From theologians they drew on the language of hermeneutics, the never-ending debate over different modes of interpreting the Bible. What they denied, emphatically, was that they were abandoning their faith in the Bible as divine, reliable, and authoritative.

When native churches were allowed to interpret the gospel in terms of their own worldviews, unfortunately, some of the results did not appear "biblical" to many missionaries and their home supporters. Nonfundamentalist interpretations of the Bible were, by definition, not acceptable. Fundamentalists continued to insist that there was a single correct interpretation of the Bible—their own— and that anyone of good will and sound mind could arrive at it. To admit the variation and ambiguity implicit in talk of contextualization, hermeneutics, or ethnotheology would be death to their whole system.

Evangelizing non-Western cultures by working through their worldview, rather than trying to breach it, had subversive implications. As evangelical anthropologists acknowledged, discussion of how the gospel message was culturally conditioned could discredit them in the eyes of brethren. In the words of one scholar, contextualization inhabited "the nether regions of evangelical discussion."[56] Confronting the question could split the evangelical establishment down the middle.

In the meantime, anthropologists were helping to train much of the next generation of missionaries. But for all the talk about cultural sensitivity, skeptical Latin Americans such as Jorge Lara-Braud believed that most North American brethren reaching their shores did not possess the intellectual tools for missionary work.[57] Joining the pessimists was Eugene Nida, the Bible society consultant who had long urged anthropology on his brethren. Unimpressed by claims of an enlightened generation of recruits in the 1970s and 1980s, Nida believed that the socialization of missionaries continued to produce workers ill suited to the task. True, the traditional mission compound walling off missionaries and converts from the rest of the society was gone. But according to Nida, agencies were still promoting the kind of in-group behavior they felt essential to holding their enterprise together.

Missionary training continued to revolve around inculcating established truth, Nida argued, not developing critical judgment, which was still foreign to much evangelical education. Certain features of North American culture—a sense of cultural superiority, priority to programs over people, preoccupation with quantifica-

tion, personal success, and upward mobility—seemed to be deepening in the "me generation." Ever more insecure North Americans, Nida suspected, were less and less capable of dealing with
other cultures. Much of the missionary movement continued to be
driven by the assumption that the wealth of American churches was
God's great resource for evangelizing the globe, that what worked
in America would work abroad, and that, practically overnight, a
flood of young people could win the world for Christ.[58]

Christ, Inc.

The Lausanne Congress had declared world mission to be a world
effort, by Christians everywhere, not just those from North America and Europe. Under pressure from Third World nationalism,
leading U.S.-based missions such as the Latin America Mission,
World Vision, and the Wycliffe Bible Translators internationalized
their administrative structures. They talked of partnership in missions, building up the local and national church to meet their responsibilities, and encouraging Latin American churches to send
their own foreign missionaries.

None of this meant diminishing the North American presence,
however. It meant expanding it, in what became an era of headlong
growth for the largest agencies including Wycliffe, World Vision,
Campus Crusade for Christ, and Youth With A Mission, each headquartered in southern California except for the last, whose founder
came from there. Wycliffe's U.S.-origin income alone increased
from $18 million in 1978 to $48 million in 1985, while World Vision's—boosted by famine in Africa—soared from $39 to $232 million.

By the standards of the business world, these were not especially
large organizations, but their volunteer nature meant that they
fielded large numbers of personnel. On $105 million in global in-
come in 1984, Campus Crusade supported sixteen thousand full-
time and associate staff. The following year Youth With A Mission's
five thousand full-time staffers supervised fifteen thousand short-
term missionaries: in the future, they hoped to build up to fifty
thousand. Much of the money of such organizations was spent in
the kind of place where a few thousand dollars went a long way, to
give villages their first wells or to make pastors the first educated

men in their communities. In 1985, World Vision reported 3,900 such grass-roots projects assisting an estimated 16.8 million people. The field of these organizations was indeed the world. Wycliffe worked in over forty countries, World Vision in eighty-four, and Campus Crusade in one hundred and fifty including protectorates. Youth With A Mission reported centers in sixty countries and claimed to have evangelized nearly everywhere except a few high-risk polities such as Libya and North Korea.[59]

In contrast to churches, which usually were supposed to function as membership-based democracies, parachurch agencies were less accountable to their financial supporters. They tended to be run in a top-down, corporate manner by the men who had started them.[60] The epitome of the corporate style was Campus Crusade for Christ. It was the creation of Bill Bright, a small-town boy from Oklahoma who went to Los Angeles to make his fortune in the confections business. As Bright prospered, he was attracted to the wealthy, influential Christians of Hollywood's First Presbyterian Church. At the time, Hollywood Presbyterian was engaged in witnessing to stars who became some of the first evangelical media celebrities. Not far away was the University of California at Los Angeles, where Bright started his campus ministry in 1951. With public universities growing rapidly, he offered students, typically from religious backgrounds, a new family away from home, middle-class standards, and a model of upward mobility—the Christian way. Bright's relentless positive thinking also appealed to parents worried that their children would not withstand the temptations of college. In Campus Crusade, young Christians would be too busy witnessing to their faith to get into trouble.

To Bright, Christianity was a product to be advertised like any other. Evangelism was a kind of salesmanship, best conducted in a business suit. And the clearest sign that he was carrying out the Lord's work was his success in using contributions from wealthy business executives to build up a corporate organization.[61] No one claimed that Campus Crusade was a democracy. Staff turnover was high, owing to what even a sympathetic observer, Richard Quebedeaux, termed the authoritarianism of the movement's founder and president. Following the departure of Bright's closest lieutenants in the late 1960s, he established a policy of "noncriticism."[62]

Beyond the universities, Campus Crusade became famous for its mass media approach to evangelism. In 1985 the main attraction was "Explo 85" (for "Explosion of Love"), a technological extravaganza bringing together three hundred thousand Christians in ninety local conferences via satellite hookup.[63] A decade earlier, it was the "I Found It!" campaign. Following an advertising blitz on billboards and over the airwaves, Campus Crusade sent in student volunteers to spread the message person to person. This was "saturation evangelism," intended to confront entire populations with Bright's "four spiritual laws," a seventy-seven word prescription for salvation. Despite all the hoopla, saturation evangelism seems to have been ineffective. In Arcadia, California, the result of 29,000 phone calls, 6,000 explanations of the four spiritual laws, and 1,665 decisions for Christ were fifty-five new church members, twenty-three of whom had some previous ecclesiastical involvement.[64]

Among evangelical detractors, Bright's four spiritual laws, along with his obsession with numbers and setting statistical "firsts" in the history of Christianity—323,419 of this, 1,000,000 of that—became synonymous with turning faith into a commodity. Outside the United States, Campus Crusade acquired a reputation for failing to adjust its message to local situations. Evangelicals trying to adopt more diplomatic, cultural approaches were not impressed by rhetoric about Great Commission armies conquering the world for Christ. They interpreted Campus Crusade's publicity campaigns as competitive and grandstanding. In Colombia, the "I Found It!" campaign—intended to generate curiosity about who was behind the advertising and what had been found—had the misfortune to coincide with the Jonestown Massacre in Guyana and a wave of paranoia about North American sects.[65]

Another parachurch making itself evident around the world was Youth With A Mission. YWAM (pronounced why-wham) was the leader in an evangelical growth industry rivaled only by relief and development groups. The idea was to send legions of North Americans on short mission tours, often the length of a summer vacation. The group's founder, an Assemblies of God minister named Loren Cunningham, started out in 1960 with a vision of waves of young Christians evangelizing every continent. Parachurches were often accused of offering less participation to their financial supporters than churches did, but YWAM was the epitome of participation; it wanted to send everyone to the mission field.

Short-term missions were made possible by cheap international air fares. Interpreted as tourism or worse by suspicious Latin Americans, they functioned like a mobile version of church camp. Short-termers—thirty thousand a year in the 1980s[66]—were usually students subsidized by their parents or church. Without much language capability, they probably did not make many converts. But that was not necessarily the point: short-term missionary work was a Christian way to see the world, exposing provincial North Americans to other cultures but protecting them from the dangers of immersion. A gospel choir of attractive young North Americans was a good way to advertise the next revival. When not singing, they could help construct a new church building nearby. Most important, such experiences hooked participants on evangelism, boosted the enthusiasm of prayer groups back home, and fed volunteers into longer mission commitments.[67]

Charismatic in style, YWAM made much of signs from the Lord. These were strokes of good fortune, often donations from other Christians, which it taught members to interpret as divine providence. Influenced by the shepherding movement, YWAM also emphasized the establishment of spiritual authority over recruits, sometimes to the point that other evangelicals wondered whether they were dealing with a cult.[68] Under the guidance of staffers who seemed free to do just about anything they believed the Lord was telling them to, recruits went through "discipleship training schools," which turned them into evangelizing teams. YWAMers inundated international sporting events (eleven thousand of them at the 1984 Olympics in Los Angeles), evangelized red light districts, put on street theater, worked in orphanages, distributed Bibles, sent out medical teams, even ran refugee camps in East Asia.

Around the world YWAM operated from what it called "bases"— two hundred of them—each of which was supposed to operate as a more or less independent "franchise." To this decentralized structure was sometimes attributed the misunderstanding and conflict which YWAM's hit-and-run ministry could leave in its wake. In Guatemala, the 1983 arrival of the YWAM's good ship *Anastasis*, loaded with relief supplies and hundreds of short-termers, convinced Catholics that they were being invaded by an army of sects. According to YWAM, it sent almost two thousand short-term mis-

sionaries into Guatemala over the next two years.[69] The group's
methods also aroused objections from some of the local churches
and missions it said it was helping. When its visiting teams made
cultural and political blunders, such as spilling out right-wing
North American attitudes in door-to-door evangelism, resident
brethren took the blame.

"YWAM comes in and goes out and seems never to pay attention
to the ministries already there," a missionary to Africa complained.
"When they came into our area, they didn't have any idea how what
they were doing was going to affect those of us who were there on a
longer-term basis. A lot of governments are so concerned for the
tourist trade that they will do nothing to hinder the activities of
people like YWAMers. But as soon as a group like that leaves, the
national Christians and long-term missionaries feel the backlash.
Surveillance is increased, people are jailed, houses searched,
Bibles confiscated."[70] YWAM founder Loren Cunningham believed
that his short-termers should be allowed to make mistakes.[71]

Church versus Parachurch

Youth With A Mission was far from the only North American parachurch agency accused of pursuing its own agenda at the expense
of local churches. "Bringing your own program, talking about col-
laboration, and ending up doing your own thing is every outfit that
comes down from the U.S.," Washington Padilla told me.[72] The
larger parachurch organizations, such as the Billy Graham Evangelistic Association and Pat Robertson's Christian Broadcasting
Network, could have quite an impact on evangelical movements
abroad. So could smaller coalition-builders such as the Luis Palau
Evangelistic Team and O.C. Ministries.

To make matters worse, now that some older missions were slowing down and reflecting on their experiences, many domestic North
American ministries were launching overseas ventures, in yet another wave of brash entrepreneuralism. More often than not, the
new groups were pentecostal or charismatic. Each justified its ambitious plans for expansion as humble obedience to the biblical
mandate to evangelize the world. The most revealing indictments
of these groups, generally, came from other evangelicals. Common
complaints included failing to consult with established churches

before entering new areas; duplicating the efforts of brethren in wasteful, competitive ways; attracting the most promising young leaders with higher salaries than local churches could afford; and failing to investigate the background of new employees, who sometimes turned out to be on the lam from their original church owing to moral lapses.

Enlisting local churches in one parachurch campaign after another was not the solution because such efforts tended to be a tremendous financial and psychological burden. At the end of the excitement, the parachurch agency left town, local churches were exhausted, and their members felt in need of new forms of extraneous excitement. If that were not enough, the impressive number of decisions for Christ at parachurch-organized events usually did not translate into new church members: it was not unusual for 90 percent of such converts to vanish into thin air.

The stated objective of parachurch agencies was, by definition, to multiply and build up local churches. Yet they could only justify themselves by claiming that existing churches could not handle the job of evangelism alone. According to two church researchers in India, Vinay Samuel and Chris Sugden, what they called "multinational missions" were systematically bypassing Third World churches, subordinating them to their own agendas, and imposing their own leaders. Such agencies recognized the formal autonomy of national churches, Samuel and Sugden argued, but were incorporating them into a more sophisticated form of dependency.

Many Third World denominations were descended from what were now ecumenical Protestant bodies in North America and Europe. When new evangelical agencies arrived on the scene, according to Samuel and Sugden, they assumed that the leadership of the daughter groups was nonevangelical, too. They then bypassed the national church authorities whom they distrusted, went straight to local pastors, and gradually recruited, trained, and financed their own "national evangelical leadership," backed by the multinationals but without real accountability to established denominations. Such leaders were "evangelical pirates," Samuel and Sugden claimed: "they control the seaways and commandeer resources but are beyond the law."

Parachurches were interested above all in maximum growth, tempting them to substitute an easy-to-market form of salvation for difficult gospel imperatives such as repentance and justice. According to church-growth experts, for example, attracting the maximum number of people meant keeping the church away from social issues that caused controversy as well as minimizing demands on new believers. At home, to appeal to the widest spectrum of donors, parachurch agencies tended to take the most inoffensive, middle-of-the-road positions, at the cost of failing to inform their supporters about social realities on the mission field.

The implications of continuing dependence on North American agencies were dramatized by the Latin American debt crisis. Although Latin American denominations had taken steps to nationalize mission functions, Al Hatch pointed out, now economic collapse made it impossible for them to keep up the funding. That meant either shutting down the program or returning to dependence on foreign money. Meanwhile, the stronger buying power of the North American dollar in ruined Latin American currencies was widening the disparity between expatriate and national institutions. Although it was easy for U.S.-based organizations to build up their infrastructure, it was almost impossible for Latin evangelicals to hold so much as a conference—unless underwritten by North American funds. As a result, more evangelical leaders would decide that the Lord was calling them to minister to Hispanics in the United States.[73]

Not only did evangelical multinationals display a formidable appetite for building up clienteles; they were also adept at wrapping their drive for influence in the language of completing the Great Commission. As Samuel and Sugden pointed out, they continually redefined world evangelism such that the requirements for carrying it out were always beyond the reach of the national churches, therefore requiring the intervention of the multinationals. If national churches responded to the need as defined by these agencies, they became dependent on foreign sponsors for technology. Once the national church was equipped to handle the task as defined by the multinationals, the latter leapfrogged ahead with new definitions of the challenge.

To Samuel and Sugden, therefore, calls to world mission sounded suspiciously like sales pitches for the mission agencies themselves. Instead of serving national churches, as the multinationals claimed to be doing, they were persuading Third World

Christians that they needed products only the multinationals could offer. By multiplying the apparent need for missionary work and assuming that nationals alone were unequal to the task, Samuel and Sugden argued, the multinationals were inventing rationales for bypassing the national church.[74]

Talk about unreached people groups was a case in point. As it turned out, Ralph Winter's figure of 16,750 "hidden peoples" proved more a publicity device than a hard statistic. But it impressed so many uninformed churchgoers, the editor of *Evangelical Missions Quarterly* reported, that missions under pressure from supporters to find and evangelize hidden peoples were complaining about "foggy, bizarre numbers."[75] The idea was so elastic ("nurses in St. Louis" have been advertised as a hidden people) that it could be used to justify missionary intervention anywhere.

Still another problem was how to define "unreached": what about the many indigenous churches which had rebelled against missionaries, turned heretical, and were now immune to further evangelism because they insisted that their own interpretation was correct? Were they reached or unreached?[76] Distinctions between "true" and "nominal" Christians were being made arbitrarily. While Peter Wagner hailed the influx of Africans into independent churches, some of which regarded their leaders as messiahs, in Latin America he excluded all Roman Catholics from his calculations of church growth.[77]

Remorselessly, evangelical strategists expanded their definition of the need for missionary work. One Lausanne consultation decided that the unreached consisted of any social group with 20 percent or less Christians, prompting complaints that such a definition included everyone outside the Bible Belt.[78] Generally speaking, enthusiasts were pushing the meaning of "unreached" from "untouched" to "untransformed." Simply broadcasting the message was not good enough; instead, evangelists would have to continue targeting a group even if it had rejected Christianity.

Despite quibbles, most of the missions movement seemed quite taken by the logic of the hidden peoples. Its most fascinating feature was the way it expanded the need for their services. As to the charge of inventing rationales for bypassing Third World churches, advocates were unrepentant. Claims by churches to be *the* national church with jurisdiction over new missionary initiatives, the Missions Advanced Research Center claimed in 1979, were blocking the evangelism of hundreds of unreached groups.[79]

As a matter of policy, the Assemblies of God refused to "succumb . . . to nationalist interests which would impede completing the Great Commission." Peter Wagner decried "hypersensitivity to . . . ecclesiastical nationalism."[80] It was true that some of the more established Protestant denominations were not vigorous evangelists. Just as the Roman Catholic structure had stifled the autonomy of local dependencies for centuries, William Burrows pointed out, bowing to the wishes of Protestant elites headquartered in Latin American capitals could stifle evangelism at the grass roots. Did evangelical critics of North American missions really want centralized authority instead of evangelistic free-lancing?[81]

But to evangelicals concerned about U.S. influence and the rise of the religious right, it was easy to read political motives into the burgeoning parachurch agencies. What if they were contributing less to church growth than they were feeding off it, by using the accomplishments of Third World Christians to raise money in the United States, then spending it to subordinate those same Christians to their own agenda? Perhaps they were trying to undermine intermediate levels of leadership and replace them with their own, George Pixley suggested, to establish direct control of Latin American evangelicals through show business personalities like the television evangelists.[82] Applied to some of the older, more cautious missions, this kind of speculation seemed paranoid and unfair, until the arrival of the religious right appeared to confirm it.

Chapter Five

The Evangelical Awakening in Latin America

Since the Sandinista revolution, Margaret Randall claimed in 1982, more than ninety new sects, pseudo-religious in nature, had sprung up throughout Nicaragua. They were most noticeable in poor neighborhoods of the cities and close to the Honduran border, wherever poverty, illiteracy, and ignorance made people vulnerable to religious propaganda. The sects urged people not to participate in the revolutionary process, not to join the militia or community organizations, not to honor Sandinista symbols, not to defend the revolution. In almost all the battles between Sandinistas and counter-revolutionaries, their presence supposedly could be felt. According to Randall, even a summary investigation revealed that they were funded by the Central Intelligence Agency.[1]

This was how much of the left and the Catholic Church perceived evangelical growth in Latin America. Alarmed by sectarian inroads in their constituencies, perplexed over how to respond, they accused evangelicals of being a fifth column for U.S. imperialism. Actually, there was no firm evidence of CIA funding, at least not yet.* Whether such evidence surfaced, there was a larger problem: the right wing of the evangelical missions was all too pleased to serve Washington at its own expense.

---

* According to *Newsweek*, June 15, 1987, the Catholic archbishop of Nicaragua, Miguel Obando y Bravo, had received funds from the CIA through a maze of fronts intended to create "double deniability" by donor and recipient. (For further details, see the Council on Hemispheric Affairs, *Washington Report on the Hemisphere*, March 16, 1988, p. 5.)

Back in the war zone of northern Nicaragua, the Sandinistas and their supporters found it hard to understand why, at a time when the poor needed to defend their gains against the United States and counter-revolution, so many were spending their nights clapping and singing to no apparent purpose. For the administrators of a new socialist society, it was easy to conclude that fervent evangelicals had lost their bearings. Indeed, when I asked some Matagalpa believers what their church's name was, it set off a debate. Before finally agreeing on who they were—the United Pentecostal Mission in Nicaragua-Matagalpa—they proposed and rejected four similar appellations, apparently the names of other churches from which theirs had descended in a series of splits.

Matagalpa was the home of the "firebrand" (*tizón*) movement, a stirring of the Holy Spirit which began in the politically conservative Assemblies of God. The churches, leaders of the movement held, had become like burned-out firebrands. Quenched by worldliness, they needed to be rekindled. The movement was said to have started in 1983 or 1984, with a Sandinista soldier's resurrection from the dead. No one had gotten the man's name before he walked away, but subsequently there was speaking in tongues and laying on of hands; those filled with the Holy Spirit were knocked to the ground. The local pastor's committee refused to supply its endorsement: one reason was that the firebrand image had come to the initiator in a prophecy rather than from the Bible. But the revival was still going on in the hills and was said to have spread as far as Cuba.

As the evangelicals of Matagalpa pondered the meaning of these events, they and their pastors were on the fringes of a power struggle in the capital, between two groups claiming to represent Nicaragua's Protestants. One was a pandenominational development agency working closely with the Sandinistas; the other was a fundamentalist-led body that wanted nothing to do with the revolution.[2]

Typical of such contests in ecclesiastical affairs, each side accused the other of being a political front, an instrument in the struggle for power. Each suspected the other of representing an international conspiracy that was ensnaring Christians in false ideology and manipulating them to unholy ends. Implied in this kind of exchange, ironically, was a shared denigration of Latin Americans' ability to act for themselves. Left out of the polemic was how religious movements flowed out of popular experiences, how they expressed popular struggles in ambiguous new ways, and how they could burst the forms into which pastors and politicians channeled them.

To make sense of the Protestant effervescence in Latin America, church watchers have talked of successive "waves" of evangelism. The first, starting in the nineteenth century, came from the mainline denominations of North America. Their missions led the struggle for religious liberty against the Catholic Church, built hospitals and schools, but usually produced only small enclaves of converts. Within a generation or two, such Protestants tended to climb out of the lower classes and lose interest in evangelism.

The second wave of evangelism was fundamentalist. It consisted of faith missions and conservative denominations, who arrived in the belief that mainline agencies were not doing enough. After the Second World War, these groups—such as the Central American Mission, the Christian and Missionary Alliance, the Gospel Missionary Union, and the Latin America Mission—replaced the mainline denominations as the mission establishment. But they tended to be too straitlaced for Latin Americans. They opposed emotional forms of worship, for example, and were slow to let converts run their own affairs. As a result, even these fervently evangelical groups produced only small churches.

By the 1960s, both kinds of Protestantism had clearly been overtaken by a third, pentecostalism. Two-thirds of Latin American Protestants were pentecostals and that proportion was increasing, to three-quarters by the 1980s.[3] Some of the most successful pentecostal bodies were missionary in origin—including the Assemblies of God (Springfield, Missouri), the Church of God (Cleveland, Tennessee), and the Four-Square Gospel Church (Los Angeles, California). But more were national-led breakaways from mission-dominated churches. Protestantism was becoming Latin American in two ways, as Emilio Willems pointed out. The first was organizational, in revolts against missionary control. The second was liturgical and to a lesser extent doctrinal, in a shift to the enthusiastic forms of worship characteristic of pentecostals, even among evangelicals who said they were not.[4]

One feature of the resulting scene, Jean Pierre Bastián has noted, was an explosion of competing groups. Evangelical churches had always suffered splits, but now the atomization seemed to intensify. Contributing to it were North American agencies whose money, personnel, and ideas still mattered. From the great mainline-evangelical split in the United States, conflicts ramified into Latin churches and polarized them along new lines. Mainline and evangelical agencies backed rival leaders, widened differences, and tried to influence the churches—mainly pentecostal—in their own direction.

Stressing expansion above all else were U.S. parachurch agencies and their Latin American allies, men whose favorite subject was the latest technique to market the gospel. Opposing them was a small radical wing, associated with the World Council of Churches and stressing the need for structural change—that is, a revolution against the same power structure that conservatives taught was ordained by God. Playing an ambiguous role between the first two tendencies was a third, led by Latin American theologians who were critical of the right as well as the left but usually spoke in subdued tones, to avoid being accused of liberalism. This was the triangular confrontation of the 1970s into which a fourth group erupted in the 1980s, the religious right. It viewed the Reagan administration's war in Central America as something on the order of the divine plan and tried to push evangelical churches into its forefront.

Church-growth conservatives and the religious right dominated the scene. But as Jean Pierre Bastián noted, the wishes of competing leaderships could have little influence in the churches. He detected a division between city and country, between urban ecclesiastical bureaucracies and rural churches which he thought were escaping their control.[5] The language of salvation had to be prevented from referring too directly to the here and now.

Adventists, Mormons, Witnesses

A missionary knew few afflictions greater than to be confused with another group that he regarded as a false sect; that, at the same airport where he met a single new assistant from the United States, unloaded a dozen such helpers; and that was growing several times faster than his own church. As Protestants introduced the dissenting church into Latin America, their heels were dogged by still other dissenters. The most numerous were pentecostals, with whom other evangelicals gradually came to terms. But some of the most visible were three churches from the United States which evangelicals found so difficult to accept that, in varying degrees, they classified them as separate religions: the Adventists, Jehovah's Witnesses, and Mormons.

In the 1970s, the Seventh Day Adventists seemed to be the largest non-Catholic church in Mexico, Honduras, Costa Rica, Colombia, Ecuador, Peru, and Bolivia.[6] The church grew so rapidly in Latin America and Africa that only 15 percent of its 4.4 million members in 1984 were North American.[7] One reason for success, according to a church-growth study, was transfer of leadership to converts. Another was a medical and educational program tied closely to evangelism.[8] For peasants who desired a school for their children, an Adventist teacher complete with salary was a powerful inducement; in exchange, he organized them into a congregation.

The Adventists were particularly controversial owing to two of their doctrines based on the Old Testament. The first, observing a rigorous sabbath on Saturday, disrupted many a community work day. The second, prohibiting pork and certain other kinds of meat, encouraged malnutrition when converts lacked other protein sources. Such idiosyncrasies did not impede growth, however: in Peru, a splinter group known as the Israelites carried such rules even further, to the point of returning to the sacrifices, long beards, and white robes of the Aaronic priesthood. Identifying their promised land as the Amazon Jungle, the Israelites founded colonies and by the 1980s rivaled the largest evangelical denominations in size.[9]

Returning to the Adventists proper, their obsession with ritual purity and the end of the world gave them an authoritarian reputation. They dismissed as apostate other fundamentalists, who reciprocated the opinion, on grounds that Adventists placed an unbiblical reliance on the visions of their founder, the prophetess Ellen G. White (1827–1915). But many Adventists also wanted to be accepted as evangelical Christians. In the 1960s and 1970s a more "biblical" tendency emerged, one willing to shelve Adventist teachings if they seemed to contradict scripture. Although members of this wing were occasionally purged, they helped the Adventists win a measure of acceptance.[10]

As for the Mormons and Jehovah's Witnesses, they showed no

sign of being admitted to the evangelical fraternity, but that did not prevent Catholics from lumping everyone together. According to a Costa Rican survey, the two kinds of *evangélicos* most familiar to Catholics were the Mormons and Witnesses, suggesting that they were the most influential in shaping Catholic perceptions of Protestants.[11] No doubt this was due to their astonishing capacity for door-to-door visits, which other evangelicals sometimes blamed for their own bad image. In Costa Rica, an evangelical historian complained that the Witnesses "destroyed the field of colportage by their boorish and brazen methods."[12] In each country I visited one year, I thought I saw the same pair of tall young North Americans, dressed in dark business suits with black nameplates on their chests, striding side by side down the street. These purposeful apparitions were Mormon missionaries, just a few of the thirty thousand who spend two years of their lives going from door to door around the world.

Owing to the recent foundation of Mormonism—formally the Church of Jesus Christ of Latter-Day Saints (LDS)—its supernatural claims have been subject to historical tests and exposés in ways that mainstream Christianity is not, owing to its more distant origins. The founder of the church, Joseph Smith (1805–1844), grew up in a part of the North American frontier known as the "burned-over district" for its incessant revivals. The mockery started after Smith reported that he had been visited by an angel, who directed him to a set of golden tablets buried near Palmyra, New York. On the tablets were written the scriptures of the new faith, the Book of Mormon. According to the book—which bore a certain resemblance to the King James Bible and other religious works popular in the early nineteenth century—the lost tribes of Israel reached the Americas around 600 B.C., were visited by Christ in A.D. 34, and subsequently turned into American Indians.[13]

Following Smith's murder, his followers were driven across the United States to their inhospitable Zion, the Great Salt Lake, where they erected one of the great utopian experiments of the nineteenth century. Much has changed since then: the communalism of the early years gave way to capitalism; polygamy was abandoned to gain U.S. statehood; and in 1978 black males, previously excluded from the priesthood for bearing the mark of Cain, were granted equal status. What did not change was the church's emphasis on patriarchal authority, hard work, and family unity.

In the late 1970s, Mormon values attracted the religious right in its search for a new "moral majority." Among other things, the religious right admired the de facto alliance between church and state in the heavily Mormon state of Utah.[14] But many fundamentalists continued to recoil from the doctrines of the LDS church and fear its growth rates, the highest of the major North American denominations. By 1985, with 3.8 million members in the United States and another 2 million abroad, the church's gains in the southern United States led to a backlash from Baptists.[15]

In Latin America, Mormon growth rates were even higher, and they prompted the same kind of evangelical reaction. "A temple of darkness was opened last month in Guatemala," Gospel Outreach reported of an LDS dedication ceremony.[16] The first Mormon temple in Latin America—something like a Catholic cathedral in ritual significance—opened only in 1978. But by the middle of the next decade, seven more were being consecrated. From 1965 to 1975, Latin American membership tripled to 337,000, then over the next decade more than tripled again, to 1.2 million by 1986, with the largest concentrations in Mexico, Brazil, Chile, Argentina, and Peru.

Despite hopes that Israelite-descended American Indians might be predisposed to LDS teachings, the church tends to find its converts elsewhere, such as among upwardly mobile urban dwellers.[17] Door-to-door evangelism apparently is not very productive, but recruiting along social networks is.[18] Sociologically, Latin American Mormons are hard to distinguish from more orthodox evangelicals. But their phenomenal growth statistics are said to be inflated by competition between Mormon dioceses (called "stakes") and pressure to meet quotas. In Oxapampa, Peru, a couple who told me they were Mormons ran a bar.

Still, the missionary effort is impressive. In Colombia, other evangelicals accused the Mormons of alarming the authorities into tightening up visas, by asking for five hundred at one time.[19] In all of Latin America, 8,136 missionaries were serving in 1985—only 27 percent less than the 11,196 non-Mormon Protestant missionaries from North America.[20] Perhaps due to reports that CIA recruiters favor former Mormon missionaries for their patriotism, strict morality, and overseas experience,[21] the church seemed to attract more than its share of harassment. In Chile, LDS meeting places were hit by twenty-two bomb and arson attacks in sixteen months. The perpetrators left behind pamphlets attacking the Mormons as agents of yankee imperialism.[22] But the church's political conservatism did not necessarily protect members from the same kind of repression experienced by other Latin Americans. In Guatemala, one labor leader murdered by government death squads in 1980 was a Mormon bishop.[23]

The second great pariah of evangelical Christianity in Latin America were the Jehovah's Witnesses. Their nineteenth-century founder, Charles Taze Russell, calculated that the messiah would return to earth in 1914. Many disappointing years and several postponed predictions later—including 1975 and October 2, 1984—the leadership was battling a heresy that the messiah had returned in the person of pop singer Michael Jackson, who was raised as a Witness and claimed to be one still.[24]

Even more so than the Mormons, the Witnesses owed their omnipresence not to vast numbers—in 1982 they claimed 2.4 million members around the world, of which 392,000 were in Latin America—but to compulsive evangelism. Each member was expected to spend much of his or her life knocking on doors and distributing the publications of the group's Watchtower Bible and Tract Society. According to the group's zealously kept statistics, the 172,859 members with the most time for evangelism spent 384,856,662 hours at it just in 1981. Some 2,000 to 3,000 hours were spent for each convert baptized, in contrast to the Mormon ratio of 710 hours for each baptism. By knocking on so many doors—an average of 740 for each baptism according to a 1976 estimate—the Witnesses located people facing crises without anyone to turn to. They offered the afflicted a shoulder to lean on, then encouraged them to identify the source of their problems as the "world" and take refuge in a sectarian group. Critics accused the Witnesses of making converts too dependent on them, but they introduced a note of order into disorganized lives.

Wherever the group's "kingdom halls" sprang up, they seemed to go through a time of trouble with the authorities. One reason was the refusal of Witnesses to accept blood transfusions, based on an Old Testament prohibition against eating blood. But the main issue was their refusal to salute national flags, sing national anthems, vote, or submit to military conscription because they regarded such activities as idolatrous. "We believe nationalism is a perversion of loyalty to God," a member told me. In the United States, this stand led to judicial decisions broadening the right to freedom of conscience. Elsewhere it meant being banned, in 1982 in twenty-eight countries. In the late 1970s, the military government of Argentina prohibited the Witnesses from worshipping in public, a measure which eventually was repealed. In 1980, Fidel Castro put a number of them on the Mariel boatlift to Florida. But they appeared to be growing more rapidly in Latin America than anywhere else.[25]

The Assemblies of God in Brazil

Pentecostals were often thought to be rather independent of missionary influence, and many were. But the giant of the pentecostal denominations was the Assemblies of God, based in Springfield, Missouri. In 1984, 9.9 million of its 12.9 million "members and adherents" outside the United States were in Latin America. That 9.9 million figure was 2.1 million higher than the 1983 figure—a 27 percent increase—and supposedly did not include children who had yet to be baptized. With 67,375 ministers serving 81,836 churches and another 25,715 students training for the ministry in 145 Bible schools, the Assemblies accounted for approximately one of every four evangelicals in Latin America. More than six million of these were in Brazil, where the Assemblies claimed to have more than half the country's Protestants.[26]

The Assemblies in Brazil traced its origin to two Swedes who, at a pentecostal revival in South Bend, Indiana, in 1902, received a prophecy that they were to do mighty works for the Lord in a place called Pará. At the public library they located the Brazilian state of that name, booked third-class passage on a freighter, and arrived at their destination penniless in wool clothing. When they learned enough Portuguese to preach in the local Baptist church, their sermons split it in two—the start of the largest evangelical denomination in Latin America.[27] From 1934 to 1964, William Read discovered, the Assemblies of Brazil grew at about 23 percent per year. From 1949 to 1962, it increased almost fivefold.[28]

Significantly, the Assemblies received its first great impetus in the Northeast, a region famous for its messianic movements. In 1964, Donald Curry was able to trace an Assemblies congregation in this drought- and strife-ridden part of Brazil back though several messiahs to Antônio Conselheiro, the doomed prophet of Canudos memorialized by both Euclides da Cunha in his *Rebellion in the Backlands* and, more recently, Mario Vargas Llosa in his novel *The War of the End of the World.* Charismatic leadership in the region was intimately connected with the migrations of the poor, Curry observed. Like so many Brazilians in flight from hard times and in search of work, religious visionaries were usually on the move.

In the case of the aforementioned Assemblies of God congregation, a local Catholic prophet claiming to incarnate past messianic figures had gathered migrants around him into a large settlement. A newer prophet had led a split-off into a new settlement, which eventually entered into the Assemblies of God. In each case, communities organized around the religious visions of prophetic figures provided seasonal labor for plantation owners and votes for political bosses. They also became way stations for migration into the cities.

According to investigators, the majority of urban pentecostals converted in chapel-centered rural settlements. "I have made many of the pastors of those great churches in the [cities] wealthy men with the converts I have sent them," a chief pastor in the countryside told Curry. "I estimate that in the past ten years alone no less than 10,000 people have become believers in the little churches under my jurisdiction and moved on." As a missionary had observed in 1910, Brazil was being evangelized "not from the coast to the interior, but from the interior to the coast."[29]

In just this way, the Assemblies learned to fish in the streams of rural-urban migration across Brazil. After starting churches in the towns, it extended them into the surrounding region and harvested bountifully from the migratory flow. Poor people felt at home in the informal, rhythmic services. When they went to strange cities, sister churches provided fictive kin and served as a referral agency. Assisted by a strict moral code and fervent exhortations to improve oneself, many poor members and their children were able to move upward in the social structure.

A second reason for the Assemblies' success was its expectation that every member evangelize. Instead of building up institutions that failed to generate new converts, the Assemblies produced armies of open-air preachers, Sunday school teachers and deacons, who organized satellites of their huge "mother church" in every neighborhood and village within reach. The idea that, inspired by the Holy Spirit, the ordinary person was capable of leadership ran through the entire pentecostal boom. "Theoretically this is in every evangelical church," a nonpentecostal missionary told me, "but among the pentecostals it really gets through. Ordinary people are persuaded to lead the Wednesday night prayer service and, even though they think they can't do it, they do." [30]

A third reason for the Assemblies' success was the transfer of leadership to Latin Americans. [31] It is unclear whether this was intentional or accidental, a consequence of rapid growth outstripping the mission's ability to supervise. But without much in the way of subsidy from the United States, Brazilian pastors were forced to find enough believers to support themselves. That made them alert to responsive areas and led to considerable emphasis on the duty of believers to tithe into the Lord's—that is, the pastor's—storehouse. The rapid growth of the Assemblies brought local leadership to the fore to such an extent that, in 1962 in Brazil, there were eight North American missionary couples for a million adherents. [32]

The home office at Springfield and its 328 missionaries to Latin America continued to have influence, however. When I talked to Nicaraguan pastors expelled by the Assemblies for their support of the Sandinista revolution, they described various requests from Springfield—to suspend a pro-Sandinista pastor touring U.S. churches, to pardon an anti-Sandinista leader who had fallen into a financial scandal—which national church leaders had honored.

The mission's $15.9 million Latin American budget in 1984, for special projects such as tent campaigns and new Bible schools, was certainly a factor. [33] Another was the awe with which many Assemblies pastors regarded their North American mentors, for one virtue the Assemblies could not claim was democracy. The organization was authoritarian, the very model of patriarchy, in which local congregations depended on parent churches for all instruction. [34] Even after national churches were granted independence, the chain of authority seemed to stretch back to Springfield. So did an undercurrent of resentment, over the superior living standards of missionaries, their imposition of unwanted rules, and political meddling.

A person might make an individual decision to join the Assemblies, Judith Hoffnagel observed in Pernambuco, Brazil, but staying with the group required total submission to authority. In such a legalistic minded institution, gossip over breaking the rules was an effective form of social control, especially when it reached church authorities and they called members to account.[35] The denomination might emphasize "the primacy of the laity" in reaction to Catholic tradition, as Emilio Willems pointed out, but its pastors also tended to imitate Catholic tradition, by assuming the stature of bishops.

The *pastor presidente* of a "mother church" was a commanding figure, even the object of veneration owing to his charismatic authority. "It is surprising to observe the care and reverence which the people show to the pastor," an observer wrote in 1951 of such men. "They do everything for him. Besides monetary support, the members of the church bring him meat, fruit, and vegetables. His table is usually abundant. He entertains lavishly and never denies help to a member in need. But it needs to be emphasized that the pastor controls everything, as much the finances as all the other activities. Nothing is done without his consent."[36]

Such a pastor was clearly descended from the authority figure in a tributary mode of production. He was a political as well as a religious personage, conceived of as the father of his people, to whom they owed their surplus by divine law but who would generously give of his reserves in time of need.[37] In churches such as this, the uncertainty and hardship of capitalist development for the poor seemed to generate, not a protest against the status quo, but a revamped form of the traditional social organization.[38]

The Assemblies was not without its internal rivalries. The pastor presidentes of different mother churches often vied for peripheral territory by planting satellite congregations next to each other. On one street in Brazil, an Assemblies official told me, three satellites from different mother churches were competing against each other with loudspeakers.[39] Because pastor presidentes appointed their own subordinates and successors, the only way to decentralize a church or change its leadership could be through a full-fledged re-volt.[40]

It was not long before politicians realized that senior pastors could perform miracles of a worldly nature, in the same manner as a traditional *patrão* or hacienda owner. As lord and master of a closed community, the pastor presidente turned into a middleman in the political economy of bossism or patronage.[41] This was the source of the famous duality in the political attitudes of the Assemblies, frequently interpreted as hypocritical. On the one hand, as preachers of separation from the world, leaders claimed to have no interest in politics. On the other hand, as pastors of large lower-class flocks, they told their followers to obey the government because it was ordained by God, discouraged political dissent, and generally behaved like bulwarks of the status quo.

Thus in northeastern Brazil in 1974, Hoffnagel discovered, Assemblies leaders were encouraging their members to vote for the candidates of a military dictatorship. To secure a block vote, the ruling party was careful to choose a few of its candidates from the Assemblies, each subject to the pastor's approval. Just like other "apolitical" evangelical pastors in Latin America, Assemblies leaders were joining political machines to obtain building and pa-rade permits, neighborhood improvements, and government jobs for their members.[42]

Pentecostalism as Power Encounter

For a left accustomed to dealing with the threadbare fabrications of dictatorships, it was difficult to handle anticommunist ideologues imbued with charisma, men who claimed to be filled with the Holy Spirit and convinced multitudes that they could work miracles. The most well-known case of pentecostal support for right-wing dicta-torship occurred in Chile, where pentecostals made up more than four-fifths of the evangelical population.[43] Some years earlier, in 1960, Emilio Willems found that Chilean pentecostals were staying away from politics unless their sect leaders exhorted them to get involved, perhaps in the name of defending religious freedom.[44] But under President Salvador Allende (1970–1973), the churches divided over his attempt to institute socialism. Numerous pentecostals responded to their class interests and supported the revolutionary program; however, pastors feared their followers were being seduced from the church.[45]

This was the context in which evangelical leaders are said to have organized secret meetings, to pray for deliverance. The September 1973 military coup, which led to the murder of an elected president and thousands of his supporters, they hailed as an act of God. "The pronouncement of our Armed Forces in the historical process of our country," leaders of thirty-two mainly pentecostal denominations declared a year later, "was God's answer to the prayers of all the believers who recognized that Marxism was the expression of satanic power of darkness. . . . We the evangelicals . . . recognize as the maximum authority of our country the military junta, who in answer to our prayers freed us from Marxism."[46]

Grateful for the endorsement, the new dictator, General Augusto Pinochet, became a patron of the country's largest Protestant denomination, the Pentecostal Methodist Church.[47] One miracle the church reported under the Pinochet regime was oral in nature. Because Pentecostal Methodists were poor and could not afford dental care, an adjunct professor of the Fuller School of World Mission explained, "they pray and receive new fillings in their mouths. The fillings just seem to grow there overnight or over a period of time, but they appear, they are not planted by any dentist. This is generally the first thing to be shown to foreign visitors, a parade of young people pass by with open mouths."[48]

Whatever one makes of this—similar reports emanated from Jorge Raschke's campaigns for the Assemblies of God in El Salvador[49]—it should remind us of the tremendous demand for magical relief from affliction. Frequently, evil spirits are the terms in which the poor and not-so-poor understand their difficulties. This is why the social disruption caused by capitalist development can be counted upon to multiply evil spirits, and why the march of "progress" over the last several centuries has, if anything, increased the demand for exorcism. As for pentecostalism, it is Christianity's main bid to subdue or, as a faith healer would put it, "rebuke" the clouds of demons swarming around the planet.

The eruption of pentecostal phenomena in many cultures has led scholars to posit a "pentecostal complex" that is highly adaptable to local circumstances.[50] In Latin America, pentecostal movements obviously rechannel the popular religiosity of folk Catholicism. As Karl-Wilhelm Westmeier points out in a study of churches in Bogotá, Colombia, pentecostalism expresses popular traditions of holy intoxication, mystical unity with the divine, and miraculous healing, all of which, until recently, have been thought of as Catholic. For the poor in a harsh milieu like Bogotá, Westmeier writes, the ecstasy generated by pentecostal worship "melts the . . . world of changing realities and rampant uncertainty into a cohesive whole on a direct experiential level of absolute certainty."[51]

Throughout Latin America, instead of praying to the Virgin for a cure or going to a folk healer, pentecostals pray for deliverance by the Holy Spirit. In Mexico, a country with a strong indigenous heritage, many rural pastors are former shamans who, in effect, continue to divine and cure under the new religion, as a more effective source of power and legitimation.[52] In Haiti, according to Frederick Conway, pentecostal healing tends to validate belief in voodoo and represents "an innovation within the traditional belief system rather than a restructuring of it."[53]

For just this reason, from an orthodox point of view, faith healing, prophecy, and the like are ambiguous and risky. Such phenomena are so common in other traditions that they are not necessarily Christian. Even if reports of miracles are true, are these the work of God or the devil, demonstrations of Christian power or of witchcraft? When converts interpret Christianity as a superior form of magic, in any case, they are bringing their traditional belief in magic into the new religion. That means they could be carried off by the next miracle-worker to come along, even if he is a raging heathen.

These were the kinds of questions which skeptical missionaries were asking about "signs and wonders," the wing of the church-growth movement stressing the importance of pentecostal weaponry for the "power encounter." The power encounter is a crisis, such as a confrontation between a missionary and a shaman over a dying patient, in which the Christian tries to prove that his religion is stronger than the traditional one. On certain golden opportunities this is not so difficult, especially when Christianity is accompanied by the power of the printed word, guns, or antibiotics. But when the new religion fails to address basic problems and creates new ones, as it certainly will, then it too will be easy to discredit.

At the Fuller School of World Mission, the reaction to "signs and wonders" reached such a point that the school discontinued its course on the subject.[54]

Even in Brazil, where pentecostalism seemed so successful, there were doubts that it was competing successfully for hearts and minds.[55] However rapidly Brazilian pentecostals had grown, to the majority of the country's ten to thirteen million Protestants, forms of spiritism such as the Africa-based Umbanda religion had grown faster and were absorbing the energies of many more Brazilians.[56]

According to Gary Howe, Umbanda's ad hoc, contractual transactions with magical power reflect the kind of ties that hold Brazilian society together, the personal favor or "fix" which the power-holder grants his dependent client. Protestantism, in contrast, attempts to internalize personal responsibility, establish universal ethical rules and centralize spiritual power in a single godhead, in a way which assumes the rational bureaucratic state. If that rational bureaucratic state is actually a fiction in the patronage-ridden reality of Brazilian society, Howe argues, then perhaps pentecostalism is a marginal, isolated vanguard.

Judging from studies which identified converts to pentecostalism as the rootless and disconnected, it was made up of those whose extended family networks had disintegrated, and who therefore had lost much of the social infrastructure needed to survive in the pervasive clientelism of Brazilian life. Although the churches that pentecostals joined might give them a new community, it was arguably a community out of touch with the way Brazilian society worked.[57] When church-growth experts talked hopefully about faith healing as their open door to Brazil, maybe it was the only way to keep the door from slamming shut.

Pentecostalism as Conformity and Protest

The dreams of pentecostals for a new heaven and new earth often seemed to contribute to preserving the old one. In a 1966 study of two low-income neighborhoods in Guatemala City, Bryan Roberts found that pentecostals and other evangelicals were refugees from harsh conditions in the countryside. They explained their many misfortunes in terms of the succession of apocalyptic disasters through which the world was passing. Meanwhile, however, they were attempting to improve their situation, with a certain amount of success. Abandoning vices and maintaining a close-knit congregational life gave Protestants more economic security and family stability than many of their Catholic neighbors. But because church activities consumed as much as 15 to 20 percent of their income, they did not seem much better off than Catholics. Those Protestants who were getting ahead seemed to do so through contacts with nonbrethren. The more prosperous they became, the less active they tended to be in church, as if they did not want to tithe away their newfound gains.

The evangelicals of these poor barrios were more outspoken about the Guatemalan social order than Catholics, but they were not about to revolt against it. One convert narrated a lifelong struggle against soldiers and landlords. But he also thanked God for helping him realize that suffering in this world was beside the point—and no reason to lose one's life in futile efforts to change the government. Most Protestants in the two barrios refused to join even nonpolitical neighborhood improvement associations. They spurned Catholic invitations to join committees and even engaged in active sabotage, by spreading rumors and voting for political parties opposed to neighborhood associations. In the two barrios, then, pentecostals were serving as "blocking groups" against efforts to improve the lot of the poor.[58]

Not all pentecostals can be accused of this behavior. Even the subjects of Roberts's study have probably changed in the two decades hence. But the combination of recognizing oppression, yet refusing to organize against it, is reported often enough to suggest a pattern. In a study of pentecostals in the United States, *Vision of the Disinherited,* Robert Mapes Anderson attributes their "curious mingling of revolutionary and conservative impulses" to an underlying conflict between rebellion and submission in the attitude of the lower classes to capitalist society. According to Anderson, North American pentecostals repressed feelings of rebellion toward their employers and the state, against which they felt more or less helpless, and displaced this hostility into the religious sphere, from which they attacked established churches, other members of their own class, and each other. Pentecostalism may have helped rural Americans adjust to more urban environments, Anderson writes. But it also transformed their millennialist hopes for a better world into ecstasy, escapism, and political conformity, turning them into a model proletariat.[59]

Still, this denouement was associated with considerable movement of North American pentecostals into the middle class: their escapism had been rewarded by advancement. Would evangelicals in Latin America be rewarded in the same way? During prosperous times, it seemed that they might. But the debt crisis of the 1980s pauperized the majority of the population and undermined the new middle class, with no improvement in sight. Capitalism in Latin America simply did not work well enough to deliver the things of this world to large numbers of fundamentalist Christians. Even in the less desperate 1970s, Cornelia Butler Flora found that the ability of Colombian pentecostals to accumulate capital was negligible. Their lack of upward mobility meant that they continued to identify with the lower classes, and they occasionally joined populist campaigns which spoke to their interests.[60]

In a Mexican case, Carlos Garma Navarro has described how indigenous pentecostals challenged a local elite for control of a town government. The largely Totonac municipality of Ixtepec, Puebla, was dominated by mestizos, who owned much of the land and relieved the Totonacs of their coffee crop at low prices. Protestantism had emerged in step with coffee cultivation, winning over better-off campesinos who were diverting their savings from community religion to personal accumulation. As in so many other places, the Bible translators of the Summer Institute of Linguistics helped disseminate the new religion. The resulting believers were deeply divided, with pastors competing bitterly for converts and a pentecostal wing emerging from the turmoil. As churches split, then split again, leaders maintained that true Christians remained apart from politics.

This might not seem a very promising basis for civil rights organizing. But then the pentecostals of one church joined with Catholics to organize first a good-government group, next a union of coffee producers and cooperative store. Basking in the approval of their fellow Totonacs, the interfaith coalition took the audacious step of running in the 1983 municipal election. Led by a capable young pentecostal pastor, who had once worked in the Volkswagon factory in the state capital, the reform slate offered itself to the winner of most elections in Mexico, the Institutional Revolutionary

Party. But the government party chose to continue supporting the mestizo incumbents. Next the pentecostal preacher appealed to his friends at the Volkswagon factory, where union leaders put him in touch with their own political party.

Soon the pentecostals and their Catholic allies were on the ticket of the United Socialist Party of Mexico. The largest constituent of this political coalition was the former Communist party: like the rest of the Mexican left, its representatives regularly denounced the penetration of the country by North American sects. Neither side in the new alliance seems to have known much about the other. But when the official party won by a narrow, suspect margin, the reform slate occupied the town hall and, backed by the Totonac majority, remained there defying mestizo authority for months afterward.

Another instance of evangelical activism in Ixtepec was confrontation with witches. In the satellite community of San Martín, a Totonac ally of the mestizo elite was not just that settlement's president and only storeowner: he was also feared as a witch. But Protestants had their own source of spiritual protection, which enabled them to brave the president's sorcery and convince Catholics that it was ineffective. The Protestants were also sophisticated enough to take the witch-president's abuses directly to the state authorities, who forced him to leave his post.

How did evangelicals come to lead these struggles? According to Garma, their pastors cut a more independent figure in relations with the outside world than traditional Catholic leaders, who tended to be very dependent on mestizos. In establishing ties with denominations outside the town, pastors learned how to line up political allies in the larger world. Despite the sectarianism of evangelical Protestantism, it could also be a school for politicians. A pastor who had managed to attract followers, then hang onto them despite the blandishments and imprecations of other men of God, was capable of wider responsibilities.[61]

Evangelism in Depth

Owing to the growth of pentecostalism, Protestant missionaries began to realize that they were being left behind by Protestantism. In the 1960s—the era of the Cuban revolution, of John F. Kennedy's

Alliance for Progress and the Second Vatican Council, of guerrilla movements and counterinsurgency, land reform and mass migration to the cities—the North American evangelical mission to Latin America seemed like a sideshow in the great changes sweeping the region. Confirming that assessment was the first major study by the Fuller School of World Mission, *Latin American Church Growth* (1969).[62]

The Fuller researchers discovered that, after three quarters of a century of work in Ecuador, there were only thirty-four Protestants for each missionary in the country. After half a century in Nicaragua, the Central American Mission's church membership peaked at seven hundred souls; then it began to fall.[63] The team heard many a story like the one from Cochabamba, Bolivia, where the Andean Evangelical Mission, after painstaking preparations, managed to attract one thousand people to a revival. A few weeks later, a pentecostal faith healer drew five times as many.[64] Nonpentecostal churches accounted for 90 percent of Protestant missionaries in Latin America but only 37 percent of the converts, the Fuller team calculated. The other 10 percent of the missionary force, the pentecostals, accounted for 63 percent of the faithful. Making the worst showing were the faith missions, the backbone of the fundamentalist missionary effort: their 32.4 percent of the Protestant missionary force in Latin America accounted for 1.5 percent of the church members.[65]

Fuller's church-growth team called for radical, ruthless changes in the way missionary work was done.[66] Obviously, the faith missions had something to learn from pentecostals. Taking the lead in doing so was the Latin America Mission (LAM), a group that specialized in support services for other agencies and churches. Founded by a British couple, Harry and Susan Strachan, LAM had always been on the innovative edge of evangelism. In the 1920s and 1930s it organized the first pandenominational campaigns. In the 1950s, it incorporated Latin Americans into its work on an equal basis with North Americans. By the 1960s, it was leading the way in civilizing relations with the Catholic Church and warning against communism.

LAM's drive to imitate pentecostal methods is sometimes dated to its 1958 Billy Graham crusade on Barbados. One-fourth of the island was said to have stepped forward to make a decision for

Christ. But the effect on church attendance was minimal, and afterward the bars and jails were just as full as they had ever been. The same thing was happening everywhere, the mission discovered.[67] The hoopla of its evangelistic campaigns attracted people who, for the most part, were already going to church. It got them accustomed to the excitement of a big-name event. And after the revivalist imported for the occasion left, their enthusiasm evaporated. Now they were bored by ordinary church life. Few newcomers who did sign decision cards actually joined churches.

How could missionaries turn the emotions generated by mass evangelism into institutional growth? To answer the question, the son and successor of LAM's founders, Kenneth Strachan, looked at why pentecostals, Jehovah's Witnesses, and communists were more successful than evangelical faith missions. The reason, Strachan concluded, was that they mobilized their entire memberships to bring new people into the movement. Instead of relying on a few pastors and famous revivalists, they made each member an evangelist.

This was the idea behind the Latin America Mission's influential new strategy, Evangelism in Depth. Throughout the 1960s, in country after country, LAM brought together missions and churches in yearlong national campaigns. The first step was to train the members of each congregation in personal evangelism. Then they were organized into prayer cells and sent out to evangelize entire populations on a one-to-one basis. Finally, the campaign culminated with parades through the streets of Catholic cities, with rallies addressed by famous evangelists, and exchanges of mutual respect with the president of the republic.

What LAM called "total mobilization" had a political dimension—the wish to compete with the left. Recognizing the social origin of revolutionary unrest, the mission placed some hope in the Alliance for Progress reforms being pushed by Washington.[68] Fear of communism was also one reason for LAM's decision to adopt a more conciliatory attitude toward the Catholic Church.[69] Hostility from Catholic authorities had long moved evangelicals to ingratiate themselves with governments, to assure themselves of official support. Now, worry over revolutionary agitation reinforced that habit.

The attitude evangelicals took toward the authoritarian, anticommunist regimes of the 1960s and 1970s was illustrated by one of the first Evangelism in Depth campaigns, in Guatemala in 1962. The final rallies in the capital were inaugurated by the president of the republic, the honorable Miguel Ydígoras. But on the last day of the campaign, the air force revolted against Ydígoras's corrupt, repressive rule. Even before the fighting in the capital had died away, to show the power of their faith, the campaign's organizers decided to go ahead with the march they had planned. As the march ended inside the city's Olympic stadium, a triumphant Ydígoras rode into the rally in a motorcade, according to *Christianity Today* with the barrel of his submachine gun still warm. The crowd cheered, and evangelical leaders gave thanks for his victory.[70]

LAM's approach, as Rubem César Fernandes and Enrique Domínguez have pointed out, had paradoxical results. For one, the mission alienated fundamentalists with its sociological frame of reference, talk about the need for Christians to address social needs, and tolerance of different opinions. For another, LAM became aware of the need to decolonize missionary work. By incorporating Latin Americans into its program on an equal basis with North Americans, it internalized the tensions between the two in a creative new way.[71]

Still another result was dissatisfaction with the superficial quantification of the Evangelism in Depth campaigns. Were they really producing more converts? Despite all the fanfare about a new strategy, the fifteen thousand decisions for Christ in the 1965–1966 campaign in Peru produced no rise in church membership figures. The program also failed, by and large, to decentralize and invigorate church life. Instead of every member becoming an active gospel witness, congregations tended to return to the old pattern of an all-powerful pastor and a passive laity.

In 1971 LAM therefore abandoned nationwide campaigns, resolving to work locally from the grass roots.[72] That same year the mission decentralized its structure and renamed itself the Community of Latin American Evangelical Ministries (CLAME). Members went to work for various institutes and programs, which came under the direction of Latin Americans and whose agendas began to diverge. In this manner, as we shall see below, the market-oriented Evangelism in Depth campaigns eventually led to trenchant critiques of church life.

But on a wider scale, Enrique Domínguez argues, Evangelism

in Depth reinforced a narrow growth mentality. To bring evangelicals together in national campaigns, the Latin America Mission argued that sectarianism was getting in the way of the most important task, evangelism. By imitating the most rapidly growing churches, the pentecostal ones, and inviting them to join evangelical alliances, LAM helped establish their legitimacy. As a result, even though LAM abandoned strident anticommunism, its campaigns amplified the apocalyptic views of pentecostal leaders. Moreover, because pentecostals were best positioned to incorporate the converts generated by Evangelism in Depth, they continued to increase their lead over other churches. Now nonpentecostal evangelicals felt even more pressure to compete with them than before. Even as the Latin America Mission became more sensitive to social issues, therefore, many evangelical leaders narrowed their concerns to numerical growth. Ultimately, Evangelism in Depth reinforced the idea that making the maximum number of converts was the only mission of the church.[73]

The Billy Graham of Latin America

Fearful of another Cuba, many evangelicals welcomed the right-wing dictatorships that, in the 1960s and 1970s, took over much of Latin America. Despite some Protestants who joined with Catholics to denounce human rights violations, many others defended military rule as a lesser evil, one needed to protect the church's freedom to spread the gospel. When Catholic hierarchies refused to bless military dictatorships, prominent evangelicals were quick to provide their own brand of legitimacy. In return, authoritarian governments gave them full liberty to spread their version of the gospel, sometimes with free access to the airwaves.

The best known Latin American evangelist came to attention in the 1970s in this way, in nationwide media blitzes carried out with the help of governments. Luis Palau (1934–) was from a hard-luck family in the provincial bourgeoisie of Argentina, where he came to the attention of O.C. Ministries. As part of its effort to train Latin American leaders, O.C. brought him to the United States, which he liked so much that he married there and became a U.S. citizen.[74] For Overseas Crusades, however, Palau returned to Latin America to pursue Evangelism in Depth, by capturing public attention in rallies and over the airwaves while churches mobilized their members to go from door to door.

An admirer of Billy Graham, Palau imitated his methods and was successful enough to go independent in 1978. As the most attractive evangelical personality on the scene, he provided a Latin face for the latest in North American-style, market-oriented evangelism. His meetings were designed, above all, for television. At a 1982 crusade in Guatemala City, for example, the audience filled only part of the stadium. The organizers therefore seated the crowd behind the evangelist, to give the cameras out on the playing field the impression of a full house. When Palau waved the Bible over his head, it was at the camera lenses, not the people who were there.

Like other evangelists, Palau said he wanted to avoid politics. But that did not prevent him from making friends with the authorities, perhaps due to the experience of having one of his first crusades canceled by the Mexican government.[75] Like Billy Graham, again, he made a point of witnessing to presidents—Alfonso López Michelsen in Colombia, Alfredo Stroessner in Paraguay, Ríos Montt in Guatemala, Fernando Belaúnde in Peru—in the hope, among other things, of free air time. When successful, Palau called on the president, held a prayer breakfast for him, broadcast his talk show and rallies over government-controlled networks, and called the nation to repentance. Given his rather nonsectarian approach to evangelism, Catholic church authorities usually held their peace. Apparently they had not heard that his goal was "to see three Latin American republics become predominantly evangelical during his lifetime."[76]

The risk of swapping blessings for broadcast time caught up with the evangelist in Bolivia, where the well-connected Summer Institute of Linguistics introduced him to army dictators Hugo Banzer (1971–1978) and Juan Pereda Asbun (1978). He addressed presidential prayer breakfasts for them and, over government airwaves, exhorted Bolivians to obey their government because it was ordained by God. Eventually, under still another army dictator, Luis García Meza (1980–1981), Palau's call for a "new emphasis on morality" was being sponsored by a regime which was, not just extremely violent, but dedicated above all to the cocaine trade.[77] By this time, despite the García Meza administration's promise to hold a national Bible quiz, the evangelist's modus operandi was making some of his brethren uneasy.

Palau was sensitive to such criticism, making it harder to finance expensive broadcast time. Because he was reluctant to solicit his audiences for money as faith healers did, he turned to evangelical foundations such as the Billy Graham Evangelistic Association, as well as to Christian business leaders in the United States. With only $1.88 million in revenue in 1983, $2.56 million in 1984, and a disappointing drop to $2.48 million in 1985,[78] his Portland, Oregon–based organization also depended on contributions of funds and labor from Latin American churches.

Yet church leaders were starting to balk at the necessary commitments. Palau's *Continente 1985* campaign, based in Puerto Rico, deflated when evangelical leaders there said they needed more time to get ready. Owing to the lack of commitment in Puerto Rico, a televised extravaganza had to be canceled, and satellite transmission replaced by video tape.[79] By this time, Palau seemed to be eclipsed by other evangelists. Aside from the handicap of not being pentecostal, his finances were far inferior to a figure like Jimmy Swaggart, who used footage from his Latin American crusades to harvest donations from North American television viewers, part of which was then plowed back into new crusades.

In appeals to North American donors, Palau sometimes played on fear of social disorder and anti-Americanism as well as the need to save the lost. On the road, he seemed to welcome attacks from Marxists, as if they were validating his message and helping to draw the crowd. He told the usual evangelist's stories of how his gospel message had triumphed over communism, by converting a guerrilla sent to kill him and preventing a revolution in Ecuador, and how the only ideology that could stop Marxist-Leninism was evangelical Christianity.[80]

But Palau was not a standard-bearer of the religious right, at least not in the North American sense. At the February 1986 convention of the National Association of Evangelicals, he served as point man for moderates criticizing the jingoism and partisanship of the NAE's National Religious Broadcasters.[81] One reason was that the bellicosity of right-wing North Americans was triggering reactions against him. When he arrived for a crusade, he did not like to be greeted with newspapers charging that he was a "preacher of Reagan." Although he protested such reports as calumnies, the exploits of the religious right were putting him on the defensive.[82]

In his campaign messages Palau stayed away from politics, focusing instead on personal moral issues like drug addiction and paternal irresponsibility. During Holy Week, a time of repentance in Latin America, he intended to play off any feelings of guilt that Catholics might have acquired during the preceding debauchery of *Carnaval.*[83] To bring a person to God, Palau explained, it was necessary to provoke crises in his or her spiritual life.[84] Overtly at least, Palau's discourse centered on how to change one's disorganized, guilt-ridden life and keep one's family together. But he also played on the sense of crisis in Latin America to sound an apocalyptic note, as if history were a race between impending chaos and the chance to redeem it through religious faith. Palau was appealing to the need for order during a time of rapid change, and he was promising that the solution to one's personal problems would also solve Latin America's. If enough people set their lives straight, Palau claimed, Latin America would see a new day.

Church Planting

Behind the evangelists like Luis Palau, whose coming was announced in posters and ads, and who temporarily occupied the public eye before disappearing to the next engagement, were numerous developments in evangelical strategy. By the 1970s it was obvious that delivering appeals and collecting decisions for Christ was not enough. Congregations had to be built up, tens of thousands of them, which meant systematic, relentless organizing at the grass roots. Because only large numbers of Latin Americans could cover the territory, many North American missionaries withdrew from mud-on-the-boots field assignments to become researchers and planners.

Exemplifying the behind-the-scenes approach was O.C. Ministries, operating through its SEPAL (*Servicio Evangelizador para América Latina*) offices in Brazil, Colombia, Mexico, Guatemala, and Argentina. From O.C.'s origin in the Far East in the early 1950s, it specialized in helping other agencies and churches develop national leadership. Three decades later it was making much of missionaries from the Third World, apparently in the hope of increasing North American support for them.[85] O.C. was also the main channel for church-growth thinking in Latin America. With a $5.1 million income in 1985, its forte was bringing other agencies and churches together in nationwide growth programs. In effect, it was stepping into the role vacated by the Latin America Mission when the latter abandoned large-scale Evangelism in Depth campaigns. O.C.'s approach was to bring a country's evangelical church leaders together, encourage them to compare their growth rates, and calculate the year when they would constitute a majority of the country—if the slower growing churches could match the fastest.[86]

To arrive at their figures, church-growth experts first added up the memberships reported by all the denominations in a country. Then they multiplied that figure by another number, to account for unbaptized children, converts attending services but not yet baptized, and so forth. The multiplier was usually 2.5, 3, or 4, depending on "sociological factors," whatever those were construed to be. The result was supposed to be the total evangelical community. In the case of Guatemala, a church-growth investigator named Cliff Holland noticed that, in a government census, five times as many people claimed to be non-Catholic Christians as were enrolled in evangelical churches. To leave out unacceptable groups such as the Mormons, Holland multiplied evangelical church memberships by four. That was the origin of the widely quoted figure that evangelicals were 22.4 percent of the Guatemalan population in 1982, for a total community of 1.73 out of 7.71 million people.[87]

What such figures seemed to gloss over was the "circulation of the saints," the revolving door quality of many congregations. Numerous converts seemed to drop out of church life after a short time but continued to describe themselves as evangelical to avoid Catholic obligations. Others who did not wish to identify themselves as Catholics probably never had anything to do with a non-Catholic church. Still others hopped from church to church in search of spiritual excitement. Pastors under pressure to show impressive statistics failed to purge the rolls of lapsed members. Among recent migrants to the city, some lost interest as they prospered, and many children drifted away from the convictions of their parents. Owing to the vicissitudes of the faith, one evangelical investigator pointed out, the human base on which church growthers calculated their figures was not stable like the financial base on which capital increases.[88] "At times, in certain places," another put it, "we have the impression that there are more evangelicals outside the churches than inside them."[89]

However questionable many of the statistics, evangelical growth was rapid enough to outstrip the supply of trained leaders. Even rudimentary Bible courses could not churn out enough graduates to keep up with the demand. Missionaries shuddered at the exegetical results of unschooled preaching. Seat-of-the-pants leaders were also unlikely to build congregations much beyond their own family network. Without pastoral training, the Southern Baptists found, their congregations leveled off at twenty to thirty people.[90]

Behind the lack of training was a deeper problem, the wrong kind of training, thanks to the importation of inappropriate expectations into Latin American churches. Seminaries and Bible institutes were a case in point. While denominations were putting a few choice young men through years of such training, often they did not get much for their investment. Of 264 students who attended the Presbyterian Seminary of Guatemala over a twenty-five-year period, according to Ross Kinsler, only fifty-two graduated, and of these only fifteen were serving their church in the late 1970s.[91] Seminarians from the countryside who became accustomed to city life were often unwilling to return to their people. More than a few immigrated to the United States. Even if they consented to remain in church work, they were professionalized into the middle class, creating a gap between themselves and the majority of their brethren.

This was not the way to evangelize the vast lower reaches of Latin American society. Meanwhile, mature men, more likely to persist in their humble surroundings, were unable to acquire training because they could not meet entrance requirements or had to support a family. Some pentecostal denominations had a solution: instead of investing in seminaries, they put potential pastors through lengthy apprenticeships by promoting them through a series of levels—street preaching, Sunday school teaching, and so forth—in a way that built up their religious skills without professionalizing them.[92] Another solution was to open extension programs with lower admission requirements. The first such effort, started by Presbyterian missionaries in Guatemala in 1963 for rural pastors, was called Theological Education by Extension (TEE) and inspired many others.

The cities were also in fashion in the 1980s, accounting as they now did for the majority of the Latin American population. Most cities were already jumping with evangelical churches. But North American missions had been slow to shift from previous frontiers of the faith, so that much urban evangelism was pentecostal or heretical in nature. Often it was also confined to the lower classes, the usual milieu for Protestantism in Latin America, with spiritual commitment waning as evangelicals rose into the middle class.

That made saving souls higher in the social scale a related subject of keen interest. Only by expanding upward in the class structure could Protestants win a nation to their faith politically as well as religiously, in the sense of claiming professionals and executives as well as the common people. "Witnessing to the upper classes," as this congenial branch of world mission is known, was especially appropriate for North Americans. As persons of high status, they were more likely to appeal to Latin American elites than lower-class evangelists from the same country, no matter how well educated and presentable the latter might be. Based on the church-growth movement's "homogenous unit principle"—that persons prefer to become Christians together with members from their own social group—it became common to appeal separately to the upper class. In one such country club movement, the leaders noticed that "as soon as people from the lower and middle classes began attending their churches, ingathering from among the upper class ceased." In keeping with the Apostle Paul's injunction to be all things to all men, they therefore organized separate churches for the plebeians. [93]

Despite criticism that evangelicals were "buying" converts, many missionaries recognized that such practices backfired. Subsidies, except for pastoral training or strategic building sites, tended to be death to evangelism. "Every time a new work began, it decreased the subsidy the other churches were receiving," a Southern Baptist in Guatemala explained. "There was no initiative . . . to expand the work." Like the Assemblies of God, the Southern Baptists discovered that one of the best ways to make churches grow was to refuse to pay pastor salaries. That forced aspiring men of God to follow up personal contacts, knock on doors, start Bible studies, and convert enough people to make a living. [94]

In Lima, Peru, the Regions Beyond Missionary Union came in from the jungle to pursue a typical program for planting urban churches. Starting with a careful selection of target areas, it planned to go from door to door, then hold brief, intensive evangelistic campaigns, followed by Bible studies for new believers and lengthier training for potential leaders. The whole effort was to be spearheaded by missionaries, ideally a team consisting of an evangelist, a Bible teacher, a pastor, and a youth director, who were gradually to turn over leadership to the Latin Americans they trained, move on to other neighborhoods, and repeat the process.

A high profile without putting up sectarian barriers was the ideal in these ventures, at least at the start. In an Assemblies of God text on how to plant churches, evangelist David Godwin stressed the importance of keeping the crusade as open as possible to newcomers. For example, a good way to start out was by reciting core doctrines shared with the Catholic Church; campaigning against the Catholic clergy was to be avoided at all costs. The model evangelist, according to Godwin, even tried to avoid premature classification as a new religious group. Construction of a church building was to be put off as long as possible, for up to several years, to avoid erecting walls that would discourage people from wandering into the festive meetings.[95]

To keep the church and its members close to the street, where they could win new converts, Regions Beyond planned to organize small Bible studies to meet in homes during the week, in the kind of familiar, nonintimidating surroundings most likely to attract neighbors. On the weekend, everyone was to gather at the central church for the edification provided by professional religion. Eventually, some of the Bible studies—also known as satellite, daughter, or house churches—could mature into central churches with their own offspring. As weekday conduits into mother churches on Sundays, such cell groups were a popular way not just to stay close to the grass roots but to prevent converts from being carried off by rival sects.[96]

Political Polarization

In 1969, the authors of *Latin American Church Growth* decried the "importation of foreign theological problems irrelevant to Latin America." The disputes between liberal and conservative North American Protestants were irrelevant, the researchers from the

Fuller School of World Mission believed, because their Latin American brethren agreed on the essentials of the faith. But now agencies of cooperation such as the National Association of Evangelicals and the World Council of Churches were becoming instruments of power politics, needlessly polarizing Latin Americans.[97]

Even in the new era of supposed independence from North American missions, many Latin American churches remained dependent on foreign funds for new initiatives. Both the ecumenical and evangelical wings of North American Protestantism were bringing up promising young leaders like Luis Palau to study in the United States, then hiring them, and financing efforts to make Latin American churches more "national."

The original bone of contention between the North Americans was theological: how to interpret the Bible and whether to give priority to evangelism or social action. But Latin Americans were less inclined to turn social and spiritual work into a dichotomy, and they had never worried overmuch about the precise nature of biblical authority. It could even be argued, as did the Latin America Mission, that the problem of "modernism" scarcely existed.[98] What certainly did exist were serious ideological and political differences.

In the early 1970s, José Miguez Bonino distinguished three such tendencies in Latin American Protestantism. The first was engaged in what Christian Lalive d'Epinay had recently termed a "social strike." Consisting primarily of pentecostals, these Christians professed to be turning their back on the world and its wicked ways. But through a curious inversion which we have already glimpsed, leaders of the tendency sometimes seemed preoccupied with maintaining the status quo.

The second group, which Miguez Bonino called "liberal," was a product mainly of the older denominations. In the late nineteenth and the early twentieth century, its struggle for civil liberties against the clerical power of the Catholic Church led to support for bourgeois revolution. In Cuba, Protestants played a conspiratorial role in the war of independence against Spain.[99] Early in the century, many Protestants fought for the Mexican revolution, the majority in the constitutionalist faction.[100] In Guatemala, evangelicals were strong supporters of the reformist Arbenz administration overthrown by the Central Intelligence Agency in 1954.

Such Protestants faced difficult choices when, in the name of fighting communism, a curtain of dictatorship rang down on Latin America in the late 1960s and early 1970s. Forced to choose between submission and protest, their churches were torn by power struggles between right and left.[101] The polarization gave rise to a third grouping, whom Miguez Bonino called "revolutionary" and who usually lost.[102]

As a result of these disputes, Latin American church life came to be seen in terms of a confrontation between a small progressive or radical camp on the one hand and a reactionary or conformist one on the other. A first sign of the split was the backlash against a World Council of Churches affiliate, Church and Society in Latin America (ISAL). The theologians of the movement, organized in 1961 in the Southern Cone, upset conservatives on two scores. First, they lost interest in proselytizing Catholics, feeling liberated from that responsibility by the Second Vatican Council. Second, they became convinced that evangelism alone would never address the misery of the Latin American masses. Only the kinds of structural change brought about by social revolution could.[103]

The Protestant intellectuals of ISAL were, in a sense, the first liberation theologians in Latin America.[104] But conservatives felt that the innovators were making revolution their supreme value and turning Christianity into a political instrument. Although ISAL considered itself the vanguard of Latin American Protestantism, it was unable to build bridges to many churches. As its members quarreled over a diminishing institutional base, they were pushed out of the Southern Cone by the military dictatorships of the 1970s and ended up on the fringe of Latin American evangelicalism.[105]

To North American evangelical missions, ISAL was a vivid example of how Christianity could be corrupted from within. They feared that the WCC's ecumenical bodies—the Provisional Commission for Latin American Evangelical Unity (UNELAM), the Latin American Union of Evangelical Youth (ULAJE), and Christian Student Movement (MEC), as well as the Latin American Evangelical Commission for Christian Education (CELADEC)—could attract the churches they themselves had founded.

To guard against that, in 1969, the NAE and the Billy Graham Evangelistic Association financed the First Conference on Evangelism in Latin America.[106] CLADE I, as the gathering came to be known, defended soul winning against Protestants trying to replace it with social issues. Laced heavily with North American mission-aries, the conference illustrated what would become a recurring phenomenon: support from U.S. parachurch agencies for "biblical" breakaways from existing Protestant associations, to organize more conservative ones to compete for influence over Latin American evangelicals.

The Latin American Theological Fraternity

CLADE I was not a complete success for its North American orga-nizers. Once Latin churchmen were brought together, they discov-ered that they were all tired of North Americans telling them how to think.[107] The conference organizers made the mistake of circulat-ing missionary Peter Wagner's attack on ISAL as the "new radical left" betraying the gospel to Marxism. Enough Latin delegates were offended to push through a call for evangelicals to meet their social responsibilities, by contextualizing their faith in the Latin American context of oppression.[108]

This might seem like an innocuous resolution. But it was the point of departure for a new movement, the Latin American Theo-logical Fraternity (FTL), which aimed to be distinctively Latin American as well as distinctively evangelical. The fraternity wanted to pursue social issues without abandoning evangelism, deal with oppressive structures without endorsing violence, and bring left- and right-wing Protestants back together again.

Two theologians involved in the FTL—Orlando Costas of Puerto Rico and René Padilla of Ecuador—played an important part in the 1971 restructuring of the Latin America Mission, several of whose offshoots provided an institutional base for their thinking. Another, rather unlikely supporter was the National Liberty Foundation, since renamed the Arthur S. DeMoss Foundation after its now de-ceased founder, an insurance magnate and board member of Cam-pus Crusade for Christ. The foundation sought to advance the evan-gelism of the world from a conservative point of view. But to further this task in Latin America, it backed a "Partnership in Mission" pro-gram intended to assuage relations between Latin churches and North American missions. As it turned out, Partnership in Mission was administered by an FTL thinker, the British-Peruvian theologian and former Billy Graham representative Pedro Savage.[109] Before the funding was cut off, Savage sponsored the kind of questioning that, in the 1980s, would be stigmatized as liberation theology.

Like liberation theologians, FTL's members defined sin in social as well as individual terms. They recognized that the fundamentalist dichotomy between evangelism and social work was not in scripture. They also recognized that one's reading of the Bible was shaped by history and culture. Because it was impossible to be above politics and the time to realize the values of the kingdom was now, FTL theologians rejected the otherworldly position taken by North American fundamentalists. But they were also critical of liberation theology. Liberationists had subordinated biblical reflection to Marxist theory, they argued, replacing the need for individual regeneration with political organizing. Instead of "liberation" as a paradigm, the fraternity chose another term: "contextualization."[110]

The outlines of the "third way" advocated by FTL thinkers remained hazy. But they impressed North American mission executives looking for an appropriate response to revolutionary upheaval. As Enrique Domínguez has pointed out, here were orthodox evangelicals in favor of social engagement but against commitment to revolutionary politics. The combination so impressed the North Americans that, at the instigation of two FTL members at Lausanne, René Padilla and Samuel Escobar, they wrote social responsibility and contextualization into the Lausanne Covenant in 1974. But while the more flexible North American missionaries adjusted to the FTL's critiques, many Latin American church leaders did not.

CONELA

In 1978, at a meeting in Oaxtepec, Mexico, ecumenical Protestants pushed through a proposal to create a new Latin American Council of Churches (CLAI).[111] Hoping to make the new organization inclusive, they pledged to promote evangelism as well as social change. More than a hundred denominations and agencies signed up, including some pentecostal ones. But conservatives at the meeting objected to the agenda: they were wary of the new organization's financial dependence on the World Council of Churches, and they were offended by what they felt were radical political pronouncements.[112] Here, they feared, was another front for the WCC to mis-represent them. In some haste, opponents therefore set up a counter-organization, the Latin American Evangelical Confederation (CONELA).

But CONELA was not just a reaction to the organizing efforts of ecumenical Protestants. It also expressed a division among evangelicals claiming to uphold the Lausanne Covenant. This was apparent from the very germ of the new body, in 1980, at a Billy Graham-financed conference in Pattaya, Thailand. The men who set up the first organizing session for CONELA wished to keep out, not just clearly defined ecumenical Protestants, who were few at Pattaya, but the larger number of evangelicals who wished to remain in dialogue with them. That meant excluding evangelicals pledged to uphold the Lausanne Covenant, in particular, several of the best known members of the Latin American Theological Fraternity. CONELA's leadership proved to have few members of the fraternity, which declined to affiliate either with it or CLAI, in the vain hope of serving as a bridge between the two.[113]

What pulled CONELA together was the evangelist Luis Palau. Two Palau executives were among the organizers of the first caucus at Pattaya; his people played a major role at the founding conference, in Panama in 1982; he himself was the star of the show there; and his team provided CONELA's first president, all of which led to the perception that CONELA was Palau's show. His people disavowed any such intention, but they did admit to wider goals. "It's hard to over-emphasize the importance of CONELA right now in Latin America," Palau executive Bill Conard explained. "Leftist ideologies are penetrating the church, and there is no united defense of the biblical gospel, nor offense [sic] as to how to apply biblical principles in our churches and life. CONELA offers a real solution to this impasse."[114]

The new confederation's leaders defined their separatist identity by denouncing CLAI and liberation theology; that was the explicit enemy. But implicitly, they were also setting themselves against the Lausanne Covenant. While claiming to uphold the covenant, they feared that evangelicals pursuing its call for "social responsibility" were compromising their faith with left-wing ideology. As a result, CONELA's architects concluded that the kingdom of God should not be confused with food or drink, that churches should not become involved in struggles for political power, and that Christians should render unto Caesar what is Caesar's.[115] In keeping with church-growth thinking, they relegated social responsibility to specialized relief and development agencies.

CONELA claimed to represent twenty million evangelicals. It did incorporate existing associations, such as the Evangelical Council of Venezuela (CEV), and proceeded to organize new ones in countries where they were lacking, including Mexico, the Dominican Republic, and Panama. But while delegates from eighty-four denominations attended CONELA's founding conference, three-quarters of the 4.2 million church members represented directly belonged to just one group: the Assemblies of God in Brazil. Unfortunately for CONELA, the more fundamentalist churches tended to be very difficult to organize. Their reason for existence was splitting off from other churches, after all, and they distrusted any attempt to organize them into something larger.

The majority of Latin American evangelicals probably did not even know what CONELA was, let alone feel represented by it. But the new confederation did have the support of the North American mission establishment, including Billy Graham, Campus Crusade for Christ, and O.C. Ministries as well as the Palau organization.[116] Present at the founding conference were sixty-four parachurch agencies, with media organizations comprising the largest number and mass evangelists the next.[117] At the mercy of government fiat for their access to airwaves and coliseums, such operations tended to be among the most conformist toward political authority. Many of the broadcasters and evangelists were also, of course, headquartered in the United States. As a skeptical observer from World Vision asked, did they really have a Latin American identity, or were they simply trying to justify themselves?[118]

Chapter Six

The Religious Right Comes to
Latin America

*A Christ-centered counter-revolution is saving lives in Central
America. . . . Find out how you can join the counter-revolution before it's too late.*

World Literature Crusade, 1987[1]

In a 1984 television special on Central America, the babble of conflicting claims in the media gives way to a familiar voice rising above
the confusion. "There's a fire starting and burning on our doorstep,"
declares Ronald Reagan, kicking off a fundraiser by an organization
called Open Doors with Brother Andrew. Open Doors' specialty is
smuggling Bibles, but now it is branching out. As a country-by-
country profile of Central America reaches Mexico, a pink arrow
flashes into the soft underbelly of the United States. If Mexico cannot put its house in order, a voice intones, millions more of its desperate citizens will flee to the United States.

"The revolution now in Latin America," explains actor Dean
Jones, Walt Disney nice guy and born-again Christian, "is only a
foretaste of what will happen once the Russians have a strong foothold in Africa. Once they can afford the men and military power,
they will move into Latin America in full strength, concentrating
on Central America. [Open Doors' founder Brother] Andrews believes that their purpose is to first cut off North America from South
America, then to engulf all of the southern hemisphere in revolution. And then, finally, to isolate North America from the rest of the
world."

"Perhaps for now we can ignore the crisis on our doorstep," continues Jones. "But if Latin America falls to the forces of Marxist revolution now at work throughout the continent, there is little doubt that its impact will reach deeper into our lives than we can possibly imagine. The military implications alone are staggering. Perhaps the question of the hour should be, *how* will we be involved in Latin America? For now, we have a choice. For *now*." To the sound of drumbeats, the slight, intense figure of Brother Andrew appears, amidst Salvadoran troops on a search-and-destroy mission. "Better to go to them before they come to us," the veteran Bible smuggler warns North Americans in his clipped Dutch accent. "If we do not go to the heathen with the gospel, they will come to us with revolutionaries and occupation armies."[2]

For right-wing evangelicals, 1979 was the year the alarm began to ring and refused to shut off. The Sandinistas had come to power in Nicaragua, making them the first successful revolutionaries in Latin America since Fidel Castro rode into Havana two decades before. They proceeded to support insurgencies in neighboring countries, raising the specter of a Red isthmus cutting the hemisphere in two. Hard to believe as it might be, the Sandinistas owed their victory to support from Christian churches. Certainly, the Catholic clergy was known to harbor leftists, but they were not the only guilty party. Young people from Nicaragua's evangelical churches had also helped the Sandinistas overthrow the old regime. "Pastors reported that they were losing their youth almost completely," an Open Doors executive reported.[3]

In the western Guatemalan highlands, whole congregations of Mayan Indians seemed to be going over to the guerrillas. Elsewhere, entire seminaries were said to be infiltrated by subversive doctrine. Unless something was done, the Interamerican Mission's Ray Hundley declared, Protestant churches would be reduced to strategy centers for guerrilla warfare and Marxist revolution.[4] "Daily more and more Latin American Christians are obeying the liberationist call: 'Put down your Bibles, take up your rifles, and join the revolution!'" Hundley warned. "Churches once known for their evangelistic fervor are being converted into centers for subversive guerrilla action. Seminaries that were once world-famous for their Bible-centered training are now mass-producing Marxist leaders expert in using God's Word to stir their congregations into violent uprisings."[5]

This was the kind of hysterical assessment that raises money. What better way to get attention back home and justify hanging on in the field than to protect converts from communism? Clearly liberation theology was being used as a bogeyman. But the rhetoric suggests that revolutionaries were not the only ones worrying about the churches multiplying among the poor; so were conservative evangelicals. Detecting a subversive potential in their churches, they conceived of liberation theology as a doctrinal virus originating in communist capitals, capturing the minds of recklessly liberal Christians, and now infecting their own impressionable churches.

Usually we think of liberation theology in terms of the Catholic Church, sometimes in association with ecumenical Protestants, but never with fundamentalists or evangelicals. The latter's case against liberation theology was simple and often seemed unanimous. Whereas Christ located sin in the hearts of men, evangelicals argued, liberation theology attributed it to social structures. And whereas Christians believed that salvation was achieved through personal rebirth, liberation theology reduced it to revolution, to the idea that only a social upheaval could redeem humanity.

Ultimately, then, liberation theology was about people improving their own condition rather than being saved through faith in Christ. By viewing sin as a social rather than a personal phenomenon, liberation theology tended to merge religion and politics, replace evangelism with political organizing, and advocate revolutionary violence. That made it a deceptive, falsely Christian vehicle for Marxist indoctrination. When the revolution came to power, it would surely turn against the church, destroy its independence, and reduce it to a hollow, spiritless shell. To join hands with liberation theology, then, was an invitation to suicide.[6]

Even politically daring evangelicals repeated much of this indictment.[7] At their kindest, they thought that liberation theology was too dependent on Marxist analysis and too selective in its use of scripture.[8] They did not agree with its interpretation of the Bible, and they thought it neglected the importance of personal salvation. But they did admire one feature of liberation theology, "Christian commitment"—not the kind displayed by guerrilla priests, but that of all the men and women who had disregarded threats, refused to take up arms, persisted in their ministry, and given their lives. Some evangelicals were ashamed that they could claim few such martyrs of their own. They wished to match the dedication of such Christians without losing sight of their own commitments.

On liberation theology, then, evangelicals were more divided than might appear from the chorus of repudiation. In the atmosphere generated by heresy hunters, in which any assessment other than total condemnation could be interpreted as sympathy, some evangelicals maintained a discreet silence. To suggest, as others did, that at least liberation theology had placed scripture in the Latin American context and encouraged evangelicals to pay attention to social issues, such a response was risky because it drew accusations of falling into liberation theology oneself. Conservatives were using the label to discredit and expel brethren with a critical attitude toward their domination of church life.

Numerous tensions sharpened by economic depression and war—between missionaries and Latin Americans, rural and urban evangelicals, young leaders and old ones, the poor and the well-off—were generating a counterculture in the evangelical churches. That was the case with the Interamerican Mission, the group to which the alarmed missionary Ray Hundley belonged. Interamerican had a long history of conflict with its churches in Colombia, the kind caused by a mission not ceding control to local people. As a result, some of its spiritual charges had turned antimission, then anti-North American. "By charging that missionaries are CIA agents or unconscious dupes of 'yankee imperialism,'" Hundley complained of such nationalists, "they have succeeded, in many cases, to paralyze or at least cripple foreign missionary involvement."[9]

From radicals declaring for social revolution to fundamentalists pledging to stop it, left-right politicization was the new style in religious rivalry. If battles over turf used to be waged mainly between Catholics and Protestants, in terms of the honor due the pope or the Virgin Mary, now they were being overlaid by a new kind of confrontation between liberation theology and anticommunist crusades. Where right-wing fundamentalists came up against left-wing Catholics, religious and political differences overlapped and built up into what started to look like holy war.

In the belief that they were Christianity's last line of defense, missionaries inspired by the religious right made themselves eager servants of the Reagan administration's foreign policy in Central America. This new wave in the missionary effort included members of older, established agencies who had never shared in the self-critical mood of the 1970s. Alarmed by the prospect of communists in power, they polarized to the right and could be particularly influential owing to their established position in local churches.

But much of the missionary right was new to the scene, having been attracted since the early 1970s by natural disasters and then the war. More often than not, the new apostles were from the Sunbelt and part of wider pentecostal and charismatic networks—the Assemblies of God, the Full Gospel Businessmen's Fellowship, the various television ministries—extending into the region. Central America was conveniently close to home, within range of small independent mission budgets, and familiar enough culturally to get started with a few contacts and a smattering of Spanish. By the 1980s, moreover, Central America appealed to some of the deepest symbolic needs of gospel preachers. It was a next-door neighbor under the menace of communism, and it was already coming to the Lord, in the form of pentecostal movements eager to hail revivalists. Central America was the perfect stage on which to heft one's Bible aloft, cast out demons, and throw back the Satanic tide.

Encouraged by the White House, these Christians were using their foreign missions to promote the U.S. government's agenda in Latin America. As Deborah Huntington pointed out, they tried to dissuade Central Americans from joining movements for social change, by holding out the hope of a spiritual alternative to political action. They also assured U.S. supporters that the Reagan administration's version of events was correct and attacked critics as communist sympathizers.[10] They were, in effect, cheerleaders for U.S. military intervention. To support the Nicaraguan contras, they worked closely with organizations studded with former military and intelligence officers.[11] In joining the contra war, they seemed bent on confirming fears that North American missions were CIA fronts.

Liberation Theology

When evangelical missionaries encouraged Latin Americans to read the Bible, they did not anticipate that it would be interpreted in terms of liberation theology. But where North American ideas of development had failed, the Bible's many references to the poor and to social justice were hard to ignore. Instead of relegating such verses to the afterlife, to the millennial kingdom, or to one's spiritual state, as North Americans usually did, why not interpret them literally? Much of the Catholic Church decided to do so, prompting reprisals from governments and feeding church people into revolutionary movements.

The intent of Catholic reformers had been to avert a violent social revolution, not become part of one. In the 1960s and 1970s thousands of Catholic volunteers forsook middle-class comforts, went to live with the poor, and tried to respond to their material as well as spiritual needs, to save them from the blandishments of communism. One of the first obstacles church workers encountered was the resignation of the people they planned to uplift: many of the poor were so downtrodden that they seemed to have given up hope. Hence the interest in the Brazilian educator Paolo Freire's *concientización* or consciousness-raising technique, a Socratic-style device for organizing people to change oppressive conditions. Propagated through networks of lay catechists, the new approach led to forming thousands of "ecclesiastical base communities," small, grass-roots groups that studied the Bible and often moved on to analyze local problems such as the lack of secure land titles.

Analyzing the local situation led to a second kind of problem, with the authorities. The original idea had been to resolve conflicts peacefully, before revolutionaries moved in to exploit them. But that required making changes which the oligarchies and gendarmes of Latin America were unwilling to accept. It meant confronting the state, to whose security forces the Christians were soon denounced as subversives. Nor were such fears entirely groundless, due to the parallel emergence of armed insurgencies. Led by urban intellectuals, a number of these revolutionary groups wished not just to organize the same people as the church did but also to organize through the church, whose religious purpose would provide cover—for a while, anyway.

Along with certain ecumenical Protestants, Catholic theologians were, meanwhile, increasingly receptive to Marxism as a mode of analysis. They had already turned to social science as a framework for applying church teaching to social problems. Now they were attracted to dependency theory, a revisionist form of Marxism concentrating on the exploitative relations between the imperialist core and its Third World periphery. One reason dependency theory appealed to Latin Americans was that it located the source of the region's difficulties, not in its class structure as did orthodox Marxists, nor in its religion and culture as did Protestants, but in subordination to the United States. If Washington was ultimately to blame for frustrating social reform in Latin America—an attractive proposition following its overthrow of democratically elected governments in Guatemala, Brazil, and Chile, its war on Cuba, and the 1965 invasion of the Dominican Republic—then here was a doctrine to rally a broad anti-imperialist front.

Liberation theologians refused to dichotomize the spiritual and material by, for example, suggesting that the poor accept their lot in this life and look forward to their reward in the next. In contrast to conservatives who claimed to be above politics, liberationists showed that, whatever one's theology, it had political implications. Although the church had long justified an oppressive social order, they continued, the Bible promised salvation in this world, not just the next. Drawing on Latin American experience with capitalism and the United States, these thinkers Christianized anti-imperialism, class struggle, and social revolution. The result was a God of the poor who, as in the exodus of the Israelites from Egypt, would deliver his people from bondage.

This is not to say that Catholic activists were enthusiastic about Marxist-Leninist vanguard parties, armed struggle, or the dictatorship of the proletariat. Most were not. It is important to note, as does Philip Berryman, that categories such as class and exploitation are as pervasive in the Latin American vocabulary as psychobabble is in the North American: it is practically impossible to refer to life without them.[12] Even when desperate for allies, the majority of progressive Catholics were not impressed by the available left. Experience taught that, while its parliamentarians were ineffective, its insurrectionists were immature, manipulative, and hazardous for anyone else advocating social change. Most armed uprisings were unsuccessful, the main result being government reprisals against anyone unlucky enough to be in the vicinity.

Most clergy working at the unprotected, lower end of the social scale did not wish to alienate the authorities for any but the best of reasons. It was lonely and violent out there. Hoping to avoid bloodbaths, social activists usually concentrated on their own parish-level efforts. As for the big picture, they contented themselves with hopes for some kind of democratic socialism, visualized in terms of cooperatives or egalitarian communities.

In the United States, the political system could have accommo-
dated many of the programs that progressive Catholics were organizing in Latin America. But in Latin America, activists were
quickly treated as subversives. As dictatorships suppressed church
organizations, they became bridges to the armed left. Seeing their
people slaughtered for trying to exercise their rights, and basing
their counsel less on liberation theology than on the traditional doctrine of the just war, Catholic clergy in Guatemala and El Salvador
told peasants that rising up against the authorities could be a Christian cause. In Nicaragua, base communities became what the Sandinista guerrillas called "quarries" for their movement.[13]

Hearings in Washington

Word of these events was quick to reach Pharaoh. Liberation theology could be scapegoated for the revolutionary turmoil in Central
America, and North Americans influenced by it were hindering the
Reagan administration's effort to overthrow the Sandinistas in Nicaragua. Through their churches, North American Christians were
creating sympathy for Marxist revolutionaries. It was for these reasons that liberation theology was taken up on Capitol Hill, by a
Senate subcommittee investigating terrorists.

The October 1983 hearings, on "Marxism and Christianity in
Revolutionary Central America," were chaired by Senator Jeremiah
Denton (R-Alabama), a former Navy pilot who had spent eight
years in a North Vietnamese prison camp. The National Council of
Churches and the U.S. Catholic Conference declined to testify,
fearing an inquisition. Owing partly to Senator Denton's reputation
as an extremist, the hearings did not attract much attention. But
they did fill out the Reagan administration's indictment against liberation theology, arming the religious right on the subject for years
to come.

Leading off the testimony was a representative of the Council for
Inter-American Security. This was the think tank which, in its 1980
Santa Fe report, called on the U.S. government to counter liberation theology and also helped formulate the Reagan policy of bank-
rolling right-wing guerrilla movements.[14] Working closely as it did
with Washington's military-intelligence bureaucracies, the Council
apparently found it hard to conceive of religious developments ex-

cept as a reflection of political conspiracies. According to the Council's witness, a Catholic priest named Enrique Rueda, liberation theology was a Soviet-Cuban strategy to subvert the hemisphere.

The next five witnesses were exiles from Sandinista-controlled Nicaragua. They pointed to a handful of priests who, under the Somoza dictatorship, had worked with the Sandinista guerrillas, then allegedly manipulated fellow clergy into supporting a Marxist takeover. According to the witnesses, the chief villain was poet-priest Ernesto Cardenal, an early admirer of the Cuban revolution, a clandestine member of the Sandinista guerrilla movement, and now the Sandinista minister of culture. Under the old regime—which had crushed peaceful opposition and come to be universally repudiated—Cardenal and a few other clergy had recruited young people for the Sandinista movement, raised money for it abroad, sheltered guerrillas in their rectories, encouraged confrontations with the authorities, even helped organize surprise attacks. When the Somoza dictatorship retaliated against the Catholic Church, they had concealed their use of it for revolutionary activities and accused the government of religious persecution.

Now that the Sandinistas had taken power, Cardenal was the most well-known figure in the revolutionary religious community, sometimes referred to as the Popular Church. While most clergy supporting the Sandinistas were "naive romantics," one witness told the Denton committee, Cardenal was an atheist who merely paraded as a Christian. According to another witness, the Sandinistas were using the image of revolutionary Christians like Cardenal to disguise the Marxist-Leninist nature of their regime, reinterpret Christianity in terms compatible with Marxism-Leninism, and conceal the persecution of Christian opponents. Still another witness, a Sandinista defector named Miguel Bolaños Hunter, described the manipulation of revolutionary religious groups by security agents from the Ministry of Interior.

What is to be made of such testimony? Without discounting everything said before the Denton committee—certainly liberation theology could be manipulated like any religious movement—it should be noted that histories of polarization can, in hindsight, be misread as conspiracies. Each side interprets the symbolic linkages tying together the other as proof of premeditated, centralized direction, often incorrectly. By glossing over the many tensions and cleavages in the enemy camp, such interpretations produce a police state version of history.[15]

The Denton committee's star witness in this regard was Luis Pellecer, a young Jesuit "disappeared" by Guatemalan security forces in June 1981. Presumed dead like so many other political detainees, Pellecer was resurrected four months later at a government press conference where he confessed a vast conspiracy of the Catholic Church, private development agencies, and his own Jesuit order, which he identified as the mastermind of the revolutionary movement.[16] Pellecer had in fact been recruited as a collaborator of Guatemala's Guerrilla Army of the Poor, but only at the late date of mid-1978, after a government massacre of Kekchí Indians spurred recruitment into revolutionary groups. Like many other Christians who have joined rebellions, Pellecer did so only after witnessing the kind of crimes of state which, according to theological tradition, may justify such an action.

Later, when Pellecer described Catholic social programs as a Marxist-Leninist conspiracy, he seemed to be regurgitating the rationalizations of his kidnappers. Contrary to the Guatemalan government's version of events, most observers would agree that army and police atrocities, not guerrilla organizers, turned the bulk of the country's Catholic clergy against the regime. By reducing the Catholic social outreach to a communist conspiracy, Pellecer's captors were projecting the paranoia and conspiracy of their own, highly centralized death squad state into a less organized opposition.

The hearings on liberation theology may have shown how the Sandinista regime was using religion to suppress domestic opponents and defend itself against U.S. attacks. But they were also a mirror image of how the Reagan administration was manipulating religion. If we reverse the religious right's indictment of the Sandinistas, it becomes clear that the Reagan administration was using the banner of Christianity to justify the capitalist system, interpret Christianity in terms compatible with it, cover up the persecution of Christians opposed to it, and identify religious opponents as subversives. Just as the religious right saw liberation theology as proof of communist subversion, it was easy for the left to interpret the religious right as an instrument of Washington.

Cuba and Grenada

To prove its views on liberation theology, the religious right pointed to Cuba and Grenada. Conservatives had long accused the Castro regime of persecuting Christians at home and infiltrating churches throughout the hemisphere. After U.S.-sponsored exiles unsuccessfully invaded Cuba in 1961, then continued to raid the island with CIA backing, the Cuban government arrested clergymen for preaching against the revolution, spying, and changing money on the black market. The government also adopted a Soviet-style policy of state atheism in which it tried to structure religion out of national life. Christmas was knocked off the vacation calendar; Holy Week was preempted by annual celebrations of the defeat of the U.S. invasion. Christians were barred from the Communist party, unbelief propagated in the schools, and evangelism forbidden outside church walls.[17] Scheduled services were allowed, but only seminary graduates could preach.

Ironically, Protestants had played a significant role in the 26th of July movement that brought Fidel Castro to power in 1959.[18] But evangelical support did not survive the revolution's transformation into a Marxist-Leninist one. The most popular response was to leave for Miami, a move undertaken by a large fraction of the faithful and at least half the clergy. Congregations dwindled, from perhaps two hundred thousand persons at the time of the revolution to some fifty thousand in the 1970s.[19] Evidently Cuban Protestants had identified strongly with the United States. Since the revolution occurred before many missions turned over control of their churches to Latin Americans, many property titles were still in the name of U.S. organizations; a number of churches were still part of U.S. ecclesiastical jurisdictions; and numerous North Americans were still pastoring congregations.[20]

Evangelicals who stayed in Cuba felt that their leaders had abandoned them. Exiles in the United States suspected those who remained behind of becoming collaborators.[21] At the evangelical seminary in Matanzas, a small group of pro-Castro Protestants tried to build a new kind of church. Despite all the hardship the revolution had brought, they asked, what if it was part of God's plan to build his kingdom?[22] In what must have been the most difficult circumstances, this group overidentified with the regime and ruined its credibility with brethren. After 1968, official pressure relented and more acceptable leaders emerged. Conservative enough to maintain a following, they were willing to cooperate with the government, with which churches started to come to terms.

Hanging back was a dissident sector, apparently in the majority, which continued to abstain from the revolution. Consisting of people too poor or tied down to leave the country, these Christians tended to be independent pentecostals, Assemblies of God, Jehovah's Witnesses, and Seventh Day Adventists. They considered themselves outcasts, as if they were exiles in their own country, and were treated accordingly, so that they settled into a circumscribed existence on the margin of Cuban society. According to Margaret Crahan, their congregations were "alternative communities for those who resist integration" into the dominant order. The fastest growing groups appeared to be the most disaffected, such as the Witnesses.[23]

No matter how much church-state relations improved in Cuba—and by the 1980s they had improved quite a bit—the grievances of dissidents enabled Cuba to be painted as a vast concentration camp. That made it a target for adventurers, prompting further official reactions. In May 1979, a small plane from Florida crash-landed on a Cuban highway after littering an international air corridor across the island with gospel tracts. To the Cuban authorities, the fact that the pilot had flown helicopters in Vietnam suggested that he was a CIA agent. The other miscreant, a product of the Gulf Coast Bible College, was acting in the belief that forty to fifty huge prisons housed 5 percent of the Cuban population. He hoped to sow the island with "spiritual bombs." The two were sentenced to twenty-four years, then released.[24]

The Cuban revolution's response to religious opponents had not been subtle. But when Fidel Castro held out the olive branch, as he did in the 1970s, then more frequently after the Sandinistas came to power in Nicaragua with church support, the religious right credited him with a diabolical new strategy to destroy Christianity. Wasn't his talk about a "strategic alliance" between Marxists and Christians proof that he was trying to manipulate the latter? If the best way to make a revolution was through the churches, wasn't the Cuban dictator simply replacing force with cooptation? There was no doubt about it, the religious right decided: Castro had masterminded liberation theology.

In Cuba, for what it is worth, pro-Castro Christians were very slow to accept the new theology. In their context, it seemed to imply challenging the existing revolutionary order, which they wished to justify rather than oppose. But for the religious right, the short-lived revolution on the island of Grenada confirmed that liberation theology was Fidel's latest trick. From the tons of files captured when the United States overthrew the revolutionary New Jewel Movement on Grenada, analysts produced several memoranda as evidence of a communist master plan against the island's churches.

Keeping in mind that the Central Intelligence Agency occasionally forges such mementos, one is signed by New Jewel security chief Major Keith Roberts. Dated three months before the October 1983 U.S. invasion, the memo calls the churches "the most dangerous sector for the development of internal counter revolution." As revolutionary regimes usually do, New Jewel had alarmed church leaders by drawing Sunday worshippers into voluntary work brigades and recruiting their children into its Young Pioneers youth organization. Fearing for religious freedom, the Catholic clergy mounted protests and Protestant groups stepped up evangelism. Although the memo describes the main threat as the Catholic Church, the largest on the island, its author is alarmed by the "flood of new-fangled religious sects" in recent decades and their "frenzied drive" to win new members. Church leaders are all hostile to the revolution to one or another degree, the memo's author states, then lists various steps to defend the revolution against them. The proposals include promoting contacts with sympathetic liberation theologians outside Grenada, tightening work permits for the evangelists flocking to the island, removing deeply religious head teachers from primary schools, cutting back religious broadcasting, and stepping up surveillance.[25]

Given the Reagan administration's preparations to occupy Grenada, it would have been hard to ignore church services like the one where, according to Open Doors News Service, a "member . . . stood up well before the invasion took place and said that without a shadow of a doubt the Lord had told her that the president of the United States would invade Grenada. He would set up his armies in the Caribbean Sea and he would invade Grenada."[26] "We considered Ronald Reagan's liberation of our island a true act of God," a like-minded Christian leader said. "Just days before it happened, we had a prophecy in our church that God was going to deliver us through Reagan. So when it happened, we were not surprised, but very grateful."[27] To the religious right, what had occurred in Cuba justified what the United States did in Grenada and what it was preparing to do in Nicaragua.

Marching as to War

The Reagan administration's invasion of Grenada and its contra war in Nicaragua did not arouse universal enthusiasm in the evangelical missions. There were moral reasons, but the main consideration was survival. With the American defeat in Vietnam, a wider spectrum of evangelicals had recognized the cost of riding Washington's coattails. The advantages of disassociating from U.S. policy were further underlined by the 1975 exposé of the CIA's use of missionaries.[28] When President Reagan loosened restrictions on the agency six years later, mission executives fretted about returning to the old days. The Southern Baptist mission board asked Congress to forbid the CIA from setting up missionary fronts.[29]

Following Vietnam, many evangelicals concluded that God was humbling the United States for its sins. For moderates, the repentant mood provided a chance to engage in gentle critiques. In step with the human rights campaign of President Jimmy Carter, they suggested that maybe God intended Christians to listen to victims of oppression even if they lived under pro-American governments. Maybe God did not intend Romans 13:1 ("Let every soul be subject unto the higher powers. For . . . the powers that be are ordained of God") to apply to any anticommunist regime that welcomed evangelists, no matter what it did to its people.[30]

Such critics continued to be theologically conservative—insisting, for example, that the only path to social improvement was faith in Jesus Christ. They also refused to support revolutionary violence, but they understood how it originated. "By not being violent," a couple with the Latin America Mission reported of their failure to prevent a large landowner from stealing the water rights of small farmers, "we acquiesced to the destruction of twenty families."[31] Like this couple, some missionaries tried to explain the social context of rebellion to their home supporters and spoke against heavy-handed U.S. policies.

The religious right drew different conclusions from the era of chastisement. If America did not restore its military might, preachers warned, communism would go on to conquer the world. It was therefore obvious who was to blame when Central America exploded at the end of the 1970s. The war was close enough to insist that the United States was in danger: if nothing was done, America's southern borders would be inundated by millions of refugees intermixed with terrorists. Even Christianity was at stake, the religious right believed, because Marxist revolutions inevitably turned against the churches as their final and greatest enemy. Along with the Middle East, some argued, Central America was one of two places in the world for which the Lord had special plans. Bornagain religion was Latin America's last line of defense.

Groups of the old religious right dating to the McCarthy era were one source of this kind of thinking. With little experience in Central America, they talked as if they were returning to the days of their youth to repulse the Red hordes in Korea. Unlike organizations that sounded an occasional anticommunist note but concentrated on the spiritual, these made occasional references to salvation and concentrated on fighting communism.

The most extreme, the Christian Crusade of Billy James Hargis, defended the death squads in El Salvador and detected Nazi conspiracies in the Kremlin.[32] Billy did not seem active on the ground, perhaps because he was still recovering from a scandal over his seduction of students of both sexes at his Bible college.[33] From Glendale, California, Dr. Steuart McBirnie of the "Voice of Americanism" radio broadcast asked for contributions to distribute millions of copies of Sergey Nechayev's *Revolutionary Catechism* in Central America. McBirnie felt that this work, an anarchist manual dating to 1869, would inoculate Central Americans against the blandishments of communism.[34] He was a member of the Coalition for World Freedom, an organization founded by General John Singlaub, one of the agents of the Reagan administration organizing mercenaries and men of God to support the Nicaraguan contras.[35]

The most active of the old religious right groups in Central America was the Christian Anti-Communism Crusade of Dr. Fred Schwarz. Salvadoran, Honduran, and Guatemalan officials welcomed the ideological support provided by the crusade's lecturers, whose literature the Costa Rican police as well as the Salvadoran and Guatemalan armies distributed to their ranks. The crusade held seminars for much of the evangelical pastorate in the three countries and reported warm receptions from the National Alliance of Evangelicals in El Salvador, the Ministerial Alliance of Costa Rica, and two officers from the Salvadoran Department of Psychological Warfare.[36]

Other stridently anticommunist groups interested in Latin America, especially Cuba and Nicaragua, were agencies specializing in persecuted churches. Known to the evangelical public as Bible smugglers, they found their calling when Eastern European borders closed during the Cold War. Their favorite symbol was the barbed wire atop the Berlin Wall. Because of the undercover nature of their work, they occupied a mysterious corner of the mission movement. To penetrate closed borders, some adopted outlandish tactics such as dumping tracts into ocean currents or sending them aloft in balloons. A recurring figure was the refugee pastor, a man said to have narrowly escaped death at the hands of his atheistic captors. Now that he had miraculously reached the West with his unbelievable testimony, he was using it to compete for funds against other refugee Christians with their own dramatic stories.*

In Latin America, the most active such organization was Open Doors with Brother Andrew, founded by the most appealing and

*The capital of this branch of Christian mission was Glendale, California, home of a group called Underground Evangelism (UE). UE's founder and president, L. Joe Bass, got his start in the early 1960s by having himself filmed addressing another man's revival meetings in Yugoslavia. Back home, he turned the footage into a story of religious persecution, then used it to raise money in churches. To keep the operation going, Bass signed up newly arrived refugees with promising testimonies. In 1973 one such Christian, a Soviet sailor who had jumped ship, accidentally killed himself while playing Russian roulette in bed with his pentecostal girlfriend.

Two other Bass fundraisers quit to start their own organizations, Richard Wurmbrand (of Jesus to the Communist World) and Haralan Popov (of Evangelism to Communist Lands). The disagreements between the Wurmbrand clan ($5.8 million in 1977) and Bass ($8.2 million that same year) culminated in reciprocal lawsuits after the former accused the latter of lying to donors, misusing contributions, and engaging in sex orgies. In 1985, Bass and another of his organizations, International Christian Aid, achieved notoriety once again, for siphoning off money raised for Ethiopian famine victims (*Christianity Today*, April 13, 1973, pp. 44–47; March 2, 1979, pp. 50–57; and March 1, 1985, pp. 36–39).

respectable of the Bible smugglers. A Dutchman operating under a pseudonym, Brother Andrew had learned his trade in the harsh eastern Europe of the 1950s. Not content to sneak printed matter over borders, in the 1970s he went on the offensive, by going to Asia, Africa, and Latin America to prepare the church for persecution wherever it might be threatened. The idea was to set up "delivery systems" for Christian literature before countries fell under communist domination and persecution began.[37] In a larger sense, the program seemed to entail organizing Christians to oppose every revolutionary movement in the Third World.

Before Brother Andrew found his calling, he became personally acquainted with the reality of defending Western interests. As a Dutch soldier fighting the independence movement in Indonesia, he participated in a massacre of civilians.[38] Yet despite this demoralizing experience, he continued to interpret social conflict everywhere in the world according to the same rigid East/West perspective. "God has his hand especially on the United States of America," he explained, "because in America there is all the potential for world evangelism, and world evangelism is God's primary purpose. God will protect any nation in which he sees the potential for world evangelism. I don't have to agree with its president or its way of capitalism, but I have to learn to look at that country the way God looks at it."[39] So concerned was Brother Andrew to look at the world the way God looks at it that, in 1978, his board of directors included a retired U.S. army general, Raymond O. Miller, and a former Navy secretary, J. William Middendorf, soon to become the Reagan administration's ambassador to the Organization of American States.[40]

The most visible transmitters of religious right ideology were pentecostal television evangelists. They were, by the nature of the enterprise, successful capitalists, generally from humble backgrounds, who by force of personality and business acumen had built up media empires. Presenting their success as a divine blessing, they promised viewers that they, too, could be blessed abundantly by the Lord. What often seemed overlooked in their messages was repentance and moral exertion. Beneath the talk of redemption and miracle, their Christianity was a harmonious mixture of North American patriotism, capitalism, and anticommunism, in a born-again version of the civil religion of the United States.

The television broadcasters did not, as we have seen, reign unchallenged in the evangelical world: many leaders with less spectacular callings distrusted them. Particularly resented were the hundreds of millions of dollars they drained from North American churchgoers to the greater glory of their ministries. Television evangelists justified their appetite for contributions by appealing to the need for evangelism. But judging from viewer surveys, their audience was mainly evangelical, suggesting that they did not win many converts. Casting about for an alternative function, they claimed to "reinforce" existing believers. But according to critics, what they reinforced was the dissatisfaction of viewers with their own congregations. Their example encouraged viewers to switch to pastors who, in worship style and doctrine, imitated television.[41]

In Latin America the impact of televangelists on church life was unclear. Much of the population lacked access to television, for one thing, leaving them to radio evangelists such as the relatively apolitical Paul Finkenbinder ("Hermano Pablo") operating out of Costa Mesa, California. But those people who did watch television had fewer channels from which to choose, so that they were more likely to tune in. Of the three television personalities who achieved substantial penetration, one was Pat Robertson, founder of the Christian Broadcasting Network and candidate for president of the United States. Another was the PTL Club's Jim Bakker, defrocked by the Assemblies of God in 1987 for sexual and financial abuses.

The third and most well-known television evangelist in Latin America by the late 1980s was Jimmy Swaggart, the Assemblies minister who publicized the charges against Bakker. Not given to modesty, Swaggart claimed to air his revivals on more than 3,000 stations, in more than 140 countries, and to staggering viewer totals—half a billion people including 70 percent of the population of El Salvador.[42] Jimmy Swaggart Ministries was an independent organization, headquartered in Baton Rouge, Louisiana, but it was also the single largest contributor to the Assemblies foreign missions—$7.9 million in 1984 and $12 million in 1986[43]—and claimed to support more than six hundred of its missionaries.

In Central America, Jimmy Swaggart Ministries was known for working so closely with the Assemblies of God that it could be hard to tell the difference between the two. The idea was to build up local Assemblies churches, already perhaps the largest denomination in the region. The partnership included constructing handsome new sanctuaries for central congregations. Compared to the modest dimensions of most evangelical meeting places, these structures could seem like cathedrals, and they were subsidized by Jimmy Swaggart. There were Bible institutes to train a new national church leadership, subsidized again by Jimmy Swaggart. And in poor urban neighborhoods there were Jimmy Swaggart schools, to provide children with hot meals, clothing, education, and spiritual growth.[44]

With the help of footage from an active schedule of crusades, Swaggart made himself a hero to constituencies in the United States and Latin America. Back home on North American television, he used the footage to bring in part of the $150 million a year on which he was operating by early 1988. Part of the money then went to Latin America, not just to organize new crusades and build up local Assemblies churches, but to buy time on television stations and put his ministry on further display.

It was quite an arrangement. Images of Jimmy Swaggart flashing a gospel sword in unsaved, war-ravaged countries were bringing in North American dollars for building up the Assemblies churches there. The Assemblies missions were benefiting not just from his contributions but from his powerful image. It was the most dynamic revival style in the business, what Swaggart regarded as his anointing in the Holy Spirit. The resulting chain of crusades and purchase of television exposure gave him the highest profile in the region. In a survey of Central American audiences, he had the highest name recognition, was the most tuned-in of four leading programs, and generated the highest confidence levels among the poorest sectors of the audience.[45]

Jimmy Swaggart's impact on popular consciousness was unclear. But he attacked the Catholic Church more openly than other major evangelists did, and his view of the politics of the region was a simple one, derived mainly from rhetoric about the evil empire. As a result, the religious right regarded Swaggart as its strongest bulwark against communism in Latin America. In 1987, he was received by President José Napoleon Duarte in El Salvador and General Augusto Pinochet in Chile.

"History is going to treat the measures which you took years ago to stop communism here in Chile as one of the great acts of this century," he told Pinochet, referring to the bloody coup that had brought the latter to power. "We will tell the world that Chile is a free country."[46] The following year, he was received by President Daniel Ortega in Managua, Nicaragua. Just as he had for Pinochet, Swaggart asked evangelicals to pray for their leader and called down God's blessing upon him.

Hanging Back from War

Outsiders could have a hard time telling the mission movement apart from the religious right. The two certainly overlapped: like any political tendency within North American evangelicalism, the religious right extended into the missions. Both movements spoke the language of evangelism and were prone to slip into military metaphors. They looked to a number of the same evangelical leaders, drew their support from some of the same North American churches, and shared some of the same fears about Latin America. When the religious right tried to recruit the missions into its political agenda, however, it was resisted by vested interests.

Established agencies were usually led by older men who had spent decades in Latin America. They claimed to be apolitical, avoided speaking out on controversial issues, and wished to concentrate on their religious message, usually rather unpolitical at least to appearances. Unlike religious right activists, who tended to be new to Latin America and looking for local churches to sponsor, these men already had constituencies to protect. They knew that U.S. military strikes could make it impossible for them to continue. After the Reagan administration bombed Libya in 1986, missionaries throughout North Africa and the Middle East were forced to rein in their already constricted activities, even leave. Mission leaders in Latin America did not want to suffer from more backlash than they already did. Their first reaction to a political issue was: let's stay out of it; they wanted to stay out of trouble.

The same attitude prevailed in the two principal mission associations. The Interdenominational Foreign Mission Association (IFMA) dated to 1917, a product of the fundamentalist split from the mainline denominations. It consisted solely of faith missions, that is, nondenominational bodies drawing recruits and funds from a variety of conservative churches. The Evangelical Foreign Missions Association (EFMA) included conservative denominations as well as faith missions: it was organized by the National Association of Evangelicals in the 1940s. Although the IFMA initially held back from working with the EFMA, by the 1960s the two cooperated in joint ventures, and together they formed the evangelical mission establishment.*

These were conservative bodies, wary of theological contamination even at Billy Graham-sponsored conferences and the mission think tanks of southern California. They both covered approximately the same fundamentalist-to-evangelical spectrum in terms of theology (although the IFMA did not include pentecostals and charismatics). But when it came to politics, conservatism meant caution. In the 1970s, for example, the EFMA turned down a membership application from Open Doors with Brother Andrew. EFMA members were not above smuggling Christian literature into closed countries when all else failed. But Brother Andrew's practice of publicizing his exploits to excite donors could lead to reprisals against their own efforts. The drift of opinion in the two associations was to accommodate hostile governments, not confront them.

Sharing the same caution was the World Evangelical Fellowship (WEF), another integrator of the mission movement and its Third World offspring. Originally based in Europe, WEF's headquarters moved to the United States after the Second World War, with assistance from the National Association of Evangelicals. One of its accomplishments was the idea of "evangelical alliances" or "councils," loose associations of independent evangelical bodies that emerged in most countries. WEF was slow to sign up affiliates in Latin America, however; evangelicals in Africa, India, and the Far East showed more enthusiasm, and in the 1980s its headquarters

*Among the IFMA's members were the Central American Mission (CAM International), Gospel Missionary Union, South American Mission, World Literature Crusade, and World Radio Missionary Fellowship. The EFMA included the Assemblies of God, Bible Literature International, Campus Crusade for Christ, Christian and Missionary Alliance, Church of God (Cleveland, Tennessee), Compassion International, Foursquare Missions International, Latin America Mission, Luis Palau Evangelistic Team, Nazarene Division of World Mission, OMS International, Overseas Crusades, World Concern, World Vision, and Youth for Christ International. Some groups, such as Mission Aviation Fellowship and Trans World Radio, belonged to both.

moved to Singapore.[47] But WEF's members and leaders ranged from Campus Crusade for Christ to theologians of the Latin American Theological Fraternity, a spectrum it was able to maintain in part by avoiding political stands.

Significantly, the EFMA, the IFMA, and WEF did not include some of the most politicized groups, the charismatic missions inspired by the latter rain and the restoration revival. These latest stirrings of the Holy Spirit also tended to administer their missionaries differently. Each congregation became a "sending church" by dispatching its own members to the field. A common result, in the view of more established agencies, were missionaries operating without proper guidance or support. Such missionaries were more likely to act out the fundamentalist imperatives of their home body and less likely to be influenced by missiology.

The most obvious test of whether a mission was part of the religious right was whether it identified evangelism with North American interests, harped on the Reagan administration's propaganda themes, and supported its war in Central America. One sign that missionaries did not identify with the religious right was worry over backlashes against their churches. Although such missionaries often feared communism as much as the religious right did, they were less likely to conceive of their government as the Seventh Cavalry riding to the rescue. Instead, many recognized that U.S. intervention was part of the problem.

These were significant differences. But it could be difficult to distinguish between missionaries caught up in the religious right and those who were not. Political differences cut across mission organizations and were the subject of internal debates, albeit poorly reported ones. Missions and their members also showed different faces in different situations and changed over time, so that they could not be frozen in one category. When a usually cautious agency found itself in a crisis, members could rise to the occasion with behavior they usually avoided. That was the case in Guatemala with the Wycliffe Bible Translators, several of whose members served informally in 1982–1983 as pacification advisers for the Guatemalan army.

With such caveats in mind, one way of visualizing religious right influence in the mission movement was in terms of a series of concentric circles. At the core were the groups promoting the Reagan administration's contra war in Nicaragua, including Pat Robertson of the Christian Broadcasting Network and small charismatic groups such as Maranatha Campus Ministries and Trans World Missions. In the second ring were agencies which refrained from explicit support for the contras but identified so closely with North American interests that they made evangelism sound like a geopolitical insurance policy for North American churchgoers; Open Doors with Brother Andrew was a prime example. In the third ring were agencies that, like the first two, had definite ties to the religious right and supported the Reagan administration's policies in Central America. But they were less likely to identify explicitly with the cause, laboring instead to maintain an apolitical front. Campus Crusade for Christ was one example, Youth With A Mission another, and also the Assemblies of God.

In the fourth ring were equally conservative organizations who, owing perhaps to their long experience in Latin America, were more likely to display discomfort with the religious right and the Reagan administration. The Southern Baptists belonged in this category, along with many older faith missions such as the Central American Mission and two of the most influential new groups, O.C. Ministries and the Luis Palau Evangelistic Team. The greater part of the mission establishment was to be found here. In the fifth ring were those groups most likely to show signs of opposing the religious right. They included two of the more established relief and development organizations, World Vision and World Relief; the Latin America Mission; and the various Mennonite missions.

Pressure from the Right

Missionaries who distrusted the religious right often said they were not aware of heavy pressure from that direction. Perhaps all they noticed were occasional challenges from home supporters, who wondered why their missionaries were not jumping on the Reagan bandwagon in Central America. But in various situations—El Salvador and Costa Rica, the Guatemala of General Ríos Montt, and the Sandinista-Contra war in Nicaragua—the curtains parted to reveal an interesting scene. In each case, the religious right was attempting to draw the evangelical missions into orbit around the Reagan administration's foreign policy.

The two succeeding chapters will suggest the degree to which the religious right succeeded in Guatemala and Nicaragua. For now, let us simply note some of the vulnerabilities of evangelical missions to pressure from the right. One was the ease of feeding them U.S. propaganda. Like conservative North Americans in general, evangelicals tended to distrust big government at home but be naively patriotic about it abroad. It was hard for them to conceive that a system showing a relatively high regard for human rights in the United States was so indifferent to them in Latin America. As a result, even cautious missionaries were inclined to give more credence to Washington's view than this deserved, dismissing contrary press and human rights reports. Reinforced by active distrust of left-wing movements, they tended to assume that whatever Washington wanted was the "lesser evil."

The ease with which evangelical opinion could be manipulated was illustrated by the case of Humberto Belli, a Nicaraguan exile accusing the Sandinista regime of religious persecution. Pushed by Open Doors News Service, Belli's views received wide currency in the evangelical press and filtered into mission publications, even of middle-of-the-road groups such as the U.S. Center for World Mission.[48] While scathing in his indictment of the Sandinistas and accurate in some respects, Belli downplayed that they were responding to attacks by the United States. He also ignored the human rights violations of their opponents, the Nicaraguan counterrevolutionaries. According to a former contra leader, one reason for such omissions was that, for his first book *Christians Under Fire,* Belli and his "Puebla Institute" were on the contra payroll with money from the Central Intelligence Agency.[49]

Generally speaking, evangelical missions were so accustomed to conforming to right-wing biases that they did not seem aware of them. This made it easier to engage in withering criticism of the left while remaining silent on the abuses of the right. When the Luis Palau Evangelistic Team mentioned human rights violations in its magazine for home supporters, it never assigned responsibility to governments. Governments, after all, would have to give permission for the next crusade. Instead, the Palau publication assigned responsibility to guerrillas or implied as much; to uninformed readers, it therefore looked as if revolutionaries were guilty of all the violations—a common misperception among North Americans.

Another vulnerability was financial in origin. Raising money for missionary work was not getting any easier. More and more groups were crowding television screens, mailboxes, and pulpits to vie for evangelical contributions. As old agencies struggled to dramatize activities which had become routine and unexciting, new ones elbowed in promising to evangelize every household in the world. With the television evangelists sensationalizing and debasing spiritual language, some agencies were turning to professional fundraisers and making more strident appeals. In the catalogue of possible pitches, red-baiting could be a profitable one, and Central America an opportunity to bring it back into fashion. It was a chance to recover from the L. Joe Bass/Richard Wurmbrand scandals of the 1970s, which seem to have undermined the income from hardcore anticommunist appeals. Open Doors, for example, seemed to be struggling to keep its head above water. Despite glossy presentations, it suffered a small decline in North American contributions in 1983–1984 and only managed to inch above its 1982 level three years later, to five million dollars.[50]

Another group that employed the color red in asking for money was Bible Literature International (BLI), a refugee from lost wars in the Far East. In Guatemala, this Columbus, Ohio–based group distributed quantities of New Testaments to government forces under the name of "Operation Whole Armor." According to fundraising appeals, Guatemalan soldiers needed to put on the "whole armor" of the Bible to protect themselves against guerrillas.[51]

"Do these Communist rulers *like* the Bible?" BLI headlined in one solicitation. In this case, ironically, it was defending its new alliance with the communist government of Poland. Together with Bible Pathway Ministries, a stalwart of the religious right in Murfreesboro, Tennessee, BLI had the approval of the Jaruzelski regime for mass distribution of a Bible study guide. Material from a like-minded agency, the southern California–based World Literature Crusade, was being printed on Polish government presses.[52]

"Ever since the days of Solidarity," a BLI fundraising letter sagely observed, "the Communist rulers have been seeking ways to undermine Catholic power. Is our invitation into Poland a result of this church-state struggle? Are Jaruzelski and his friends simply trying to hurt the Catholics by helping the Protestants? We may never know. But we do know that there's a marvelous opportunity before us."[53]

Missions fearful of reliving their experiences on the Asian mainland did not necessarily fall in with the religious right. One such agency was O. C. Ministries, which dated to 1950 when Madame Chiang Kai-shek asked a missionary named Dick Hillis, just expelled from China, to evangelize her demoralized soldiers on Taiwan. Supported by the Republic of China's president and first lady, who identified themselves as Christians, the group expanded to other countries along the U.S. perimeter in the Far East, and in the late 1950s to South America.[54] Owing to the bitter experience of its founder in China—one repeated by supporting the American intervention in Vietnam—Overseas Crusades conceived of itself as strengthening the church in prerevolutionary situations such as Allende's Chile.[55] Yet by the 1980s, like its most well-known product Luis Palau, it seemed to be keeping its distance from the religious right.

One figure who did lurch to the right was Alberto Mottesi, a rising mass evangelist and broadcaster. Like his fellow Argentine Luis Palau, Mottesi moved to the United States and started an evangelistic association there, preparatory to competing with Palau for the limelight. Emotional rallies in Central America raised his profile, and, in 1985, he organized the Hispanic Congress on Evangelization, a southern California extravaganza sponsored by Billy Graham, Campus Crusade, World Vision, and other pillars of the mission establishment.[56] Earlier in his career, Motessi is known to have sympathized with the Allende government in Chile. But a decade later, he was claiming to preach a pure gospel unsullied by politics while simultaneously blasting revolutionaries. Although claiming neutrality in Nicaragua, to avoid commenting on U.S.-sponsored violence there, on U.S.-controlled ground he identified leftist guerrillas as "revolutionaries for Satan" and presented his revivals as an alternative to revolution.[57] In his drive to be evangelist number one, Mottesi was exploiting the opportunities provided by the war in Central America.

One place to watch the contest between right-wing, centrist, and left-wing tendencies was the National Association of Evangelicals.

As we saw in a previous chapter, the NAE reached across much of the evangelical spectrum in the United States. Although the majority of its constituents were pro-Reagan, a vocal left wing agitated on peace and justice issues. To maintain a politically diverse membership, the NAE's leaders tried to keep to the middle of the road, disappointing activists at both ends of the spectrum. But given the predominance of conservatives, the NAE's course was determined more by pressure from the right than the left. When evangelicals opposed to U.S. military adventures became too vociferous, the NAE was interested mainly in disassociating from them.

In 1983, the NAE cosponsored an evangelical conference on nuclear arms. To its embarrassment, the event turned into a peace rally. Three-quarters of the two thousand participants seemed to be wearing nuclear freeze buttons. To the dismay of NAE officials, those few affiliates who did systematically address foreign policy tended to be Mennonites, Brethren, and other advocates of pacifism. At evangelical colleges, where children from conservative families came under the influence of academics, the disarmament lobby was putting in a strong showing. Two anti-interventionist voices, the *Sojourners* monthly and Evangelicals for Social Action, seemed to be gaining influence.

For NAE officials, these developments suggested vulnerability to political pressure and disproportionate criticism of the Reagan administration. After several years of right-wing ascendancy in the federal government, we may infer, the countervailing efforts of the evangelical left were threatening to tarnish the NAE's reputation among conservatives. This was the origin of Peace, Freedom, and Security Studies, an attempt to work out a balanced approach to Washington's latest weapon systems and wars.[58] The human rights issues that moderates harped on would, for example, be weighed against the security issues preoccupying conservatives. But in working out its balance, the new NAE program drew heavily on the thought of the neoconservatives. Also known as Cold War liberals for their emphasis on fighting communism, the "neocons" boasted the most impressive intellectual credentials in the Reagan administration. Conceiving of themselves as fighters for democracy, they did much to make the Nicaraguan contras respectable.[59] It was therefore easy to interpret Peace, Freedom, and Security Studies as an attempt to hold the line against the NAE's left wing.

Meanwhile, the association was under more pressure from the other direction. On Central America, the religious right was disappointed by the NAE's failure to join wholeheartedly in the campaign against the Sandinistas. When the NAE cosponsored a conference on religious freedom with the State Department, it was not pleased that President Reagan used the occasion to lobby for the contras.[60] The new foreign policy guidelines would show, an NAE staffer explained, "why our members can be on both sides of some questions like contra aid."[61]

Campus Crusade for Christ

Evangelical ties to the religious right in the United States made it hard for Latin Americans to accept claims to be above politics. One flagrant and frequently attacked example was Campus Crusade for Christ. Funding the group's campaign to complete the Great Commission were what it called "history's handful," predominantly Texan millionaires who, by 1981, had pledged nearly $220 million. The drive's chairman was Nelson Bunker Hunt, the Dallas oilman who had tried to corner the world silver market and set off a 1980 crash requiring a federal bailout. Besides giving Campus Crusade $6 million for its globally screened epic film *Jesus*, Hunt also backed the Nicaraguan contras and the World Anti-Communist League.[62]

Whether this kind of man was investing in Campus Crusade to save souls or stabilize the business climate, what most disturbed the group's critics, including many evangelicals, was its founder Bill Bright's use of evangelism to further the political objectives of his backers. During the campus protests of the 1960s, Bright had proclaimed "spiritual revolution" as the only solution to the world's problems and led his organization against student radicals. In 1974 he fell in with an Arizona congressman, John Conlan, for a trial run of the techniques that, a few years later, created the religious right.

In a secretive manner, Conlan used Campus Crusade's network to turn Bible studies and Sunday schools into organizing sessions for political candidates. Moderate evangelicals were offended to learn that the only "real Christians," according to Conlan, were right-wing ideologues like himself. Meanwhile, Bright was opening a Christian Embassy on Capitol Hill, to evangelize the elite of

Washington, D.C. When the Christian journal *Sojourners* blew the whistle in 1976, Bright took refuge in what sounded like plausible denials. Campus Crusade was never politically motivated, he insisted.[63] Like other prominent mission leaders, including Jimmy Swaggart of the Assemblies of God and Youth With A Mission's Loren Cunningham, by the 1980s he was on the board of various religious right coalitions.[64]

Despite Bright's claims to be above politics, he was obviously engaged in what could be called "pre-politics," that is, the use of religion to lay the groundwork for mobilization. His widely distributed pamphlet on the duties of Christian citizens advertised the services of Christian Voice, a descendant of the Conlan scheme, which targeted liberal congressional representatives for smear campaigns.[65] According to Christian Voice's scorecards for rating representatives on their votes, godly positions included supporting the predictable range of weapons systems, dictatorships, and CIA-sponsored guerrilla movements.[66] In practicing "pre-politics," of course, Campus Crusade was like a socially conscious priest who, on the basis of the Bible, urges parishioners to join a peasant league. The difference was that Campus Crusade steered Christians toward supporting U.S. foreign policy and the status quo, instead of questioning it.

Campus Crusade was just one of a number of North American missions with a special interest in Latin American students. Conservative evangelicals envied and feared the influence of Marxist academics on this part of the population. Judging from what some agencies told their U.S. donors, one of the main reasons for ministering to students was to prevent them from turning into communists.* In Latin America, however, student evangelists tended to deny any such ambition, least of all to confront radicals. Even if they wanted to, they were usually too few and too weak to stage anything but their own downfall. Under the Pinochet regime in Chile, an Open Doors student group calling itself the "Jesus Christ

---

*Not all student ministries hankered to start a counter-revolution. The International Federation of Evangelical Students was affiliated with the World Evangelical Fellowship. It was not, one of its officials informed me, a "reaction" or "fighting organization" against left or right. In May 1983, the Salvadoran government arrested the group's Central American director on charges of subversion, apparently due to his work with refugees and visits to Nicaraguan chapters (*Missionary News Service*, June 15, 1983).

Revolution" tried to hold a march in the capital on the theme of "no to atheistic Marxism!" Hecklers infiltrated the march and provoked security forces into tear-gassing the evangelicals. The "Revolution's" leaders were hauled off to jail.[67]

Given Campus Crusade's well-known history, it is important to stress that usually it was not overtly political in its ministry. Compared to the religious right, in fact, it often appeared to be moderate. "There is no politicization in Campus Crusade for Christ," Latin America director Sergio García Romo assured me. "We're not trying to rescue the youth of Latin America from revolution. That would be ahistorical. Social revolution here is inevitable, and it would be naive to think that it is not. One can be a Christian under any political system." Of five hundred full-time staff in Latin America, García said, maybe five were North Americans, and 50 to 100 percent of the group's financing in Latin America was national, depending on the country. "How can you prove that we push political slogans?" he challenged. Leftists accused Campus Crusade of "depoliticizing" students just because it did not share their version of Christianity, Garciá complained.[68]

One reason for inaccurate allegations against Campus Crusade was confusion over what it was. Contributing to the uncertainty was its use of dissembling tactics to approach Catholics, by operating under the name of, not just the Professional and Student Crusade for Christ, but the Alpha and Omega Movement. In 1978 in Colombia, a Catholic cardinal accused Alpha and Omega of using Bible studies and charismaticism to wean Catholics away from their church.[69] Campus Crusade denied encouraging charismatic practices,[70] to avoid alienating anticharismatic backers in the United States. But the group's impressive *Jesus* movie, dubbed into more than one hundred languages by 1985, was credited with setting off many a miracle.[71] In practice, Campus Crusade apparently used charismaticism as a way to reach Catholics and funnel them into the pentecostal churches with which it often worked.[72]

In a further complication, around 1980 a Colombian leader carried off a large faction which, under the Alpha and Omega name, spread into neighboring countries. Upset by its poaching in their flocks, the Catholic hierarchy of Panama consigned Alpha and Omega to the same "non-Christian sect" category as the Moonies and the Children of God.[73] In southwest Colombia, a related

"Agape" organization—functioning like an evangelical Peace Corps and apparently belonging to the splinter—won the backing of area politicians and used its aid program against the local civil rights organization, the Regional Indian Council of the Cauca.[74]

As for the main Campus Crusade, its literature was bland and apolitical in the extreme. When Sandinista security agents arrested Campus Crusade's director in Nicaragua for possessing counter-revolutionary literature, they were reduced to identifying the incriminating material as Bill Bright's "Four Spiritual Laws."[75] This is a pamphlet distributed around the world: if it makes any reference to politics, I was unable to find it.

Campus Crusaders were supposed to absorb themselves in the group's time-consuming program of spiritual discipleship, not become political activists. They did explain that, if enough people accepted Christ, there would be no need to join radical political movements. "The student conglomerate is one of the most powerful forces in society," a staffer in Ecuador told me. "If we can save the students, society can be saved. Change the individual first, that will change the structure." The idea of transforming society through a spiritual movement was opposed to another concept, the staffer added, of transformation through violence.[76]

Some Campus Crusade leaders were explicit about defeating communism and liberation theology.[77] In El Salvador, the group's executives told the *New York Times* that their purpose was ideological as well as religious. "Our main objective is to influence the university," Manuel Martínez explained. "All mass movements and revolutions begin there. The conflict we have in El Salvador today began in the universities."

"The Marxists infiltrate the universities," added national director Adonai Leiva. "So do we. Marxism is the first thing humanities students hear. It's planned that way. Therefore we try and get to them first. So we start work in high schools and prep schools. . . . In our methods and strategy we emphasize the personal contact. We usually follow a person through visits and contacts for three months, like a soccer player follows the ball. Then, if the person still resists, we incorporate him into a cell, a small group that often meets for prayer and discussion. Of course, not everyone lets you go all the way."[78]

However well Campus Crusade might be doing in El Salvador,

generally its results in a hundred and fifty universities across Latin America were not impressive. While taking up the rhetoric of changing society, in practice it channeled recruits into further evangelism. In Bible studies and leadership training seminars, it stressed the cultivation of personal virtue and how to function smoothly as part of an organization. The underlying message, to play according to the rules, did not seem very appealing to young Latin Americans who were familiar with how the system worked and knew that it offered them little.

"It's more or less true that we're not harvesting multitudes," regional director Sergio García conceded. Of another organization's goal, Open Door's talk about evangelizing ten million Latin American youth in 1985, García regarded it as a fundraising gimmick. "It doesn't appear to be a serious program" was his assessment, one shared by other evangelicals. "They speak glibly of reaching millions. How can they do in months what it's taken us years to do?"[79] Student ministries were supposed to reach out to Catholics, but often they seemed more like holding actions against the defection of youth from evangelical backgrounds.

The Campaign to Save El Salvador

Amidst a counterinsurgency war, the religious right's identification with Washington could appear to pay handsome dividends. Between 1977 and 1981, government forces in a country named after the Savior murdered four Catholic sisters from the United States, eleven Catholic priests, and an archbishop. Not without coincidence, evangelicals in the, to appearances, devoutly Catholic El Salvador were growing at one of the fastest rates in the world. The Central American Mission reported that, among its churches there, one hundred members had been killed in four years of fighting between government and revolutionary forces. Approximately one-fourth of the membership—two to three thousand mainly middle-class people—had left the country. But the mission hoped to recoup this figure in a single year of evangelism.[80] For as violence spread throughout the country, growth shot upward. From a 4 percent rise in 1979, the Central American Mission's churches grew 30 percent the following year.[81] From 1976 to 1985, the Assemblies of God registered an increase from 63,000 to 200,000 members.[82] By

1986, evangelicals claimed to have tripled, even quadrupled, and represent up to one-fifth the population.[83]

One reason evangelical churches were growing so quickly was that they served as a haven from government violence. According to an evangelical leader, soldiers dragged him, his wife, and four children out of their car, put them up against a wall, and were about to shoot them as a Marxist cell group when he persuaded them to look at the religious literature in the vehicle; it saved their lives.[84] Gospel tracts could serve as a safe-conduct pass because, despite occasional professions of neutrality, the majority of evangelical leaders supported the U.S.-backed regime. Their habit of denouncing revolutionaries as servants of Satan made it easy to identify evangelicals as a progovernment bloc.

When Salvadoran dictator Carlos Humberto Romero is said to have given his heart to Christ shortly before being overthrown in 1979, it was part of an attempt for a "national dialogue" in which most Catholic clergy refused to participate. He was not the last beleaguered head of state to attract evangelists. During the subsequent civilian-military junta, hopeful ambassadors for Christ claimed to have elicited professions of faith from President Duarte and Colonel Jaime Gutiérrez.[85] Although these decisions seem to have been fleeting at best, the middle and upper classes were indeed asking Jesus into their hearts in unusually large numbers, with special interest reported among military families. In effect, they were turning to a new source of spiritual solace, one that did not criticize the social structure from which they benefited but that did absolve them of responsibility for it. Yet as the story of the pastor up against the wall suggests, the motives of converts could be mixed. Another group said to be particularly touched by the Holy Spirit was university students. In a country where the military automatically suspected students of subversion and killed thousands of prisoners without trial, the ability to witness to one's faith provided a sense of security in more ways than one.

Appearances to the contrary, the evangelical community was divided, between social activists on the one hand and those who wished to play safe on the other, between those reacting to killings by the government and those reacting to killings by the guerrillas. Official repression in the late 1970s and early 1980s radicalized numerous evangelicals, especially among the Baptists, Lutherans, and Episcopalians. They felt a call to help the refugees from the government's bombing campaigns and counterinsurgency sweeps. Because the refugees tended to support the guerrillas, the government suspected religious workers of serving as a communication channel between the two.

Something like that suspicion is apparently why, in 1984, soldiers murdered a Lutheran pastor named David Fernández.[86] The incident was one of a number of government reactions against evangelicals helping refugees, including the torture of a Lutheran bishop and the 1985 arrest of a U.S.-born Assemblies of God pastor.[87] Even CESAD, the conservative evangelical relief and development committee, was red-baited for helping peasants in guerrilla areas.[88] Judging from conservative observers such as the Southern Baptists and the Central American Mission, rural evangelicals suffered approximately as much from the government as from the guerrillas. Such sources depicted guerrillas pressuring believers into joining them, assassinating suspected informers, and shooting other persons by mistake, but they also referred to government massacres and the destruction of churches in aerial bombardments.[89]

Encouraging the dominant progovernment mood were North American missionaries. For the Salvadoran army and the U.S. embassy, groups such as World Relief and Paralife Ministries were a welcome alternative to agencies that refused to participate in government resettlement programs.[90] Inside the Salvadoran military, Youth With A Mission was setting up a chaplaincy training program under a U.S. colonel.[91] When new charismatic groups arrived in search of worthy Christians to sponsor, men who had started store-front churches lined up with their hands out. Meanwhile, para-church agencies organized Salvadorans for door-to-door proselytizing. Campus Crusade for Christ was especially active in this kind of "saturation" evangelism, backed up by films, rallies, and street-corner preachers. Operating in conjunction with local churches, Campus Crusade's first campaign in 1978–1980 claimed 64,000 decisions for Christ.[92]

By 1986, Campus Crusade's director in El Salvador, Adonai Leiva, was working with one of the tract societies involved in Poland, the World Literature Crusade (WLC). With two thousand volunteers from three hundred local churches, the organizers planned to reach one-quarter of the country's population in two days. Lest rebel-held areas be missed, a Salvadoran denomination throughout the mountainous and devastated north, called the Church of the Apostles and Prophets, would take the campaign there as well. "We want to give every person in the region an opportunity to look past the false hopes of Communism and find true salvation in Jesus Christ," the WLC explained.[93] This was the start of its campaign to visit every home in what it called the "strategic triangle"—Central America, Mexico, and the Caribbean. As a region of strategic importance to the United States, the WLC argued, it needed to become a top priority for every Christian.

The strategic triangle was an idea advanced by evangelical anthropologist Dale Kietzman, a former official of the Wycliffe Bible Translators, who had previously helped Open Doors organize a similar campaign: "Project Crossfire."[94] Crossfire and the like might be appropriate fundraising motifs in the United States, where so many Christians talked like frustrated Pentagon strategists. But they did not sound very Christian in countries that suffered from the kind of violence North Americans fantasized so glibly.

The idea, in any case, was to use Latin American evangelicals to fight revolutionary ideologies. "Christ has entered my heart and has led me to see and think differently than before," Open Doors quoted a former guerrilla. "Today I realize that the cause that I had been working toward was completely utopian and useless."[95] Now the same young legions enlisted by Project Crossfire were to go to work for the World Literature Crusade, spreading out and enveloping the strategic triangle, in Kietzman's words, "with the fire of Spirit-directed evangelism."[96]*

---

*As this book was going to press, I received the following comment from an evangelical living in El Salvador: "It is true that leaders are likely to have that underlying conservative political agenda. This is certainly true of U.S. organizations such as Campus Crusade for Christ, Salvadoran affiliates of such organizations, rich Salvadoran evangelicals, and Salvadoran evangelical leaders from whatever class. However, most Salvadoran evangelicals are poor campesinos and city dwellers, and most of them would probably describe themselves as apolitical. In guerrilla-controlled zones you would find evangelicals from a number of churches sympathetic to the guerrillas. [But elsewhere] 'I'm not political' or 'I don't get involved in politics' are refrains one often hears. The main political reason that the poor turn to evangelicalism is not anticommunism but safety. . . . [Besides], evangelical doctrine gives a reason—not a solution—for the suffering faced by the poor. Many poor have given up on solutions. I don't know how many times I've

The Witch Hunt in Costa Rica

Conservatives in Latin America were especially worried about their seminaries. Populated by youth, taught by theologians, and open to new ideas, they were a chink in fundamentalist armor against social criticism. Among conservatives, the favorite horror story was the Latin America Biblical Seminary in San José, Costa Rica. Started by the renowned Latin America Mission (LAM), the seminary exported Evangelism in Depth in the 1960s. By the late 1970s and early 1980s, there were students who smoked cigarettes, a president who said he couldn't tell his pupils what to believe, chain resignations from the faculty, and alleged replacement of God by the Revolution. According to opponents, the seminary had become a hotbed of liberation theology. Although it turned back attempted purges, the Costa Rican Evangelical Alliance disfellowshipped it, the Latin America Mission withdrew endorsement, and it lost much of its church constituency.[97]

Unable to recapture the seminary, Costa Rica's evangelical leaders rid themselves of what they considered fellow travelers, that is, brethren with political opinions significantly to the left of their own. There were more than a few within reach because Costa Rica had become a regional headquarters for evangelical agencies, home to at least twenty Bible institutes and the like.[98] Despite its relative stability, the country was full of apprehension: U.S.-supported rebels were using Costa Rican territory to attack the Sandinista government in Nicaragua, prompting Sandinista reactions which the U.S. embassy was using to drum up fear of a red invasion. Among those who suffered were twenty-five pastors and leaders of the LAM-descended Association of Costa Rican Bible Churches (AIBC). For connections with the proscribed seminary or sympathy for the Sandinistas, they were forced out of the denomination and took seven of its hundred churches with them.[99]

Now that the post-Vietnam mood of contrition had drawn left-of-center evangelicals out of the closet, they were under attack from the right. According to an evangelical journalist in Costa Rica, any-

---

heard people say: 'This war is never going to end.' They settle for an explanation to make sense of their chaotic world. The one most often given is that the war is a biblical sign of the end of this world and the coming of Christ."

one who talked about social responsibility or opposed the U.S. war in Nicaragua could be accused of liberation theology. Among the suspects were the largest North American evangelical relief agency, World Vision, and an arm of the National Association of Evangelicals, World Relief. The Latin America Mission found itself divided. One member supported the expulsion of two others from an AIBC church. Others were brought before mission headquarters for an internal "heresy trial" in which they were, however, found innocent.

Because evangelicals accused of supporting liberation theology usually denied it, acknowledging only that they learned certain lessons from it or wished to remain in "dialogue" with Christians of that tendency, how could you tell who was guilty? "As the saying goes," LAM missionary Jonas González answered, "if you swim like a duck, and if you walk like a duck, then you are a duck. Liberation theology is done by the people who are the best off [economically]. They produce beautiful manuscripts but don't do anything. They're more interested in communist than evangelical allies, because they fit into the scheme better. Evangelicals dabbling in liberation theology are marginal. The evangelical position is well defined: we don't want anything to do with people who talk about structural change. It's just verbiage. What's needed is practice; people who talk about practice don't do anything. What's needed is more dedication, love and denunciation of sin—including injustice and dirty politics. We have to give help to those in need. That is a very direct social responsibility."[100]

Among those accused of walking and talking like a duck, but vigorously denying it, was LAM theologian John Stam. It took inquisitors two attempts to strip him of his credentials as an AIBC pastor: the first was in reaction to his support for the Sandinistas; the second was for criticizing Ronald Reagan in a letter to a newspaper. When I caught up with him in Guatemala City, he proved to be a man of about sixty with a cheerful air, not the sort to be oppressed by his surroundings. He happened to be leading a Bible study at the Central Presbyterian Church, located behind the presidential palace and boxed in by annexes where, according to Amnesty International, the Guatemalan army coordinated its death squads.[101] He described himself as a typical Republican missionary, in the mold of his alma maters Wheaton College and Fuller Seminary, until he met refugees who had fled the Somoza dictatorship in Nicaragua. That encounter, in the early 1970s, began his transformation into a Sandinista supporter. It was not hard to see why he was in trouble with conservatives.

"Thirty years of foreign missionary service," Stam wrote about the time that he was forced out of the AIBC, "have . . . convinced me that my almost instinctive identification of the gospel with capitalism and Western-style democracy was anything but evangelical. In the Third World I have found this view . . . highly detrimental to Christian witness. . . .

"The gospel, if freed from cultural baggage, is explosive with radical significance for the people of Central America today. To discover the meaning of evangelical obedience in this revolutionary context, evangelicals are not called upon to become less evangelical or less biblical in order to become supposedly more revolutionary. They must learn to be immensely *more* biblical and *more* evangelical than ever. . . .

"Evangelicals in Central America have every reason to be thankful to God for the great tradition of which they are heirs, but little reason to feel triumphalistic. . . . [They] have been repeating all the 'saved-by-faith' formulas, but in general have tended to fall into unevangelical legalisms . . . [reflecting] all too faithfully the individualistic, competitive, success-oriented elements of their society. . . .

"Trying to understand the gospel in the midst of revolution, one can observe that precisely where traditional 'evangelicalism' has distorted the gospel into this crass blend of legalism and cheap grace seems to be the very point where [it] has been all too successfully adapted to the individualistic, success-oriented culture from which it was brought to Central America by the missionaries. What is extra-biblical and less than evangelical in this religious ethos proves to be a transplant. It reflects an imported ideology, which must not be identified with the gospel itself. . . . We must never tire of exposing our ideas to the searchlight of the scriptures."[102]

"Numerically Central America is a triumph," Stam exclaimed, waving his arm toward the street. "Walk around the market and everyone seems to be reading the Bible. But look at how they're reading it, without any sense of the essentials of the evangelical tradition. The growth is fantastic, the numbers are great, but churches are arrogantly calling themselves biblical and Christian, with no idea of what these words mean."

Contextualization

For John Stam it was important that he had lost his pastor's credentials for his politics, not his Reformed theology. Yet it is the fate of evangelicals for their arguments to end up as arguments over how to interpret the Bible. Fundamentalists accused evangelicals such as Stam of turning into liberals. Stam denied that his interpretation was somehow more liberal or relativistic than that of his adversaries. "They're the relativists, not me!" he exclaimed. "The president of the AIBC refused to engage in a biblical discussion with me because, he explained, 'there's no end to that, people can make the Bible say anything they want.' They're afraid of biblical discussion because they know they don't master it. I want reasons, they say their opinion has the right to be tolerated even if it's narrow-minded. Unconsciously, they're camouflaging their right-wing politics as theology—which they really don't have."[103]

As mentioned in the preceding chapter, evangelical innovators like Stam were practicing "contextualization." That is, they were trying to break through the literalism imported by North American fundamentalists, to interpret scripture in the Latin American context. "The North American tends to see the scriptures through the lens of a middle-class, free-enterprise, prosperous perspective, and there is nothing wrong in that, per se," a member of the Central American Mission explained to home supporters. "But godly Christians of Africa, Asia, and Latin America will see other truths within the Word. . . . They will be more oriented to a community spirit. They will see in bold relief the Bible's teaching on wealth and poverty."[104]

"Contextualization is the new buzzword in evangelical theology," another member of the Central American Mission told me. "It comes via Africa and Latin America to the United States, where you're out of it if you're not into contextualization. Even conservatives say they're doing it. But what's the context? The crunch comes when you move from the biblical context to the present one. In the current context, there's an enormous conflict between Romans 13:1

[which instructs Christians to obey the government] and the wish
to denounce abuses and change the system."[105]

As far as Latin American fundamentalists were concerned, there
was no need to explain further. Interpreting the Bible in "the Latin
American context" implied more than one interpretation; and to
have more than one interpretation contradicted the biblical foundation of the church as these men understood it. Among those
wanting nothing to do with contextualization was the Reverend
Marcelino Ortiz, an associate of Luis Palau and also president of the
Latin American Evangelical Confederation (CONELA). "Contextualization really isn't necessary," he told me. "The message of the
gospel is the same for any epoch, for every man."

But hadn't CONELA subscribed to the Lausanne Covenant,
which talked about contextualization and social responsibility, too?
The only reason CONELA pledged itself to Lausanne, Ortiz explained, was to avoid spending weeks haggling over its own statement of doctrine. As for social commitment, he thought that it
should be confined to the task of reforming individual lives. "Conservative Christians really do more in social responsibility," he told
me. "It's not just pie in the sky. A Mexican is transformed! Money
spent on alcohol turns into bread, shoes, shelter, education. Children get educated. The next generation is stronger and more prepared. Christian social work is lifting up men. Giving them a new
heart, not a new suit. Now many Nicaraguans believe that, when
they tried to change the structure, the cure was worse than the
disease. So the real solution is changing the heart of man. But social
responsibility is not our emphasis, we admit it. It is very difficult to
know when the time arrives to denounce abuses. It is not our task
to denounce."[106]

CONELA had been organized, Ortiz explained, because "at international meetings we were being represented by people who
were not really representative, [that is,] conservative, evangelical,
and biblical." He was referring to various leaders of the Latin American Theological Fraternity. As we have seen previously, the FTL
hoped to give the churches a sense of social responsibility without
losing sight of evangelism. For the most radical Protestants, the
fraternity's rejection of liberation theology made it merely the left
wing of the fundamentalist movement.[107] But it was questioning the
reproduction of authoritarian, politically conservative churches

preoccupied with numerical growth. That made CONELA organizers suspect that some of the FTL's most prominent members were playing both sides of the fence. For discussing the issues posed by liberation theology, acknowledging the validity of some of its positions, questioning the Pax Americana and evangelical support for right-wing dictatorships, men like René and Washington Padilla, Orlando Costas, Samuel Escobar, and Plutarco Bonilla were suspected of being liberation theologians themselves.

The reason CONELA was waging a "silent war" against such theologians, Samuel Escobar argued, was that its leaders were tied to North American organizations and felt threatened by the FTL's theological and financial independence, its refusal to repeat formulas learned from North Americans. "When we insist on taking our own road," Escobar wrote, "then come the accusations of heresy and the institutional struggles. There is disrespect for a national effort to think for ourselves, there is a lack of understanding what is Latin American. Unfortunately, there are Latin leaders who lend themselves to this fundamentalist maneuver, because they often thrive within the paternalist scheme and benefit from it. If servile translation and repetition provides benefits and advantages, why bother to work for indigeneity?"[108]

Reformation in the Reformation

The conservative leaders whom Stam and Escobar criticized were, for the most part, products of closely supervised missionary training, of the Bible institute variety. Their feelings about theologians were reciprocal. Seminary professors did not produce new believers, they grumbled, just speeches and complicated intellectual formulations. When the Latin American Theological Fraternity held its CLADE II conference in 1979, conservatives complained, it was more interested in theological foundations and social responsibility than in the latest evangelistic techniques.[109] For most dispensationalists and pentecostals, Bible training was supposed to consist of indoctrination in the truth, not hermeneutics or those other big words being thrown around. In the view of fundamentalists, theology was getting in the way of simple faith in God's Word.

This kind of tension between theologians and conservative church leaders was a sign that, socially, the evangelical movement was moving beyond the stage of a simple agglomeration of sects. Once upon a time, Latin American evangelicals had little to do with fellow Protestants outside their own small denominations. Each confession was walled up in its own sectarian world, but now that was changing. Encouraged by North American agencies such as the Latin America Mission and O. C. Ministries, pandenominational campaigns and organizations were bringing churches into sustained contact with each other. Out of these interchanges was emerging a less sectarian evangelical Protestantism. It identified itself as a bloc; aspired to take consistent positions toward the great issues of the day; and was developing its own parachurch sector, of Bible schools, radio stations, and the like, subsidized by North American agencies and staffed by middle-class professionals.

Along with these new possibilities for reflection and debate were growing class differences within evangelicalism. In the early years, pastors were unlikely to live and eat much better than their flocks. But now huge churches had emerged, run by prosperous men of God who collected tithes from thousands of followers. Other evangelical leaders raised money for their projects in the United States or took well-remunerated employment with North American ministries, opening up wide income differences with pastors who did not enjoy such good fortune. As pastors turned into professionals and bureaucrats, upward mobility worked against progressive evangelicals as well as conservatives. Calls for radical change lost credibility when the prophet lived so much better than his brethren.

Yet conservatives were reacting to theological innovation as if it seriously threatened their position. The challenge came in forms that were easy for outsiders to overlook, such as the pastoral training movement known as Theological Education by Extension. As mentioned in the preceding chapter, TEE originated as an attempt to keep up with the rising demand for trained ministers, by turning them out in quantity. It was also intended to prevent seminary training in cities from maladapting pastors to the needs of poor, rural congregations. The idea was to deprofessionalize theological education. Yet for established leaders, TEE could have disturbing consequences. It could popularize theology, by moving away from some of the conceptions imported by North American missionaries, and alter the power balance in denominations, by producing so many new "cornpatch" pastors that they outvoted the established leadership.[110]

Even though evangelical Protestantism represented "religious free enterprise" in societies dominated by a state religion, it too had developed authoritarian tendencies, in imitation of figures such as the foreign missionary, Catholic priest, plantation owner, and political boss. National leaders could be more domineering than the missionaries they replaced. "The churches in Latin America . . . are dominated by the clergy, by ecclesiastical structures that place power and privilege and initiative in the hands of a few, and by . . . imported patterns of . . . ministry that stifle indigenous, popular leadership," TEE founder F. Ross Kinsler wrote. Instead of serving vested ecclesiastical interests, Kinsler suggested, TEE should subvert those interests. He hoped that it would "help the churches to throw off the bondage of a professional clergy, the ideology of the middle classes, the legalisms of the past and the cultural forms of a foreign church and an alienated society."[111]

In the 1970s, this kind of thinking came together with the effort to go beyond Evangelism in Depth. As Orlando Costas of the Latin America Mission pointed out, in-depth evangelism had implied breaking with the usual pastor-follower relationship, by training members of congregations to become activists who would each carry on evangelism. No longer would all initiative rest on a lone pastor. But such changes were hard to make: after the campaign was over, pastors and followers usually returned to their old active/passive relationship.

Some organizers concluded that "total mobilization" of the Christian community for "total evangelization" would not occur without a permanent transformation of pastoral structures. The prayer cells into which Evangelism in Depth organized church members began to take on some of the attributes of the base communities in liberation theology. Out of the study of the Bible, a reformation was to well up and democratize the church.[112]

In Costa Rica, Orlando Costas and John Stam were part of a LAM offshoot called the Latin American Center for Pastoral Studies (CELEP) pursuing this line of thinking. Like their colleague Plutarco Bonilla, both resigned from the Latin American Biblical Seminary in protest against some of the changes taking place there.[113] If seminarians who smoked cigarettes had no chance of being accepted by evangelicals, what was the point of training them?[114] In the hope of not being associated with such behavior, CELEP tried to concentrate on grass-roots work with churches. But it was still located next to the seminary, a constant reminder of the danger of burning bridges to conservatives. Upstairs was the local branch of Pat Robertson's Christian Broadcasting Network.

TEE did not always have a democratizing impact: a pastor with a sixth-grade education could be just as distant from his people as a seminary graduate, and just as oppressive. TEE could also be used to extend the reach of conventional hierarchies. But when combined with efforts to change pastoral relationships, it challenged the way older pastors had been trained to run their churches and generated stiff opposition.* In a movement preoccupied with spreading its message and setting up new forms of spiritual authority, the study of how to market the gospel more effectively had led to the scrutiny of pastoral relationships. The attempt to reform these relationships was serving as an evangelical parallel to liberation theology.

Evangelicals engaged in such critiques were a definite minority. Congregating in seminaries and other small religious bureaucracies, they usually seemed under siege from conservatives. But the dissenters believed that their day would come, and conservatives had reason to fear them. Defining the gospel in terms of social justice as well as personal salvation had the potential to appeal to the millions of evangelicals whose economic position was deteriorating. Under different conditions, new leaders might be able to replace the conservatives who had flourished under right-wing regimes.

Something like that happened in Argentina, where a succession of military governments culminated in a death squad state. As the

---

*In Nicaragua, pastoral training was one issue disputed by the pro-Sandinista Evangelical Council for Aid to Development (CEPAD) and its anti-Sandinista offshoot, the National Council of Evangelical Pastors (CNPEN). As a development agency and the older of the two bodies, CEPAD started a pastoral training program emphasizing lay activism and leadership. When the new pastor's council asked CEPAD to shut down the program so that it could organize its own, the development agency refused, on grounds that the rival body represented pastors rather than churches. Whereas CEPAD was part of the movement to decentralize congregational authority, CNPEN was operating on the traditional premise that the pastor runs the church. "We're the pastors," CNPEN's president told me in 1985, "and it's the pastors who represent the churches. That's how we look at things."

dictatorship tortured more than twelve thousand citizens to death in the late 1970s, its evangelical supporters remained firm, as did a reactionary Catholic hierarchy. "If something happened to [victims], they must have done something wrong," such Christians argued, or "you have to remember what the guerrillas did," or "the military has saved us from Marxism." But after 1981, another wing of the evangelical churches played a leading role in the Argentine human rights movement. When economic collapse and the unsuccessful Malvinas War with Great Britain brought down the army dictatorship, its evangelical supporters were also discredited. The turn of events covered religious activists with glory, giving them a strong position in middle-class churches as well as the newly elected government of Raúl Alfonsín.

But the gain was fragile, warned José Míguez Bonino, a Protestant liberation theologian who had seen many a setback for his cause. The new leadership could get too far out in front of its congregations and discredit itself.[115] Meanwhile, pentecostals reported that, under a new democratic regime that was failing to make much headway against the country's terrible economic crisis, their churches were growing like never before.

Chapter Seven

The New Jerusalem of the Americas

Guatemalans are the chosen people of the New Testament. We are the New Israelites of Central America.

Efraín Ríos Montt[1]

The prayers for Brother Efraín were not answered. After a sixteen-month march toward the New Jerusalem, the first born-again dictator in history was shunted aside, by the same army that had placed him in power. But while General Efraín Ríos Montt occupied the presidential palace in Guatemala, he drew the world's attention to the evangelical awakening in Central America. According to church growth projections, in 1981 that movement claimed 21 percent of the Guatemalan population—probably a majority of active churchgoers. If 10 percent and higher annual growth rates continue into the 1990s, Guatemala will be the first country in Latin America with a Protestant majority.[2]

Ríos Montt and his supporters hoped to turn this religious movement into a new political order. Protestants typically have ascribed violence and backwardness in Latin America, not to foreign dependency or the class structure, but to Latin Catholic mores. If poverty and civil strife are fundamentally moral problems, it follows that only a moral reformation can solve them. What Latin America lacks, they believe, is a "biblical" foundation.

This was the premise on which Ríos Montt announced that he would moralize national life from the top down. Guatemala would not be liberated by a revolution overthrowing oppressive structures, he preached. Instead, it would be liberated by a revolution in the hearts of men. In the person of an erratic army general describing himself as God's chosen representative, what the Melvilles call "power in search of legitimacy" turned to a religion of Guatemala's powerless for justification.[3] To the astonishment of world opinion, which continued to receive horrifying reports about the Guatemalan army's human rights violations, that institution's new commander-in-chief made moral renovation his favorite topic.

Ríos Montt's urgency stemmed from the fulfillment of long-held fears. As long ago as 1936, a U.S. missionary wrote a novel in which a Russian Bolshevik leads an uprising of Guatemala's Mayan Indians, only to be foiled by a Mayan evangelist wielding God's word.[4] Under the lawless Praetorian regime that preceded Ríos Montt's, Indians throughout the western highlands joined Marxist guerrilla movements. The threat was materializing, moreover, in what the new dictator and his brethren regarded as a particularly insidious guise: a revolutionary interpretation of their own Christian faith.

We can therefore imagine the hymns of praise which greeted a true soldier of God. The confrontation between North American fundamentalism and liberation theology made Central America, in the words of an evangelical missionary, "one of the strategic battlefields in the spiritual warfare over the allegiance and eternal destiny of the world's inhabitants."[5] The fundamentalist gospel, an elder of Ríos Montt's Word Church stated, was a "stabilizing factor." It would transform Guatemala into a "spiritual stronghold," prevent Guatemala's rich oil and titanium reserves from falling into Marxist hands, and become a buffer between the United States and communist advance. "After Guatemala," warned Word's parent church in the U.S., "only Mexico remains!" But that was not all. For a Latin America which these Christians considered lost in the darkness of Catholic idolatry and liberation theology, Guatemala was to become a beacon of light. It would serve as a model of biblical righteousness for other countries threatened by the same satanic forces: it was to become a theological "New Israel" of the Americas.[6]

The geopolitical faith of the men surrounding Ríos Montt seemed to confirm the worst fears of the left. Now that revolutionaries had begun to extol the virtues of Christian consciousness-raising, the Guatemalan army was not only crushing church activists but also promoting a more amenable form of worship. Catholic Indians were said to be converting to Protestantism en masse to save their lives. Here was a true alternative, television evangelist Pat Robertson explained, "between the oppression of corrupt oligarchies and the tyranny of Russian-backed communist totalitarianism."[7] Encouraged by men like Robertson, North American evangelicals were said to be pledging millions of dollars for Ríos Montt's pacification campaign.

Evangelical relief in Guatemala was coordinated by Gospel Outreach, the California-based ministry to whose Guatemalan branch, the Word Church, Ríos Montt belonged. Assisted by the Summer Institute of Linguistics, Word started a much-publicized effort to help indigenous war victims. Soon its pronouncements were flouting the findings of human rights organizations, in an attempt to justify Ríos Montt's "rifles and beans" policy of concentrating Indians into resettlement camps and conscripting them into army-supervised civil patrols.

Reports of continued army atrocities did not affect Ríos Montt's stock with conservative evangelicals in the United States. Even after his overthrow, they showered him with applause and prayer. Back in Guatemala, however, evangelical leaders were full of apprehension about the way Ríos had politicized their faith. Nor was that the only reason they were being sucked into the political arena. While conservative churches had grown mightily by declining to confront army and police depredations, now they were inheriting the survivors, masses of people being impoverished at a rapid rate. Church growth had a price not mentioned by church-growth salesmen. Even conservatives who had condemned reform-minded Christians for "getting involved in politics" were being forced to confront social issues. Not unlike the Catholic Church in the 1950s and 1960s, they were responding with a wave of social programs. "Even though conservatives are in control," a lonely in-country dissident predicted, "they're not going to maintain it, because the people are learning to speak, in their own terms and in their own forms."

Gospel Outreach

For spiritual guidance, Efraín Ríos Montt looked to the elders of the Word Church. And for their own spiritual direction, Word's

young North American and Guatemalan leaders looked to Eureka,
California. North of San Francisco along the coast, the town was
named for the "Eureka!" ("I have found it" in Greek) which pros-
pectors shouted during the California gold rush. Several booms and
busts later, the area's leading industry was growing marijuana, introduced by hippies from San Francisco. Early in the 1970s, some
of these flower children rediscovered the traditional opiate of the
people. A decade later, they were the spiritual advisers of a military
dictatorship.

The leader of the new movement in Eureka was a generation
older than his followers: alcohol, not hallucinogens, had brought
the portly, avuncular Reverend Jim Durkin to ruin. But the same
Lord had saved them both. Under the guidance of this real estate
broker and lay preacher of the Assemblies of God, the long-haired
penitents acquired the Lighthouse Ranch Commune, a nearby social experiment also evolving from drugs to Christianity. Here Durkin put his followers on a strict regime, perhaps already influenced
by the shepherding wing of the charismatic movement. Haircuts
were only the beginning. Moral discipline was so severe that members of the opposite sex reputedly could not be alone in the same
room together. Originally, the ranch had tried to model itself after
the primitive communists of the first century church. Durkin decided to teach his followers how to run a business and support their
ministry, too, by starting commercial enterprises, where members
could earn their room and board out at the ranch. In exchange for a
multiple tithe of the profits, businesses were then turned over to
members to operate as their own. If man is made in the image of
God, then the Lord started to look like the confident young graduate of a business school.[8]

Journalists who met the Word elders during their days of glory
were quick to note a peculiar combination of good nature and meg-
alomania, common sense and fanaticism, which can be traced to
their peculiar training. Durkin's followers had been supreme relativists. Hippies just wanted to do their own thing, anything was
okay as long as it didn't hurt anyone else, and everything would be
beautiful if you just let it happen. But Durkin told his young people
not just that this tolerant philosophy had worn down their sense of
right and wrong but that it was how the devil had taken over their
lives. Now, were they to keep the smallest part of their lives from
God, that was where the devil would return and drag them down

to hell. If something in their lives was not of the kingdom of God, then it was of the kingdom of darkness—otherwise known as "the world," this world, which belonged to Satan.

The main target of Durkin's moral formation program was what he called the "I-centered" approach to life. But after he had brought his egotistical young followers face to face with their true worthlessness, he showed them how, with God's help, they could take their place in an awe-inspiring millennial drama. In fulfillment of Biblical prophecy, Durkin said, they had been put on earth to change history. They would evangelize the world.

The world Durkin presented to his followers was a stormy one. Approaching was an awful retribution for the sins of mankind, a great tribulation that would end with the Second Coming of Christ and his thousand-year reign on earth. This was the reason for the group's survivalist tendency. Profoundly pessimistic about the future of what he called "debt-capitalism," Durkin advised his flock to prepare for the coming financial crash by staying out of debt, diversifying investments, and storing food supplies.

The Lord would probably return in his own lifetime, Durkin believed, but only after true Christians had multiplied over the earth. The mission of his church was therefore serving as a base for evangelism: sending out the shepherding-style "elders"—formerly of the Lighthouse Ranch Commune, now in their thirties—whom he trained to start churches elsewhere.[9] Hence the group's name, Gospel Outreach. In 1983, four thousand people were said to be attending its services.[10] There were forty congregations in the United States, with the majority on the West Coast, and six abroad, in Europe as well as in Guatemala City, Managua, and Quito.

Guatemala appeared on Gospel Outreach's horizon following the 1976 earthquake. As its volunteers from California helped rebuild low-income neighborhoods around the capital, they blended into a charismatic movement which was recruiting from the upper classes and spinning off into a number of churches. Participants in this move of the Holy Spirit often knew some English and had become infatuated with North American culture. But they needed something more than the pursuit of profits and pleasure as Guatemala's masses hungered outside the gate. Gospel Outreach's moralistic young North Americans had the answer. Being filled by the Holy Spirit gave upper-class Guatemalans a sense of vindication at a time when their way of life looked increasingly uncertain. By early 1982, a well-heeled, enthusiastic congregation of five hundred was meeting under a circus tent, staked in an expensive neighborhood next to the Camino Real Hotel.

Could the Lord Have Something in Store for Brother Efraín?

When the Word elders found themselves in the middle of a military coup, on the morning of March 23, 1982, they were not totally unprepared. They already knew that, thanks to the remarkable correspondence between the East-West conflict and the impending millennial showdown, any outbreak around the world was a step on the march to Armageddon. But until swept along by events, the Word elders were far from political activists. Even as their brethren in the United States joined the religious right, the North American elders in Guatemala tried to keep their distance from politics Central America-style.* They were well aware that the administration of General Romeo Lucas García (1978–1982) left much to be desired as a defender of religious liberty. Anxious that church and union activists were fronting for revolutionary organizations, Lucas unleashed death squads. Coordinated from an annex of the presidential palace, the death squads destroyed Guatemala's political center and pushed thousands of survivors into guerrilla movements.

The Word elders were not alone in feeling detached. Evangelical church leaders in general were not eager to address the disintegration of the country. Their upbeat centennial history of Protestantism in Guatemala, published at the height of the violence in 1982, managed to avoid the subject.[11] Corruption, disrespect for authority, communism, and evil were on the increase, these men preached, but their kingdom was not of this world. Such reasoning did not, of course, prevent certain of them from enlisting in the 1982 presidential campaign of the official party, a creation of the

---

*Illustrating this sense of detachment, one remonstrated anti-Sandinista pastors in Nicaragua for "depart[ing] from the pure preaching of the gospel to actively support anti-government forces." Satan was using such people to make the Sandinista government distrust Christians, the Word elder continued, and "make the gospel seem an instrument of external—rather than internal—revolution (James Jankowiak, *Radiance*, April 1982, p. 3).

army high command, and a sure winner judging from its theft of the two previous elections. Now that official murders had alienated most of the Catholic Church, the dictatorship was eager to enlist alternative men of God.

A month before the March 7, 1982, national election, a conference of five hundred pastors was honoring the hundredth anniversary of Protestantism in Guatemala. They were interrupted by the arrival of helicopters bearing the official presidential candidate, General Aníbal Guevara. Prominent pastors in the general's campaign had arranged the appearance, promising free chalk and notebooks for all who attended. To hallelujahs from the audience, General Guevara shouted "praise the Lord" and, observing Christian etiquette, asked for prayer that the Lord's chosen man win the election. Their daughter-in-law was an evangelical, Guevara's wife mentioned, and although they themselves had not taken the big step, they certainly were considering it. At noon, the cafeteria buzzed with recriminations: this was like selling one's birthright for a mess of pottage. The church was supposed to be above politics. Suddenly guerrillas appeared, to distribute pamphlets from the Vicente Menchú Revolutionary Christians.[12]

Over at the Word Church, meanwhile, the elders were keeping an eye on another army general, a retired one in their congregation named Efraín Ríos Montt. Eight years before, Ríos himself had run for president and probably won. He had been the reform candidate, campaigning on the Christian Democratic ticket in a convincing manner, and was far ahead on election night 1974 when, suddenly, television screens went blank. Broadcasting did not resume until the next morning, by which time the official candidate was the winner by a large margin. The army clique ruling the country had imposed its own candidate.

Four years later, when Ríos Montt started showing up at functions of the Word Church, the elders of Gospel Outreach wondered why such a big league politician was coming around to see them. He proved himself, they relate, by cleaning out toilets. Fortunately, the Word Church's 1983 biography of Ríos provides a revealing account of his frustrations and dreams. His religious conversion, it emerges, grew out of frustrated ambition for the highest office in the land. Bitterness over how fellow army officers had cheated him out of the presidency, the Word elders discovered, was the deepest wound of his life. When Ríos came home from exile in 1977, it was in the vain hope of winning a second nomination from the Christian Democrats, for the next year's election. Only after this second, seemingly terminal disappointment did the general find his way to the Word Church. There the elders said that God had a very special purpose in store for him.[13] Charismatic religion became a balm for his wounded ambitions and transfigured them. From now on he was God's soldier, whose duty in life would be realized in the Lord's way.

The Word elders remained of two minds on the privilege of ministering to a Guatemalan general. Yes, as a brother in Christ, Ríos had made a "covenant" with them and submitted himself to their authority. This was the essential relation of trust among Word members, and it is a main theme of the biography.[14] Yet as the political parties settled on their candidates for the March 7, 1982, national election, the elders were not pleased to pick up their newspapers and read that Brother Efraín was considering a third run for the presidency. Hoping to keep him and their church out of the race, the elders made Efraín's never-quenched presidential ambitions the subject of three days of prayer and fasting. Various prophecies indicated that participating in these elections was not of the Lord: Efraín's time was yet to come. Although the elders would support him if he chose to be a candidate, the Lord was telling them that "another door" would open for him. But only the collapse of the party coalition offering him the candidacy—not their three days of advice and prophecy—settled the matter against running.[15]

Two weeks after the official candidate stole the election, on March 23, 1982, young army officers called Ríos to the national palace to take charge of their coup d'etat. He was at his job administering Word's day school that morning; he seemed genuinely taken aback, even afraid, and professed no involvement in the conspiracy. But with his sudden appearance on television that night in battle fatigues, as the head of a new military junta, it occurred to more than one Word elder that their brother in Christ had broken covenant with them.

Was it simply coincidence that the planners had struck on the eighth anniversary of the day he went into exile in Spain?[16] If certain conspirators are to be believed, Ríos took Word's prophecies so seriously that he helped plan the revolt that brought him to power.

In view of the early 1982 consensus that the Lucas regime had to go, not to mention Ríos's prominence as a defrauded president-elect from eight years before, it would be little short of miraculous for him not to have been involved at least peripherally. Of the two groups who planned the March 23 coup, Ríos is accused of having dealt with each.

The first was the National Liberation Movement (MLN), placed in power by the CIA in 1954 and known as "the party of organized violence" for its reliance on strong-arm tactics, including death squads. Ríos Montt was no enthusiast of the MLN: its 1982 presidential candidate, Mario Sandoval Alarcón, had supported the theft of his presidency eight years before. But Ríos's wife, Teresa, was from an important military family enmeshed with the MLN, the Sosa Ávilas, and worked in its 1982 presidential campaign. Ríos himself, according to a political enemy, headed an MLN paramilitary group which was supposed to protest the coming electoral fraud by starting riots.*

The second group plotting the March 23 coup was the young army officers. Some were MLN supporters, others not. But all were disenchanted with a corrupt high command which was losing the war against the guerrillas. According to one of the young officers, Ríos had been chosen to head the new junta from the start of their plan, due to his upstanding reputation and election as presi-

*The source of this accusation is Danilo Roca, an MLN ally in the 1982 election. According to Roca, the MLN's agents inside the government had confirmed that the ruling party would steal the March 7 election. The MLN therefore planned to turn its victory celebrations, at Catholic churches around the capital, into a riot to burn trucks and blow up bridges in the early morning hours of March 8, to shut down Guatemala City and force the army to intervene against the ruling clique of senior officers.

An associate of Roca's provided me with a detailed (but uncorroborated) account of nightly planning sessions chaired by Ríos, in his home during the month preceding the election. According to the source, at these meetings Ríos said that he was not going to let happen to Mario [Sandoval Alarcón, the MLN candidate] what had happened to him in 1974. The last time he had not been prepared, Ríos is supposed to have said, but this time they would be ready. He also stressed that the MLN provocateurs were under no circumstances to confront the army, which was being brought into the conspiracy by another route. The night of the election, according to Roca and his associate, Ríos aborted the plan (author's interview, Guatemala City, August 24, 1985).

The MLN's Leonel Sisniego Otero charged that, prior to the March 23 coup, Ríos had agreed to head a joint civilian-military junta, then betrayed his MLN coconspirators after taking power (*This Week*, July 4, 1983, p. 193).

dent in 1974. But Ríos had not been informed beforehand, the young officer insisted, because if word leaked their chosen leader would have been killed.[17]

Following the successful coup, the MLN's conspirators were flabbergasted to hear Ríos Montt denounce, not just the deposed Lucas regime, but them as well. They too were among the rotten civilian politicians responsible for Guatemala's sorry straits, the head of the new military junta declared. It was the Lord who had placed him where he was, Ríos announced, closing ranks with fellow army officers and shutting the MLN out in the cold.

As far as Ríos was concerned, his deepest ambition had become God's purpose for him. It might seem implausible that a Guatemalan general could lead a coup he had not planned. But for the Word elders and other evangelicals, all hinged on Ríos Montt's claim to innocence. To them, the most important question was the purity of his motives. Only if his arrival in the palace had been undefiled by the filth of Guatemalan politics could it be of the Lord. Efraín insisted that he had nothing to do with planning the coup, and the Word elders decided to honor their covenant by believing him. The drama of the moment touched their own sense of destiny: hadn't they received a prophecy saying that they would counsel heads of state?[18] Through nothing but prayer on their part, they concluded, the Lord had placed his servants at the center of the cosmic struggle between good and evil. With two Guatemalan elders at the presidential palace as Ríos Montt's advisers, and other elders joining weekly prayer sessions with him, the Word Church had become, in fulfillment of its own prophecies, a door for Brother Efraín and a leader of nations.

The International Love Lift

As Guatemala's first evangelical president reined in government death squads in the capital and pushed back the guerrillas in the countryside, a noteworthy date was approaching. November 1982 was the hundredth anniversary of the first Protestant mission in Guatemala. Surely, many evangelicals believed, this convergence between the centennial year of their faith, the country's first Christian leader, and national deliverance was a sign from the Lord. Like the Word Church and Ríos Montt himself, they concluded that he was God's man to save Guatemala from communism and lead the nation to Christ. For believers who previously had preferred not to discuss politics, a taboo subject suddenly turned into an act of God.

The Word elders, enemies soon alleged, had a Rasputin-like influence over the new president. But their only visible function in the new regime was vouching for its integrity. This was no small or unimportant task, to be sure, and they addressed it with great energy. For despite the announcement of a new era of morality, the Guatemalan army's strategy in the western highlands was producing unprecedented numbers of Indian refugees. Their needs were not being met, and their stories of army barbarism contradicted Ríos Montt's claim to respect human rights.

In public, the Word elders never faltered. On arrival at the presidential palace, they had stressed the evils of the preceding regime and how Ríos was going to end them.[19] Now he had done so, they argued. As personal friends of the president, they knew that he could not be ordering massacres of civilians. Of course, they admitted, Ríos could not be held responsible for every act committed by an army of twenty thousand individuals. But now that he had brought the security forces under control, it could not be guilty of such crimes. The blessings unleashed by the Holy Spirit on March 23 were so powerful, according to the Word Church, that they produced a 180-degree turn in the respective behavior of soldiers and guerrillas.

Regrettably, not everyone was willing to recognize this new fact. Soon the Word elders were locked in spiritual warfare with two of the most insidious manifestations of secular humanism in the world today. The first was fellow Christians, or at least that is what they called themselves, for in the persistent slanders from certain so-called church groups, the Word elders detected the influence of liberation theology—that Marxist, man-centered attempt to replace evangelism with politics and twist the gospel into a justification for violent revolution. But Ríos's most deadly enemy was the liberal media, with their blatant biases and propaganda. Blinded by the night and fog that shroud the vision of unbelieving men, journalists were not reporting the truth as the Word Church so clearly perceived it.

Where could the Word elders find fellow Christians to help them fight these lies? A few years before, the western highlands had been populated by missions, agencies, and centers for the development of this or that, usually financed by foreigners. Then the previous regime had identified such efforts as the Trojan Horse of subversion, placed their local Indian coordinators on death lists, and diligently hunted them down.[20] Now, shocked benefactors were wondering how to help the survivors without stimulating further bloodshed. Most decided to wait.

But two—the well-known community health promoter Dr. Carroll Behrhorst and certain members of the Summer Institute of Linguistics (SIL)—did not wait. Behrhorst's development program had ended when eleven of his forty-seven Mayan extension agents died mysteriously under the Lucas García administration. As for the Summer Institute, it had joined that same regime's literacy program. Although the new literacy drive was administered by the national police, who might be less interested in producing new readers than in gathering intelligence, this had been just SIL's chance to pursue its policy of serving God by serving the government. But while eager to cultivate those in authority, most of SIL's Bible translators had been reluctant to waste time thinking about politics: that got in the way of their mission. Yet as threats and violence mounted, the translators were forced to respond. They did so by pulling out, taking Mayan assistants to the capital to finish their New Testament translations as quickly as possible. These groups would not return to the countryside until it was brought under control, which included bringing the army under control. Could the new president provide that guarantee?

To prove that he could, Ríos Montt appointed a board member of the Behrhorst Foundation, Harris Whitbeck, to serve as his personal representative in relief work. A former U.S. Marine sergeant and construction contractor who proved to have pull in Washington, Whitbeck served as liaison between the military and private relief efforts. Thus reinforced, by July 1982 the three groups—the Word Church, the Behrhorst Clinic, and several Summer Institute translators—were organizing the Foundation for Aid to the Indian People (FUNDAPI). Behrhorst personnel and the Summer Institute translators would serve as field agents, while the Word Church would provide staff in the capital and raise funds in the United States. There had been much talk about how North America evangelicals would come to the aid of their fellow believer, with Ríos

Montt tossing out the figure of a billion dollars. Late in July, he announced that an arm of Gospel Outreach would administer contributions from the United States: it was called International Love Lift.[21] In Guatemala, the new FUNDAPI officers braced themselves for an avalanche of funds.

Providing food, medicine, clothing, shelter, and tools, the Word elders anticipated, would meet the needs of refugees, win their support for the new government, and create openings for evangelism. An evangelical presence would also, they hoped in private, restrain the army from crimes which they knew it was still committing. Finally, they hoped to bolster Ríos Montt's credibility in the United States. The appeals for funds would lend the names of spiritual leaders such as broadcaster Pat Robertson, Bill Bright of the Campus Crusade for Christ, and Moral Majority founder Jerry Falwell to the cause of the new Christian president.

Soon, FUNDAPI was taking visitors to a place where it could show them, first-hand, "how it really is"—in startling contrast to the picture painted by refugees, journalists, and human rights and revolutionary groups. However brutal the army had been prior to Ríos Montt, FUNDAPI told visitors, the violence had been provoked by the guerrillas. Why didn't the army's critics ever mention that the guerrillas used unarmed, unwilling civilians as shields against army firepower? The people had been caught in the middle, FUNDAPI maintained, and now they were fleeing to the army for protection. Other refugees were said to be still held captive by the guerrillas, who killed those who tried to escape. There was simply no proof that Ríos Montt had ordered atrocities, FUNDAPI staffers argued. In many cases, they further insisted, supposed army massacres had turned out to be perpetrated by guerrillas, who wanted to discredit the new government and prevent the United States from resuming military aid.

Many evangelical missionaries did not, to be sure, share the thunderstruck vision of the Word Church. Two other schools of thought emerged as reports of new massacres flooded in from the countryside. A few missionaries decided that Ríos Montt was using their faith to cover up an escalation of army terror; they were soon forced to leave the country. Another, much larger group of missionaries discounted those reports, accepted Ríos Montt's good intentions, and hoped that he would stabilize the situation. But they continued to harbor doubts about the idea of a born-again dictator, and they did not really believe that the Guatemalan army had been transformed into a humanitarian institution. Unlike the hallelujah wing of North American evangelism, these more pragmatic, experienced missionaries accepted the new army regime and its promises of reform as a lesser evil than a revolution.[22]

Church, Army, and Guerrilla in the Ixil Triangle

FUNDAPI gave visitors a "true" picture of the war in its main theater, the Ixil Maya country of northern Quiché Department. The Ixil municipalities of Nebaj, Cotzal, and Chajul were a bitterly contested stronghold of the Guerrilla Army of the Poor (EGP). The road into the Ixil Triangle switchbacks up the wall of the Cuchumatanes range, wraps around a mountain shoulder, and disappears into the clouds. As the road drops into a mountain valley, the white walls and red roofs of Nebaj in the distance seem as remote as Shangri La. That, unfortunately, is not the case. Around the turn of the century, white merchants began to arrive. Through an attractive combination of liquor and credit, they trapped the Ixil into debt, seized their best land, and forced them to work on plantations.[23]

In 1955, a new Catholic order took charge of Quiché Department. The Missionaries of the Sacred Heart arrived the year after the Catholic hierarchy supported the CIA's overthrow of the leftist Arbenz government. It would have been hard to predict the eventual fate of these Spanish priests, murdered or expelled as alleged subversives: in the beginning, their job was to defend Quiché from evangelical missionaries and communism. But they were shocked by the way plantation owners and merchants treated Indians. For collateral on loans, it was not unusual for local patróns to demand Ixil girls, then boast of the number of children they had sired.

Armed with Catholic social doctrine, the Spanish priests launched development projects which upset the equilibrium of oppression in Quiché. New village committees organized cooperatives. Indians started to buy back land. The first Mayan professionals graduated from teacher training institutes and universities. Part of the population started to organize, first in the Catholic Action movement and then the Christian Democratic Party, and demand better salaries.[24]

It was not long before local power brokers attacked such movements as communist.[25] When security forces began to eliminate leaders suspected of subversion, they engaged in self-fulfilling prophecy according to the human rights lobby: the murders radicalized Indians into joining a revolutionary movement. But according to the Guatemalan army, the Catholic clergy fulfilled their own prophecies of repression, by lending their churches to infiltrators. What is certain is that church reform movements and the Mayan effervescence drew in guerrillas and government forces, whose blows and counterblows swirled into a vicious war in which most of the dead were Mayan Indians.

One turning point was the March 1974 election, in which the Christian Democrats—and their presidential candidate Efraín Ríos Montt—swept Quiché. The official party blamed the Catholic Church for its defeat. According to a Protestant missionary, soon after death squads abducted their first victims from Nebaj.[26] As Ríos Montt stewed in exile in Spain, his defrauded and persecuted Indian supporters were forced to look elsewhere for support.

Another milestone was the Guerrilla Army of the Poor's first execution of a plantation tyrant in the area, in June 1975. Survivors of an earlier, non-Indian insurgency had started the EGP three years earlier, from the jungles along the Mexican border.[27] When these outsiders chose northern Quiché as the most promising terrain in the country from which to launch a liberation war, among the factors said to influence their decision was the strength of Catholic organizations in the area.[28]

To the disgust of more cautious priests, in the late 1970s a few of their colleagues apparently turned church organizations into vehicles for guerrilla organizing. In defense of the radicals, it can be said that Guatemala's army regime was already responsible for thousands of political murders and showed no sign of changing its ways. Peaceful opposition was dangerous and ineffective.

A group of itinerant Jesuits was particularly active in using consciousness-raising techniques to train catechists and cooperative leaders. As these priests became disillusioned with the results of development schemes, the Guatemalan Church in Exile has ex-

plained, they directed their message "not to solve economic problems through a new technology or financial organization . . . [but]
to free the mind from traditional constraints, the . . . most profound being respect for the authorities. It was a message which
subverted the law."[29]

According to Luis Pellecer, the Jesuit EGP collaborator kidnapped and "turned" by Guatemalan security forces in 1981, the
catechists provided, not just a new form of communication between
the masses and Catholic clergy, but a new collective consciousness
among Indians previously divided by ethnic barriers.[30] As the army
reacted against the movement, it became a bridge into the EGP.
When a priest objected to catechists getting involved with guerrillas in 1979, he reports, a colleague challenged him: "Are you afraid
of the army?" He was, and with good reason.

The army was soon on the rampage against Catholic organizations, in the belief that it was finding guerrilla leadership there.
From 1975 on, as the EGP staged rallies, ambushed soldiers, and
assassinated informers, security forces responded with wider and
wider reprisals against the Ixil—from kidnapping and murdering
virtually any kind of Indian leader, including Protestant pastors, to
wiping out villages. From 1976 to 1979—that is, before the worst
violence—the Guatemalan Church in Exile claims that more than
350 leaders were kidnapped from the three Ixil municipalities
alone.[31] Among the victims were three Sacred Heart priests, none
of them political activists, who were methodically hunted down. In
1980, the bishop of Quiché ordered his clergy into exile, and at
least three priests of the diocese went over to the guerrillas, along
with many parishioners. By the end of that year, the three Summer
Institute teams assigned to the Ixil region had also pulled out.

Unfortunately for the government, its violence did not have the
intended effect. Instead of suppressing the guerrillas, it multiplied
a small band of outsiders into a liberation army, mostly Indians
drawn from local communities. By the end of 1980, government
atrocities seemed to have alienated the entire Ixil population. Ex-
uberant over the Sandinista victory in Nicaragua, the EGP rushed
into the political vacuum and organized across the western highlands. By early 1982, guerrilla armies seemed to control all of
Quiché and Huehuetenango departments except for a few garrison

towns. They were on the point of cutting the Pan-American High-way. With the Indians of the western highlands behind them, they could have marched on the capital half a million strong.

But the guerrillas had few weapons to give their followers, and fear of soldiers did not necessarily mean solid support for the revolution. Unlike several smaller, more cautious guerrilla groups, the EGP organized entire communities into its ranks. Not only did the EGP do so very openly and quickly: its mass organizing strategy destroyed the "neutral" middle ground where many Ixil would have preferred to stay. In the Nebaj township of Salquil, government-controlled refugees told me, EGP militants would plant revolutionary flags at night. If neighbors removed the flags, they identified themselves as progovernment. But if the flags remained until the army arrived, the entire neighborhood would be suspected of supporting the guerrillas.

Evangelical missionaries called this kind of polarization tactic "provoked repression."[32] Initially it worked in favor of the guerrillas; then it backfired. Once a neighborhood was under attack from the army, its guerrilla defenders could scarcely tolerate neutrality, let alone any sign of support for the government. They, too, were forced to crush dissent. But the people had become all too aware that EGP organizing had provoked the army's fury, and that the guerrillas were not protecting them from the army as they had promised to.

Shortly before Ríos Montt replaced Lucas García in the presidential palace, the Guatemalan army turned its full force on the Guerrilla Army of the Poor. One of the first areas it decided to retake was the Ixil Triangle.

Pastor Nicolás

FUNDAPI missionaries attributed the turn of the tide in the Ixil area to a single believer, Pastor Nicolás Tomá in the town of Cotzal.[33] When I met him one night there in December 1982, this thoughtful, articulate man seemed haunted by the choice he had made. After a July 28, 1980, EGP raid on the Cotzal barracks, his own brother and brother-in-law had been among the sixty-four townsmen hauled out of their houses and butchered by the army in reprisal. But when the guerrillas hit the Cotzal garrison a second time, on January 19, 1982, the pastor helped the army track the retreating insurgents.

"The guerrillas only provoke the army and then they go," Pastor Nicolás said bitterly. "We are the ones who suffer the consequences." In the course of several hours discussion, he did not cite a single religious or ideological justification for his decision to support the government. Apparently the only reason was survival, for his people as well as himself. The army had killed "thousands"of unarmed civilians just in the municipality of Cotzal, the pastor claimed. Had he not helped the soldiers, Nicolás told me, they would have killed him, too.

When a new military commander arrived after the second EGP raid on the barracks, he told Pastor Nicolás and other religious leaders that, at the present rate, the army would have to "finish with" Cotzal. If the entire Cotzal population supported the guerrillas, the entire Cotzal population would have to be eliminated. Despite pledges of cooperation, troops and helicopter gunships continued to rampage through the countryside, killing anyone they found. "I can no longer control them," the commander told Nicolás, pointing out that the soldiers were from other garrisons. Later that year, a young government official came out from the capital. He discovered that, of Cotzal's twenty-nine rural neighborhoods on his list, only three were still in existence.[34] Soldiers had, during the anti-guerrilla offensive, burned the others to the ground.

The army had announced that everyone who did not come into town would be considered a guerrilla; that is, they would be shot on sight. But while a number of survivors had surrendered to the army, the town remained paralyzed with fear. To the commander, therefore, Pastor Nicolás offered his own life as a guarantee for the good behavior of the inhabitants. Soon Nicolás was playing a leading role in the civil patrol which the army now imposed on the town. Through the civil patrol, the information and the captives it brought in, the army was finally able to strike at EGP combatants, extract more information, and dismantle guerrilla infrastructure.

A Summer Institute of Linguistics (SIL) prayer letter describes what happened next. "We have been . . . spectators, only able to watch from far away . . . but we are cheering wildly," one of the SIL-Cotzal translators wrote in May 1982. "Beginning in January, the believers, led by Pastor [Nicolás], have taken desperate risks and aligned themselves with the national army. Civil patrols have been organized and given arms. The incredible result has been the eradication of guerrilla revolutionary forces from the Cotzal area!"[35]

Actually, a war between the army and the Ixil population had turned into a civil war, among the Ixil. The local army detachment had not lost a single man since it organized the Cotzal civil patrol in January 1982, the head of the latter force told me at year's end. Of the nine hundred civilians in his patrol, this Cotzal elder said, seventy-six had died fighting the guerrillas. Pastor Nicolás found himself on an EGP death list. Still, by December 1982, he thought that the people had "more confidence" because the army "cares for the people; the people are aware that being on the side of the army is the solution to their problems." Yet the new civil patrols, compulsory public meetings, and work days were taking people away from worship service, Pastor Nicolás complained. His protests had only earned the enmity of the local authorities.[36] One Sunday morning in March 1983, a few weeks after a crisis in the civil patrol led to his appointment as its chief, Pastor Nicolás was shot and killed on his way to preach at an outlying church.

But before Nicolás died, FUNDAPI missionaries claim, word of his arrangement with the army spread far and wide through Ixil country. By his example in Cotzal, the pastor is said to have proved to Ixil in Nebaj and Chajul that they, too, could survive the holocaust by cooperating with its perpetrators. According to the Guatemalan army, Cotzal provided the model for the civil patrols which, under Ríos Montt, drafted three-quarters of a million Indian men—many of them guerrilla sympathizers—into the antiguerrilla cause.[37] The elders of the Word Church drew their own conclusions: were they to back up pastors like Nicolás with relief supplies and political influence, they could humanize the army's treatment of civilians and win Indian support for Ríos Montt.

Providing an Alternative

On July 5, 1982, a Summer Institute couple who had spent three decades in Nebaj translating the Bible returned for a visit, to interpret for International Love Lift's first project in the area. As a North American dental team pulled nine hundred aching teeth, the Bible translators heard many stories contradicting Ríos Montt's claims to

respect human rights. Evangelical converts told them of beatings
and death threats from soldiers. Were the army commander to discover that victims had complained, they could expect worse. Teenage girls feared that they would be dragged to the barracks, to be
gang-raped and killed like others had.

The missionary couple was horrified. But they regarded army
victory as a lesser evil than continuing warfare, with its appalling
cost for civilians, and guerrilla victory, which they feared would
turn Guatemala into a communist prison camp and destroy freedom to spread the gospel. Besides, to the Summer Institute
couple, Ríos Montt's leadership seemed to hold out the possibility
of a new deal for Indians, a middle way between right- and left-
wing oppression. With the army still mistreating civilians and thousands of refugees still afraid to surrender, the couple decided that
the Ixil "need an *alternative* to the pressures being put upon them
by the guerrillas."

To Ríos Montt the missionaries recommended that the army:
(1) refrain from shooting unarmed civilians just because they were
running away or digging holes to hide in; (2) start remunerating its
forced labor crews, many of whom had no way to feed themselves
or their families; (3) provide the refugees it had created with corn
and blankets; and (4) provide its compulsory civil patrols with arms,
instead of sending them out to fight guerrillas with machetes and
hunting pieces.

Judging from what I was able to see in Nebaj five months later,
the missionary linguists' advice was being followed. But perhaps
the best gauge of the North Americans' influence was their success
in having the previous army commander—whom a civil patrol
leader blamed for the murder of his own father and ninety-six other
civilians—transferred to another job.

The Summer Institute couple was especially concerned for the
evangelicals of Salquil, an EGP-controlled township to the north-
west. How could they be persuaded to surrender to the army? Few
of Salquil's inhabitants had done so, for reasons the missionaries
understood all too well. Word that the army was now respecting
the lives of the innocent needed "to trickle up to them," one of the
missionaries wrote in early July. To that end, he pondered using a
light airplane with a public address system or airdropping packets
of scripture.[38]

Less than a month later, several hundred evangelicals fled from guerrilla control in Salquil under cover of darkness. Their leader, like Nicolás a pastor of the Full Gospel Church of God, told the mission couple that his people had escaped murderous religious persecution. The guerrillas "insisted that we should oppose the President," the pastor explained. "But we kept remembering that the Bible says that we should obey the President. . . . The Bible tells us that we shouldn't join ourselves to the guerrillas. . . . Here we were in a situation where the guerrillas would kill anyone who refused to do what they said. And they've actually killed some of us."[39]

Like a number of other refugees under government control, the Salquil pastor told me that the guerrillas had "deceived" his people. EGP combatants had promised that they would feed the people who fed them, provide arms for defense against the army, and win the war by the March 1982 election.

When soldiers destroyed their crops and homes, however, the people went hungry. "We no longer had food, and we no longer had houses," another refugee leader explained. "We were without clothes, without medicine, and there had been many deaths among us." Because the guerrillas had taken away their government identity papers, several refugees said, they could not even flee to the Pacific Coast to work on the plantations, on which many depended for their livelihood.

Six members of his church had been killed by guerrillas, the Salquil pastor related. Four had been strangled with lassoes in the hamlet of Tu Jolom, in June 1982, for filling in stake pits the EGP had placed near their church. The booby traps would have brought army reprisals and, according to the elders, violated the biblical injunction to love thy neighbor.

But the army also had killed members of the pentecostal church, twenty-nine of them in the hamlet of Tu Chobuc on May 4, 1982. When helicopters landed, three families gathered to pray. After troops discovered an empty guerrilla storage pit nearby, they took the men, women, and children there and cut their throats, the pastor told me in the presence of soldiers.

Two days later, troops destroyed all the houses in Salquil. But over the radio, the country's new Christian president could be heard offering amnesty and praying. "Spies" from the town of Nebaj—possibly a missionary effort to advertise the amnesty—said that the people there had new confidence in the army. Fearing EGP reprisals, on August 3 the pastor led 237 evangelicals out of Salquil at night by a circuitous route. Escorted by soldiers, another fifty converts also left for government-controlled territory.[40]

Along with many more Salquileños who were rounded up by force or starved into submission,[41] the evangelicals were sent to "Camp New Life" at the Nebaj airstrip. With soldiers stationed at the highest point and refugee huts spilling down the hillside, trees felled in every direction to guard against ambushes and the occasional machine gun-mounted helicopter, Camp New Life looked like a strategic hamlet in Vietnam. It was one of the first of a number of tightly controlled resettlement camps, called "model villages" or "development poles," subsidized unofficially by the U.S. Agency for International Development.

Even in these government showcases, refugees were often willing to relate how army killings and ultimatums had driven them from their homes. "If we obey," a model villager explained, "they don't kill us anymore."[42] According to a wave of refugees who reached Mexico, from April 1982 into the new year troops supported by helicopters assaulted their villages in Chajul, killing livestock, men, women, and children.[43] But what seemed to keep the Salquil refugees at Camp New Life in late 1982 was, not physical coercion, but food-for-work and the physical security of being on the stronger side.

FUNDAPI missionaries functioned like fairy godmothers in the Ixil towns and refugee camps: besides keeping an eye on army administrators, they seemed to provide the majority of the available help—corn, blankets, and metal roofing—with preference for widows. But nothing like the billion dollars from North American evangelicals which Ríos Montt predicted ever materialized. Whether due to reports of army atrocities, fundraising costs, or the many other causes vying for evangelical dollars, money never poured into the Word Church. In 1984, as the flow of donations dried up, FUNDAPI reported having raised about $200,000.[44]

What does the Ixil area—the only one where FUNDAPI played a major role—tell us about the evangelical contribution to counterinsurgency? Until Ríos Montt arrived on the scene, Sheldon Annis has pointed out, the government had so disgraced itself that revolutionaries dominated the country's moral landscape. But the new evangelical president challenged the guerrillas "morally as well as militarily," providing a rationale for those who wished to support the army but had been stupefied by its behavior.[45] In Cotzal, Pastor Nicolás helped pioneer the amnesty and civil patrols which, under Ríos Montt, offered Indians protection from further army massacres if they turned against the insurgents. In Salquil, as violence by the Guatemalan army escalated, evangelical teachings seem to have become a wedge in the split between civilians and their ineffective guerrilla defenders. When Summer Institute translators began to return, their advice to the army may well have proved instrumental in persuading more refugees to surrender.

Evangelical churches in the Ixil area grew tremendously. According to a government health census, by 1983–1984 23 percent of heads of family in Chajul, 30 percent in Cotzal, and 37 percent in Nebaj said they were evangelical.[46] When Andrés Fajardo surveyed the model village of Salquil Grande in 1986, 44 percent of the 467 households described themselves as evangelical or were identified as such by an evangelical guide.[47] Judging from my visit in 1987, evangelical pastors in Nebaj were able to outdraw the new Catholic priest by a factor of several times. From a small minority before the war, Protestants seemed to have become the dominant religious group.

Such a religious transformation raises more issues than can be entered into here. But the testimony of Ixil evangelicals suggests that it was first of all the dictates of survival, not born-again religion or the efforts of missionaries, which pushed them into the army's hands. This raises the question of how revolutionary strategy encouraged the growth of conservative churches. If the Guerrilla Army of the Poor made Christian consciousness-raising a step in transforming indigenous resistance to the level of armed struggle, the Guatemalan army was not far behind in its use of religion. It turned politically conformist fundamentalism into a "dustpan," into which its repression pushed remnants of the consciousness-raising movements and other Ixil survivors.

As for the Guerrilla Army of the Poor, it lost most of the population it had controlled and took refuge in a few remote areas. The devastating setback eventually forced it to recognize a grave error, that of expanding too rapidly to defend the people it was organizing.[48] However much the EGP was responding to the historical struggle of the Mayan people, it channeled that resistance so as to make truly staggering demands on them, demands many could not meet. As a result, what the EGP called "popular revolutionary war" no longer looked very popular in what had been its core area. Judging from the cost of guerrilla organizing to the Ixil, the reason for the growth of Protestant churches in the western highlands did not have to be sought in Washington or the North American religious right. Rather, the leading argument for converting to an evangelical church was the cost of revolutionary strategy.

Let the Dead Bury the Dead

At the first anniversary of the March 23 coup, Ríos Montt appeared in camouflage uniform and web gear surrounded by the departmental commanders of the Guatemalan army. Hemmed in by a phalanx of impassive colonels, in a sweat with his eyes darting around the palace, he seemed like a Caesar awaiting his Brutus. To clear the way for the New Israel, Ríos had cast aside political parties and the high command. But he never threw himself against the steel paunch of the military hierarchy, the colonels in charge of the departmental garrisons. When Ríos donned his jungle fatigues on March 23, 1983, and took his place among like-uniformed fellow officers, he ritually subordinated himself to them and hailed the supremacy of the army. It had been a week of rumors about another coup, which finally came to pass four and a half months later.

As Ríos preached to the nation every Sunday, moralizing against subversion and the sorry state of private as well as public life, he never indicted the single institution which, more than any other, had devastated the country, because it was the institution which had put him in power. Even though trusted brethren were quietly confirming some of the accusations against the army, in public he issued denial after denial. Since Word's biography of Ríos does admit "some abuses" by the army despite his orders, the two it mentions deserves our attention.[49]

In the first, at the Finca San Francisco in Huehuetenango in July 1982, the army wiped out a large village of Chuj Maya men, women, and children. This was not a case of civilians caught in a crossfire because there had been no resistance. Gang-rape—the

Guatemalan army's inducement for soldiers about to massacre women—torture, execution, and ritual cannibalism were supervised by officers who alighted from a helicopter, indicating the department commander or his orderlies.[50] Although the evidence was unusually good—survivors compiled a list of 302 dead and a highly credible observer visited the remains four days later—the Word elders, their FUNDAPI advisers, and the U.S. embassy made jokes about it. This was a prime example of the smear campaign against Ríos Montt, they said. As it turned out, the U.S. embassy's investigation consisted of passing over the site in a helicopter that didn't land. When a FUNDAPI adviser finally reached the place in January 1983, he was shaken to discover skeletal remains, then confirmed the story from the nearest extant settlement.[51]

The second abuse admitted by Word was the army's February 1983 murder of Patricio Ortiz Maldonado, a Mayan professional employed by a USAID-financed bilingual education program. The army claimed that Ortiz and his three companions had been killed while trying to escape. His supervisors proved that he had been taken to the army garrison at La Democracia, the end of the road for many a disappeared person. According to an army captain who served at that base before seeking asylum in the United States, orders from the colonel to "process" prisoners were actually code for murdering them.[52] This was nothing new: every year thousands of Guatemalans were taken into official custody and never seen again, with the authorities denying all knowledge of their whereabouts. But this time a victim was on official business for the U.S. embassy, forcing Washington, Ríos Montt, and his Word Church biographers to take note.

Occasionally, the president and his advisers seemed to justify killing civilians. "The problem of war is not just a question of who is shooting. For each one who is shooting there are ten working behind him," Ríos observed on one occasion. Continued his press secretary, Word elder Francisco Bianchi: "The guerrillas won over many Indian collaborators. Therefore the Indians were subversives. And how do you fight subversion? Clearly you had to kill Indians because they were collaborating with subversion. And then it would be said that you were killing innocent people. But they weren't innocent. They had sold out to subversion."[53]

From statements such as this, some have concluded that Ríos

was in fact ordering massacres. Yet he tried to avoid repetition of some crimes by reassigning commanders, and Word elders reportedly got into shouting matches with such officers.[54] What is certain is that Ríos participated in the system of circumlocution employed by military bureaucracies to avoid responsibility for their acts.

"It could have happened," Ríos responded to reports of army massacres on one occasion toward the end of his government. "It could have. I say it circumstantially because I can't be sure. I never authorized it. That's the truth."

But in his daily briefings, had he never been informed of such events, even the burning of a village?

"Never," Ríos answered. "They never come into my office to say, 'Today we burned such and such a village.'"

But hadn't the army burned some?

"They might burn," he admitted.

How is it that this information didn't get to you?

"What information? This is all hypothetical. . . . No information came to me. . . . I didn't know about it."[55]

One sign of Ríos Montt's Christian conscience was a vague plea for forgiveness. "We know and understand that we have sinned, that we have abused power," he confessed over the radio after a year in the palace. "What can I do with a second lieutenant who won't accept my order not to kill?"[56] The pathetic nature of this admission suggests what Word elders allowed after their man was overthrown: that he had never really brought the army under control. Not a single army officer was brought to trial under his government. Because the army had never disciplined officers for even the most flagrant crimes against civilians, Ríos and his spiritual advisers generally avoided the issue. If the energy expended on denying the army's crimes had been devoted to stopping them, he might have lasted even less time at the head of the regime than he did.

After the days in the national palace were over, appealing to the realities of power did not prevent Ríos Montt's supporters from continuing to flail the human rights lobby, as if to justify themselves. Didn't the U.S. embassy declare that it had been unable to verify a single incident? Wasn't so and so of Amnesty International a communist? Weren't the refugees making the accusations really guerrillas? What else could the army do when guerrillas had fired on them from the middle of crowded plazas?[57]

As a result, the "smear" of Ríos Montt has passed into evangelical mythology. Convinced that he had been victimized by a well-coordinated misinformation campaign, even Luis Palau and *Christianity Today* lent their weight to rehabilitating his name, turning a dictator into a victim of religious persecution.[58] In March 1984, the deposed Ríos Montt made his North American debut with a tour of the evangelical talk shows. He also addressed enthusiastic meetings of the Full Gospel Businessmen's Fellowship, the National Religious Broadcasters, and the National Association of Evangelicals. According to Gospel Outreach, the visits were intended to break the silence following his overthrow, build ties with top Christian leaders, and prepare an international prophetic ministry for him, maybe even a radio or television show.[59]

The resulting legend appealed to the religious right's wish to perceive Central America as a clean, simple showdown between East and West, freedom and communism, good and evil. When North American evangelicals applauded Ríos Montt, they were celebrating the illusion that counterinsurgency in Central America was a godly struggle against a satanic foe. The selectivity of their perceptions could be astounding. One Christian returned from Guatemala to assure me that the army's abuses had actually been committed by Cuban infiltrators in government uniform. They were all over the country: he knew this for a fact because they had almost arrested him.

As for Guatemalan evangelicals, some maintained that Ríos had been overthrown because the churches had not prayed enough for him; others muttered that maybe God had put him out of office because he deserved it. But for his supporters, Ríos became something of a prophet.[60] Like every prophet, they comforted themselves, his warnings had fallen on deaf ears. Some sinners had repented; many others had not; and under a just and wrathful God, there probably would be worse days ahead. Because God alone gives and takes away authority, the Word Church reasoned, their brother had been removed from office so that he could share the gospel with the world.[61] Christians had "paid more attention to [the massacre reports in] the *New York Times* and the *Washington Post* than to the Word of God," Ríos lamented. "That is a sign of the last days because we didn't believe each other."[62]

The Struggle for Social Responsibility

When the high command threw Ríos Montt out of the palace, it announced that it was saving the government from religious fanatics.[63] The archbishop of Guatemala held an open air mass for the new president and called for reevangelizing the country. Policemen started to patrol evangelical services. Government inspectors paid unwelcome visits. Charismatic churches prophesied seven years of persecution. Hesitantly, various Protestant leaders named themselves the Coordinating Commission of the Evangelical Church (COCIEG) and went to see the new chief of state, General Oscar Mejía Víctores. To their relief, Mejía proved to be even more nervous than they were and apologized for the incidents.

Two years later, evangelical leaders—at least the nonpentecostals with whom I talked—were not shy about criticizing Ríos Montt. True, he had put the church on the map, given brethren a rallying point, and provided them with the security and confidence they needed to evangelize without fear. And yes, his use of the presidency as a pulpit, his weekly homilies to the nation as if it were a big congregation, were perhaps the Lord's design. But some of these men were not even sure that the Word Church was evangelical. At least the Word elders and Ríos never used that term, describing themselves instead as "Christians," to avoid drawing a line between themselves and Catholics.

Ríos Montt's style had offended lots of people, evangelical leaders added, and they were tired of being blamed for his policies. The basic message was fine, they thought, but it should not have gotten mixed up with politics. Whereas Protestants supported the separation of church and state, Ríos Montt's sermonizing on radio and television had given Catholics the idea that he wanted to set up a theocracy.[64]

Evangelical leaders also received the impression that, while Ríos was asking for their support and prayer, he wasn't really listening to them. "Buildings aren't necessary," he responded when told that the army was destroying Protestant chapels in the Ixil area. "At Word we're still meeting in a tent." The two hundred pastors on hand for this remark were not impressed. Because Ríos was usually too busy to meet with church leaders personally, they had to present their problems to Word elders, who were said to have proven "totally impenetrable" to suggestions such as ending Ríos Montt's Sunday homilies to the nation, his value-added tax, or secret tribunals.[65]*

For the president's spiritual advisers were reserved some of the unkindest words. "The people he surrounded himself with were extremists," a member of the nonpentecostal Central American Mission told me. "They were running around saying that they had visions. Visions? Once people think they're having visions, they're getting away from the Bible." The two Word elders who served as presidential secretaries, Francisco Bianchi and Alvaro Contreras, scarcely controlled the government machinery or army, but they did have considerable influence over Ríos. According to Word's shepherding-style doctrine of the covenant or spiritual pact, a new member submits himself not just to Christ but to the church, to the point that one is supposed to consult with elders over any significant decision. When Ríos went to the national palace, he did so under the spiritual authority of the Word church.

That said, the Word elders evidently served as scapegoats. For army officers who considered Ríos their personal chief of state, not anyone else's, his fervent talk of a new Guatemala sounded suspicious. Obviously, it was more convenient to blame advisers from a minority religion than a fellow officer. For the Catholic clergy, the prominence of the Word elders dramatized how they had been elbowed aside by the Guatemalan state, their influence supplanted by that of a North American sect. When army opponents demanded dismissal of the two elders, it was reportedly with the encouragement of evangelicals who recognized the mounting liabilities. "If they go," Ríos responded, "I go."[66]

Crowning the discontent of evangelical leaders was their discovery, after Ríos was gone, that he had granted them less access and fewer favors than his Catholic successor did. "Yes, Ríos would re-

---

*The tribunals sent accused criminals to the firing squad without due process. The executions were closed to the public after the first group of condemned men included an evangelical who sang "I have a crown in the sky" for the television cameras (Pixley 1983:10). According to Amnesty International, some three hundred people detained in the special tribunals remained unaccounted for after Ríos Montt's overthrow. Survivors of the system report systematic torture (Amnesty International 1987:101–12, 123–25).

ceive us, and hear our requests for help, but we never got it except once," states a disgruntled evangelical chieftain—when Ríos generously covered a deficit left over from the Protestant centennial. He did not accept the people they recommended for government jobs. Contrary to legend, few evangelicals populated his administration except for a limited number of Word members. Evangelicals never received the new radio frequency they solicited from him, only from General Mejía, who overthrew him. Finally, it is supposed to have been easier to see Mejía about kidnappings.

This kind of contradictory attitude—blaming Ríos for mixing religion and politics, then for not doing church leaders enough favors—was nothing new, of course. Some pastors were quite accustomed to telling their followers not to have anything to do with politics, then presenting themselves to the latest regime for favors.

Soon after Ríos Montt's fall, the COCIEG coordinating commission sought to return to principles in the first edition of *La Palabra*, an evangelical newspaper cofounded by one of the late president's press secretaries. The evangelical church was nonpolitical, COCIEG declared, and went on to claim that no political commitment had been made to the previous government.[67] Upon reflection, hailing an army general as a vicar of Christ seemed quite out of order. Having broken away from an established church and still feeling threatened by it, many Protestant leaders continued to be church-state separationists; they felt that men of God should stick to the spiritual realm.

Now that evangelicals were recovering from Ríos Montt, the second oldest North American agency in the country, the Central American Mission, decided that it had left a theological vacuum for irresponsible visionaries to fill. It therefore helped organize a pandemoninational Commission on the Social Responsibility of the Church. Building on the September 1983 CONELA meeting on the same subject, the commission laid down what missionaries hoped would become the golden rule: while Christians were to meet their civic responsibilities, they were to do so as individuals. As an institution, the church was to stay out of politics.

Enough nerves still jangled over Ríos that hopes for another born-again president were not in the fore. Still, with evangelicals supposed to total 25 percent of the population, political aspirants wondered whether the Lord might knock on their door. Ríos himself stayed out of the 1985 presidential election: although offered a candidacy by several political parties, they were deemed too small and unrepresentative to carry his spear, aside from possible reluctance by fellow Word elders who were still licking their wounds.

Stepping forward as the newly anointed was Jorge Serrano Elías, a thinker in Guatemala's business lobbies, who had served in Ríos Montt's administration and retained a reputation for honesty. Serrano had gotten saved around 1977 in Guatemala City's charismatic awakening, then gone bankrupt in the 1980–1981 crash like many others in the construction business. Another misfortune soon became an honor: he was forced to leave the country for criticizing the Lucas García regime. Under Ríos Montt, a family tie to a Word elder helped him win appointment as head of the State Council, an advisory office that gave his presidential ambitions a boost. Impressed by Ríos Montt's talk of divine appointment, he is said to have fancied himself a new David to his chief's Saul.

When Serrano first approached the elders of the COCIEG coordinating council in 1984, they told him that the churches were not ready for another evangelical president. Couldn't he wait a few years? Some were unenthusiastic about the congregation to which he belonged, the pentecostal superchurch Elim, which had drawn thousands of members from other denominations with its hypnotic preaching and eerie, electronically amplified speaking in tongues. Under Ríos Montt Serrano made "prophet," one of Elim's half dozen or so who ranked below its maximum leader or "apostle."

To distinguish himself from Ríos, the candidate cited his opposition to his former boss's tax increases and secret tribunals. But to mobilize evangelical voters, he also needed to present himself as a spiritual heir. Serrano therefore adopted something of the same messianic tone, on the need to create a new man and a new Guatemala. Although evangelical churches did not formally endorse him, the campaign clearly hoped to harness them. "This whole question is delicate," a campaign manager admitted, "because it is well established that the church does not participate in politics. This is agreed by all concerned. So church leaders have endorsed Serrano, members have too, but as organizations, no."[68]

Serrano's supporters claimed to organize only outside church walls and confine themselves to civic orientation, by urging brethren to pray, register, and vote with discernment. This was the kind of approach adopted by middle-of-the-road evangelicals in the United States. But Serrano's people also organized prayer breakfasts for pastors of each denomination and, when they asked for prayer for Guatemala, included their candidate. Out in the departments, campaigners told the faithful that, if Serrano failed to win, a terrible persecution would ensue. Skeptics worried that it was Serrano's candidacy which could stir up trouble, by reigniting Catholic fears that evangelism cloaked a drive for political power.[69]

As it turned out, Serrano won 13.8 percent of the November 1985 vote, placing him a respectable but disappointing third.[70] Many of his brethren voted instead for the Christian Democrats, the centrist party furthest to the left on the country's limited aboveground spectrum. Evangelical politicians might fantasize about a block vote of one-quarter of the electorate, but their churches were not the most promising constituency. Politics was just not their forte.

"If this candidacy depended totally on us," an evangelical in the Serrano campaign told me, "we would be totally lost."[71] He was referring to the tradition of condemning politics as sinful, discouraging activism, and even spoiling ballots. "We all have our political perspectives," the presiding elder of the Word Church in Managua explained, "yet the Lord warns us not to be troubled by the woes or wars of this world. If we take our eyes off the principles of the Kingdom, we will be swept off into the wiles of rightest or leftist philosophical persuasions. . . . One thing has to be learned, and that is that hope is not an attribute of any of the Kingdoms of the earth."[72]

Back in Guatemala, meanwhile, this man's colleagues were trying to justify their sudden promotion in a kingdom of this world. Borrowing a scripture from the religious right in the United States, they decided that, like Nehemiah in the Old Testament, they were rebuilding the walls of Jerusalem. But for evangelicals accustomed to think that the world was inevitably getting worse, the idea of building a new, reformed Guatemala took some getting used to.

They had supported Ríos Montt because God had miraculously placed him in charge, not because they had changed their minds about the futility of politics.

Now, in a change from the traditional stance, much of the evangelical leadership was talking about the duty of Christians to get involved. The Latin American Theological Fraternity had been encouraging social engagement for more than a decade. But in Guatemala, some of the same arguments were surfacing among a new social group, evangelical professionals who faced a limited future in a country run by an army. They talked like reformers and were finding a hearing in middle-class congregations, something of a new phenomenon. Among this class of Christians with more than a little to lose was a feeling that, if they didn't pull Guatemala together now, they would lose it completely. And here they were, in the words of Marco Tulio Cajas, "the best organized minority in the nation," with a responsibility to offer an alternative to the squalid prevailing norms.[73]

From this evangelical sector, a number of whose churches worshipped in or near the city's luxury hotels, not a whole lot was heard about social justice.[74] But churchmen had been impressed by the loss of entire Mayan congregations to the guerrillas. Now that the revolutionary movement had failed, Indians were being treated worse than ever. With more of the poor professing to be evangelicals than ever before, social responsibility clearly included doing something for them, forcing evangelical churches into what a Presbyterian missionary called "an interesting political dilemma."[75] Because the army and large landowners seemed to find subversive intent in any scheme that benefitted Indians, conservative evangelicals faced a difficult choice. They could do nothing and risk losing their Indian clienteles; or they could try to help, which would arouse the suspicion of Guatemala's neanderthal ruling class and push evangelicals down the same road as the Catholic Church.

Presbyterian work among the Kekchí Maya illustrates the problem: the Kekchí have a long history of opening up virgin land, to which they have legal rights, only to be forced off by landlords, who use their connections in the capital to obtain title for themselves. Protestantism was introduced by plantation owners, who hoped that the gospel would make their sullen Kekchí workers more reliable. The despot who brought in the Presbyterians considered himself a consecrated Christian even as he partook of haremlike sexual privileges. In the ironic words of a Presbyterian writer, his threat to whip peons for failing to attend the chapels he built led to an "extraordinary revival."

Justice arrived in the late 1960s, in the form of guerrillas who chased the owner out of the area. Ironically, they also cleared the way for an autonomous Kekchí church. Evangelicals multiplied, and the new religion stiffened Kekchí resistance to further expropriation. With political violence sweeping the land, an alarmed pastor from the capital noted that converts were ready to defend themselves by force. How could Kekchí evangelicals be convinced that armed struggle was not necessary?[76] Well, the Presbyterians could help them defend their land through the law. And if that failed, maybe they could help a community or two buy the land in question. But as a newly organized Presbyterian Defense Commission came to the aid of first one community and then two others, disappointed land monopolists accused it of subversion.[77]

According to one source, the 1981–1982 violence in the area (mostly the army's) cost the Presbyterians six of their seventeen Kekchí churches and left more than five hundred widows and a thousand orphans. In August 1982, soldiers arrested a Kekchí pastor serving in Ríos Montt's civil defense patrols and repeatedly tortured him before realizing that they had the wrong man. But now that they had abused the pastor, they could not just let him go. Every week on television, after all, Ríos Montt was claiming that this sort of thing no longer happened.[78*]

Ríos had repeatedly called on such victims to come forward and press charges: he would protect them. After the pastor managed to escape, his colleagues decided to make the incident a test case. A few weeks later, in September 1982, a Christian Reformed mission-

---

*"[The soldiers] say the guerrillas are the killers, but they are the ones who kill," the pastor later reported. "They told me so when I was their prisoner. They said the order comes from General Ríos Montt that they are free to kill whoever they want. They come to 'save,' but they come to kill and cause panic and terror. . . . Many poor people have fled to the mountains in fear. Others are in the mountains because they have been abandoned. Men without children or wives. Women without children and with no one to help them. The army searches for these people in helicopters. They kill them as if they were animals, cutting them into pieces and throwing the pieces into pits. The women are raped by many soldiers" (In Communion, July 1983, p. 3).

ary connected to the plaintiffs was abducted and thrown into the back of a van filthy with vomit and blood. During the interrogation, he was threatened with torture instruments, had a gun put to his head and the trigger pulled. Pressure from the U.S. embassy saved him but not two Indian church workers—Ricardo Pop and Alfonso Macz. A year later, one was reported to have been seen in an underground cell, where he had gone insane and was whimpering to see his wife and children. The church committee trying to protect Kekchí rights was forced to disband, four of its five members fleeing the country.[79] Presbyterian officials decided against trying to find their disappeared church workers. An army officer had informed them that, because the two were guerrillas, excessive concern over their fate would mean that the Presbyterian church was guerrilla, too.*

The toll of pastors and evangelical congregations under Ríos Montt never was reported because churches were afraid to. Let the dead bury the dead was their attitude. Otherwise, one was likely to join them. Yet now that the guerrillas were a distant presence, the main enemy, even for many businessmen, seemed to be the army high command—for its economic incompetence, looting of the national treasury, and brutality. By 1985, the military hierarchy had reached the point of killing spokesmen for the private sector as well as Ríos Montt's brother-in-law, General Sosa Ávila, apparently for consulting with young officers about another change of administration.

Early the next year, under an elected but weak Christian Democrat government, the president of the Evangelical Alliance of Guatemala (AEG) committed an unprecedented act for this conservative organization; he denounced the continued depredations of the army. "The assassination of evangelical leaders is now almost a daily occurrence," Pastor Guillermo Galindo declared. If the Evangelical Alliance did not get a response from the government, it was going

---

*All this blood and tears should have, through the church's land purchase program, provided one Kekchí congregation with titled land. But after the Presbyterians invested sixty thousand quetzals in the mortgage, it turned out that the landowner—the same Manuel de la Cruz who had been driven out by guerrillas in the late 1960s, still a Presbyterian in good standing—had sold it a nonexistent tract. If the church sued Cruz for fraud, he could countersue for the sixty thousand quetzals it still owed him on the mortgage; so the church dropped the matter and lost its money.

to join the human rights protests of the Mutual Support Group, the organization of relatives of the "disappeared."[80]

When the Saints Come Marching In

One Christian skilled at placing adverse events in eschatological perspective was John Carrette, owner of the Pan-American Hotel in downtown Guatemala City and an active member of the Full Gospel Businessmen's Fellowship. Still in his thirties, Carrette had trained as a Green Beret and served as a platoon leader in Vietnam, then had come home to Chuck Smith's Calvary Chapel near Los Angeles, a charismatic superchurch for young people determined to get right with God. Here he imbibed the doctrine of the rapture, the quintessence of evangelical escapism. According to this teaching, let us recall, just before the world ends in the great tribulation, true Christians will be whisked up in the air or "raptured" to be with Christ.

In the late 1970s, Carrette says, he thought that he had his cake and could eat it, too. Not only was he saved and assured of escaping the great tribulation: the tourist boom in Guatemala made his hotel produce profits like a money machine. Then, unexpectedly, communist guerrillas overran the western highlands. The tourist trade evaporated. Bankruptcy loomed. And Carrette felt abandoned by his Lord. What was this Job trip? Now that the world was rushing to perdition, where was the rapture? Why wasn't he being taken up to meet the Lord in the air?

Estranged from the Lord a good six months, one night Carrette was looking down on the lights of Guatemala City when he realized that God was speaking to him. Down there is a great army, the Lord told Carette, but they don't know they're in a war, that they are a great army, or who the enemy is. Who's the army, Lord? Carrette asked. It was not the guerrillas or the Guatemalan army, the Lord told him. It was the church, whose struggle was not against flesh or blood but against the principalities and powers of evil. His job was to stay, the Lord told Carrette, not to be raptured out. His job was to mobilize the church to pray for the overthrow of the devil's government in Central America.

Latin America, in Carrette's view, had been under the dominion of Satan since before the Spanish Conquest. The Indian nature gods had been the devil's hierarchy of authority. True, the light of Christianity had started to shine through the overcast with the arrival of the Catholic Church. But now the radiant beams of Christianity were shining even stronger. This was the reason for the terrible conflict in which Central America found itself today. The preaching of God's word in Catholic as well as Protestant churches was ripping the entire area from the hands of Satan, Carrette believed. It was a contest over who would rule, God or the devil, in a full-fledged spiritual war.

Carrette's wing of the church had taught Christians to pray for each other as the nation went down into the chaos of the great tribulation. The only hope, the church had taught, was the light beyond the grave and God's thousand-year reign on earth—*after* the tribulation. But according to the Bible, Carrette realized, this place Guatemala was the land of milk and honey. It was necessary to pray for the nation. So it was that, in the months preceding Ríos Montt's eruption on the scene, in the darkest days of the Lucas García regime, Carrette began to urge church leaders to pray for Guatemala. In the name of Jesus, he exhorted them, command Satan to leave this country!

The palace coup of March 23, 1982, then, was a miraculous answer to prayer. "What we had done in the Spirit was made visible in the streets," Carrette explained. "Ríos Montt was put in because the church did its job in the spirit. He brought the church together for six to eight months, astounding it into unity and intercession— for a while. Ríos Montt was taken out again because the church didn't do its job of intercession. The church didn't do its job and so the devil was not bound."

Three years later, Carrette felt, the country was going through a time of wrenching, of birth pains. But he was confident that Satan was going to be taken off Guatemala, that Jesus would soon be free to pour out his blessings. Strikes over wages, protests over prices, and corruption in the army high command, Carrette predicted, were about to set off a civil war inside the country's very power structure, in the Guatemalan military. There were all the makings of a real bloodbath. But along with it would come a mighty revival in Guatemala, a revival that would spread throughout Central America. By the end of 1986, he was convinced, the entire region would be on the mend.

"The body count concept rules the evangelical church here," Carrette said. "There's an emphasis on sales, like the commercial chain concept, of putting a McDonald's on every corner. That's the American concept of missions in Latin America. But the Lord is coming back, and he wants more than numbers. The church that is well organized and reports back to Springfield doesn't cut the mustard. He wants us to bind the devil. He wants signs and wonders here in Latin America. Bureaucracies concerned about body counts are not important; spiritual warfare is the thing. We're on the brink of a real transformation. God is going to put his man in. God will heal the economy, the guerrilla situation, the army, everything. The kingdoms of this world have become the kingdoms of Christ. That's Revelation 11:15."[81]

Chapter Eight

Evangelicals in the
Sandinista-Contra War

*"You may think the world has the answer to your problems. But I
tell you Havana doesn't have the answer. Moscow doesn't have the
answer. And Washington doesn't have the answer. Jesus Christ is the
only answer! He alone can change your life and give you peace."*
Evangelist Alberto Mottesi, Managua, January 1984.[1]

If Pastor Fernando were to be believed, he had been delivered out
of Nicaragua trailing miracles behind him. According to this young
peasant preacher, a pentecostal from the northern part of the country, the Sandinista revolution was being turned into a concentration
camp. He had seen Sandinista thugs attack a peaceful revival in Yali
on May 8, 1982, beat up the women, and put acid in the pastor's
eyes. There was just one thing the revolutionaries could not withstand, and that was the power of God. When the Sandinistas sent
informers into church services, the Christians just converted them.
Once when the Sandinistas shot at a believer, the bullet turned
around and hit the man who fired it. Another time, when a security
agent tried to shoot a sister who was preaching, he became stuck to
the floor. Now that same man was a great preacher for the Lord. As
for Pastor Fernando, he had preached in the very battalions of the
Sandinistas. On one occasion, three hundred of them accepted
the Lord, laid down their weapons, and defected. That was why
the Sandinistas wanted him dead or alive: angels had protected him
from their wrath.[2]

Fernando was now a refugee in Costa Rica. His problems with

the Sandinistas had started around July 1981, two years after they led the overthrow of the old regime, when he and his congregation refused to join the militia. To the Sandinistas, that meant refusing to defend the revolution against U.S.-backed counter-revolutionaries. After a long history of confrontations and detentions, Fernando escaped to Costa Rica. But his troubles were not over. As he testified about his experiences in church services, he was interviewed by a U.S. television crew, from the Christian Broadcasting Network, which was using stories like his to build support for the contras. Whether or not Fernando had intended to be part of the Reagan administration's war, now he was. When I interviewed him in July 1985, he was a frightened man who claimed that Sandinista security agents were trailing and threatening him even in exile.

The question of how much of this man's testimony to believe was important because, up and down the hemisphere, Christians were looking to Nicaragua for inspiration or warning. They were looking to the Sandinista revolution because it was supposed to be different. Throughout Latin America, church people had been caught up in revolutionary movements. Now they had come to power with one. Here was a chance for the churches to help build the new society instead of, as usually occurs, becoming a refuge from it.[3] Here was a new kind of laboratory for revolutionary Christianity, a way to prove that a liberated church and a revolutionary state could, in a realistic sort of way, bring the kingdom of God to Latin America.

The Sandinistas encouraged these hopes. They were the first regime in the world to give liberation theology something like official status, as a faith appropriate to their new order. Suddenly, a revolution in an obscure Central American republic was the supreme test for liberation theology. And a cruel one, because when prophets gesture toward the promised land, they tend to be vague about the exact time and place, to avoid disappointing the faithful. But when prophets hail a particular political movement, they stake their credibility on its fate. Welcoming revolutions is especially risky. The Sandinista experiment was a golden opportunity to discredit the alliances between Christians and Marxists, in a social revolution that could turn out like others have before.

The Sandinista National Liberation Front (FSLN) originated in the early 1960s, led by students who saw themselves as the vanguard of the proletariat. Perhaps because that class scarcely existed in Nicaragua, they named themselves after a more traditional figure, General César Augusto Sandino, the Liberal war leader who led the resistance to U.S. occupation in the 1920s and 1930s. Stepping into the Sandino legend, his namesakes mounted dramatic raids on the regime which the U.S. Marines left behind, that of the Somoza family. When entire neighborhoods rose up against the Somoza dictatorship, in 1978–1979, the Sandinistas descended from the hills to provide leadership.

Few question the Sandinista Front's popular support at the July 19, 1979, triumph over the old regime; it had led all social classes to victory over a tyranny of forty years. During that struggle, the FSLN won over much of the country's elite by claiming to have transcended its Marxist-Leninist origins and to be Sandinista, not communist. But in power, its militants did not prove masters of negotiation and compromise. Young and heroic, the survivors of years of conspiracy and gun play, they were not about to hand over the revolution to bourgeoise politicians who would fail to attack Nicaragua's terrible social inequities. Instead, building on their position as vanguard of the revolution, they took full credit for the victory against Somoza and claimed to be the sole representative of the people. Critics they accused of being counter-revolutionaries, while identifying the new revolutionary state, its armed forces, and educational campaigns with their own party apparatus.

Anti-Somoza allies who had expected to take power found themselves sidelined. Soon they were accusing the Sandinistas of totalitarian ambitions. Despite considerable space for dissent, the Sandinista idea of government was indeed centralized. "We always have to go to a commandante to resolve something, because intermediate levels don't have any power of decision," an employee of a pro-Sandinista church agency explained. "The line of the Sandinista Front is what's important, not the opinion of the bases. Democratic centralism is the real model."[4] Suddenly, an old-fashioned family dictatorship, careless and even laissez-faire in its attitude toward much of social life, was replaced by young militants bent on revolutionizing everything. Although the Sandinistas felt that they were bringing social justice to Nicaragua—and in fact managed impressive results in popular organization, land distribution, and social services—their achievements often seemed to entail bringing everything under their personal control. "Commandante" was not just an honorific title.

Once under attack from the United States, of course, the Sandinistas had no choice but to put the country on a war footing. Fighting for their lives against the Reagan administration, they were captive to an old theme in Nicaraguan life, that power comes out of the barrel of a gun. Throughout the nineteenth century it had been peace which interrupted war in Nicaragua, owing to the interminable strife between Conservatives and Liberals. The country became a plaything for foreign interests.[5] In the twentieth century, perhaps only the U.S. Marines and the Somoza dictatorship provoked enough nationalist reaction, enough common feeling among warring elites and their peons, for Nicaragua to be called a nation. Even then no one could expect to take or hold onto power without guns because peaceful alternation between competing blocs was unknown. In a country where losing politicians had the habit of appealing to foreign powers to make their comeback, loyal opposition was an improbable concept. Sedition was more or less inevitable, due not just to the Sandinista Front's drive to monopolize power but to where it knew opponents would go for help, to the United States.

The FSLN's contest with its main religious foe, Archbishop Miguel Obando y Bravo, illustrates the resulting spiral of distrust, violence, and self-fulfilling prophecy. As head of the Catholic Church, the archbishop had occasionally aided the Sandinistas during the struggle against Somoza. But at the fall of the old regime, he also tried to prevent the Sandinistas from taking power, by supporting a more conservative alternative. In the belief that a split in the church was inevitable,[6] the Sandinistas took a step they came to regret; they began to denounce the counter-revolutionary church of the rich, of Archbishop Obando y Bravo. The real Christians, they proclaimed, were to be found in that part of the church which supported the revolution, the church of the poor.

To Obando, this kind of language proved that the Sandinistas were not just consolidating a one-party state. As a jealous defender of the Catholic hierarchy's prerogatives, he feared that they were also setting up their own "popular church" in order to "confiscate" religion,[7] for an inexorable transition to a Marxist-Leninist totalitarian society. Meanwhile, his own behavior confirmed Sandinista suspicions of church sedition. Although the archbishop claimed to be neutral and working for reconciliation, he took every opportunity to attack the Sandinistas, pointedly refrained from condemning the contras, and took no exception to U.S. aid to them. The contras, meanwhile, hailed him as their spiritual leader and recruited members of his clergy.[8] Looking back on the sequence of events, it is as if Obando and the Sandinistas each fashioned their own nemesis out of the accumulated treachery of Nicaraguan history and North American intervention.

The main contra group, the U.S.-backed Nicaraguan Democratic Force (FDN), came to include politicians, businessmen, and peasants alienated by the Sandinista process. But the Reagan administration played such a prominent role in organizing, financing, and periodically rearranging the FDN that it seemed little more than a huge, poorly controlled CIA front. The leaders who counted—the military commanders who survived every U.S.-imposed shakeup—were from the National Guard of the old regime. Their behavior made the Sandinistas look like models of restraint. During a March 1983 trip with FDN forces into Nicaragua, journalist Christopher Dickey saw men pulling Bibles out of their knapsacks to read. At night, their former National Guard commanders admitted killing their prisoners.[9]

Back in the United States, the Reagan administration and the religious right baptized the FDN as "Christian freedom fighters" and projected all their misdeeds onto the Sandinistas. If the contras were accused of atrocities, then it must be communist propaganda. Maybe the Sandinistas were dressing up in FDN uniforms and, just to discredit the freedom fighters, committing the atrocities themselves.[10] Right-wing evangelicals supporting the contra war described the Sandinista revolution as a furnace of religious persecution. They claimed that pastors were being mutilated for their faith in front of congregations, believers locked into churches and burned to death, Christian ministers murdered by the thousand[11]—at a time when there were only sixteen hundred pastors in the entire country.

Nicaraguan evangelicals were of special importance in the propaganda war. Thought to number 15 percent of the population, without centralized leadership or a tradition of political activism, they were not a cohesive force in the same sense as Archbishop Obando's wing of the Catholic Church. But many were unenthusiastic about the revolution and professed neutrality in the contra war, forcing the Sandinistas to question their loyalty. Many also had institutional ties with North American evangelicals, that is, with supporters of a U.S. president waging war against their own government. For the same North Americans, they were the single most important index of the revolution's popular support and legitimacy—or lack thereof.[12] Given their highly charged position, evangelicals became key figures in the claims and counterclaims of ideological warfare: while the Sandinistas applied the more cooperative to the task of defending the revolution's image, the Reagan administration used them to justify a war.

To persuade North American churchgoers to support military intervention, Washington needed to make Nicaragua conform to stereotypes of the communist state. To accomplish that, it had to show that the Sandinistas were guilty of religious persecution. But the only way to produce much evidence was to goad the Sandinistas into taking harsher security measures. Then, when the Sandinistas suspected evangelicals of counter-revolutionary ties, the Reagan administration could rail at them for persecuting Christians. According to Open Doors with Brother Andrew, Central American evangelicals were caught in a "crossfire" between right and left.[13] But the Reagan administration seemed to be using Nicaraguan evangelicals to direct a "crossfire" at another government. Suffering in rough proportion to U.S.-backed attacks on the Sandinistas, Nicaraguan evangelicals were being used to polarize the situation. By presenting Nicaraguan evangelicals as victims of religious persecution, the religious right was setting them up for real persecution, in a self-fulfilling prophecy.

To look carefully at evangelicals in the Sandinista-contra war, this chapter will avoid reducing their situation to monolithic conceptions of left and right. For me at least, that requires a painful step: leaving open questions such as responsibility for the civil war bleeding Nicaragua in the 1980s. Did the Reagan administration alone launch the counter-revolution, or had it also been generated by the Sandinistas' heavy hand? Were the Sandinistas remarkably flexible, pragmatic revolutionaries who, when they cracked down on their domestic opponents, were simply reacting to a war situation? Or were they thinly disguised Marxist-Leninists erecting a police state?

Except in the broadsides hurled by the Sandinistas and the Reagan administration, the answers to these questions were not simple. Answers depended so much on contradictory testimonies, on events, on how the different factions responded to and shaped each other in an endless series of polarizing reactions. Answers also depended so much on personal experiences. My own point of view was shaped partly by a security crackdown in late 1985, when the Sandinistas arrested the conservative wing of evangelical leadership in the capital. Included in the mostly brief detentions were five men who, a few months before, had helped me understand the viewpoint of evangelicals opposed to Sandinista rule.

One detained pastor had invited me along on his confrontations with Sandinista bureaucrats. Twice he had also taken me to the U.S. embassy, where he was in the habit of trading gossip with a member of the political section. My notes of these visits do not record anything of great significance. But in a war situation, Sandinista security agents were forced to draw their own conclusions. Here was an evangelical leader providing information to a hostile foreign power. As to be expected, the pastor's contacts with the embassy came up during his interrogation, as did his relationship to me. Wasn't I his CIA contact? As to how these events influenced what follows, readers will have to judge for themselves.

The Sandinista-Evangelical Courtship

Protestants did not suffer a great deal at the hands of the Somoza dictatorship (1932–1979). "We're not going to let anyone bother the evangelicals," a pastor recalls one of the regime's National Guardsmen saying as he threw a drunk out of church. "If everyone was an evangelical," the guardsman remarked, "we would sleep better at night." Apparently fitting into the Somoza political order was a group that later would be attacked for supporting the Sandinistas, the Evangelical Committee for Aid to Development (CEPAD). A service agency claiming most Protestant denominations as members, CEPAD got its start coordinating foreign relief after the 1972 Managua earthquake.

In its first years, the group did little that could be described as revolutionary. On one occasion, it asked President Anastasio Somoza to investigate the crimes of his National Guard against pentecostals in a guerrilla zone. To get political prisoners out of Nicaragua, it became adept at bribing the dictator's officials.[14] As the Somoza regime reacted to Sandinista attacks by butchering young people, CEPAD's funding sources—ecumenical bodies in North America and Europe—wondered why it was not taking a public stand against the dictatorship.[15]

Just like other Nicaraguans, however, evangelicals were alienated by Somoza's reprisals. Some broke with the teaching of their North American mentors that they needed to obey the government because it was ordained by God. As the fighting escalated, evangelicals churches became places of refuge, and CEPAD distributed emergency supplies which, intentionally or not, helped sustain the insurrection.[16] Numerous evangelical youth joined the final street battles.[17]

Relief at having survived the carnage released long-suppressed hopes for social change. Perhaps feeling guilty for having bent the knee to Somoza, many Protestant church leaders swung left and seemed more enthusiastic about the new order than the Catholic hierarchy did. In October 1979, CEPAD sponsored a meeting at which five hundred pastors thanked God for the Sandinista National Liberation Front and pledged to join its neighborhood Sandinista Defense Committees.[18] They hoped that support for the government would prevent it from turning sharply to the left, for their revolutionary gestures were tinged with anxiety. Fearful that the days of religious freedom were numbered, many churches planned campaigns to take advantage of it while they could, producing a surge in evangelism.[19]

Perhaps the strangest courtship during the first year of the revolution was between the senior Sandinista commandante and the Full Gospel Businessmen's Fellowship. The Fellowship was a charismatic boosters' club started by a wealthy Armenian-American dairy processor, Demos Shakarian, in Los Angeles in 1951. Thirty years later it had 2,700 chapters at home and abroad, making it probably the most widespread interdenominational network in the pentecostal-charismatic world. The idea was to draw men who didn't like to go to church into a male setting, then expose them to the warmth of fellowship and repentance in the Holy Spirit. Rotary club-style meetings were organized around powerful testimonies by reformed sinners—tax chiselers, drug pushers, motorcycle outlaws, combat veterans—who told how the Lord had set them straight. Small businessmen, many of them from the Assemblies of God,[20] made up the bulk of members.

The bulk were also the kind of self-made men who try not to discuss liberals in polite company. But Demos Shakarian wanted to keep the door open to everyone, even Fidel Castro. In 1974, he was invited to the Vatican and commended for his group's role in renewing the faith of millions of charismatic Catholics. South of the border, where the Fellowship began to organize chapters in the mid-1970s, it made other daring alliances, with a particular vision for witnessing to heads of state.[21]*

For a time in Nicaragua, the Fellowship thought it had acquired Tomás Borge, the Sandinista interior minister. Borge's interest dated to border clashes with Honduras, in December 1979, when the Fellowship arranged a parley between the leaders of the two countries. The commandante became an enthusiastic participant in religious functions, talked about his "personal experience with Christ," and, for the Nicaraguan literacy crusade, asked the Fellowship to provide 800,000 copies of the New Testament.[22] Afterward, like junta president Daniel Ortega, Borge continued to attend private Bible studies, a participant in which claimed that, while Borge remained a paradoxical case, Ortega at least was a genuine, God-fearing Christian. With friends like that, pro-Sandinista evangelicals could claim to be exorcising the communist demon.

Subsequent events were too much for Full Gospel's headquarters in the United States, however. Despite the rhetoric of fellowship, its impressive roster of military officers and Pentagon contractors, early Reagan backers and investors in religious right television[23] were not about to tolerate a ministry to Sandinista commandantes, for it contradicted their identification of the Reagan administration's policies with God. Succumbing to the pressure, De-

---

*On an expedition to Guyana in November 1978, two Texan businessmen converted the country's leading criminal defense lawyer, Sir Lionel Luckhoo. An adviser to Guyanese prime minister Forbes Burnham, the inimitable Sir Lionel was said to have defended 229 accused murderers without losing a case. At the time, he happened to be defending a Christian minister from California against a couple trying to regain custody of their child. The reverend's name was Jim Jones, and he was holding the child at a place called Jonestown. Following the mass suicide and massacre later that month, the repentant Sir Lionel persuaded his friend the prime minister to hold a state dinner with the Full Gospel Fellowship. Carried away by moving testimonies, the avowedly socialist Burnham declared for Christ. Local evangelicals living under his rule "expressed doubts" (*Christianity Today*, March 7, 1980, pp. 48–52).

mos Shakarian claimed that he had been hoodwinked. The Texan businessmen who had organized the banquets left Full Gospel and tried to carry on by themselves, in a more and more difficult environment.[24] It was hard for everyone to be brothers in Christ when, as minister of interior, Borge's job included defending the Sandinista revolution from its enemies, who were starting to be bank-rolled by the Central Intelligence Agency.

Just as it was hard for the Sandinistas to distinguish CIA assets from opponents who were simply exercising their right to dissent, it was hard to discern a Christian transformation in the Sandinista security apparatus. In particular, what Borge called "divine mobs" did not seem very Christian. These were crowds of demonstrators who, in their harassment of opposition figures, claimed to represent Sandinista mass organizations and occasionally even Christian base communities.

Such attacks occurred at an early date, before the country was on a war footing. One took place during "Nicaragua '81," a nationwide Assemblies of God effort. According to a refugee pastor I interviewed four years later, the April 1981 campaign in Estelí was being held with the permission of Commandante Christian Pichardo when, after several nights of enthusiastic revival, it was attacked by a mob of young men hurling bricks and slashing people with broken bottles. When the Sandinista police finally interrupted the melee, they did arrest those attackers who had not been carted off to the hospital. But the prisoners never made it to jail, apparently because they were immediately set free. When the Assemblies tried to pursue the matter, the authorities showed more interest in questioning their motives than in finding the hoodlums.[25]

Exactly who was responsible for such incidents is unclear. Possibly party militants or Sandinista youth were acting on their own, contrary to the wishes of Sandinista administrators. But according to a Sandinista defector presented by the Reagan administration in Washington, the mobs were actually organized by state security officers in the Interior Ministry.[26] The issue, in any case, was how to handle opposition to the revolutionary process. Evangelicals were far from the only group to manifest unease over the direction taken by the Sandinistas. But as a religious minority, they were easy to single out, and some were starting to react against revolutionary regimentation in visible ways.

One of the first innovations to upset many pastors were the San-

dinista Defense Committees (CDS), which extended Sandinista administration and vigilance down to the level of every neighborhood. People with objections to how the Sandinistas were running
things began to feel that they were being watched and controlled.
From 1980 on, a letter from the CDS on one's block was increasingly necessary to get a government job.

Numerous pastors also began to fear that the Sandinistas were
draining away their authority and followings. They were especially
alarmed by the new Sandinista organizations, which were turning
some of their youth into political militants. The 1980 literacy crusade, which sent students into the countryside to tutor peasants
and brought many of them back spouting slogans, stirred up deep
feelings. One church supervisor, evidently upset by women's liberation, went so far as to call the literacy crusade public prostitution. The seemingly noble effort had a dual purpose, he claimed, to
break up families and encourage sexual license.[27]

Clearly, conservatives were frightened by the Sandinista campaign to inculcate Nicaraguans with revolutionary ideology. In reaction, they insisted that the church of Jesus Christ was apolitical
and neutral. They resisted the idea of volunteering to pick cotton
or coffee, of identifying with the Sandinista Front, or even of denouncing U.S.-backed counter-revolutionaries. Instead, they said,
their job was to preach the gospel. "We haven't made any declaration against the CIA or the contras because the situation is so mixed
up," a leader of a conservative pastor's association told me in 1985.
"Everyone is calling for an end to the war anyway. If the evangelical
church calls for an end to hate and war, we can be accused of placing
ourselves on the side of the revolution. If we don't say anything,
then we're accused of being with the contras. If evangelicals help
with the cotton and coffee harvests, then the newspapers say that
we support the revolution. If not, then you're a contra. So if you
participate you're manipulated, and if you don't you're in trouble
too. Our mission is clear and specific—it's spiritual, that Jesus
Christ is the only answer. We know that this isn't the answer people
want to hear, but this is what we believe."[28]

The first revivalist whom the Sandinistas prevented from entering the country was a North American, Morris Cerrullo, in May
1981. In the words of Brother Cerrullo, at his miracle crusades the
hands of thousands reached up toward heaven. The deaf began to

hear, cripples rose out of their wheelchairs, and miracles exploded beyond counting. His 1981 journey of love through Central America had rocked governments and shaken nations, Cerrullo reported. In Costa Rica, the prayers of his crusade had been responsible for the government breaking ties with Cuba. Through prayer and "God's army"—the local evangelists he trained—Brother Cerrullo vowed to reverse the Satanic communist tide.

As the language suggests, Cerrullo was not the most diplomatic of evangelists. In Argentina, he was proud to say, his sensational tactics had landed him in jail three times.[29] But in Nicaragua, the authorities didn't even let him in. There Cerrullo's idea of advance work was to have pastors informed that he would liberate the country from the demons which had taken possession of it. The Sandinistas interpreted this as a reference to themselves. "You're talking to a demon," Tomás Borge protested to an evangelical trying to intercede for the faith healer. Cerrullo would arrive in his private jet, rake in money from the Managua poor, then use it to buy gasoline for his jet, and take off again, Borge said.[30]

Conservative evangelicals were also alarmed by the departure of some of the established missions, squeezed out by new rules and pressures. One was Compassion International, the child sponsorship agency: when the Sandinistas ruled against conditioning aid on religious instruction, it preferred to close shop.[31] Other departures included two Southern Baptist couples, whom the Nicaraguan Baptist Convention asked to leave in April 1982, and the Central American Mission, which two months later ended eighty-two years of work in the country.[32]

Throughout, the Sandinistas were developing an acute sensitivity to religious language that expressed opposition to their rule. "Thou shalt not kill thy brother" might seem like an unimpeachable injunction, but it could also be used to tell evangelicals not to join the national defense effort.[33] When men of God attributed the floods of early 1982 to divine wrath, and slogans such as "Christ is coming" proliferated on walls, the Sandinistas suspected that CIA-inspired propagandists were at work.[34] "Christ is coming," a Sandinista supporter argued, "is threatening and lying . . . in direct opposition to the Christ that has already arrived in Nicaragua with . . . the revolutionary triumph."[35] It is said to have been Interior Minister Tomás Borge who decided that the slogan "Christ is coming" was intended to mean "the contras are coming." He was correct that the contras were coming.

The Miskitos

Sandinista distrust of evangelicals was fed by events on the Atlantic Coast. Cut off from the rest of the country by mountains and jungle, the Atlantic Coast was incorporated into Nicaragua only at a late date. Even then, communication with the United States was easier than with the government in Managua. Much of the population were Amerindians and Caribbean blacks, or Creoles. They spoke more English than Spanish and tended to regard Latins from the Pacific Coast as colonizers. From the beginning, the Sandinistas worried about the region's separatist tendencies: here, they felt, was a contradiction that enemies of the revolution were sure to exploit.

The Creoles were the first to protest, in October 1980, against economic mismanagement and an influx of Cuban technicians. A number of the sixty-five people arrested were Protestant church leaders, and at first Interior Minister Tomás Borge called it a sectarian conspiracy.[36] Although he soon backed off, Protestant churches were such a fixture on the Atlantic Coast that they were likely to be involved in any significant event. The Moravian denomination, introduced by German missionaries in the nineteenth century, had become the main authority structure in remote areas. Soon further equations between Protestantism and counter-revolution were being produced, by a collision between Sandinista administration and autonomy drives by the main native group, some hundred thousand Miskito Indians.

The resulting Indian war was a trial not only of Sandinista behavior toward Protestants but of the Latin American left's attitudes toward native people. Throughout Latin America, Amerindian civil rights movements have usually found their allies on the left. But these alliances have been fraught with tension. Because Indians have always suffered discrimination, they tend to organize along ethnic lines and insist on some kind of autonomy from Latin-run organizations. Most of the left distrusts ethnic appeals, however, due to the potential for dividing its own class-based organizations along racial lines. In the wake of lengthy theoretical discussion of this contradiction, the Sandinistas were among the first Latin American Marxists to have the chance to overcome it. By all accounts, including their own, they failed. The most generous assessment was that they were learning the hard way.

To guard against North American meddling, the Sandinistas wished to knit the Atlantic Coast into their administrative structure along the same lines as the rest of the country. That is, they wanted to organize Protestant English-speakers into class-based "mass" or "popular" organizations under their own party loyalists, most of them Hispanic. Only reluctantly did the Sandinistas bow to Miskito sentiments by accepting an ethnic-based association, MISURASATA.[37] When the Sandinistas launched the 1980 literacy crusade in Spanish, the new organization led a boycott until Miskito and English were added. By organizing against the ruling party's alien bureaucrats, MISURASATA quickly outstripped their influence.

When the Sandinista Front decided to bypass the native organization as ungovernable, disagreement over land rights led to war.[38] At issue were the seemingly empty spaces of eastern Nicaragua, which the Sandinistas wished to open up for colonization and production and for which MISURASATA was preparing a sweeping land claim. MISURASATA was also claiming subsoil mineral rights, which in Latin America, unlike the United States, belong to the state. Its game plan seems to have been inspired by contacts with the Native American movement in the United States, where huge claims based on eighteenth- and nineteenth-century treaties serve as bargaining chips for more immediate goals. But to the Sandinistas, such tactics smacked of separatism. In February 1981, following MISURASATA's decision to organize mass demonstrations to claim 31 percent of Nicaraguan territory, the Sandinistas arrested all the organization's leaders. Four Miskitos and four soldiers were killed when a patrol tried to arrest a MISURASATA figure during a church service at Prinzapolka. The Miskito population rose up in civil disobedience, the Sandinistas responded with force, and the first wave of refugees—young political activists—crossed over into neighboring Honduras.[39]

This is the chain of events cited by anti-Sandinistas to show that the Miskito insurrection was indigenous, the product of Sandinista repression rather than counter-revolutionary plotting. Ordinarily, however, eight deaths do not lead to war. To understand how they did, we must bring the external forces seeking to overthrow the Sandinistas into the picture. The central figure here was one of the arrested MISURASATA leaders, Steadman Fagoth, who had been released on condition that he calm down his agitated followers, then go study in Bulgaria. Instead, the impetuous Fagoth escaped to Honduras, where he joined forces with the Somoza supporters being reorganized by Washington. Over their radio station, he began accusing the Sandinista revolution of genocide; the charges were untrue but many Miskito believed them. Soon he was being touted as the U.S. government's best chance to get rid of the Sandinistas.[40]

In the United States, the religious right lionized Fagoth as a Christian freedom fighter. Meanwhile, his murders of fellow Miskitos were alienating other insurgents, to the point that his own organization disowned him. Fagoth may have been on the payroll of the U.S. government at an early date. According to another Atlantic Coast dissident jailed by the Sandinistas, in March 1980 he was approached by a North American who offered him $100,000 in a briefcase to turn his organization into a front for separatists. After turning down the offer, this Nicaraguan claims, one of Fagoth's associates told him that Fagoth had accepted the money.[41]

By November 1981, in any case, the contras of the Nicaraguan Democratic Force and their Miskito allies were financed by the Central Intelligence Agency.[42] In anticipation of just that, the Sandinistas had continued to take a hard line with the remaining MISURASATA leadership, most of the rest of whom also left for Honduras. In December 1981, raids from Honduras took the lives of sixty Nicaraguan soldiers and civilians. The Sandinistas denounced the attackers as former Somoza National Guardsmen of the FDN: actually, they seem to have been Miskito recruits who became disgusted with the FDN, escaped, and went into action on their own.[43] Interpreting the raids as a CIA plan, the Sandinistas evacuated eighty-five hundred Miskitos from forty-two villages along the border to resettlement camps in the interior. To deny crops, animals, and shelter to the enemy, the Sandinista forces destroyed everything, including village churches. The evacuees had not been consulted beforehand, and even more than that number fled to Honduras, from which Miskito insurgents redoubled their attacks.

The Taking of the Temples

Among the Miskitos who fled the country were two dozen Moravian pastors. In Honduras, these men applied their spiritual authority and organizational experience to help Steadman Fagoth lead an armed insurrection. With most Sandinistas from another region, culture, and religion, this kind of provocation made it easy to stereotype evangelicals as traitors to their country. In March 1982, the FSLN's newspaper *Barricada* denounced the "invasion of the sects."[44]* That same month, the war started in the north with the FDN blowing up two important bridges, and the Sandinistas declared their first state of emergency.

In Chinandega, Catholic catechists claimed that relatives of former National Guardsmen were pretending to be evangelical pastors, to undermine resistance to counter-revolutionary raids. First these wolves in sheep's clothing told people not to join the Sandinista militias, the report went; then former National Guardsmen came to torture and kill.[45] Sometimes the preaching and the attack were said to be led by the same men. "An enormous quantity of ex-National Guardsmen are now evangelical pastors," Commandante Luis Carrión declared, without evidence. For popular antipathy toward the revolution he blamed religious sects.[46] Tomás Borge denounced the Jehovah's Witnesses, Mormons, and Seventh Day Adventists, for allegedly receiving funds from the CIA.[47]

As Sandinista rhetoric escalated, churches were vandalized and their members threatened by mobs. A few days after Borge denounced the "ninety-nine sects" that supposedly had invaded the country, the Sandinista Defense Committees of a Managua barrio occupied three temples belonging to the Jehovah's Witnesses, Church of God, and Assemblies of God. According to *Barricada*, an Assemblies pastor had made the mistake of telling the local CDS chief to take a complaint about a loud worship service to the devil.[48] Nervously, the Evangelical Committee for Aid to Development (CEPAD) tried to enlighten commandantes on the difference between its member denominations and "sects." It persuaded them to

*Because CEPAD surveys show a 1978–1981 increase of only ten new groups, half of them splits from existing ones, perhaps *Barricada* was misinterpreting stepped-up evangelism by established churches.

return the Assemblies and Church of God buildings.[49] Among the Adventists, unfortunately, a mentally unbalanced pastor's assistant chose this moment to dynamite a power pylon, providing the newspapers with what seemed a clear case of counter-revolutionary sabotage.[50]

When Sandinista Defense Committees seized more than twenty Adventist, Mormon, and Witness churches on August 9, the Sandinistas claimed that no one in their own command structure had been responsible. Instead, they said, the popular masses had been reacting to the theological backwardness of the groups in question.[51] But the truth seems to have been otherwise. CDS barrio chiefs and neighbors, some of them embarrassed by the seizures, told evangelicals that the order had come from above, apparently CDS commander Leticia Herrera, who worked next door to one of the choicest buildings seized.[52]

According to a Baptist missionary who participated in the ensuing CEPAD-arranged dialogues, the Sandinistas required a great deal of education. They had a hard time distinguishing between evangelical organizations hostile to the revolution and those that were not.[53] As commandantes and church people tried to establish a mutually acceptable distinction between counter-revolutionary activity and propagating the gospel, junta president Daniel Ortega admitted that seizing churches had not been a correct revolutionary attitude.[54] Commandante Bayardo Arce admonished CDS coordinators to refrain from harassing, imposing voluntary tasks upon, seizing the property of, or withholding sugar ration coupons from citizens professing nonrevolutionary ideologies.[55]

Adventist properties—nine churches plus an office building—were returned minus their archives and a safe containing several thousand dollars. Three of the six Mormon churches seized were returned that same year, plus a fourth much later. In 1985, two Mormon churches and three lots were still in Sandinista hands. "We're practically the only church that isn't resisting military conscription," a law-abiding Mormon official puzzled. One reason that the church failed to recover property was probably that it had declined to negotiate through CEPAD, on the Mormon principle of not working with other religious organizations. Jehovah's Witnesses were the biggest losers: apparently none of their buildings were returned. In 1985, a member recalled the location of seventeen kingdom halls taken by mobs or closed. I found four more locations listed in press reports. According to a couple who showed me the deed to the unpretentious structure which had been their own kingdom hall, neighborhood authorities had informed them that it would not be returned because the seizure had been a political act, not a religious or legal one. A lawyer would cost too much, the Witness couple told me; besides, it was against their principles to file suit. Even where kingdom halls were still in the hands of Witnesses, they usually confined themselves to small house meetings.[56]

The Popular Church

The seizure of a few dozen buildings cost the Sandinistas dearly, at home and abroad, because it contradicted their claim to respect religious freedom. Part of the blame, conservative evangelicals said, belonged to church leaders who supported the revolution, men who were worshipping the Sandinistas rather than God and setting up an apostate, separatist "popular church." That expression was avoided by some pro-Sandinista Christians: they referred to themselves as the revolutionary wing of the church and denied any intention of dividing it.

The revolutionary church could be traced to the long years of conspiratorial organizing against the Somoza dictatorship, when the Sandinistas wished to have religious fronts for the admirable cover they provided.[57] Opposition politics was necessarily conspiratorial at that time, it must be remembered. Although the Sandinistas incorporated Christians into their ranks, they may not have achieved quite the Christian-Marxist synthesis sometimes claimed. Even if their popular base maintained a vital, traditional faith, this attribute appeared to thin out higher in the FSLN hierarchy.[58]

Once the Sandinistas took power, their church allies organized various study centers and professional organizations—the Antonio Valdivieso Ecumenical Center, the National Association of Evangelical Pastors of Nicaragua (ANPEN), the Evangelical Commission for the Promotion of Social Responsibility (CEPRES), and the Ecumenical Axis—to defend the revolution against religious backlash at home and abroad.

On the Catholic side, the Sandinista wing of the church could claim a certain number of ecclesiastical base communities. But base leaders tended to move onto wider responsibilities in the Sandinista political apparatus, and some communities declined.[59] As for the Catholic clergy, as few as 15 to 25 percent supported the revolution.[60] That left, as visible head of the popular church, the various organizations in Managua. Staffed by church professionals, they operated on grants from ecumenical bodies in Western Europe and North America. Besides representing Nicaragua in the exterior, they received delegations from abroad, tried to organize Christians to support the revolution, and quoted Scripture against its enemies.

Anti-Sandinista "seminars" held outside the country, especially in Costa Rica, were one challenge these groups faced.[61] The events were organized by U.S.-based religious organizations, often with political axes to grind, such as Morris Cerrullo World Evangelism and Trans World Missions. In the case of the Christian Anti-Communism Crusade, its traveling pastoral teams specialized in McCarthyist displays for Central American security forces as well as church audiences.[62] But the most worrisome conferences were for Nicaraguan pastors, invited out of the country temporarily to strengthen their Christian fortitude. In the case of Open Doors with Brother Andrew, its "Victory Seminars" in Costa Rica focused on how to ensure the survival of the church under communist persecution. That led to talk about setting up underground churches,[63] which the Sandinistas interpreted as an attempt to set up a political underground.

Tangled in the question of the seminars was another scheme run from Costa Rica, to supplement the inflation-ravaged salaries of Nicaraguan pastors. Now that the missions had pulled out and left pastors to their own devices, were decades of work going to be ruined by allowing hardship to divert them from their spiritual responsibilities?[64] In 1983 six hundred pastors—about 40 percent of the country's total—were on the dole from across the border. Although the amount of money was small—$5,000 a month—even divided six hundred ways it could double a pastor's salary. The missionary administering the program from Costa Rica, John Kessler, was frank about his anticommunist views but felt unable to disclose the source of the money, arousing further suspicion.[65]

At home in Nicaragua, the pro-Sandinista church faced an elusive foe. Conservatives were expressing their disapproval of the FSLN's rule in apocalyptic language and calls for repentance. Meanwhile, based on Marxist thinking about ideology and class polarization, revolutionary Christians were convinced that no act or group was really politically neutral. Therefore, failing to support the revolution meant opposing it. What might seem spiritual escapism, they began to argue, was actually an attempt to stab the revolution in the back. To prove it, they pointed to a "hidden discourse" lurking behind the otherworldly language of conservatives.

Some conservative teachings—"the true Christian is not to the left or the right, but in the center with Jesus Christ"—carried a clear enough message. Conservatives also preached that "you can't serve two masters," that is, the revolution and Christ. Having always told their flocks to stay apart from "the world," now they were extending the meaning of "world" from smoking, drinking, and other vices to Sandinismo. But if the Sandinistas were so worldly, why hadn't conservatives ever condemned the worldliness of the Somoza dictatorship?[66]

For such attitudes, Sandinista supporters blamed the influence of North American theological training. It was true that, of the eighteen hundred evangelical congregations in Nicaragua, one thousand to fifteen hundred were thought to be affiliated in some way with the National Association of Evangelicals in the United States.[67] Decades of anticommunist indoctrination had laid a certain foundation.

But the Sandinista Front's militant episodes seemed to be leaving conservatives with little choice but to oppose the revolution. According to one pastor, when he criticized television for taking people's time away from the Lord, the authorities told him that he was preaching against the state broadcasting network and its revolutionary programming.[68] Now if a pastor couldn't fulminate against the idiot box, what could he preach against? This was how attacks on the hidden counter-revolutionary discourse could seem to turn into attacks on evangelism itself. If evangelicals insisted on a spiritual dimension apart from politics and that was inevitably escapist, as Sandinista militants seemed to argue, then wasn't traditional soul-saving inherently counter-revolutionary?

In the eyes of conservative evangelicals, revolutionary Christians were encouraging the Sandinistas to regard them as a threat and leaving them less and less room to practice their faith. "This is the place to study liberation theology," a conservative said a few months before fleeing the country. "Because here it is not just a plan, here it has been carried out. What have its people turned out to be? They've turned out to be security agents for the government."

"The dispute is over what is a Christian," he continued. "They define it in detail in their documents. If you don't fit, you are a sect, alienating, diversionist. Nowadays, to say that you are Sandinista in an evangelical church is almost to say that you're not a Christian. Five years ago, a Sandinista soldier in church was just like a soldier belonging to any army in church. But after the harassment began in 1981, not any longer."[69]

Patriotic Military Service

Even if Sandinista Christians were as wise as serpents and as gentle as doves, the hard realities of revolution and counter-revolution were placing them in a difficult, unpopular position. Inflation, rationing, and the collapse of purchasing power were not the only reasons evangelicals were going sour on the revolution. There was also Patriotic Military Service—the draft. Dodging the draft had been a real survival skill in nineteenth-century Nicaragua, as political rivals depopulated the countryside of males to fight their interminable civil wars. In the 1850s, the American filibuster William Walker is said to have attained a brief popularity among the poor because, unlike local war leaders, he took only volunteers.[70] The grievance went dormant under the Somozas, who also relied on volunteers. But with the military necessities of the Sandinista revolution, talk of pacifism flooded the churches.

It was easy to detect a hypocritical note in this moral awakening. Only a few of the smaller Protestant denominations in Latin America had ever troubled themselves over the morality of war. Consistent pacifists—opponents to all violence—were as rare as Buddhists. Now conservatives sprouted an antiwar conscience, using scriptures such as "thou shalt not kill" to tell their young men not to submit to Sandinista military service and ostracize those who did.[71] Two groups traditionally committed to pacifism were the first to suffer from this theological twist. In March 1982, twenty-five Mennonite missionaries were given twenty-four hours to leave the country before being reprieved at the airport.[72] Actually deported were nine foreign Jehovah's Witnesses, for endangering national defense.[73]

At issue in 1981–1982 were the Sandinista militias. These were supposed to be voluntary in nature. But if the local Sandinista Front decided that it needed to build up forces against contra attacks, it brought pressure to bear, as did community opinion. According to an American Baptist missionary, Sheila Heneise, talk about the sinfulness of carrying a rifle died down as contra atrocities increased. But then, when an all-inclusive draft was declared in September 1983, pacifist sentiment rolled forward. Opposition to the draft could not be blamed on right-wing North American missionaries, Heneise believed, because the same feelings were strong in churches without them.[74] For a short time, there were case-by-case exemptions for conscientious objectors. But so many stepped forward that the exemptions were restricted to seminary students, leading to a boom in seminary enrollment. For those not lucky enough to serve God in this manner, the last resort was alternative service within the army—if that could be worked out with local commanders, some of whom did not like the idea. Conservative pastors who detested the Sandinistas, men with a high opinion of the United States, stood by helplessly as their young men marched off in Sandinista uniform to be killed by U.S.-supported forces.

"No, we're not pacifists," an Assembly of God leader told me. So if his church did not object to military conscription in El Salvador, Honduras, and Guatemala, then why here? "Because it's for an ideological war . . . to impose communism," he explained. The objection was "to the ideology, not to military service in itself." According to the Sandinistas, such pastors were responsible for many of the thousands of young men sneaking away to Honduras and Costa Rica. But this Assemblies leader denied that his denomination was spiriting its young men out of the country. The Assemblies might not like the law, he and a colleague claimed, but their church was obeying it. Besides, they said, draft-age youth were needed to testify for their faith inside Nicaragua.[75]

What the most pro-Sandinista evangelical organizations lacked, it became obvious as the revolution wore on, was a popular base. The Ecumenical Axis was the most extreme example: its leaders had been among the young Baptists expelled from their churches in the 1960s for contacts with the outlawed Sandinista Front. They found a home in World Council of Churches organizations such as the Christian Student Movement (MEC) and the Latin American Evangelical Commission for Christian Education (CELADEC).[76] After the Sandinistas took power, the Axis claimed that, led by the FSLN, its members had fought for national liberation for fifteen years.[77]

"Whenever there was a problem in Nicaragua," a church worker recalls of the Ecumenical Axis, "it would leave for Europe with a plan and go around to agencies raising money." Back home, meanwhile, the organization was identifying with the Sandinistas in an uncompromising manner, as if evangelicals should hail the FSLN as their spiritual vanguard. When the churches were seized in 1982, the Axis delegate to the Council of State issued a warning. If religious groups failed to obtain their incorporation papers under the auspices of his organization, it would not be able to vouch for their integrity. That is, they would be suspected of counter-revolutionary tendencies.[78] By mid-1985, the Axis had so alienated everyone from left to right that it seemed moribund.

Other casualties were a handful of pro-Sandinista pastors in the Assemblies of God, one of the country's largest denominations and also the most defiantly conservative. In February 1984, the Assemblies suspended two of the men for defending the revolution in print. Their criticism of "apolitical" evangelicals had not been taken kindly by the denomination's leaders, who interpreted it as an attack on themselves.[79] After another Assemblies churchman tried to mediate, he too was drummed out.[80]

"The true Christian doesn't like to get into politics," an Assemblies pastor told me. "If we see a pastor come out of church to join a march, we know that he's not really a Christian." Although members were free to join the Sandinistas or the contras as they wished, another Assemblies figure assured me, he doubted that it was possible to be a good Sandinista and a good Christian.[81] Mixing politics and religion was a sin, these men felt. Yet if supporting the revolution was politics, resisting it was not. As for the pro-Sandinista pastors, they had a pessimistic assessment of their support within the Assemblies—almost nil.

Evangelicals were not a monolithic, committed anti-Sandinista block, as some conservatives claimed. For one, there were pockets of grass-roots appreciation for revolutionary achievements in land reform and the like.[82] For another, withdrawal from the revolution did not necessarily mean support for the opposition: while the Sandinistas might not be very popular by 1985, evangelicals tended to perceive the contras as too brutal to be an alternative. Withdrawal could also mean fearing the consequences of being identified with the Sandinistas, owing not only to contra raids but also to the possibility of a U.S. invasion followed by mass reprisals.

In Managua, the number of people whom revolutionary evangelicals could attract to their functions dwindled. Crowds that had been substantial in 1981 now consisted chiefly of foreign well-wishers, middle-class church delegations from the United States and Europe. As the revolution demanded heavier sacrifices, evangelicals who had joined the national celebration at the fall of the Somoza regime were returning to their previous abstention from politics. What had gone wrong? From the agitational, expectation-raising politics of a revolutionary party seeking power, pro-Sandinista evangelicals found themselves trapped in the politics of austerity and sacrifice, discipline and control of a revolutionary party hanging onto power.[83] When they reacted against evangelical tradition as alienating, their message seemed less spiritual than political, in the form of constant appeals on behalf of the revolution, of which the population was already getting a full diet from the Sandinista Front itself.[84] By trying to defend a revolution under siege, they put themselves under siege as well.

The Battle of the Pastors

An uneasy member of the Sandinista wing of the church was the Evangelical Committee for Aid to Development (CEPAD). This pandenominational body defended the revolution, but it was selective about what it supported, in deference to the many conservatives it was supposed to represent. The Sandinista Front did not trust it completely: in 1985 one board member was detained for three days in the Solentiname Islands because the wife of the local commandante suspected him of contra activities.[85] But as the more revolutionary church leaders lost their constituencies, the Sandinistas turned to CEPAD for mediation on such issues as the church seizures, the Atlantic Coast, and the draft. When evangelicals suffered abuses, CEPAD presented the grievance.

Relief and development was the agency's original purpose, not representing Nicaragua's seventy plus denominations. The idea of CEPAD serving as a church council was anathema to conservatives, many of whom had never trusted it in the first place. They were not pleased by the liberalism of its foreign financial backers, its attempt to infuse evangelicals with new ideas like getting along with Catholics, and its emphasis on social service rather than evangelism. Wasn't all the talk about development diverting attention from saving souls? But under the Somoza dictatorship, conservatives were too busy quarreling with each other to devise an alternative.

Meanwhile, CEPAD's forty or so denominations, and working relations with twenty more, made it function like a church council anyway. Reinforcing that tendency were first the emergencies of the insurrection, then the Sandinista wish to deal with a single entity rather than one denomination after another. Because member churches claimed 80 percent of Nicaraguan evangelicals, CEPAD might seem like the most representative body. Not so according to an organizational rival, the National Council of Evangelical Pastors (CNPEN). Claiming to represent 520 pastors by 1985, CNPEN was not a church council either; instead, it was an association of religious professionals, a guild. But it claimed to represent a majority of the country's 1,600 pastors, in spirit at least, and on that basis the majority of Nicaraguan evangelicals.

CEPAD itself had sponsored the formation of CNPEN, in August 1981, as part of its ceaseless efforts to placate conservatives distrustful of the revolution. Once provided with their own platform, the anti-Sandinista leaders of the new pastor's council proceeded to declare themselves apolitical as well as antiecumenical. But their subsidy from CEPAD ended sooner than expected, and by 1983 they were bankrupt and foundering. As disgusted members jumped ship, CNPEN's Managua council decided to make one last try, by organizing the country's first pandenominational crusade since the 1975 Luis Palau campaign.

The evangelist they invited was Alberto Mottesi. At the press conference opening his week-long "Nicaragua '84" campaign, he refused to condemn the Reagan administration's war on the Sandinistas. "The true church," he declared, "is not going to get mixed up with any [particular] current."[86] The small, pro-Sandinista National Association of Evangelical Pastors (ANPEN) denounced him as evasive and cowardly.[87]

But Mottesi's scorn for politics brought the crowd to its feet. "You may think the world has the answer to your problems," he preached. "But I tell you Havana doesn't have the answer. Moscow doesn't have the answer. And Washington doesn't have the answer. Jesus Christ is the only answer! He alone can change your life and give you peace."[88] Turnout was unprecedented for an evangelical event, making CNPEN's name as an organization. The Mottesi campaign also began to make the group's name in the United States, for it was advertised as a triumph over Sandinista religious persecution. What the organizers interpreted as politically motivated harassment—restrictions on publicity, a last minute change of location for safety reasons, a power outage, a delay in the radio broadcast—enabled CNPEN to present itself as a plucky defender of religious liberty.

One reason for CNPEN's difficulties with the Sandinista bureaucracy was its lack of legal incorporation papers. Despite having many more members than the pro-Sandinista pastor's association, its application had been sat upon by the Ecumenical Axis in the State Council.[89] Without legal papers, the pastor's organization was often forced to ask its rival CEPAD to intercede with the authorities. Lacking legal papers also meant less protection from the Ministry of Justice, particularly its Division of Civil Associations—a new office with discretion to demand reports from and impose requirements upon organizations it suspected of counter-revolutionary tendencies. The month after the January 1984 Mottesi crusade, this regulatory agency informed CNPEN that, as an organization, it was canceled.[90]

More summonses to the Ministry of Justice came out of an exposé of the linkages between Central American evangelicals and the religious right in the U.S., by the New York-based North American Congress on Latin America (NACLA). Anti-Sandinista CNPEN churchmen interviewed by NACLA found themselves being interrogated on the same points by Sandinista authorities.[91] With national elections approaching in November 1984, however, the Sandinistas switched tack. When the usual bureaucratic rigamarole threatened to strangle the annual Day of the Bible celebration in September, Commandante Dora María Tellez took the beleaguered organizers under her wing. She even offered to obtain the long-awaited incorporation papers. In the United States, however, CNPEN boosters painted the resulting Sandinista-supported march as another triumph over Sandinista religious persecution.[92] When a small group of Sandinista supporters tried to join the CNPEN-organized rally with slogans such as "The Bible Condemns Imperialist Aggression," marchers tore up their banners and pamphlets, and the two sides nearly came to blows.

Nothing exercised CNPEN's directors more than their estranged parent organization, perhaps because CEPAD could still claim to represent the same evangelicals which the pastor's council believed it represented. Then too, the Sandinistas had made CEPAD their preferred intermediary, guaranteeing trouble on several scores. First, under pressure to prove that evangelicals supported the revolution, CEPAD made more pro-Sandinista statements than it might otherwise have cared to. Even when it organized evangelical gripe sessions with commandantes, the official press invariably focused on the ritual eulogies for the Sandinista Front, emblazoned them with CEPAD's name, and downplayed the objections it was raising. "We want more respect for the use of the term 'the evangelical people,'" a CNPEN leader told me. "No more political statements implicating evangelicals in what they do not support."[93]

Second, representing evangelicals also meant becoming a transmitter for Sandinista demands. CEPAD's liaison between the government and the churches was Sixto Ulloa, a Baptist development worker elected as a Sandinista congressman in 1984. Sixto had rescued conservatives from many a brush with the authorities. Yet they distrusted him totally. If they failed to go to Sixto or were not associated with CEPAD, conservatives complained, the Sandinistas would not listen to them. "It's a type of domestication," a pastor insisted. "If we want something, we have to go to CEPAD and to Sixto, who is lord and master of all the evangelical field. It's like the Office of Religious Affairs in Cuba, the same politics of monopolization." More efficiently than any government bureaucracy could, conservatives argued, CEPAD was carrying out Fidel Castro's game plan for the evangelical churches—cooptation. "Sign up with CEPAD," a North American missionary claimed, "and you end up being used as a rubber stamp."[94]

Behind complaints that CEPAD had sold out to the Sandinistas was a third objection, the kind against any well-financed organization in a poor country, to its patronage power. "CEPAD is like city hall," a critic claimed. "You can fight it, but you're not going to win." With a 1985 budget of around $2 million, plus whatever arrived in the way of emergency aid, it was the only source of financial help for most churches. That led to a great deal of envy. By mid-1985 CNPEN was insinuating logistics scandals and arguing that it ought to administer the money—without any administrative apparatus to speak of.[95]

"Sometimes we're a bit egotistical," a Matagalpa pastor belonging to both CNPEN and CEPAD explained. "CNPEN's idea is that help should go to the evangelicals." More precisely, the pastor's council felt that the money should be channeled through its members, a feeling heightened by the mounting relief effort for war refugees, of which pastors saw little. "We're the biggest denomination here," an Assemblies of God leader volunteered, "and we think we've done a great deal for CEPAD. But it does unfair things. For example, we asked CEPAD to help the pastors of Ciudad Sandino. Some are getting by on starvation wages as low as four thousand cordobas a month (about $6 in 1985). They're nearly going around without shoes. But they just gave us a bunch of jackets, which we don't even need [because of the tropical climate]. So we've realized that, while CEPAD has done great things for nonevangelical communities, giving them millions of pesos, the money should be for us."

More was involved than who would get to drive around in imported land rovers. CEPAD hired its employees for competence, not theology, which meant that many of them—Catholics and liberal Protestants—could be accused of violating evangelical mores. "There's a great deal of liberation in this sense," a CEPAD official admitted, invoking German theologians who smoked pipes and drank beer. Although the agency distributed some relief supplies through pastors, it administered the bulk without religious criteria. To guard against using aid as an inducement for conversion, it left soul-saving to the churches. Such policies made CEPAD seem like an ecumenical body, even if it avoided that term and its member churches remained firmly committed to evangelism. As far as conservatives were concerned, CEPAD was using ecumenical money from the United States and Europe to buy up their constituency.

Besides the rebellious pastor's council, another index of the pressure against CEPAD was conservative protest within the Baptist Convention. That was the affiliation of much of CEPAD's leadership, who had made their denomination the one most closely identified with the revolution. Now they faced a revolt by the conservative wing of their pastorate. At a session attended by sixty Baptist dissenters in July 1985, one grievance consisted of the anti-imperialist statements the denomination's leaders were accustomed to make. Another was the Baptist seminary, which the conservatives accused of liberation theology and ecumenism. Hadn't it been visited by a radical theologian from Mexico? Didn't it admit five students from the Catholic Church?[96]

A third index of the pressure against CEPAD was the Assemblies of God. The Assemblies were the mainstay of the rival pastor's council. As the country's largest evangelical denomination, their resignation from CEPAD was a perpetual rumor. But the Assemblies remained and, out of either conviction or necessity, many CNPEN pastors continued to work with CEPAD. In the Assemblies of God stronghold of Matagalpa and Jinotega, the local CEPAD office claimed to be working with 180 of the area's 300 pastors. At the neighboring office in Jinotega, CEPAD's president was vice-president of CNPEN, and CNPEN's president was vice-president of CEPAD. The entire Jinotega directorates of the two organizations were supposed to be identical.[97] However polarized evangelical leadership might be in Managua, out in the countryside many pastors seemed to be keeping a foot in each camp.

The Propaganda War

Another service CEPAD performed for the revolution was in the United States. Invoking the Bible, it denounced the Reagan administration's support for the contras and, in two years, brought eighty-five foreign delegations to Nicaragua.[98] It mobilized so much North American church opinion against military intervention that it became the target of an influential political lobby in Washington, the Institute on Religion and Democracy (IRD).

The IRD dated to the start of the Reagan administration and was led by conservative dissidents in the mainline Protestant denominations. Mainly theologians and academics, they said that they wished to rededicate their churches to democratic values. In practice, that meant attacking mainline church officials for such causes as opposing U.S. military intervention in Central America. On the subject of Nicaragua, the IRD accused pro-Sandinista church groups of being political fronts and campaigned against their North American funding.[99]

As the IRD's targets were quick to point out, it too could easily be analyzed as a front, for the neoconservative movement and the Reagan administration.[100] More than half its first budgets came from a foundation chaired by Richard Mellon Scaife, a millionaire financier of the New Right.[101] It rarely criticized the contras, and its attacks on pro-Sandinista church groups were quickly picked up by the White House. When the U.S. Congress refused to approve aid for the contras in April 1985, one of the IRD's luminaries, Michael Novak, lent his name to a new Nicaraguan Freedom Fund to raise money for them.[102]

Perhaps inadvertently, the IRD set off a backlash against the National Council of Evangelical Pastors (CNPEN). It did so by accusing CEPAD of using church funds to buy eleven jeeps for the Sandinista police, then suggesting that U.S. churches should send their money to the more worthy pastor's council.[103] For CNPEN, this meant endorsement by a Washington lobby which the Sandinistas regarded as a CIA front. It meant big trouble. After lengthy meetings with CEPAD and Commandante Dora María Tellez, CNPEN leaders denied all knowledge of the eleven jeeps.[104]

Was the accusation true? IRD's source was a staff member of Open Doors with Brother Andrew. A popular source of information in the evangelical press, Open Doors News Service was heavily influenced by the mystique of its parent organization's main activity, smuggling Bibles into communist countries. So great was the mystique of Bible smuggling that, even in a country like Nicaragua where Bibles were sold in supermarkets, its correspondents operated under aliases, collected rumors in a hurry and, without much checking around, rushed into print with sensational charges. Never figuring in Open Doors news stories were the human rights violations of the contras, U.S. support for them, or the U.S. contribution to provoking Sandinista crackdowns. Always figuring in its stories were the brutal human rights violations of the Sandinistas.

In this case, Open Doors' source consisted of "several pastors" in the department of Matagalpa. No one with whom I spoke in Nicaragua in the course of a month—including half a dozen pastors in Matagalpa—would admit to having heard the accusation before it appeared in the newspapers. Even those who said they believed the charge could not provide details. The CEPAD office in Matagalpa boasted a total of two jeeps and three motorbikes, it should be noted: the man in charge told me he had traded in a truck for a jeep so that it would not fill up with hitchhiking Sandinista soldiers and become a target for ambushes.[105] True, in an emergency such as evacuating wounded, CEPAD (like anyone) could be required to loan vehicles to the government. According to a CEPAD official, on different occasions three such vehicles had been recovered only after great delay.[106]

Judging from what anti-Sandinista evangelicals in Managua told me, many accusations of religious persecution from outside the country were outlandish. For example, according to a newsletter run by Juan Isáis, head of the Latin America Mission in Mexico:

- church treasurers were being named by the Ministry of Interior;
- obtaining a new Bible required filling out a sixty-two part questionnaire from the Ministry of Interior, to which the response was generally no;
- believers were being condemned to thirty years in prison for painting slogans on walls;
- the Sandinistas had forced the superintendent of the Assemblies of God to parade through the streets of León in his underwear.[107]

Each accusation was false according to conservative evangelical leaders in Managua. They also doubted another story which, judging from anti-Sandinista propaganda in the U.S., seemed to be on the lips of every Nicaraguan refugee who stumbled across the border into Costa Rica or Honduras. Sandinista teachers were said to be telling children to hide their faces in their hands and ask God for candy. When they opened their eyes, there wasn't any. Then the teachers told them to pray to Marx or Lenin or Fidel for candy. When they opened their eyes, lo and behold, a sweet was on the desk before them. According to a veteran of many confrontations with the Sandinistas, they were too subtle to employ this kind of tactic.[108]

Lending weight to any accusation against the Sandinistas, no matter how far-fetched, was the Reagan administration. To recruit North American evangelicals into its war, the White House held numerous briefings on the theme of Sandinista religious persecution. An indication of what evangelical leaders were being told is provided by Trans World Missions. A shoestring operation despite the name, Trans World was descended from the "Airmail from God" organization, which used to evangelize Mexican villages by bombing them with tracts from small planes, until two pilots were shot down. [109] Now it raised money through a daily radio broadcast from Glendale, California. Frustrated by the poor response to appeals for orphans, Trans World president John Olson replayed the Reagan administration's line on his mission program.

"Last night I dreamed that I saw a squadron of 200, perhaps 300 American phantom jet fighters flying over Nicaragua," Olson quoted a persecuted Nicaraguan Christian. "I heard them coming and ran out of my house screaming, WELCOME! WELCOME!, because I thought they were coming to liberate us." [110] Olson also explored such topics as the degree to which the Nicaraguan people would resist U.S. invaders. [111] He proudly reported attending a briefing by Lieutenant Colonel Oliver North, the Reagan administration's secret coordinator of the contra war after Congress voted to cut off funding. [112]

What Trans World described as ferocious religious persecution was not backed up by one of the leaders of its small youth church in Managua. "We don't have so many problems with the government," the young man claimed. "We're free to preach even though Sandinistas live on this same block." He did refer to a brush with a local Sandinista Defense Committee, which decided that the group's evangelism in a public park was competing with its own activities; the evangelicals withdrew. The church's founder had left the country to keep a son safe from the draft, after his political beliefs got him in trouble with the Sandinistas. But the young evangelicals he left behind did not set great store by the "freedom fighters." "What the contras do in the name of Christ makes me laugh," the co-pastor told me. "It's terrorism they're doing. There's nothing good about it." Recently a contra unit had killed one of his friends. [113]

The man responsible for the most open, influential religious pitches for the contras was Pat Robertson. Amplified by his Christian Broadcasting Network (CBN), Robertson served as Christian cheerleader wherever CIA-supported movements fought Marxists. Causes lionized on his talk show included Jonas Savimbi's guerrilla war against the Marxist government of Angola, the Son Sann faction in Cambodia, the Afghan rebels, the Christian militia of Major Saad Haddad in Lebanon, and Ríos Montt in Guatemala.

For the contras, Robertson's coverage was timed to coincide with the Reagan administration's aid packages, for the passage of which he urged viewers to pressure their congressional representatives. The tone of CBN reporting can be judged from its "Inside Nicaragua" series in July 1984. "The attack on the Catholic Church is mild," CBN correspondent John Hasbrouck declared, "when compared to the vicious and often deadly assault the Sandinistas have made on Nicaragua's evangelicals." Christian freedom fighters had been driven to take up arms by religious persecution, torture, and mass execution, Hasbrouck told North American viewers. "We can do all things by the power of God," a young FDN-allied Miskito declared with weapon in hand. "All of us young people involved in this struggle have our weapons in our right hand and our Bible in our left."* "The real solution for Nicaragua's problems may well lie in the faith of the people," Hasbrouck concluded. The last scene was of a fervent gospel meeting, leaving the impression that the Sandinistas would be overthrown by evangelicals wielding AK-47s.

Helping the Freedom Fighters

As Pat Robertson denounced the Sandinistas for their treatment of the Miskitos, he never mentioned how the Reagan administration had exacerbated the conflict. Instead, along with like-minded brethren, he was joining in the effort, by helping to feed the Miskito refugees in Honduras back into the war. The main agency on the scene was the World Relief Corporation (WRC), an arm of the National Association of Evangelicals in the United States. Given the enthusiastic reception for Ronald Reagan at NAE functions,

*About the time this program aired, a Miskito commander allied with the FDN stated that his men routinely executed prisoners after torturing them to obtain information. "I love killing," another Miskito commander told an associate of Jack Anderson. "There's nothing I like better. If I could, I'd kill several people a day" (Jack Anderson, *Washington Post*, September 30, 1984, p. D4).

World Relief was quickly suspected of being another component of Washington's strategy, to build up a refugee population in Honduras as a base for contra raids. It was true that World Relief came on the scene with the approval of the U.S. embassy; it was also true that its aid helped turn the refugees at Camp Mocorón into a rear base for the Miskito rebels, and that some of its supplies flowed into the contra effort. Initially helping coordinate the World Relief effort was the wife of the U.S. ambassador to Honduras, John Negroponte, who happened to be supervising the CIA war against the Sandinistas.

But when U.S. strategy diverged from guidelines of the United Nations High Commissioner for Refugees (UNHCR), World Relief sided with its UNHCR funding source despite UN restrictions on evangelism of refugees. The first collision was over the UNHCR/WRC decentralization plan for Camp Mocorón, where Miskito refugees were sinking into mud, disease, and dependency on handouts. The idea of scattering them to various sites, where they could support themselves, did not please the U.S. embassy or the Miskito insurgents.[114] Fearing that dispersal would make it harder to use the Miskitos for war, rebel leaders accused the UN agency and World Relief of being communist. By 1984, with Miskito refugees in Honduras asking to go home, World Relief's coordinator Tom Hawk arranged reconciliation talks on both sides of the border. The son of a U.S. missionary known for his anticommunist views, Hawk was now considered a CIA operative by some and a communist sympathizer by others.[115] When the U.S. Congress voted $7.5 million for Miskito refugees in 1984, World Relief was kept out of the disbursement because of its scruples against supporting the war.[116]

After May 1984, the U.S. government unofficially shifted its support to religious right groups entering the area. The first, organized by an evangelical state legislator from Louisiana, was called Friends of the Americas. By operating from Rus Rus, headquarters of the Miskito rebel group MISURA just seven kilometers from Nicaragua, Friends of the Americas violated UNHCR guidelines calling for refugee camps to stay fifty kilometers away from borders. The new group's paternalistic hand-out mentality also disrupted efforts to promote self-sufficiency. It and the U.S. Agency for International Development poured so much money into a small population, World Relief suspected, that they were drawing people out of Nicaragua for economic reasons. Another result was to pull four thousand refugees toward a MISURA military base at Rus Rus.[117] At a 1985 banquet in Washington, Friends of the Americas received a humanitarian award from President Reagan.[118]

"There are at least twenty groups in the area now, a lot of weird groups," World Relief's David Befus complained. "They don't speak Spanish or anything. It seems like there's a new group here every day. You wouldn't believe what they do. They drop candy out of a plane. You can hurt kids by dropping candy on them from 200 feet. And they think they're doing something great for God."[119]

"The Holy Spirit continued to open doors," one such ministry reported of a 1986 meeting with contra leaders Adolfo Calero and Enrique Bermúdez. "Chopper visits to training camps inside communist Nicaragua enabled Phil Derstine to give the Kingdom of God message to many new recruits. In fact, arrangements are being made to include part of our Video Institute of Ministry directly into their new recruit training! . . . Freedom fighters systematically support with food, clothing and medicines the civilian population surrounding the Command Headquarters. . . . Highlighting our visit was an evening service at the Strategic Command Headquarters . . . [where] the four of us ministered the Gospel to 2,000 enthusiastic freedom fighters."[120] According to this group, Gospel Crusade of Bradenton, Florida, its previous visit to the contras had followed a personal invitation from Lieutenant Colonel Oliver North and a briefing session at the National Security Council in Washington.[121]

Estimates of the contributions made by the Christian Broadcasting Network through its Operation Blessing started at $2 million a year.[122] Pat Robertson aired footage of himself reviewing contra troops. "Everything they do is justified as long as they're fighting 'communists,'" Tom Hawk complained. "They are a bunch of thugs down there. Steadman Fagoth is a thug. He has killed innocent people. The contras are constantly terrorizing refugee camps, forcibly recruiting people. That's the kind of people that Friends of the Americas, CBN, and CERTs (Christian Emergency Relief Teams) are supporting." People whom the Christian Broadcasting Network claimed to be helping—the refugees—were being prevented from returning to Nicaragua by the people CBN was really helping—the contras. In one incident recorded by a film crew, a MISURA mob armed with machetes surrounded and threatened seventy refugees responding to Sandinista peace overtures. Although this group was rescued, other refugees trying to go home were killed. "I'm very disillusioned with [the Christian Broadcasting Network] after what I've seen them do in the name of God," Hawk said.[123]

When CBN and company used evangelical religion to push the contra war, they did not seem to give any thought to how this could backfire against their unprotected brethren in Central America. Or did they, in a right-wing version of the "provoked repression" tactic attributed to leftist guerrillas? By identifying Nicaraguan evangelicals with the contras, were they trying to provoke Sandinista reactions, to build a case for U.S. intervention?

Provoking repression was an axiom of the CIA's contra manual, which surfaced in 1984. According to the agency, the manual was intended to dissuade the FDN from killing civilians.[124] But the manual also described how to create martyrs, by "taking the demonstrators to a confrontation with the authorities, in order to bring about uprisings or shootings, which will cause the death of one or more persons, who would become the martyrs, a situation that should be made use of immediately against the regime, in order to create greater conflicts." By exploiting propaganda themes such as religious freedom, the CIA manual advised, counter-revolutionaries could build up "a fury of justified violence" against the Sandinistas.[125]

"Pat Robertson is out in right field on Central America," an evangelical businessman in Costa Rica told me. "By taking a side in a polarized situation, he's simply dividing the church more. What he's doing is creating more hatred and more death, which is the work of the Devil."[126]

Religious Persecution in Nicaragua?

In April 1985, at a fundraiser for the contras in Washington, D.C., Ronald Reagan presented a victim of Sandinista atrocities to the world. Bayardo Santaeliz, the president declared, was a lay preacher of the Pentecostal Missionary Church. One night after a prayer meeting, the Sandinistas had tied him up inside a house and set it afire. The flames severed the bonds and Santaeliz was able to escape, with terrible burns whose scars now proved his story.[127] Or so it seemed. But as the Sandinista press was able to establish in some detail, Santaeliz had acquired the scars while fighting for Somoza as a National Guardsman. Sentenced to thirty years for alleged war crimes, he had been pardoned and released before disappearing in 1983.[128]

The war between the Sandinistas and contras provided a steady stream of refugees fleeing Nicaragua. When they crossed over into Honduras or Costa Rica, they were without resources, unwelcome, and sometimes willing to play any tune which elicited sympathy. War, hardship, and the draft seemed to be their main reasons for leaving, but some of their benefactors had a keen interest in finding victims of religious persecution. There was no shortage of raw material into which such motives could be read, whether correctly or incorrectly was difficult to tell.

One refugee had a long story, corroborated by hideous scars, of how the Sandinistas tried to kill him for his Christian objections to military service.[129] He had taken refuge with Costa Rican evangelicals, who during the week I visited were about to baptize him. In a case publicized by the Reagan administration, Sandinista soldiers arrested a lay pastor of the United Pentecostal Mission named Prudencio Baltodano. According to Baltodano, they took him apart, cut his ears off, stabbed him in the neck, and left him to bleed to death—an error because he subsequently reappeared minus his ears.[130] Did he suffer because he was a preacher? Or because, as one of just two men with forty women and children fleeing a counterinsurgency sweep, the soldiers suspected that the other men were off with the contras?

Baltodano was from Nueva Guinea, an agricultural colony started by evangelical churches and the Somoza regime in the southeastern jungle. If the FSLN was to be believed, the struggling, independent-minded colonists of Nueva Guinea were the kind of people for whom it was making the revolution. But that is not the way it looked to many of them. Throughout the backwoods of Nicaragua, the Sandinista Front alienated small ranchers and farmers in several ways. Price and marketing controls on what they produced, together with inflation, ruined their purchasing power. If they did not sell at government prices, their crops could be confiscated. Soon their standard of living was lower than it had been under Somoza. They also felt pressured to join "popular organizations" the Sandinistas considered essential to defense, turning participation into a test of patriotism.

All this antagonized many peasants. But as journalist Christopher Dickey was able to establish, they did not begin to go over to the contras until the Reagan administration further polarized the situation. Prior to the injection of U.S. funds, the former National Guardsmen who formed the core of the contra had been operating on the level of cattle thieves. By turning them into a serious threat, the Reagan administration aggravated tensions between Sandinista supporters and families whose members had served the Somoza dictatorship. Each contra raid and Sandinista countersweep sowed suspicion that neighbors were serving as informers for one side or the other.

This was how, in the north, in the area that had sheltered General Sandino in his war against the U.S. Marines in the 1920s and 1930s, Sandinista administration and North American intervention turned part of the population into supporters of the counterrevolution. The stronghold of Sandino, the "general of free men," had become contra country.[131] By 1984–1985, the Sandinistas were moving the people in the hardest hit areas into resettlement camps, to protect some of them from the contras and to prevent others from joining the contras. The relocation strategy was not unlike that employed by the United States in Vietnam.

To the south in Nueva Guinea the "sects," with their loudspeakers, sermonizing, and uncooperative attitudes, were what a Sandinista commentator called "the headache of the revolution."[132] Pastors were under special pressure: as community leaders, as representatives of a religion the Sandinistas distrusted, and as exponents of anticommunist ideology inculcated by their Bible training. If you collaborate with the government, an Assemblies of God refugee in Costa Rica reported, you have liberty. If not, you're denounced at local Sandinista meetings.[133]

Stepping into the gap in Nueva Guinea was CEPAD: it helped refugees and persuaded the government to release detained pastors.[134] But according to an anti-Sandinista church worker, the entire area was now run like a resettlement camp. Although some pastors had turned into Sandinista agents, he said, others were playing both sides of the fence. They had to be careful not to use scriptures that could be interpreted to have a double, counter-revolutionary meaning. As for the resettlements, they were "practically concentration camps" where children had to be turned over to the Sandinista children's organization, the women went to work in a cooperative, and the men had to join a territorial militia.

Twenty-four of his denomination's sixty church buildings in the southeast of the country had been destroyed, the church worker said. First the contras would visit an area; then the Sandinistas would clear everyone into resettlement camps. Once converted into no man's land, the churches were scavenged for scarce building materials or—if made of thatch on the Atlantic coast—torched. The church worker did not know of rapes or sacrileges by Sandinista forces. He thought that prisoners could suffer physical mistreatment—such as being threatened, beaten up, deprived of sleep or water—without being tortured in the more technical sense. But if too affected by the mistreatment, the church worker believed, a prisoner might be killed to destroy the evidence.[135]

To what extent were evangelical pastors involved in the contra? Just as some had worked for the Sandinistas—according to one source, at least ten had fought for the FSLN or worked full-time organizing their neighborhoods[136]—others were fighting for the Nicaraguan Democratic Force. The Reagan administration published a photo of two "former evangelical pastor[s]" carrying AK-47s and commanding FDN units.[137]

The hardest hit denomination was clearly the Moravian, owing to its association with Miskito Indians, the rebel portion of which claimed to be devout Christians going into battle with prayers on their lips. Prior to the hostilities, it is interesting to note, evangelical missionaries had considered most Miskitos nominal rather than committed Christians.[138] Their belief system was too indigenous by evangelical standards; moreover, the Moravians belonged to the distrusted World Council of Churches. But now that some Miskitos were fighting a leftist government, the religious right in the United States baptized them as Bible Christians and publicized their case as a Sandinista assault on religion.

Evidence of severe persecution seemed close at hand. Of some 100,000 Miskitos, the Moravian Church estimated that 36 percent became refugees in the course of the war.[139] Of the church's 166 pastors on the Atlantic Coast before the war, 24 went to Honduras. While most of the 24 supposedly confined themselves to chaplaincy

for the Miskito insurgents, one—Wycliffe Diego—replaced Steadman Fagoth as the head of the FDN-allied MISURA forces. A total
of 5 Moravian pastors died or disappeared in Sandinista custody.
The government claimed that one was killed trying to escape (at the
age of sixty-two), and that another died when insurgents ambushed
the patrol he was guiding. Three more pastors were among 70 Miskitos who disappeared in Sandinista hands in 1982–1983, the most
vicious period of the war on the coast, and were never accounted
for. Eighteen other pastors were imprisoned: 6 to 10 were mal-
treated in one way or another before all were freed by the government's December 1, 1983, amnesty. When the Sandinistas burned
Miskito villages in the 1982 relocations from the Coco River, they
destroyed Moravian buildings as well; others they used as barracks
and jails. Of 164 Moravian churches on the coast before the war, 44
were closed or destroyed.[140]

The fighting forced the Moravian hierarchy into an unhappy me-
diator role like CEPAD's, distrusted and pressured from both
sides. When the army tried to impose prior censorship over sermons at relocation camps, the Moravian bishop had to go to Interior
Minister Tomás Borge to have the rule lifted.[141] At the church's
February 1983 synod, government security agents lobbied against
the election of certain pastors to church posts, even offered their
suggestions on a church-state resolution.[142] But the Moravian leaders insisted that religious persecution was not the problem, pointing to many an open, full, and growing church. Instead, they
blamed the Reagan administration for making a bad situation
worse, by using Indians as surrogate fighters and distorting the
facts to justify a war.

Inconveniently for the persecution lobby in the United States,
Nicaraguan evangelicals were doing very well in some respects.
The government's 1980 literacy crusade enabled hundreds of thousands of people to read the Bible for the first time. Due partly to a
new import arrangement with the Catholic Church, New Testaments distributed by the Nicaraguan Bible Society increased nine-
fold. Even in 1983, the U.S. ambassador was saying that Christianity was in no danger in Nicaragua.[143] Five years after the Sandinista
takeover, the number of evangelical churches had doubled to three
thousand.[144]

In the case of the Church of God (Cleveland, Tennessee), its

Puerto Rican supervisor was expelled from the country on a visa technicality in November 1981. But the same denomination was allowed to set up a Bible institute among former National Guardsmen in the Sandinista prison system: at the main institution, almost one-third of the 2,500 prisoners were evangelical.[145] The Church of God reported complete freedom to worship and rapid growth, from 5,250 members in 116 churches in 1979 to almost 10,000 members in 150 churches by 1984.[146] That same year the Assemblies of God reported 679 churches and branches, double the figure six years before.[147]

The fate of the Assemblies was an important index of Sandinista policy. Its churches were concentrated in the north, the principal war zone, and its leaders were quick to proclaim both their distrust of the Sandinistas and their neutrality regarding the contras. In San Juan de Limay, a northern town with a 90 percent Catholic majority, the local Assembly's refusal to help defend the community against raiders killing noncombatants was not popular. Four members were in prison, the Assemblies pastor told visitors: two for refusing to join the army and two after being accused of supporting the contras. But the church was free to evangelize, the pastor said, and had grown substantially under Sandinista rule.[148]

Of 217 Assemblies congregations in the north, 20 had been forced to disband due to the fighting.[149] But according to an Assemblies official, only 10 or 12 of 400 Assemblies pastors had left the country. "The pastors who have left did so for economic reasons," he told me. "We all have a history of persecution. But if the Sandinistas want us to leave, it has to be asked, what's best for the church? Why haven't [the ones who left] stayed with the rest of us, suffering like Jesus Christ? We're called reactionaries. We're marginalized, we're watched and we suffer, but we stay independent, and there is liberty to preach."[150]

Away from the fighting, in the capital, it was easier to distinguish between the random violence of counterinsurgency and Sandinista behavior toward evangelicals. In Managua, the barrio where religious liberty was most often in distress was probably Ciudad Sandino. Here the first churches were seized in July 1982. Despite the usual attempts at conciliation by a dwindling number of pro-Sandinista pastors, in October 1983 a Ciudad Sandino mob harassed an evangelical meeting and the Sandinista police hauled off thirteen pastors for allegedly preaching against military conscription.

"We're not that stupid," one of the accused pastors told me two years later, claiming that he and his colleagues had done nothing to provoke the crackdown. Strangely, while he was enjoying total freedom to start a new church in a community one hundred kilometers away, at Ciudad Sandino even an all-night vigil could prompt official reactions. It sounded as if relations between evangelicals and the revolution were improving by 1985: the Sandinista Defense Committees had even asked an old antagonist in the Assemblies of God to serve as neighborhood coordinator, and he was building a new church. But the open-air campaign that Ciudad Sandino pastors were planning was moving indoors: in exchange for authorizing outdoor meetings, the Sandinistas wanted access to the microphone each night. The pastors refused, convinced that the Sandinistas would use it for inappropriate purposes such as shouting slogans against U.S. imperialism.

One Ciudad Sandino pastor laid part of the blame on his brethren. As a nonpentecostal, he had no use for open-air revivals; they attracted drunks and trouble. Somoza had looked upon all that singing, shouting, and clapping as a harmless diversion for the poor, the pastor explained, but the Sandinistas did not. Responding to noise complaints, they started to enforce preexisting public nuisance laws which, for example, regulated loudspeakers and required a certain distance between churches. Shouting matches erupted between Sandinista cadre complaining about disorder and church members wrapping themselves in the mantle of religious liberty.[151]

In Managua, conservative evangelical leaders related interminable difficulties with government bureaucracies. "Simple things they always make complicated," a CNPEN leader fumed in 1985. "They never admit that it's political, they just use their regulations to foul everything up."[152] According to the religious right in the United States, these men were being persecuted for preaching the gospel. But when asked to detail their experiences, they did not attribute them to expounding salvation because they were doing so without hindrance. Rather, their difficulties with the Sandinistas seemed related to visits to the U.S. embassy, or leadership roles in CNPEN, or ties with anti-Sandinista foreign organizations such as the Latin American Evangelical Confederation (CONELA), which CNPEN was in the process of joining. Above all, these men were in trouble for associating with North Americans who supported the contra war, criticizing the government's restrictions, and insisting on continued independence from the Sandinista-approved CEPAD.

Were conservative evangelicals being persecuted for their faith in Nicaragua? In the strict sense, no, because even pastors in trouble with the government seemed free to engage in essential religious activities such as holding meetings, issuing altar calls, and the like. Obtaining permission for revivals and marches was a bureaucratic nightmare, but that was not unusual in wartime, and everyone had problems with the Sandinista bureaucracy. Freedom of worship was not at issue, as one anti-Sandinista author explained, because the Sandinistas were not trying to restrict it.[153]

At stake was the right of evangelicals to refuse to participate in the Sandinista revolution—or from the Sandinista point of view, to fulfill basic duties of citizenship, particularly defending the country against foreign aggression. This posed a difficult question for the ecumenical Protestants supporting the Sandinistas, because for them religious freedom had acquired a broader meaning than the right to worship inside a church building. It included the right to address political issues, criticize the government, and maintain independent organizations.[154] In that wider sense, the Sandinistas were not putting in a credible performance, at least not in 1985 when I visited. Even granted the need for emergency measures, they seemed unwilling to allow CNPEN to operate as an independent organization.

Conservative evangelicals and their boosters in the United States were also in a contradictory position, however. Under the previous regime, they had insisted that the church confine itself to spiritual matters and conform to the powers that be. "Obey the government because God has put it over you," inspired by Romans 13:1, had been a favorite teaching. Claiming to abstain from politics, they had not criticized the Somoza dictatorship for suppressing opinionated churchmen. Instead, they had condemned the victims for "getting involved in [left-wing] politics." Now they were insisting on the right to dissent themselves, while continuing to condemn pro-Sandinista brethren for contaminating the gospel with politics.

The response of conservatives to the problem of violence also tended to be inconsistent. One of their main arguments against liberation theology was that it condoned bloodshed. "We call it a theology of violence" was a typical reaction. Yet when the religious right promoted the contras as "Christian freedom fighters," conservatives criticizing liberation theology rarely objected: some joined the chorus. Then there was Ríos Montt: what conservatives found abhorrent in the Sandinista revolution—soldiers burning churches and killing pastors—they averted their eyes from in a country presided over by a fellow evangelical. "There's more torture in Guatemala than Nicaragua any day," a Gospel Outreach elder in Managua told me. "I know I'd rather be taken off to jail by one of these Sandinista boys than a Guatemalan soldier any day. Those guys in Guatemala are something. . . . I've never met a Christian here who was tortured."[155] Ostensibly above politics, conservative evangelicals ended up supporting a right-wing equivalent of what they said they rejected in left-wing Christianity and a more violent regime than the one they condemned.

Clearly, the tables had turned. Dissidents had become the establishment; the establishment had become the dissidents; and neither side was accustomed to its new role. Left-wing Christians were using the language of revolution to justify conformity, and right-wing Christians were using their old language of spiritual escapism to justify political dissent.

State of Emergency

When I left Nicaragua in August 1985, the worst seemed over, at least in terms of church-state relations. On the Atlantic Coast, the Moravian hierarchy was helping the Sandinistas start an autonomy process for the ethnic groups there. Over the next several years, many Miskito fighters accepted a truce. The majority of Miskito refugees returned from Honduras to rebuild their churches and communities. In Managua, the Sandinistas seemed to be learning to manage their domestic religious opposition without violence. Mobs were a memory and, as a method of control, were being replaced by bureaucrats. CNPEN was, once again, negotiating with the Sandinista Front for its incorporation papers. Even the testimony of anti-Sandinista evangelicals contradicted the portrait of persecution painted by the religious right in the United States.

But the gradual improvement in Sandinista-evangelical relations was not without setbacks, the kind that kept conservatives pessimistic about their future. The month after my departure in 1985, for example, the annual Day of the Bible celebrations did not go well. Pressing its luck, CNPEN organized a week-long revival in Managua, apparently without official permission. According to a visitor who participated in the event, the authorities prohibited advertising, refused to allow a parade, turned back guest preachers at the airport, and allowed thugs to molest the crowd.[156]

Then in October, the Sandinistas declared a new state of emergency. Because the contras were in retreat, the decree was not in response to a military crisis. Instead, it was intended to root out the "internal front," the contras' attempt to extend the war to Managua.[157] That, according to the CIA manual for the contras, included infiltrating above-ground institutions with three-person cell structures, to turn them into covers for "Christian guerrillas."[158] As interpreted by the Sandinistas, the "internal front" consisted of church, union, business, and political structures resisting absorption into their own system.[159]

Among the hundreds of dissidents called in for interrogations were conservative evangelicals in Managua—about fifteen leaders of CNPEN, the Assemblies of God, the Child Evangelism Fellowship, the Nicaraguan Bible Society, and the Campus Crusade for Christ. The Sandinistas made much of the connections they suspected with the Institute on Religion and Democracy (IRD). After several years of campaigning against the Sandinistas, let us recall, this Washington lobby published a call for North American Christians to switch their financial support from CEPAD to CNPEN. A few months later, one of the IRD's most prominent board members helped lead a fundraising drive for the contras, a cause that several other board members soon joined. For the Sandinistas, the IRD's politics and position in the neoconservative network in Washington were sufficient evidence that it was a CIA front. Now the Sandinistas were accusing evangelical opponents—particularly CNPEN—of being subsidized by the same Washington lobby.

As it turned out, the evidence for this charge was a shambles.[160] Apparently the Sandinistas were drawing a mistaken analogy between the IRD and the National Endowment for Democracy (NED), a U.S. government foundation set up under the Reagan administration, which replaced the CIA as a source of subsidies for the opposition newspaper *La Prensa*.[161] But there was indeed a connection between the IRD and the NED; both drew on the same neoconservative intellectuals helping Lieutenant Colonel Oliver North run a "private support network" for the contras out of the White House basement.[162]

It is not hard to see how the Sandinistas could get confused, and how evangelicals under their rule could suffer as a result. One victim of the strategies emanating from Washington was the director of Campus Crusade for Christ in Nicaragua, Jimmy Hassan. Hassan's troubles with the Sandinistas seem to have begun over his organization's political profile in the United States, then his complaints about bureaucratic obstacles to the 1984 Mottesi campaign, turning him into a suspected but unproven CIA agent. Summonses to the Ministry of Justice, as well as State Security raids on his unassuming, beat-up office, became regular occurrences. In November 1984, after war talk in Washington led to an invasion scare and security restrictions in Nicaragua, he was denied an exit visa to attend an evangelical conference in the United States. The following month, State Security arrested his brother-in-law, beat the man up, and tried to pressure his wife into denouncing her brother for counter-revolutionary activities.[163]

When I talked to Hassan in July and August 1985, he thought that the days of conservative evangelical leaders like himself were numbered. Like colleagues, he could relate many an incident to show that the Sandinistas were subtly, inexorably coopting the church. But he was trying to keep the situation in perspective. "In a certain sense, they have reason to suspect me," he admitted of Campus Crusade founder Bill Bright's role in the religious right. "Here in Managua," he said, "there are very few cases in which the Sandinistas have used violence since 1984. When it occurs, we appeal through legal channels, and it stops. Instead, they use legal mechanisms like the Division of Civil Associations."

The state of emergency was too much for Hassan, however. Early one morning, security forces in platoon strength arrested him at his house on vague charges. At the Ministry of Interior, he says that he was shown his young staffers standing naked in interrogation rooms. To make him confess that he was a CIA agent, according to Hassan, an interrogator put a gun to his head and pulled the trigger—on an empty chamber.[164] At the first opportunity he took his family to Mexico, then continued to the United States to denounce the Sandinistas for persecuting Christians. Although he stopped short of advocating aid to the contras, U.S. organizations such as the Christian Broadcasting Network used his testimony to agitate for just that.[165] The religious persecution lobby, which for some time had found itself recycling old, shopworn misdeeds for lack of more recent material, took a new lease on life.

Hassan's interrogation, like the others, took place at El Chipote, the sinister fortress built by the Somoza dictatorship on a hill above Managua. Under the old regime, it had been used as a torture center. These interrogations did not employ torture, at least of the kind that leaves physical marks, but some Protestants sympathetic to the Sandinistas—among them CEPAD and the United Methodist bishops in the United States—were quick to express their concern over the way the detainees were treated.[166]

"Why did we do this?" Commandante Omar Cabezas asked. "Because we are entitled to a defense. Let it be clear that we will not relinquish our right to defend ourselves. We will defend ourselves against the aircraft that the U.S. government has been giving the counter-revolutionaries. We will defend ourselves against all the aid that the U.S. government has been giving the counter-revolutionaries. In a similar manner, we will defend ourselves against all the plots that the church . . . and the U.S. institutes that specialize in this sort of thing, including the Institute on Religion and Democracy, are carrying out in Nicaragua. We will defend ourselves against this institute. . . . We will defend against the harm that the U.S. Congress has done to us by approving aircraft, trucks, and communications equipment so that they can kill us here in our own land, kill us who have done nothing to them. . . . We will defend ourselves with every means because this is our home, and we are being attacked from outside by all of these plans."[167]

Meanwhile, on any night and in any barrio of Managua, the sound of singing wafted through the soft night air. One evening, I followed it down the street to a pentecostal church, a new open air structure in a field between a shanty town and a middle-class neighborhood. In August 1983, the pastor had been holding open air meetings in another barrio, on a lot where he proposed to build a church. Night after night of loudspeakers provoked the usual noise complaints; there also seems to have been disagreement over who owned the lot, with the local Sandinista Defense Committee wishing to use it for more housing. One night, according to church members, a mob of young men from outside the neighborhood burst into the service, broke it up, and stole the sound equipment. They also dragged the pastor off a distance, beat him up, put a pistol to his head, and threw him in a canal. The neighbors thought this was going too far and did what they could to prevent bloodshed. That same night, the CDS built a shack on the lot and claimed it for the people.

When the pastor recovered—his congregation says that, after his wounds were anointed with oil and prayed over, they healed without scars—he went to see CEPAD, which arranged a dialogue to patch things up. According to a Sandinista account, a commandante was there, and Catholic CDS leaders tearfully embraced evangelicals. According to another version, there wasn't any commandante, and the evangelicals certainly did not get their lot back. Eventually CEPAD was able to arrange a new site for the congregation, however. Now it was drawing a hundred or more people, mostly young mothers with children, every night of the week.

Most of the churchgoers seemed to be from the shanty town next door, where the Sandinistas had helped the people replace their shacks with more substantial structures, which could be expanded into real houses. Yet inflation had ruined their purchasing power, and they had less to eat than before. When shoes wore out, it was much harder to buy a new pair. And now there were new shacks on the edges, built by teenage couples striking out on their own, as well as refugees from the war and the agricultural crisis. There were seventy more churches of this denomination in the countryside, members told me, and they had suffered. Maybe four churches had disintegrated in the fighting. Some brethren were in resettlement camps; pastors and deacons had been detained, and a few were still in jail. But here they were in a handsome new church, and they hadn't had physical confrontations with the authorities in nearly two years. They didn't know what would happen next. "If you want evangelical growth," a missionary remarked, "hand it over to the communists."[168]

Chapter Nine

World Vision in Ecuador

At 3,300 meters, the little town of Pilahuín huddled just under the cloud cover, on a cold, windy shoulder of the Andes, high above the modern city of Ambato. Bypassed and forlorn, it looked like many other small trading centers in the highlands of Ecuador, in need of a paint job and crumbling slowly as adobe does. But if time seemed to have stopped a generation ago in Pilahuín, the hamlets of Quichua Indians around it were not forgotten. For these peasant farmers were in the gaze of World Vision, the largest of the evangelical development agencies, and that was not to the liking of the Catholic Church.

"Ten years ago," parish priest Jesús Tamayo told me, "evangelism here was preaching the Bible, nothing more than moralism. Suddenly, in a fit of enthusiasm for social responsibility, the evangelicals changed direction and started giving out large amounts of money. Now World Vision is the most serious problem on the level of campesino development. It is undermining effort and reflection on the part of the people themselves, destroying popular organization. Evangelicals are telling our people they're stupid because they're doing something for nothing. The mentality develops that those who demand effort are the enemy of the community. Of getting all the money you can. Of opportunism and taking advantage. With so much easy money, the idea spreads that loans do not have to be repaid." The loans Tamayo himself had extended for tractors were unrecoverable now, partly because of World Vision's generous terms. "It's impossible that World Vision continues with this policy of give, give, give," Tamayo concluded, "because, once the giving slows down, people lose interest."[1]

In the hamlet of Pallaloma, there was a new evangelical chapel and a new school, the latter not quite finished. The most visible improvements were the odd cement boxes scattered at a polite distance behind each house. These were new latrines, a sign that this was a World Vision community. Strangely, there was no evangelical pastor in Pallaloma. The pastor there had started out as a Catholic catechist working with Padre Tamayo, then switched sides and been hired by World Vision as its community coordinator. Until a problem emerged. What was happening to the money? One day Pallaloma sent World Vision a petition, asking it to leave. As for World Vision—which did not like to be identified as specifically evangelical—it had not intended to finance construction of the new chapel. There it stood, an embarrassing symbol of World Vision's theological orientation. Now there wasn't any pastor either, because World Vision's attempt to fortify Christian witness in Pallaloma had forced him to resign, over approximately five hundred dollars in missing funds.[2]

World Vision had also been asked to get out of the neighboring community of Mulanleo. Among the explanations for this event, Mulanleo was said to have been offended by the photographing of their children for fundraising in the United States. According to a second version, when Padre Tamayo found out that Mulanleo had accepted money from World Vision for a water project, he persuaded them to return it. And according to a third version, the priest came close to losing the community, after suspending the sacraments for those with an ambiguous religious position. Some of the older men were afraid of going to hell, but some of the younger ones were on the point of getting their sacraments elsewhere. Fortunately, another development agency came to the rescue by offering to finance compensating projects. "World Vision is not going to fool us," a Mulanleo leader told me. "We're Catholics to the death."[3]

Judging from such incidents, World Vision was a perfect example of a wealthy North American agency trying to buy the loyalty of the poor. Since accounting was not a highly developed skill in Andean villages, moreover, this kind of generosity was likely to leave many a quarrel in its wake. In Ecuador, just a few years after World Vision's arrival in the late 1970s, it was accused of setting off or worsening conflicts in more than a dozen communities. Intimations of the same seemed to be cropping up in dozens more. The good part about World Vision, a man from a place called Yantzapután told me, was that it gave poor people money. The bad part, he claimed, was that the fighting over the money was breaking up his community.[4]

Ecuadorians began to suspect that World Vision's humanitarian rhetoric concealed a plan to divide peasant communities and break up their political organizations. Why else would it be so interested in the Quichua, a submerged Andean nationality once subject to the Inca Empire and still numbering in the millions from Ecuador to Bolivia? Hadn't World Vision come up before, in news reports about Salvadoran refugees in Honduras? There it had been accused of turning refugees over to security forces to be killed, as if it were some kind of Pontius Pilate. The Catholic human rights organization Pax Christi denounced World Vision as a "Trojan Horse" for U.S. foreign policy.[5] In the person of this CIA front, a journalist wrote, North American fundamentalism was going head to head against the theology of liberation.[6]

To many evangelicals, ironically, World Vision was a shining example of the new wave in missionary work: social responsibility. Evangelical relief ministries were not entirely new: a few dated to the massive dislocations of the two world wars, with an additional boost from the orphan industry during the Korean War. But now helping victims was distinctly fashionable, and there was also a wave of enthusiasm for development programs, as if evangelicals were resurrecting the extinct liberal hopes of the 1960s and 1970s. Together, relief and development had become a major growth area in missions, and a rising tide of financial support was helping agencies like World Vision break away from old dogmas.

It is important to remember that, unless missionaries drum doctrine into the heads of the people they help, fundamentalists accuse them of falling into the "social gospel," that is, placing worldly concerns above spiritual ones. The child sponsorship agency Compassion International exemplified the conservative approach. It worked only through evangelicals and insisted on Bible training in the schools it supported—no Bible teaching, no funding. But conditioning aid in such ways could easily produce "rice bowl Christians," converts whose main interest in the new religion was staying on the dole.

Haiti was an advanced case of this kind of mutual manipulation: according to a Southern Baptist worker, some of the more than four hundred missions in the country were outright frauds. He had seen every trick in the book, down to the organization of fake orphanages to gratify visiting donors from the United States. Even genuine missions had made Haitian churches dependent on their subsidies, which Christians had learned to demand in exchange for going along with the program.[7]

"Frequently I was approached by Haitians who thought I was a missionary," anthropologist Frederick Conway reported. "Often they proclaimed themselves fellow Protestants and would demand gifts of money on that basis. Or they would scold me for stinginess, asking how I could expect people to join my church if I didn't give them anything. . . . They assumed that I [like an active local missionary] 'needed' a mission and would be willing to pay for it."[8]

Handouts might seem to work under an old-fashioned dictatorship like the Duvalier regime. But they did not go over well when revolutionaries took power. That was what Larry Jones, the Oklahoma City evangelist and head of a group called Feed the Children, found out in Nicaragua. At his April 1985 rallies in Managua, Jones planned to distribute kilos of rice and beans to everyone who attended, along with a New Testament and a suit of clothes to each pastor. But the Sandinistas decided that favoring evangelicals with relief supplies was not acceptable in their revolution. They confiscated the bulk of Jones's material, gave it to war victims, restricted his rallies, and after he vowed to return to Nicaragua for more rallies turned him back at the airport.[9]

Especially in Central America, talk about meeting social needs could be an excuse for setting up the crudest associations between handing out badly needed aid, reinforcing images of North Americans as benefactors, and pumping for conversion. Even the most egregious promoters of dependency claimed to be promoting self-sufficiency, of course, and no one admitted to pressuring recipients. The most naive dispensers of handouts (or the most manipulative, depending on your point of view) seemed to be newly arrived charismatics from the United States intent on building up a ministry, that is, a clientele. But most of the evangelical spectrum could be accused of such behavior at one time or another.

There were several reasons why it was hard to leave behind rice bowl Christianity. First, owing to evangelical distrust of activism to change social structures, the most likely interpretation of "social responsibility" was in terms of charity to the needy. Second, among distrustful populations, even a relatively sophisticated agency like World Vision felt that it had to use handouts to gain a foothold. Finally, regardless of occasional claims to the contrary, evangelical development programs were intended to attract converts—the only basis on which most agencies could ask their U.S. public for donations. They therefore tended to reproduce the equation between handouts and conversion despite claims to have transcended it.[10]

Still, groups like World Vision were attempting to get beyond the dispensing of pills, injections, food, and clothing, through longer-term development programs that avoided close associations with church attendance. Others in the same line included World Concern, MAP (for Medical Assistance Programs) International, Food for the Hungry, and the World Relief Corporation of the National Association of Evangelicals. Each agency was, to one or another degree, participating in the self-critical approach of the wider development community. One model of forward thinking—so forward that it was easy to forget its evangelical credentials—was the Mennonite Central Committee (MCC). A consortium of seventeen Mennonite and Brethren in Christ denominations, the MCC dated to 1920, making it the oldest and most experienced of the evangelical relief agencies.

This was a new kind of Protestant evangelism which fundamentalists considered suspiciously liberal. Although subject to all the ills of parachurch largesse, it broke the pessimistic, premillennialist mold of older missions, by urging Latin American evangelicals to take an active role in improving their communities. As an alternative source of patronage, it challenged existing mission-church structures. Based on new kinds of financial support—in El Salvador, World Vision claimed that its $2-million-a-year budget gave it a working relationship with 80 percent of the country's denominations[11]—evangelical development agencies were encouraging churches to consolidate growth by responding to the economic crisis of their members.[12] Although such groups insisted that they always worked "in Christ's name," their attempt to avoid paternalism loosened the ties between aid and evangelism.

But for Latin Americans who distrusted North Americans bearing gifts, a more sophisticated approach suggested a more sophisticated form of penetration. The funding agencies could seem omnipresent yet intangible, working as they did through many local evangelical bodies. Their use of the language of self-help, autonomy, even liberation seemed like an attempt to confuse the poor and coopt radical forms of Christianity. And it was easy to draw parallels with North American involvement in Southeast Asia. One incident was Food for the Hungry's attempt to resettle Hmong refugees from Southeast Asia in Bolivia. To the alarm of native organizations, the Catholic Church and the Bolivian left, the Hmong had fought for the Central Intelligence Agency in Laos.[13]

A particular cause for suspicion was the presence of funds and surplus food provided by the U.S. Agency for International Development. From USAID's point of view, religious missions were more effective at getting down to the grass roots, had a lower political profile, and achieved more per dollar than government programs, all because of their voluntary nature.[14] Such "private voluntary organizations" (PVOs) knew the terrain where they worked; had a constituency they could feed into the program instead of starting from scratch; and were accustomed to thinking small, which was more likely to meet popular needs. Because they usually planned on sticking around, they also knew they would have to face the consequences of their mistakes.

It took little imagination to wonder whether official subsidies were being used to manipulate PVOs: as an agency linked to the State Department, USAID was staffed by the foreign service and, in some times and places, by CIA officers as well.[15] Less dramatically, what USAID was willing to fund—under the Reagan administration, entrepreneurship and export production—was obviously influencing the priorities of private agencies.[16] But as a group, evangelical missions did not seem to be receiving a very large share of USAID allocations. The $31 million the agency gave eight evangelical PVOs in 1983–1984 was dwarfed by the $264 million to Catholic Relief Services, 77 percent of the latter's $342 million budget.*

* Among evangelical PVOs, the agencies most dependent on USAID were the Adventist Development and Relief Agency, which was receiving 67 percent of its budget ($14.3 million of $21.5 million) from USAID that year, and the Salvation

World Vision's income was larger than that of the other leading evangelical development agencies combined, and it was a particularly contradictory case. Despite being accused of imperialism in Honduras and Ecuador, only a handful of its thousands of employees and local coordinators in Latin America were North American. In Ecuador, Catholic church workers regarded it as a threat, yet evangelicals also complained about it, for wreaking havoc in their churches. Some of the greatest trepidation over World Vision was in a highland province already fraught with religious tension, Chimborazo, to which we now turn.

The Protestant Boom in Chimborazo

For the consecrated men and women of the Gospel Missionary Union (GMU), Chimborazo was a real Gethsemane. It was not just that Quichua peasants occasionally assaulted them. Worse was wondering why the Lord had called them to such a spiritually barren place.[17] To baptize their first Indian convert in the province took the Gospel Missionary Union fifty-two years.[18]

The reason for the GMU's long wait was that, as far as anyone at the time could tell, the Quichua of Chimborazo belonged to hacienda owners and the Catholic Church. When haciendas changed hands, so did the Indian serfs, bound to the estate by never-ending debts. Wound up with the tribute the Quichua rendered to priest and landlord was their belief that animals, crops, and lives depended upon the entire community's propitiation of "the saints," native gods renamed and baptized into a folk Catholic religious system. Were any household to neglect its obligations to the saints, the welfare of the entire community would be endangered. When

Army World Service Office, which was receiving 44 percent ($3.1 million of $7.1 million). The World Relief Corporation obtained 25 percent of its budget from USAID in 1983–1984 ($3.1 million of $12.5 million), Food for the Hungry 9 percent ($.9 million of $10 million), and World Vision on the order of 6 percent ($9.4 million of an estimated $150 million). Other evangelical PVOs—MAP International, the Mennonite Central Committee, and the Summer Institute of Linguistics—received approximately 1 percent or less of their budgets from USAID. World Concern and World Neighbors received nothing ("Voluntary Foreign Aid Programs 1983–84," U.S. Agency for International Development, supplemented by author's estimate for World Vision).

a man succumbed to the temptations of Protestantism, a crowd of kin and neighbors quickly confronted him with the error of his ways.

Even after this tributary system began to break up in the 1960s, through a partial land reform, the future still seemed to belong to the Catholic Church. For not only was Chimborazo deeply Catholic, it was also the diocese of Monsignor Leonidas Proaño, the "bishop of the Indians," a symbol of justice for Ecuador's racial undercaste. For leading a civil rights movement akin to that of Martin Luther King in the United States, Proaño's clergy were beaten up and jailed, and he himself was denounced as a communist. In 1976, he became an international hero when the authorities burst into a retreat he was hosting and hauled off seventeen prelates at gun point, making fools of themselves.[19]

The future of Chimborazo did not belong to the Catholic Church, however, not even to the suffering, progressive church of Bishop Proaño. Partly through his reforming efforts, Chimborazo became the most Protestant province in the Ecuadorian highlands. In 1976, evangelical missionaries claimed 10 percent of its two hundred thousand Quichuas.[20] Ten years later, Quichua pastors said that they were shepherding fifty thousand people, Catholic opponents credited them with 30 percent of the Indian population, and World Vision's evangelical directory claimed even more.[21] Although the latter figures were probably inflated, no other external agent, maybe not even the bishop's Riobamba diocese, could claim such an impact on Quichua communities.[22]

To understand what happened, let us go to the area around the Gospel Missionary Union's station at Colta Lake. Before the spirit of evangelism possessed the mud and thatch villages surrounding this cold, marshy body of water at 10,000 feet, it was common to find much of the population in a state of intoxication. On Sundays, the Pan-American Highway running beside the lake was lined with drunks, male and female, staggering back from market and collapsing in the road.[23] The consumption of cane liquor seemed to accompany every social occasion and many nonsocial ones, too. At drunken fiestas, Quichua who at other times seemed dull and submissive insulted their masters and exploded in pride. Then, as the headaches took over, they quarreled murderously among themselves. The fiestas, GMU missionary Donald Dilworth wrote, provided an illusory revolution that kept the Quichua from exploding in a real one.[24]

In 1965, a team from Cornell University visited Colta for the U.S. Agency for International Development. The investigators learned that Indians still knelt to kiss the hand of their patrón— first folding a corner of the poncho over the patrón's flesh, to avoid touching it with their lips. The North Americans apparently betrayed their feelings about the methods employed by local bar owners and landlords because, fearing financial ruin, the latter gentlemen informed suspicious Quichua that the gringos were planning to steal their children. The Quichua were generally uninterested in development, the Cornell team reported. They were so uninterested that, at one point, some threatened to burn the Cornell team alive.

To withstand the insults and intimidation, the investigators concluded, a development project around Colta would require personnel with almost missionary dedication. That same year, the missionaries already on the scene, at the GMU station in Majipamba, felt obliged to call in the army to protect a handful of converts across the water at San Antonio. Catholics had blamed the Protestants for a drought and stoned them as they prepared for a baptism in the lake. After the converts fled to the GMU mission, the army arrived, hauled twenty Catholics back to its barracks, and beat them up. The next time the Protestants fled to the mission and the army arrived, much of the town headed for the hills.[25]

One bright spot, the Cornell team felt, was that some Colta men itinerated far and wide as peddlers. They were bringing home ideas that, some day, might blossom into community development. According to a later researcher, Bernhard Gellner, the early 1960s were already a time of ferment in Colta. To keep one step ahead of land reform, hacienda owners were selling off parcels to the Quichua. With many such purchasers already laboring under the financial requirements of petty commerce, their land acquisitions increased the pressure to evade the costly obligations of folk Catholicism.[26] If poverty could "be measured in the number and duration of fiestas," as the GMU's Dilworth observed,[27] then Colta was on the edge of revolt. Still, who would have thought that the lakeshore communities were about to be seized by born-again religion? Certainly, it took the missionaries by surprise, and it would have been difficult to foresee the transformation.

Just twenty years after the Cornell team's visit, Colta looked more like an up-and-coming suburb of the nearest city than a Quichua settlement. The mud and thatch huts of old had almost disappeared behind a wall of modern white houses, many of them two stories high, ringing half the lake. The Nuca Llacta cooperative maintained an impressive fleet of buses, pickups, and other motor vehicles, most of them owned by evangelicals. Because Colta's major sources of prosperity were its far-flung merchants and other migrant workers, it was subject to the usual rumors of involvement in the drug trade—a murder here, so-and-so in prison there. From across a mile of water in San Antonio, which the army used to invade to protect converts from Catholics, a loudspeaker could be heard announcing the latest Bible study.

Around Colta the majority of Quichua converted to Protestantism, ruining the local bar owners and ending the Catholic Church as a significant presence.[28] GMU churches popped up across the Chimborazo landscape. Evangelical planners made much of the movement as a model of working through the local culture: it was one of the first Protestant breakthroughs among the Quichua anywhere in the Andes. Missiologists tallied long lists of factors: the linguistic approach, an idiomatic translation of the New Testament, a radio station that broadcast hymns and popular music in the native language, medical clinics, Evangelism in Depth, Theological Education by Extension, church conferences, functional substitutes, this and that.

But the most important step the GMU apparently took was to let the Quichua run their own churches. By loosening the reins in the mid-1960s, the mission allowed its budding churches to be carried away on the back of a Quichua independence movement. At a time when the Quichua were breaking away from landlords, opening up to developmentalism, and searching for new ways to organize themselves, here was a new form of organization in which they could speak their own language and run their own affairs, where they could remain true to their sense of themselves as an oppressed group yet get ahead in the world.[29]

The Bishop of the Indians, Part I

For Monsignor Proaño, the Protestant breakthrough in Chimborazo was a real embarrassment. The country's most noticeable evangelical movement had erupted in the diocese of its most progressive bishop. Were his policies to blame? Proaño was not well physically when he gave a friend and me an hour of his dwindling energies in May 1985: he seemed less charismatic than careworn. He had just reached the mandatory retirement age of seventy-five and stepped down. But for thirty-one years, Proaño occupied a sacred position in Andean culture. Many still regarded the bishop as a saint, a breathing, talking, miracle-dispensing equivalent of the plaster images in church. To Proaño was added the aura of the progressive Catholic Church and his courageous stand for Indian rights.

Despite accusations of being a dangerous radical, Proaño's main accomplishment was to pull his diocese out of the hacienda era. Only in a backward highland province like Chimborazo could he be regarded as a red bishop, by landlords enraged that he had publicized the official minimum wage which they were neglecting to pay. The truth was that Proaño feared violent revolution, in particular the number of Indians he knew would be killed making one. Preaching against ideological borrowing from Marxism, he favored what he called an authentically Christian theology of liberation. Instead of socialism, he preferred to speak of a "communitarian option," based on indigenous campesino tradition, which would somehow save Latin America from the destruction and strife of capitalism.

Proaño had gotten his diocese out of the hacienda business by returning most of its land to the Quichua, but it could still seem like a relic of the colonial era. Headquartered in drafty monuments in the provincial capital of Riobamba, the diocese had no archive; no legal department to defend itself against government authorities, landlords and evangelicals; and (remarkable to a hurry-it-up North American like myself) no system of radio communication to make up for the general lack of telephones.

What the Riobamba diocese did have was a wealth of pastoral agents, 1,318 of them, in an impressive network of lay and clerical, local, national, and international personnel who staffed parishes, schools, centers, and institutes. Pursuing specific tasks to strengthen the church's popular base were pastoral teams, commissions, and services, including Quichua "peasant missionaries." To address material needs there were development agencies, a well-drilling program, and medical teams. To teach peasants to read and raise their consciousness there were the well-known radio schools. Still other organizations promoted solidarity with Central American revolutions, persecuted Christians, and communities struggling for land.[30]

For Proaño and his supporters, it was no coincidence that Protestant growth paralleled their confrontations with the local ruling class, which evidently saw evangelicals as allies against a socially conscious diocese. Political conspiracy was difficult to prove, Proaño admitted, but clearly North American sects had been sent to counteract the message of liberation. Just as any empire seeks to impose its religion, he observed, Protestant missionaries had been flooding into Latin America ever since the Catholic Church began to work for social justice and question North American hegemony. This was how the church was paying for its option for the poor, the bishop believed. It was being undercut by sects that Washington was using as an "ideological irrigation canal."[31]

Proaño knew that Protestant missionaries had been in Chimborazo since the turn of the century, of course, and he recognized that his reforms had helped open up the province to them. The changes had not been unusual for a forward-looking bishop, especially one who had attended the Second Vatican Council in the early 1960s. He had, for example, discouraged priests from inciting violence against evangelists. When an incident occurred, he called in his man for a conversation. He also urged the Quichua to read the Bible, but he was not entirely pleased with the results. "Yes, they took advantage of ecumenism against us," Proaño told me. "We distributed quantities of *God Arrives to Man*, the ecumenical translation of the Bible societies. The evangelicals used it to argue that, according to the bishop, it was just as good to be evangelical as Catholic."

That did not stop Proaño from promoting the Bible. Like other Catholic reformers of the 1960s and 1970s, he felt that scripture would undermine pagan aspects of folk Catholicism. In Chimborazo, purifying the church meant attacking the priest's traditional role in Quichua rituals. It seemed like a sensible move: the fiestas associated with such events were costly, wealth-leveling obligations for their Quichua sponsors, who increasingly preferred to invest their surplus in petty trade, a parcel of land, or education. Part of the financial burden, not necessarily a large part but enough to complain about, were ritual payments to the priest, and Protestantism was an increasingly popular route of escape.

But when Proaño told priests to stop charging fees for sacraments, it left Quichua traditionalists unhappy. As far as the latter were concerned, sacraments did not perform their protective function unless they were paid for. Conservative priests had their own objections. They did not wish to break with a traditional source of income, and Proaño was in a poor position to make them conform. Dismissals were difficult under canon law, and he had too few priests to begin with. As a result, the diocese found itself in a sacramental double bind, of encouraging restless Quichua to convert to Protestantism when it fulfilled traditional expectations; and of antagonizing Quichua traditionalists when it refused to fulfill those expectations. Breaking with old ways proved to have all kinds of unpredictable costs. "The effort to renew the Catholic Church produced a crisis in the people," Proaño explained. "Many have understood, others no, and of these latter the sects have taken advantage." [32]

Judging from anthropologists, a grass roots revolt against clerical authority was taking place. Like other aspects of the old order, the Catholic Church had weighed heavily on the Quichua, embodying as it did many attributes of hacienda society. [33] Rejecting the church was therefore a way to reject the traditional order. Although Proaño was seeking to head off the repudiation of clerical authority, his reforms may have encouraged it, by undermining the priest's traditional role without being able immediately to construct a new one.

To make up for the shortage of priests, Proaño trained hundreds of Quichua catechists. But they defected to leadership positions in Protestantism with enough regularity to be a problem. Even the president of the Evangelical Indian Association of Chimborazo in 1985 had worked for the Catholic radio schools for thirteen years. Now, over the evangelical radio station he administered, he was said to make biting attacks on his former employer the bishop. "They buy our catechists," diocesan workers complained, accusing evangelicals of inducing Catholics to change their faith by offering them salaries. Evangelicals, in turn, were willing to swear that the bishop was "trying to buy our evangelists," with each side denying that it paid its Quichua leaders anything.

But the Catholics suffered more of the losses, and one reason appeared to be that Quichua leaders were running up against priestly authority. Despite Proaño's promotion of lay leaders, he preferred the Roman collar when available, and men of the collar remained in charge of diocesan programs. Even progressive priests could have a high opinion of their clerical prerogatives and be resented for it, reproducing the traditional social distance between shepherd and flock. One promising solution, to train Quichua priests, continued to present many difficulties. After thirty years of reform, it was still in the planning stages. At a time when evangelical leadership had become largely Quichua, Proaño's clergy continued to be foreign to their parishioners. Clericalism was a weak point in the Catholic reform, providing an opening for evangelicals on the lookout for frustrated local leaders.[34]

Christian Violence

Chimborazo was just one of a number of places in the indigenous regions of Latin America where the spread of Protestantism was punctuated by violence. In southern Mexico, in the western Guatemalan highlands, in southwestern Colombia, around Lake Titicaca between Peru and Bolivia, some of Latin America's most oppressed peasantries were converting to Protestantism in large numbers. Small evangelical chapels seemed to be materializing everywhere.

It is not hard to see how evangelism could split communities into hostile factions. Populations which evangelicals regarded as "unreached" had already been missionized for centuries, by an established clergy which was trying to obstruct the new wave of evangelizers. At the same time, religious tradition was under powerful pressure from within. Even as some native people defended the community religious obligations of old, others were refusing to perform those duties.

In Chimborazo, trouble often broke the superficial tranquility of a Quichua village in the form of a big, colorful tent. Usually the campaign was organized by the Gospel Missionary Union's local denomination, the Evangelical Indian Association of Chimborazo (AIECH). As the meetings grew in size and enthusiasm, loudspeakers blared until late at night, not always with the permission of local authorities. Catholics retaliated by roughing up evangelicals; AIECH went to the police; and the police mistreated enough Catholics to discourage them from doing it again. When evangelicals died, it was usually after being handled by a mob. When Catholics died, it was usually from police or army bullets. Cases that went before the law were usually won by evangelicals. Although the state protected the freedom of individuals, it did not recognize the right of corporate groups to expel dissidents. Backed by the state, Protestants were driving a spike into the heart of the old form of community.

Catholic as well as Protestant leaders paid lip service to the idea of religious freedom. They each abhorred violence and said they had tried to dialogue with the other side, only to be spurned. But the prevailing attitude was intolerance, with evangelicals as likely to use inflammatory language as Catholics. The early stages of Protestant reformation were not a model of Christian humility, attacks on the parish priest being a popular tactic. Catholics tended to throw the first stone, but new Protestant majorities sometimes expropriated Catholic chapels and even tore them down.[35] One reason: Protestants had helped build the chapels when they were still Catholics and considered them community property.

Religious toleration was not in the culture, missionaries on both sides observed, sometimes with a hint of self-justification. Scandal over the latest incident could give the impression that religious violence was on the rise. But according to evangelical missionaries, Catholic hostility was not nearly as frank, consistent, and physical as it had been when they arrived in the 1950s.[36] Violence appeared to be a passing phenomenon at the expanding edge of religious change, where evangelists were probing Catholic territory and leaving behind weak, easily persecuted fringes of converts. In older areas, it was common for Catholics and Protestants to start fraternizing again.[37]

"If outsiders leave them alone," Monsignor Mario Ruiz Navas of Latacunga told me, "they come to an arrangement. After living five centuries of oppression, they are capable of getting along with each other."[38] They might learn to get along like Catholics and Protestants apparently did in a place called Santa Rosa, up an eroded valley from Riobamba. Standing two hundred yards below the Catholic church was a chapel connected to the Gospel Missionary Union. Everyone in Santa Rosa worked together in the *minga* or communal work day, a local man said. The Catholics helped repair the evangelical church, and the evangelicals helped repair the Catholic church.

Catholic and Protestant Indians also managed to work together in the same political organizations, at least until the campaign to expel the Summer Institute of Linguistics (SIL). As the field arm of the Wycliffe Bible Translators, the Summer Institute had a base in the Amazon Jungle, an open-ended government contract, and more linguistic capability than any Ecuadorian organization. That made it a predictable target for concern over North American influence in national affairs. Soon after the first anthropology department in Ecuador came into being, at the Catholic University in Quito in the early 1970s, it went on the offensive against SIL. Indian organizations and the left joined in. When Ecuador's young, charismatic president Jaime Roldós revoked SIL's contract in April 1981, the aura about the decision was heightened by his death two days later in a plane crash. According to the official investigation, it was an accident. Suspicion lingered that Roldós had been killed by the United States for his nationalist policies, however, and the controversy over SIL split the Indian movement.

Opponents pressed for the physical removal of SIL members from national soil. Otherwise, they feared, the North Americans would make a comeback with the help of military officers and U.S. diplomats, as they had in other countries. But the Summer Institute had its defenders, including native pastors and teachers convinced that the government would not replace its flight and medical service. They also felt that attacks on their missionaries were turning into attacks on them. Encouraged by SIL, they pressured the government to restore the contract. Accusations flew, with each side dismissing the other as a pawn in an anti-Ecuadorian conspiracy. Evangelicals withdrew from established Indian organizations to form their own.

As the Summer Institute hauled down its flag, there were disturbing reports of a new evangelical mission at work in the highlands. According to Catholic and Quichua sources, it was sowing conflict in native communities at a terrific rate. The group's name was World Vision. It had incorporated in Ecuador only the year before the government ended SIL's contract. The coincidence prompted opponents to identify the new organization as SIL's replacement, in what they construed as another attempt to divide and depoliticize indigenous peoples.

The Development of World Vision

One reason World Vision invited suspicion in Latin America was that it was a product of the Cold War. Its founder Bob Pierce (1914– 1978) had been one of the Youth for Christ evangelists who led the revival in the United States at the end of World War II, then poured the resulting energies into world evangelism. Overseas his first campaigns were in China, where Youth for Christ hoped that evangelical Christianity would stiffen the resistance to communist advance. After the Kuomintang regime fell, Pierce led campaigns in South Korea just before war broke out in 1950. As the red tide surged forward, he came home with movie footage showing the plight of refugees and began raising money to help them.

Pierce was a domineering man, a faith entrepreneur who clashed frequently with his board of directors over how money was spent.[39] When he resigned in a fit of temper in 1967, he was replaced by the smooth, organizational W. Stanley Mooneyham, former press secretary to Billy Graham and organizer of the first Graham-financed world evangelism congress. Under Mooneyham (1969–1982) World Vision became today's slick, efficient multinational with a 1985 income of $232 million.[40] Wherever disaster struck, World Vision made a beeline for it. In 1984 it was financing one hundred relief efforts, two thousand five hundred child and family assistance projects, six hundred community development programs, and a hundred and fifty evangelism campaigns in seventy-seven countries.[41]

World Vision developed in step with an unusually broad financial base. From the start, its founder's combination of evangelism with social work turned off the kind of fundamentalist whose shibboleths cramped so many endeavors. Another influence was financial support from the U.S. Agency for International Development, which barred the use of government money for proselytism. Because

World Vision was not supposed to condition government-provided assistance on religious criteria, it became accustomed to presenting itself as a nonsectarian, humanitarian agency like other religious groups in the same line of work. Finally, when World Vision switched from documentary films to television as its main fundraiser, that shifted its pitch from the church basement to the home, where it acquired a wider range of supporters. Although World Vision's board of directors was evangelical, a significant percentage of contributors were not. In Australia and New Zealand, 20 percent were Catholic and another 20 percent were without religious affiliation; in Europe, only 5 percent were evangelical.[42]

Stanley Mooneyham presided over several important changes that kept World Vision near the forefront of evangelical relief and development. The first was how the group spent its money. Playing on middle-class guilt, World Vision's founder had made its name by coming to the rescue of children fathered by American soldiers in Korea and Vietnam. Bob Pierce was one of the first to promote child sponsorship, the "adoption" of a child in a Third World country by a North American, who pledged to send ten or twenty dollars a month in exchange for a photo of the little one and occasional thank-you notes. The scheme produced emotionally committed, long-term donors, and by 1985 World Vision was helping 360,000 children around the world in this way.[43] The stable financial return on child sponsorship was so basic to the private relief industry that, as Alan Youngren has pointed out, its main pitch is still the photo of a child needing to be picked up and held.

Two circumstances pushed World Vision and some of the other child sponsorship agencies into experimenting with new approaches, however. First, while sponsorship was an unbeatable way to raise money, the financial adoption of individual children led to all kinds of problems. If run as a long-term system of handouts, the cash, food and/or clothes bred a welfare mentality in the recipients, made their neighbors jealous, and aroused suspicion that wealthy foreign organizations were trying to alienate children from their communities. The last point became more important as political climates became less friendly to North American philanthropy.

Second, media coverage of refugees in Africa and Southeast Asia fueled a boom in giving to relief agencies (and then a depression when the media turned to other subjects, as they did in 1986 by dropping refugees for terrorists).[44] From 1978 to 1980, World Vision's U.S. income more than doubled to $80 million. Even conservative evangelicals became more responsive to humanitarian appeals than to calls for more evangelism. The income of traditional missions leveled off and even fell behind inflation, to the point that some prefaced their appeals for the next evangelistic campaign with a photo of a lonely child or the latest catastrophe.

The relief agencies were raising so much money that they ran short of good ways to spend it, at a time when their staffers were absorbing trenchant criticisms of paternalism in the relief and development industry. To avoid making rice bowl Christians, agencies tried to move away from sponsoring individual children to community development. But when World Vision asked contributors to adopt a community rather than a child, the new pitch didn't play in Peoria.[45] Like other agencies, therefore, World Vision continued to offer donors the chance to "adopt" a child, for the defensible reason that they sent in more money.[46]

World Vision's new president Mooneyham also presided over a change in political image. The organization's founder, Bob Pierce, had conceived of his work as a bulwark against the communist hordes of Asia, due to his political formation in the Cold War and association with figures such as Chiang Kai-shek and President Syngman Rhee of South Korea. In Vietnam and Cambodia, World Vision was one of the groups heavily subsidized by USAID, raising understandable fears about its objectives.[47] But when it became obvious that a close identification with the United States was not going over well in the Third World, in the 1970s, World Vision tried to rise above East/West politics. It claimed to have no political ideology, announced its willingness to help anyone, and worked under communist regimes such as Colonel Mengistu's in Ethiopia and Heng Samrin's in Cambodia. Although World Vision continued to accept surplus food, relief funds, and development grants from USAID, the percentage of its income from that source fell significantly.[48] For its Latin American programs it claimed to accept no funds from the U.S. government.[49]

Even critics conceded that World Vision had helped make North Americans aware of human needs in the Third World. On occasion, it got ahead of the evangelical pack. When the Israelis invaded Lebanon and attacked Palestinian refugee camps in 1982, World

Vision was one of the few evangelical organizations to tell its constituents about the consequences. For the eight hundred thousand readers of its magazine, World Vision's president presented the 255 bodies and ankle-deep body fluids left in a school basement by an Israeli bomb. "David seems determined to become Goliath," wrote Stanley Mooneyham, antagonized by Israeli blockades of relief supplies. "Perhaps someone in charge should reread that Bible story."[50]

World Vision was an early supporter of the Latin American Theological Fraternity and its criticism of fundamentalist positions. Following the Sandinista victory in Nicaragua, World Vision channeled its reconstruction aid through CEPAD.[51] After Archbishop Oscar Romero was assassinated in El Salvador, World Vision reprinted his views and later called on evangelicals to deal with the challenges posed by liberation theology.[52] And when Ríos Montt raised evangelical hopes for Guatemala, World Vision provided one of the few realistic assessments in the evangelical media. "Because Montt and others in his government have histories of being intricately involved in ordering mass murders of peasant people," Faith Sand wrote, "the euphoria quickly subsided and events such as the massacre at Saquiya Dos began again. Montt, it seems, either is powerless to stop the rampaging army or he is turning his back on what is happening."[53]

But World Vision could not go far, as the reaction to the Guatemala article showed. Two months later, an administrator was still fielding complaints from offended brethren. Another predicted that World Vision would never publish a story like that again, not least because it offended Ríos Montt's government, which the agency hoped would improve the situation.[54] In general, while World Vision's fundraising literature acknowledged the structural basis of injustice in a vague sort of way, it saw no point in making its work more difficult by antagonizing the authorities.

As Jörgen Lissner has pointed out, relief agencies who wish to maximize financial contributions play to the middle of the political spectrum, with occasional gestures to supporters at either end.[55] To open up maximum access to the field, such groups try to stay friendly with everyone. This is a plausible explanation for World Vision's waffling on difficult issues. When its officials were asked where their organization stood, they launched into a series of fence-straddling equations. World Vision was not against protest but it

was against violence, they said. As for liberation theology, liberation was crucial to Latin America, and World Vision did not reject
any theological position that had Christ as its center. It wanted to
empower communities, by providing the administrative skills they
needed to run their own affairs. But World Vision wished to be free
of the tyranny of bankrupt ideologies, of capitalism and communism. It wanted to choose a third way, that of the kingdom of God.[56]

Along with this kind of equivocation, World Vision had a reputation for throwing money around and bypassing established organizations. According to one analysis, the problem was the priority
World Vision placed on maximizing income. Raising as much
money as possible, then handing it out, had become the object of
the operation. Instead of responding to the needs of existing local
organizations, an approach that called for considerable caution in
expenditure, World Vision was pumping money into as many communities as possible.

By insisting on working directly with the grass roots rather than
through intermediate organizations, moreover, World Vision was
also setting up its own bureaucracy. No one was more upset about
this than the missionaries and church leaders who had absorbed
World Vision's rhetoric about how it supported the local church. In
practice, they felt left out of the picture. "They really didn't go
through the existing structure," a member of the Christian and Missionary Alliance observed in Ecuador. "They tend to short-circuit
the existing organizations and set up their own kingdom."

Still, World Vision maintained a relatively low, hard-to-attack
profile by keeping North Americans out of the field. Of eleven hundred full-time and eight thousand part-time staff overseas in 1981,
it claimed that only ninety-one were from "the West."[57] Minimizing
foreign administration could also mean a lack of supervision, however, with programs taking on the political trajectory of the national
structures through which they were channeled.

The Scandals in Honduras

That, anyway, was the most charitable interpretation of World Vision's refugee program in Honduras. The refugees were Salvadorans, who had fled from the security forces of their country in fear
for their lives. Persecution followed them across the border, how-

ever, as the Honduran army helped its Salvadoran counterpart track down and kill suspected subversives. When the Catholic relief agency CARITAS protested, the Honduran government retaliated by placing evangelicals in charge. But continued death squad raids forced the evangelicals, of the National Evangelical Emergency Committee (CEDEN), into the same oppositional stance as other relief agencies on the scene.

All, that is, except World Vision. As other agencies refused to hand over the names of refugees to the authorities, in the belief that the information was being passed on to death squads, World Vision staffers continued to do so. What set off the uproar were refugee reports that, in May 1981, a World Vision supervisor allowed the Honduran army to take two refugees from the camps at Colomoncagua. Shortly their bodies appeared in a river. Frightened by World Vision, refugees accused its staffers of interrogating them about their political views, giving information to the Honduran military, and using relief supplies to pressure them to turn evangelical. CARITAS and CEDEN backed up the complaints against World Vision, whose staffers then accused the first two agencies of ties to guerrillas.

None of World Vision's staffers in the refugee camps, it should be noted, was North American. Most employees had been hired on the recommendation of a local coordinator, the Reverend Mario Fumero, who turned out to be an anticommunist Cuban exile. Several of Fumero's recruits proved to be rehabilitated alcoholics and drug addicts, from a program he had run in cooperation with the police—hence his ties with the Ministry of Defense according to World Vision.[58] In the camps, World Vision was the only agency pushing for evangelism of the mainly Catholic refugees, an idea the Protestant CEDEN as well as the Catholic CARITAS opposed.[59]

As the scandal ruined World Vision's carefully cultivated image, its embarrassed administrators first transferred lower-level employees to another camp, Guarita. Then they fired half their staff, chiefly for stealing food or threatening to withhold it from refugees who failed to attend evangelical services. World Vision continued to deny any complicity in the Honduran government's human rights violations. But an in-house evaluation concluded that: "in trying to be apolitical . . . we communicated . . . that we favored the status quo. . . . We were blind to the intensity of the human rights struggles. . . . Consequently, for many months we were not aware that we were being pushed . . . toward a pro-government, pro-military position and therefore, a position perceived as being contra to the Catholic Church, the relief agencies, and the people. At the same time, most of the other agencies were much more actively defending human rights."[60]

That was not the end of the affair. World Vision had omitted to fire the man presiding over the fiasco, Mario Fumero, who now succeeded in having his critics purged from the Protestant relief agency CEDEN. It was not just Fumero's doing: the Honduran fundamentalists making up much of CEDEN's base were already unhappy with its approach. They felt that it was paying more attention to its ecumenical funding sources in New York than to them, by failing to give a Christian testimony (that is, respecting fundamentalist strictures) and finance what really counted—evangelism. Now in the refugee camps, instead of evangelizing the mainly Catholic war survivors, CEDEN's staffers were cooperating with their Romanist counterparts.[61]

Encouraged by local World Vision personnel, Honduran fundamentalists began to accuse CEDEN of helping the Salvadoran guerrillas and, in January 1982, staged an administrative coup. A new board of directors voted to cut all ties with the liberal World Council of Churches. Henceforth, CEDEN would accept funds only from World Vision and the U.S. Agency for International Development.[62] For a time, the ousted ecumenical backers believed that World Vision headquarters had engineered the coup, apparently incorrectly.[63] But only after Fumero had taken his revenge did World Vision replace him and end its program.[64]

In the words of World Vision's president, Stanley Mooneyham, it felt "greatly victimized" by these events.[65] But blaming local employees for what went wrong did not satisfy critics. At bottom, World Vision had been caught trying to be all things to all men. It did not want to be accused of supporting the status quo, but neither did it want to antagonize fundamentalists or take a stand against the authorities. By refusing to take stands, a growth-oriented corporation had allowed itself to be used by right-wing forces; then it had been mistaken for a right-wing enterprise and attacked as such internationally.

One of the conflicts in Honduras was about to crop up in Ecuador. World Vision administrators said they wanted to be on good terms with the Catholic Church. They even found room for it in their definition of Christianity: clearly, they said, Catholics could come to know Christ within their own church. But to fellow evangelicals, World Vision claimed that evangelism was its "guiding force" and "a significant component" of each project.[66] To most Latin American evangelicals, that meant converting Catholics into Protestants. As a result, cooperation with the Catholic Church was not necessarily part of the program.[67] Where local evangelicals were still making war on Romanism, World Vision was not about to get in the way.

The Scandals in Imbabura

One of the first things Ecuadorians noticed about World Vision was the discrepancy between what it said and what it did. Although the group described itself as Christian, not evangelical, it was channeling its help exclusively through evangelicals. Instead of working through the *cabildo*—the elected council in Quichua villages—it was bypassing them and turning its funds over to evangelical leaders. The ensuing quarrels were breaking up *mingas,* the communal work days in Quichua culture.

Ecuadorians were still debating a similar discrepancy in the work of the Summer Institute of Linguistics. Despite claims to be a nonsectarian scientific organization, it had turned out to be an evangelical mission. Now that SIL had lost its government contract, Ecuadorian opponents suspected that World Vision had inherited the same objectives. It was as if the whole operation was calculated to sharpen conflicts between Catholics and Protestants, divide communities, and make it harder for peasants to fight for their rights.[68]

Shoving World Vision into the public eye was a chain of scandals in half a dozen communities around Otavalo, Imbabura, the home of accomplished Quichua weavers and traders. When World Vision's local evangelical administrators handed out clothes and invited children to daily feeding programs, they favored their own brethren, not those in greatest need. Then World Vision started making loans for community stores and handicraft projects, which again benefited a small evangelical minority. Soon there was a string of accounting disasters—a combination of administrative ignorance, culturally approved sharing of resources with kin, and theft.

In one incident, in September 1982, a mob stormed the house of World Vision's promoter in Ilumán. Claiming to have been cheated out of promised benefits, the attackers succeeded in distributing the contents of a World Vision–financed chicken coop. But when they tried to liberate the promoter's World Vision–financed sewing machines, the spoils were destroyed in the melee.[69] According to World Vision, the men leading the raid had been entrusted with a community store, then overseen the evaporation of its funds and, as a diversionary tactic, attacked the local administrator.[70] A year later, in La Compañía, evangelicals led by a World Vision coordinator beat up Catholics in a dispute over real estate.[71] The quarrel predated World Vision's arrival. But only then did the Quito office discover that its local representatives, men supposed to be presenting a Christian witness, had a history of grabbing other people's land.

Now that the left-wing press, the development community, and Indian organizations were nipping at its heels, World Vision tried to clean up its operation. The brawl in La Compañía, in November 1983, was the last straw. The next month, World Vision dismissed all four of its Imbabura coordinators. Apologizing for any trouble they had caused, it left the most afflicted communities. Even before the trouble broke out, World Vision officials said, they had been moving away from child sponsorship to community development projects. They also began to switch to village councils or *cabildos* as less factional, more representative local conduits than evangelical churches had been.[72]

The Bishop of the Indians, Part II

In Chimborazo, Catholic clergy and Indian organizations braced for a repetition of the events in Imbabura. For Monsignor Proaño and the Riobamba Diocese, the new wave of evangelical entrepreneurship combined two phenomena in which they had little faith, Protestants and North American development agencies. Protestants alone were enough to worry about: by 1985 the Evangelical Indian Association of Chimborazo claimed to have 280 churches. Then there was World Vision; it had entered only twelve communities in

Imbabura and thirty in Tungurahua, but in Chimborazo the figure was seventy. Worse, after starting in evangelical communities, World Vision was drawing Catholic communities into its orbit. More and more were asking World Vision to come help them, an idea the diocese feared could reach epidemic proportions. According to a rumor—apparently false—the group had received more than one hundred requests in a single month.[73]

These were the georeligious preoccupations pitting the diocese against World Vision. But the picture in Riobamba was complicated by its status as a beacon of liberation theology. Monsignor Proaño's social commitments had attracted foreign church workers, especially from Colombia, France, and Belgium. His commitments also had deepened divisions characteristic of the Catholic clergy, such that certain conservative priests wanted as little to do with Proaño as possible. But even among his supporters there was bitter factionalism. While the foreign church workers tended to regard the Ecuadorian clergy as backward, the Ecuadorians tended to regard the foreigners—especially the Colombians—as subversives. By 1984–1985, therefore, some of Proaño's people were red-baiting others as guerrilla organizers.

What Proaño's supporters needed was a new rallying point. Agrarian reform had been the motor of Christian liberation in Chimborazo. But now the traditional hacienda and its system of peonage had been abolished, removing the most obvious rallying points. Enough land had been parceled out to satisfy some petitioners and set them against other Quichua. Redistribution was sputtering to a halt. The secular left was also being defeated by modest successes: now that it had helped hacienda serfs and other landless laborers acquire bits of their own land, they seemed more interested in exercising their new measure of personal freedom than in further protest.[74] What was next? What more and more Quichua wanted was "development"—public works, education, more money, a sense of getting ahead in the world. "Are you from some institution?" hopeful young men asked North Americans.

Was the Riobamba church going to give these people what they wanted? No, because Proaño and his supporters believed that, if capitalist development took its course, it would swallow up the Quichua as an indigenous people. They knew that conventional development was widening the class differences within Quichua society; the main change was probably that henceforth the Quichua would be exploited by a bourgeoisie from their own ethnic group as well as by white landowners. The Riobamba church therefore held out for social change based on communal values rather than personal ascent. For reasons stretching back before Karl Marx, to Catholic social doctrine, a diocese was sermonizing against the combined hegemonic forces of capitalism. By way of an alternative, Diego Iturralde suggests, it was proposing a sort of Indian communalism, an all-encompassing "church of the Indians" with each Quichua community in the role of a base community, each Indian organization in the role of catechist, and the Catholic clergy in their accustomed pastoral role, in a modern equivalent of the Indian republics of colonial Paraguay.[75]

Aside from the broad outlines of the communal vision, something else on which Proaño's supporters could agree was that evangelicals were ruining it. Opposition to evangelical expansion was therefore a logical new rallying point, one even conservative clergy could share. Something similar had occurred in Imbabura, where World Vision's staunchest opponents were the Missionaries of Mother Laura, an order of sisters from Colombia who had long defended the faith against Protestantism. Like Proaño's supporters, the Lauritas believed they were opposing Protestantism on antiimperialist or political grounds, not religious ones. But they tended to regard evangelical religion as inherently anticultural, individualist, and alienating, which made the popular church exclusively Catholic.[76]

The popular church in Chimborazo was also exclusive of North Americans, who were often suspected of working for the Central Intelligence Agency. The forty-nine foreign church workers in the diocese did not include any U.S. citizens, perhaps because their presence would confuse Quichua whom the diocese was indoctrinating against U.S. influence in its sermons and publications. In this sense, anti-imperialism was the Riobamba church's defense of its clientele against the buying power of North American money.

There was also a grass-roots Quichua opposition to World Vision's buying power, stemming from past experience with outsiders and activated by disruptive incidents. But its most visible expression, the Indian Movement of Chimborazo (MICH), was connected to the diocese. Founded in 1982 by Quichua leaders and Monsignor Proaño, the movement attributed the problems of native communities to factionalism caused by outsiders, especially evangelicals and World Vision. The only solution was unity, it taught, and that entailed one religion.[77]

MICH opposed conventional, externally financed development projects, in the belief that development should be endogenous, that is, from the people themselves and based on their own resources. That was no way to produce fast, spectacular results in dirt-poor communities, however. Various diocesan organizations did sponsor more conventional development projects, but there were not enough to satisfy the petitions of hundreds of Quichua hamlets. In practice, therefore, the Riobamba church was urging communities to reject U.S.-financed development projects without always providing a ready alternative.

This, needless to say, was not an easy task. "We're getting ahead" was a phrase always on the lips of evangelical Quichua, Catholic church worker Carola Lentz noticed. At the same time, she reported an "almost idealization" of indigenous poverty in the Catholic Church, as if poverty were a necessary condition for raising the consciousness of Indians and liberating them. The implication was that Indians were only authentic when they were poor, while those moving up in the world were betraying their people.[78] It was easy for middle-class radicals to fall into the trap of denying to the poor the comforts they themselves enjoyed, on the grounds that such improvements were palliatives.

When the diocesan-connected Quichua federation of Licto signed an agreement with the U.S. government's Inter-American Foundation, Catholic church workers felt that they had "lost" the area even though the federation continued to profess its loyalty. Such Quichua wanted immediate, tangible improvements that required tangible resources, from outside. When outsiders tried to work in Quichua communities, whether they were admitted depended increasingly on whether they were bringing a project. "Organizing people isn't easy," MICH leader Ana Maria Guacho told me, "when World Vision offers money and we offer consciousness-raising."[79]

Building up the Local Church

In Chimborazo, the most telling criticism of World Vision came, not from Catholics, but from World Vision's own brethren, in the Gospel Missionary Union and the Evangelical Indian Association of Chimborazo (AIECH). Like Monsignor Proaño, they said that it was throwing around too much money and dividing people in the name of Christ.

The Indian Association had been set up in 1966–1967 as the GMU's local church body. With its tent campaigns, training programs, savings and loan, radio station, and transport cooperative, it was the most impressive evangelical Indian organization in South America. Lately, World Vision had been doing quite a bit for the Indian Association. But when I met with its directors in June 1985, they were blaming World Vision for their problems. It had been "more damage than help" and "was making robbers of our brothers," they declared.

In one case, a pastor had gone to work for World Vision, seemed to be a successful coordinator, and announced his candidacy for the association's executive committee. That was the point at which World Vision accused him of falsifying receipts to buy a piece of land and a car. A cloud also hung over AIECH's previous president. He left office to preside over the evangelical Indian federation on the national level, unable to explain a shortfall in construction funds which World Vision had channeled through him. The association's books were a mess, and the new executive council didn't know where it stood. A GMU accountant was helping them figure it out, and the former president was refusing to explain his stewardship. Everyone was pointing a finger at someone else.

In Quito, World Vision administrators blamed the dishonesty of the Quichua leaders whom they had hired out of local churches. That had been part of their explanation for the scandals in Imbabura, too. But as far as the Indian Association's leaders were concerned, the problem was World Vision's lack of administration, from the top down. AIECH's leaders were also refusing to participate in World Vision's new national evangelical directory, for two reasons. First, they feared that Catholics would use the directory to identify and persecute weak, new congregations. Second, they feared that other evangelical bodies—such as World Vision—would use the listings to bypass their association and contact pastors directly.[80]

Clearly, authority and patronage were serious business among Protestants as well as Catholics in Chimborazo. The Indian Association was headquartered in the GMU's compound at Majipamba, up a lane of houses from the highway running next to Lake Colta. With big old shade trees in the yard, and the cemetery beyond, it was easy to imagine that missionaries had occupied it for most of the century. In a two-story house, on a rise looking down on the rest of the compound, lived one of the men most responsible for the evangelical breakthrough in the province.

Popular movements were not an ordinary accomplishment for the GMU, an old-fashioned faith mission dating to 1892. But Henry Klassen's upbringing had helped him see through mission paternalism in ways his colleagues did not. He had been raised in a Plattdeutsch-speaking Mennonite colony on the Canadian prairie, learning English only when he went off to the city at age seventeen.[81] Arriving in Ecuador in 1952, he understood the importance of, not just doing everything in the native language, but letting the Quichua run their own show.

Klassen was still a presence, of course, and when World Vision started working with the GMU's daughter churches, it had been without so much as a good morning to him or his mission. When Klassen went to see the new agency, its director Frank Boshold explained that he hoped to build up the local church. Once the Quichua were developed, Boshold argued, it would be easier for them to tithe. Klassen was not impressed and said that the new program would imperil the church, not help it. "You do your thing," Boshold told him. "We'll do our thing." Now, after several years of World Vision doing its own thing, Klassen was not looking forward to being blamed for the meeting it had called for that same afternoon in the compound below, as if being from Canada and getting blamed for the U.S. invasion of Grenada were not enough.

It wasn't just that World Vision hired away the most promising leaders, with the kind of money their own congregations could never provide. No, Klassen and his wife Pat said, World Vision was just giving out too much money, to the point of demoralizing the people it said it was helping. Now Quichua believers were asking why they should tithe from their own earnings if they could receive so much more from the new wonder mission. It was as if middle-class North Americans were suddenly given a million dollars. By working through individual pastors rather than the Indian organization, the Klassens felt, World Vision was corrupting pastors, un-

dermining the association, and turning the Quichua into professional beggars. Now that the believers had their minds on money,
fewer churches were being started. Those who benefited less were
jealous of those who benefited more. World Vision was distracting
and dividing the church, not fortifying it.[82]

The association's directors professed the same opinion when they
met with Klassen and me in their offices at the GMU compound. If
they did not receive a satisfactory response from World Vision in a
few days, they vowed, they would refuse to work with it again. But
when I talked with World Vision's director a week later, he seemed
genuinely surprised by my recital of AIECH's complaints. He had
never heard about them, Frank Boshold said, least of all from the
cordial meeting a few days before. And he was not contrite about
World Vision's accounting methods. "It wasn't the fault of the system," he insisted, calling the most flagrant of the fallen pastors
"bandits" and maintaining that a new auditing department was preventing such incidents from recurring. Although it was true that
AIECH's former president was refusing to render accounts, Boshold said, there were other accusations against the man, and the
funds AIECH was handling were not just from World Vision. As far
as Boshold was concerned, his agency was being blamed for other
people's problems.

Regarding competition with other agencies, Boshold argued that
communities could not be considered the property of the first
group to arrive. If an organization came in with a heavy ideological
program like consciousness-raising, as some did, the people might
turn to a program that made fewer demands on them. It was "totally absurd" that World Vision was trying to lure Catholics away
from their own church. "We are not an evangelical organization,"
Boshold insisted. "We are a Christian organization. We don't think
development projects have a religion. We are never interested in a
change of religion or church. We are interested only in a change of
heart."[83]

Unlike most of World Vision's country directors in Latin America, Boshold was a gringo, born in Germany but passing easily as a
North American. Every inch the executive, he enjoyed defending
his program and did so vigorously and well. But perhaps too well
because, if he was correct, all the fuss was about nothing.

It was true that World Vision's problems were far from unique.

According to a study of Chibuleo, Tungurahua, by José Pereira, World Vision was the seventh development agency to provide loans there. Eighty percent of the population was in debt to previous agencies, who had little chance of being repaid. Certain members of the community were accustomed to start essentially fictitious cooperatives, use their experience with development agencies to apply for loans, then fold up shop with the funds diverted to mysterious ends. Not unlike middle-class development experts who made a good living by hopping from one mainly unsuccessful project to the next, these peasant-level empresarios had learned how to attract a development agency, milk it for what it was worth, and then lure in the next one.[84] Failing to get to know a scene before putting money into it, making local rivalries worse, promoting new elites who specialized in ripping off projects, these were facts of life in the development world.

World Vision was therefore being scapegoated to a certain extent. Bringing its pratfalls to national attention were, for the most part, other outside agencies competing with it for Quichua clienteles. In Guaicopungo, Imbabura, an ecumenical Protestant agency called the Brethren and United Foundation (FBU) found its expenditures outstripped by World Vision. World Vision's free-spending approach enabled some members of the community to reject FBU's slower pace, in which it released funds only in step with a process of "permanent reflection" on community values.[85] "In one year," FBU director Germán Salazar told me, "World Vision has damaged forty years of our own work."[86] Another agency in Imbabura, the Ecuadorian Agricultural Service Center (CESA), had the same problem: in El Topo, the community leadership defected from CESA's communally oriented approach to a World Vision project with larger and faster payouts.

World Vision's substantial budget—according to Boshold around $1 million for Ecuador[87]—was not the only factor making it difficult to compete against. Simply by acting quickly on requests, World Vision outshined other agencies, especially official ones. In contrast to one of the faster moving government institutions, which took more than a year to approve credits and months more to actually provide them, World Vision made its decision in eight days and then delivered. When one community asked the Ministry of Education to add rooms onto its school, the ministry agreed, but five years later it had yet to do anything.[88] Now some communities had their own bank account for such projects, kept stocked with money by World Vision.

A Revolutionary Outlet

The left and the Catholic Church concurred that World Vision, and evangelicals in general, were dividing, depoliticizing, and destroying indigenous culture. So did many Indians. "Every day Mormons, Jehovah's Witnesses, Bahais, Children of God, etc., appear in our country," a native newspaper complained, "confusing and dividing not only the Indians but the public in general. . . . What is certain is that, even among themselves, they criticize each other to death. One group tells the other that they are devils, the other responds by calling them liars. . . . One gives free airplane rides, the other gives away used clothes. Some have medicine, others have money for livestock, still others are going to build schools. That's how each one quarrels over how to collect the largest number of followers. As if the kingdom of heaven can be won with handouts and caramels."[89]

But the pride and energy manifested by Quichua evangelicals led some researchers to different conclusions. Two foreign anthropologists, Joseph Casagrande and Blanca Muratorio, and the Ecuadorian investigator Roberto Santana decided that Protestantism was actually an ethnic revitalization movement.[90] The idea of Protestantism as a liberating force was not new: in the 1920s, in the course of prophesying the Indian reconquest of Peru, the anthropologist Luis Valcárcel hailed Protestant missionaries—especially Seventh Day Adventists—for helping form the New Indian by extirpating vices such as alcoholism, coca chewing, and servility.[91]

According to Santana, it was the evangelical drive for ethnic autonomy which explained the hostility of the left and the Catholic Church. At a time when religious conflict among the Quichua themselves seemed to be fading, Santana suggested, these external contenders were anxious over the loss of Indian clients.[92] If his line of reasoning was correct, then Protestantism was a revolt against paternalism, including the kind still found on the left and in the Catholic Church.

It may be hard to imagine the Gospel Missionary Union as a revolutionary influence. But the thought had already occurred to a GMU member who, just before the Protestant churches in Chimborazo took off, went to the Fuller School of World Mission in southern California to write a master's thesis. Donald Dilworth never returned to Chimborazo, and his 1967 thesis may never have influenced the mission. But he did raise an interesting question. At a time when the Quichua was "smoldering under his oppression," could the spiritual prairie fire missionaries hoped to kindle go out of control? Could evangelism set off a violent revolution?

At a time when consciousness-raising had yet to become fashionable, Dilworth noticed how easily the Quichua identified with the Hebrews of the Old Testament and their tribulations. The Bible endorsed their sense of nationalism, their right to have their own land and exist as a separate people. "Every alert missionary must consider . . . his part in stimulating aggressive reactions," Dilworth wrote. "Recognizing that this reaction is directed toward a revolution, the evangelical missionary continually prays and works toward capturing the trend and guiding the revolution into the Evangelical church where, learning from the Bible, the radically changed man has a chance of radically changing his environment. . . . The Quichua who becomes involved in evangelical Christianity finds, to a certain degree, an outlet for his pent-up revolutionary animosities. The converted Quichua . . . finds a spiritual substitute for the threatened physical revolution. He is now ready to pass through a Christian social reform, the great hope of the Quichua in Ecuador . . . a controlled democratic revolution. . . . This must be done before the animosity of the Quichua explodes to create a shambles of anarchy."

Sounding unusually activist for an evangelical of his time, Dilworth thought missionaries could help the Quichua in ways the U.S. government could not, given its need to maintain good relations with the Ecuadorian government.[93] Just as Monsignor Proaño's supporters suspected, here was a North American missionary talking about the need to contain the forces of change. And in some ways, GMU churches in Chimborazo performed to expectation. Hacienda owners started to regard evangelicals as more reliable workers than Catholics. The Evangelical Indian Association of Chimborazo avoided confronting the authorities or raising issues that challenged existing institutions. Quichua pastors preached Romans 13:1 that governments should be obeyed because they are ordained by God. On occasion, they even punished church members for taking landlords to court.[94]

In 1976, however, an anthropologist discovered that the same hacienda communities acquiring land and turning evangelical were working with a lawyer of the Federation of Ecuadorian Indians (FEI), associated with the Communist party. Whatever the missionaries thought, neither pastors nor political organizers seemed to attach great importance to the fact that their constituents were working with supposed ideological enemies.[95] After all, weren't communists accused of being Protestants, and Protestants of being communists, and Quichua fighting for their rights of being both?[96] Protestants on a large hacienda joined a strike for higher wages,[97] and two evangelical communities invaded hacienda land. On October 20, 1982, as part of a national protest against increased transportation fares, the inhabitants of Guamote, Punín, and Columbe seized every bus in reach and went on strike. With the Catholic radio out of commission for repairs and missionaries absent from the GMU station, Radio Colta invited a Catholic leader onto the air to organize a protest march to Riobamba.[98]

From Evangelism to Electoral Politics

It was only a matter of time, Roberto Santana and Blanca Muratorio suggested, before evangelicals turned their energies from spiritual to political concerns.[99] This was one of the issues lurking behind evangelical complaints over World Vision in mid-1985: whether the Evangelical Indian Association of Chimborazo should take a road different from the Gospel Missionary Union, into electoral politics. The association was proud of its administrative independence from the GMU, but Henry Klassen was still an influential adviser. And there was trouble within. Catholic church workers had heard dimly of a split, around the time of the last national election. That election, according to a mission executive, had "almost destroyed the unity of the evangelical church in the mountains."[100]

The Evangelical Indian Association of Chimborazo had been an obvious political bloc for some time. Already in 1978, at least three political parties had approached it.[101] But missionaries disapproved of aligning the church with political parties, or with political demands for anything but civic improvements and protection from Catholics. Because the Quichua had reason to distrust any political party, attempts to affiliate with one were bound to produce reactions. The association therefore held back from endorsing candidates. Meanwhile, however, one of its leaders, a law student named Manuel Naula, was setting up a wider platform for himself and other ambitious young Quichua. It consisted of the Indian Evangelical Federation of Ecuador (FEINE), eventually housed in the Quito compound of the Summer Institute of Linguistics. When attacks on SIL escalated in 1981, FEINE came to the North Americans' defense and, in the heat of confrontation, organized evangelical Indian associations throughout the highlands.

The Summer Institute, in turn, helped introduce the new federation to the long political season leading up to the next presidential election. In late 1983, certain of SIL's non-Indian backers arranged a meeting at which they tried to marry off FEINE to the right-wing presidential candidate, León Febres Cordero. If evangelical Indians voted for Febres, the deal went, he would give the Summer Institute a new contract. But FEINE leaders did not like Febres's patronal air or being swapped around by white politicians. [102] In the first round of voting in late 1984, Indian evangelicals went overwhelmingly for center and left candidates. Leaders of the Evangelical Indian Associations of Chimborazo and Tungurahua told investigators that significant numbers of their people voted for the Broad Front of the Left of Rene Mauge, built around the Communist party. [103] More voted for the Democratic Left, a centrist party on whose ticket Manual Naula was elected as the country's only Quichua congressman.

Not all Naula's brethren were pleased by his accomplishment, however. Soon the Chimborazo association had elected a new, anti-Naula executive committee, which proceeded to accuse one of Naula's protégés—the association's previous president—of mishandling World Vision funds. A year later, the association's directors still were exercised at Naula for offering their votes to the Democratic Left and using the association to get himself elected. "He tried to sell us," they protested.

Was it proper for a church organization, which by the nature of its membership was an organization of the oppressed, to turn itself into an electoral bloc? The Chimborazo association had always claimed to be apolitical, but the need to defend evangelicals against Catholics had led to amicable relations with local authorities, whom the association then lobbied for civic improvements such as schools and roads. As the missionaries wished, it became an alternative to joining Catholic- or Marxist-led bodies. But now that it had become a functional substitute for rival political organizations, it was coming under pressure to express basic Quichua demands too.

When Manuel Naula and his people tried to turn the Chimborazo evangelical association into a bloc vote, they argued that the church's mission was to transform society. To the missionaries that sounded like liberation theology—and dangerous from a practical point of view, too. If foreign missionaries had become involved in partisan politics like the Catholic Church did, would they have survived so many changes of government in Ecuador's turn-table politics? Even for national evangelical bodies, what happened when you ended up on the losing side? Certainly Christians could participate in politics, missionaries conceded, but as individuals rather than the church.

As Quichua leaders pursued their ambitions, older missions worried that the evangelical Indian associations could go out of control. Around Otavalo, where World Vision had first gotten into trouble, the Evangelical Indian Association of Imbabura was split even more seriously than the one in Chimborazo. There was talk of four, seven, even ten churches breaking away from the local mission, the Christian and Missionary Alliance (CMA).

Some blamed the split on World Vision. The men whom it had hired as provincial coordinators, then fired in December 1983, led the break from the CMA less than a year later. World Vision's contribution had been to pump them up, a CMA pastor suggested. Following World Vision's departure, one of the fallen coordinators had refused to accept discipline for a moral failing, and now there were two evangelical Indian associations in the province. But according to the breakaways, they were forced to take their own road when CMA missionaries and loyalist pastors tried to tie the Indian association closer to the national church. Now the dissidents were using anti-imperialist language to agitate against their disapproving North American mentors. "Missionaries want us in their pocket," one of the disgraced World Vision coordinators of La Compañía said. "They should just get out, beat it." [104]

Pilahuín

In Pilahuín where we began this chapter, high above the city of Ambato, parish priest Jesús Tamayo found himself in a devil of a situation. Catholic church worʰers like himself had encouraged the Quichua to organize in new wa,;s to defend their rights. Invariably, however, there came a time when the people thanked them for their help and went their own way.[105] Now, as a warning against trying to hang on too long, any Catholic or Protestant missionary could look to the fate of Padre Tamayo. As a founding figure of the Tungurahua Indian Movement (MIT), he had pioneered the indigenous cause in the province and built up an impressive operation in consciousness-raising, leadership training, and community development.

But in 1981, things started to fall apart. Foreign volunteers left, followed by many of his older, more influential Indian leaders, who organized their own Tungurahua Indian Movement. According to his many critics, Tamayo had protected MIT from manipulation by outside political interests so successfully that he ended up dominating it himself. His own creation, critics suggest, had outgrown him. He had encouraged the Quichua to raise their consciousness, with the result that they were no longer willing to submit to his authority.

During the infighting, Tamayo had lost the foreign funding he needed to keep abreast of rising demands for development projects. Now he was watching World Vision move into communities that, in better days, he and the Tungurahua Indian Movement had organized. They included Chibuleo, one of the shooting locations for Jorge Sanjines's *Fuera de Aqui!* (Get out of here!), an antiimperialist film that made up for its lack of budget with what some considered an excess of ideology. The film had attacked North American philanthropists as exploiters, and Tamayo had shown it to Quichua audiences all over the province, apparently to great effect. Yet now World Vision was financing projects even in Chibuleo.

The worst from Tamayo's point of view was Pucará, a short walk from his parish church in Pilahuín. In Pucará, young Protestants had persuaded the Catholic majority to elect them to the cabildo or community council. The same young men were in charge of the Evangelical Indian Association of Tungurahua (AIET), which occasionally sponsored evangelical campaigns. If that were not enough, they were also running the local World Vision office. Using World Vision money, they were financing project after project in the sub-communities around Pucará, then—as the community's leaders—calling out the Catholic majority to do the work in the traditional communal style or minga.

Catholics who had accused evangelicals of undermining cabildos and mingas found evangelicals, not just in charge of those same institutions, but pulling together what had been a weak, divided community. The new evangelical leaders had led an impressive protest march all the way down the mountain to the city of Ambato, in a successful defense of the community against a threatening water project. Padre Tamayo had pledged his life to defending Quichua culture and the community way of doing things. But now in Pucará, in a cruel twist of fate, that meant learning to live with World Vision. For now, at least, Quichua Catholics seemed more interested in the new agency's projects than in converting to its religion. According to World Vision's coordinator, the small evangelical minority in Pucará—about three hundred people—had not grown much during its ministry.[106]

Chapter Ten

Reinterpreting the Invasion of the Sects as an Evangelical Awakening

Those Americans are the Franciscans and Dominicans of our time. They may not see it that way, but they are the religious arm of an economic, political, and cultural system.
Salomón Nahmad, National Indigenist Institute of Mexico[1]

A church is just a structure. It depends on how you fill it up.
R. Dayton Roberts, Latin America Mission and World Vision[2]

In February 1988, Jimmy Swaggart brought the gospel to the capital of the Sandinista revolution. It was just one week before he went off the air, after confessing one Sunday morning to his television audience, for a sin which turned out to be addiction to pornography. Some wondered whether the sudden confession had been extorted in retaliation for his trip to Nicaragua. By going, he had allowed the Sandinistas to demonstrate that they respected freedom of worship, even for a contra supporter like himself. During the crusade, they ran spots for him on Sandinista television and broadcast one rally live over national radio. Just a few days later the photos implicating him in sin landed in his denomination, the Assemblies of God.[3]

Swaggart's visit was arranged by the two Texan businessmen who had organized prayer banquets for the Sandinista commandantes in 1980. Year after year Newman Peyton, Jr., and Glen Norwood, the latter the largest homebuilder in the southern United States, had wandered through Central America and the Caribbean, sometimes as far as South America, witnessing to the presidents and strongmen of the region. Sometimes they brought along their good friend General Charles Duke, the eleventh man on the moon. George Price in Belize, Forbes Burnham in Guyana, Alfredo Stroessner in

305

Paraguay, Ríos Montt in Guatemala, five presidents in Honduras, president after president in Costa Rica, the Sandinista commandantes Tomás Borge and Daniel Ortega—these two good old boys had sat down with them all. You name it, they had sat down and discussed it: eternal salvation—the same simple message for everyone from Stroessner to Borge; turning Jonestown into a center for Hmong refugees; border negotiations between countries; asking Pentagon generals to treat those Sandinista boys like human beings; even an unsuccessful attempt to reason with Pat Robertson. And now getting Jimmy Swaggart into Nicaragua.

From the outside, the evangelistic excursions of Glen Norwood and Newman Peyton might look like some kind of conspiracy, a way to set up back channels to tin-horn dictators. But if this was a conspiracy, it was not a very successful one. The Nicaraguan forays proved totally unacceptable to their organization, the Full Gospel Businessmen's Fellowship. Newman Peyton had been the Fellowship's director for Central and South America, operating out of Houston. But he could not prevail against those generals in the Full Gospel network, men whose final response was always that they had their information, classified of course, which proved Nicaragua was a threat to the national security of the United States. Once a general blew up at his suggestion otherwise. So it was a deliverance to be out of there, delivered from the Full Gospel Fellowship for persisting in fellowship with Sandinista commandantes.

To those of us who are not believers, the evangelistic excursions of Glen Norwood and Newman Peyton may seem bizarre. It does not occur to everyone that the Sandinistas might be interested in the testimony of an American astronaut. Or that Daniel Ortega might pray for Ronald Reagan. Or that a paladin of the religious right would tell Nicaraguans that God loves their Sandinista president. But that was the outcome of another of their prayer banquets, for Sandinista commandantes and North American businessmen at the end of 1987. Swaggart's people began approaching the Sandinistas, only to be turned down by the junta. Then Newman Peyton got through to Daniel Ortega, who asked only that Swaggart stay away from politics.

It is not hard to guess at the calculations involved, the costs and benefits to each party in this negotiation. For the Sandinistas, they would be providing more encouragement to their recalcitrant pentecostal subjects, as they had the previous year by permitting a Yiye Avila faith healing crusade, to the dismay of the radical Christians in their midst. But in return, once North American conservatives could see Jimmy Swaggart in Managua on their television sets, maybe they would run out of arguments for the contra war. Or so the more optimistic Sandinistas hoped; others remained opposed to the idea of welcoming a figure who had endorsed the war against them. But then there was the additional benefit, a usual feature of state visits by major evangelists, of reminding the Catholic hierarchy that it no longer held a religious monopoly. For Jimmy Swaggart, this was his opportunity to preach in a country where he had been led to believe that the gospel was forbidden. And of course, more footage from Central America for the relentless maw of his television show and contributors. There would, of course, be the accusation that he had allowed himself to be used. "This will cost Jimmy in credibility. He knows there is going to be a reaction," Newman Peyton observed, a few days before Swaggart's ministry was practically destroyed.

The imperiled evangelist—he knew that incriminating material was in the hands of an enemy but not when the axe would fall— delivered his message from the Plaza of the Revolution in downtown Managua. Behind him was the gutted shell of a Catholic cathedral destroyed in an earthquake. Looking down on him were huge portraits of Sandinista political saints. Quite a situation for a redneck holy ghost preacher. Even if evangelical Protestantism is a heedless sanctifier of the powers that be, in this case Swaggart requested prayer for an unlikely Caesar. It took only a small shift in the usual message. Half the world blames the Sandinistas for Nicaragua's problems, he told the crowd of twenty-five thousand in the Plaza of the Revolution. But the fault did not lie with the Sandinistas. The other half of the world said the fault lay with the contras, he continued. But the fault did not lie with them either. The cause of Nicaragua's problems was the devil. Now it was God's hour for Nicaragua, and he was going to do mighty things.[4]

I would prefer to end with an enigmatic scene such as this. Others could serve as well. But better to conclude with a look at the main questions which have been raised and the direction in which they point. When I conceived this project, it was intended to accomplish two things. In the first place, I wanted to explain the evangelical awakening in Latin America to nonbelievers, myself included. Was it really a function of North American dollars and evangelists, as so many critics on the left and in the Catholic Church have assumed? In the second place I wanted to warn evangelicals, at least those who value the independence of their churches from the state, against allowing their missions to be suborned into the militaristic and immoral policies emanating from Washington.

Neither problem was very profound, at least at the level I wanted to deal with them. Simply registering the quarrels and debates in the evangelical world—between church-growth experts, entrepreneurs adopting transnational corporate imagery, right-wing patriots volunteering for the latest CIA operation, and dissidents calling for a reformation in the reformation—did much to clarify the subject. It is not hard to show how the religious right has tried to turn missionary work into an instrument for U.S. militarism. Nor is it hard to show that, even at its most sectarian and reactionary, Latin American Protestantism manifests vital adaptations of the poor to overwhelming circumstances.

Simple questions led to more perplexing ones, however. Why should a religion that appears to work against the interests of the poor help them in their struggle for survival? Is it not paradoxical that a man like Jimmy Swaggart, perceived by many as a bigot, should have such a powerful appeal in Latin America? Why should poor people seek miracles from religious figures who tell them to submit to oppressive governments? Could the surprising evangelical groundswell affect the course of events in Latin America?

The underlying question, as far as I can see, is the direction being taken by religious reformation in Latin America. Until a few short years ago, my reaction to evangelical talk about making Latin America Protestant was amusement. Not any longer. Evangelical Protestantism is so successful that it calls into question the claims made for its great rival, liberation theology. However much has been made of the ecclesiastical base communities of liberation theology, the corresponding house churches and home Bible studies of evangelical Protestantism may be far more widespread and incorporate many more people. From what I have seen of contests between the two, born-again religion has the upper hand.

Contrasting Visions of Reformation

Enough has been said about the conflict between evangelical Protestantism and liberation theology that it is well to remember what they have in common. On either side of this great mythopoeic divide, increasing numbers of Christians envision religious change as the prologue to social transformation. Both draw their inspiration from the Bible, place great faith in the spiritual potential of the ordinary person, and dream of redeeming—this or that side of the millennium—the oppressive and sinful order of things. Although not much effort is being invested in comparisons with the Reformation in Europe,[5] both hold that religious ferment in Latin America will produce a new social order. They further believe that it will be a Christian one.

But the two visions of reformation soon diverge. Consider, for example, their respective assumptions about the United States. Whereas liberation theologians identify the United States as the main reason for Latin America's backwardness, many evangelicals hail it as a model of progress, democracy, and redemption, a veritable chosen nation. Then there is the question of how religious faith leads to social transformation. For Christians doing liberation theology, saving souls makes little sense apart from changing a social order that ruins so many lives. Analyzing sin in terms of class structure, they understand salvation as a process of raising the consciousness of people and organizing them to take political action. Their picture of reformation is a political struggle, inspired by religious faith but fought in the trenches of class conflict.

The corresponding evangelical vision is frankly mystical, especially in its emphasis on the power of personal conversion. According to evangelicals, the first step (and often the only one) is for individuals to get saved. As people are converted out of the larger society and into new groups that are "in but not of" the world, a new morality is to emerge, then percolate back into society. Conservatives speak of conversion as it if makes structural change unnecessary: reborn men and women, not a social revolution, are to reform Latin America. Guided by the Bible, conservatives believe, soldiers will respect human rights, politicians will tell the truth, entrepreneurs will make money honestly, workers will earn their daily bread, and the unemployed will find jobs. Not all evangelicals simply dream of an idealized version of the present social order: in contrast to those who embodied their hopes in a Guatemalan army general, others have placed theirs in the Sandinista revolution. Yet all agree that the way to transform Latin America is to "save" as many people as possible.

To those accustomed to analyze Latin America in structural terms, moral uplift may sound like a naive recipe. The Protestant heritage of a Caribbean island like Jamaica has not saved it from the consequences of dependent capitalism. To those familiar with the competition and rancor of evangelical church life, it may sound implausible that such institutions could serve as a moral example for the larger society. But even if we do not take evangelical moralism at face value, we should take it seriously, for it shows that evangelicals do not just turn their backs on the world and tell the poor to await their reward in heaven. Even those who stress their rejection of society address the hopes of Latin Americans on the intimate, effective level of personal morality and self-improvement.

The way to improve your life is to improve your personal conduct, evangelicals preach. Through what may seem ineffectual admonitions, they address a level of culture which political radicals tend to ignore: morals and their social implications. To take one example, fathers evading their paternal responsibilities are not the reason so many Latin Americans are being pauperized, but they do contribute to that process in millions of lives. Or consider the abuse of public office and finance, abuse so rampant that it destroys the possibility for anything but self-aggrandizement. When revolutionaries come to power and switch from the politics of raising expectations to that of imposing discipline, their talk of creating a "new man" echoes the same theme as evangelicals: the need for a new moral authority and a new moral community.

Why Liberation Theology May Not Work

This study has not made a thorough case for why liberation theology may be better at filling faculties, bookshelves, and graves than churches. Although I have taken great pains to distinguish between different currents in evangelical Protestantism, any such distinctions concerning liberation theology have been off the cuff. Christians who have invested their lives in liberation theology, who have seen friends or coworkers die for it, may feel that I have carefully selected various debacles in order to discredit it. In particular, they could argue, I have chosen to focus on Guatemala, where repression against social activism has been particularly fierce and effective, and on Nicaragua, where divisions in the Catholic Church are particularly deep and flagrant. No doubt other cases could be found where theory and practice have been more successful. Were I to have chosen Brazil, it would be apparent that liberation theology and the Catholic Church have contributed greatly to a populist effervesence, ultimately to that country's democratic opening. Elsewhere, too, the contributions of liberation theology to thriving opposition movements may be more apparent.

But if I have chosen worst-case situations, they should provide warnings for elsewhere. In revolutionary Nicaragua, the Christians who have identified most strongly with the Sandinistas apparently have not managed to appeal to the poor as effectively as more conservative evangelicals have. In highland Ecuador, the social activism of the most progressive Catholic diocese seems to have been outmatched by an evangelical movement. In Guatemala, my account suggests, certain Catholic clergy practicing liberation theology were partly responsible for the military's identification of church organizations as subversive, which led to a wave of terror from which the Catholic Church may never recover its former stature.

Even in each of these cases, liberation theology could be interpreted in a more favorable light.[6] Perhaps I have placed too much emphasis on the contradictions involved, while discounting the struggle to overcome them. But liberation theology has achieved such paradigmatic status in thinking about the politics of religion in Latin America that I think my pot-shot approach is needed, at least temporarily, to call attention to the possibility that evangelical Protestantism is more successful on the popular level.

I do not wish to deny that liberation theology represents a courageous reformation in church life. It cannot be dismissed as a clerical maneuver to regain popular support or a Marxist front as enemies do. To the contrary, its critiques of church life are penetrating even the evangelical camp, where they could become influential. No one has written its obituary: much more is to be expected of its capacity for self-criticism and change. But while liberation theology is a vital creation of the oppositional culture of clergy and university, its reception among the poor tends to be problematical. In practice, moreover, it has been forced to carry the highest hopes in the most hopeless situations. It has been drawn into merciless crossfires. And in certain situations, it seems to encourage the growth of its nemesis, right-wing fundamentalism.

Christians doing liberation theology are the first to recognize that they take risks: this is what faith is about, they say. But now that they are alarmed by the growth of "the sects," let us consider how their efforts can backfire. For those who distrust religion or are impatient for results, liberation theology has been tempting to treat like a quick fix. It is supposed to be based on the demands of the poor and to stir them to political action. For revolutionaries in need of a bridge from their politics to the populace, it offers to turn religious symbols into revolutionary action.

There is more than one danger in this procedure, the least likely of which is success. Only in Nicaragua, under the Sandinistas, has liberation theology come to power, so to speak. Now that a new society seems within reach, does a practice of consciousness-raising and dissent become the established faith? At least a few activists talked about maintaining critical distance from the Sandinista state, but others were acting like "court prophets" for it.[7] Against the onslaughts of foreign and domestic enemies, such Christians felt a duty to defend the revolution. But by joining the Sandinista power structure and defending its unpopular measures, they risked distancing themselves from the Nicaraguan people and discrediting their talk of a better world.

The central exercise in liberation theology, consciousness-raising, raises a tangle of issues. To begin with, there is the risk of failing to speak to the actual needs of the poor, as opposed to idealized versions of those needs. Liberation theology endeavors to come out of the day-to-day experience of the poor: when successful, maybe it does. But it also originated in the crisis of the Catholic Church and its attempts to recover a popular base. Despite the struggle to build a grass-roots church, the prophets of the movement tend to be religious professionals with professional interests, a fact dramatized by their disputes with offended laities and anxious hierarchies. Consciousness-raising is supposed to be dialectical, generated out of the interaction between organizer and people. But it began by defining the poor in terms of what they lacked, then presuming that they should become something else through pedagogy.[8]

Such presumptions often become apparent in collisions with popular religion, the folk Catholic traditions that clergy left, right, and middle have often tried to suppress or reform. Under the usual conditions faced by the poor, in which open dissent is followed by punishment swift and sure, folk practices have permitted expression of popular aspirations in ambiguous but sometimes strategic ways. What outsiders interpret as resignation can serve as a protective mantle for vital traditions of cultural resistance. Expressions of subordination mingle with expressions of defiance, in complex forms of ritual communication between dominant and subordinate social classes which, over time, may redefine relations between the two. Practitioners of liberation theology differed widely on how to deal with the dilemmas posed by popular religion, such as its frequent reinforcement of exploitive patrón-client ties. But they often tried to undermine such traditions, for representing a religion of domination, with the result that they alienated the people they were trying to organize.[9]

Perhaps the basic difficulty is that a message centering around "liberation" contradicts how the poor usually prefer to deal with oppressive situations: a subtle combination of deference, foot-dragging, and evasion, as James Scott has pointed out in his work on everyday forms of peasant resistance.[10] The kinds of defiance liberation theology tends to encourage, in contrast, have been suicidal in many times and places. Given this fact of life out in the hard places where liberation theology must prove itself, the frequent assumption of the need for revolutionary upheaval indicates that more or less safely situated intellectuals have had an outsize role in its production.

Encouraging the poor to insist on their rights in explicit new ways meant throwing away the protective cloak surrounding religious activities. It meant forsaking the traditional function of religion as a sanctuary from oppression. Once landlords or the state were ready to retaliate, liberation theology demanded life-and-death commitment from the people who were supposed to be liberated. Christianity is about sacrifice, of course. But it is not about putting other people on the line. When situations polarized into violence, outsiders promoting liberation theology tended to be forced out, leaving behind their local allies to relearn an old lesson about the state's ability to put down unrest. One martyrdom after another might seem to justify armed struggle as the only way forward, but most revolutionary uprisings are unsuccessful. It was so easy to leap from a religious base into a political disaster.

In Central America, as revolutionary conflict turned into a war of attrition with no end in sight, conservative evangelicals appealed to the traditional resignation of the poor in ways liberation theology could not. However much liberation theology spoke to aspirations for a better life, the escapism of the evangelical message was more compatible with the usual posture of the poor—fatalistic acceptance of the constraints on their continuous negotiation for survival. Under such circumstances, it was easy for liberation theology to fall out of touch with the people it claimed to represent.

When the revolutionary movement was shattered in Guatemala, evangelicals took the opportunity to invite survivors into their churches. In contrast to liberation theology, evangelicals offered to improve one's life through a simple personal decision, to surrender to Christ. That sounded easier than overturning the social order. Evangelicals provided an ideology, not just of political resignation as so often noted, but of personal improvement. They told the poor not to preoccupy themselves with large events they could not influence in direct, obvious ways. Instead, a person was to concentrate on what he could change, such as his drinking habits. Evangelicals also captured the poor emotionally, in ways highly politicized Christians often failed to. In the most difficult situations, calls for revolutionary commitment were not engaging the religiosity of the people and sustaining them through long, hard years of struggle for survival, at least not in the way that evangelical sects could. As revolutionary visions faded into the grim reality of endless political violence, governments encouraged evangelicals to pick up the pieces.

Pentecostalism as a Basis for Social Reformation

This work has dealt mainly with Central America, partly because the conflicts there illuminate the politics of evangelical growth in new and obvious ways. An evangelical dictator in Guatemala and a U.S.-backed counter-revolution in Nicaragua throw our subject into the kind of high relief lacking where churches occupy themselves mainly with expansion. The center of gravity in Latin American Protestantism is not in Central America, however. It is in Brazil, which accounts for more than half the evangelicals in this part of the world.[11] What about the giant pentecostal churches of Brazil and that other early center of growth, Chile? As the largest evangelical groups in Latin America, could they become the basis for a social reformation?

The safest, most probable answer is no. Since the studies of Emilio Willems and Christian Lalive d'Epinay in the 1960s, sociologists have asked whether the churches of Brazil and the Southern Cone are best understood as a form of social protest or social control.[12] Meanwhile, these bodies have come to exemplify the same polarization between the Latin American Council of Churches (CLAI) and the Latin American Evangelical Confederation (CONELA) as have the churches of Central America. There is the same lonely struggle of dissidents, often led by members of the Latin American Theological Fraternity (FTL), against conservative leaderships which usually have the upper hand.

One need only sample the critiques by ecumenical Protestants such as Rubem Alves and Jean Pierre Bastian, and the cautious appraisals by the Latin American Theological Fraternity, to see just how conservative and restrained the evangelical milieu in Brazil and Chile is.[13] This is partly a reaction to past efforts at consciousness-raising. In Brazil, the older, "historic" churches expelled dissidents following the 1964 military coup. In Chile, the curtain rang down on progressive activism following overthrow of the Allende administration in 1973. Once military men destroy democracy, the two cases suggest, evangelical church life returns to its highly euphemized norm. Conservatives reign supreme; activists are silenced or go into exile. Under this kind of dispensation, challenging the system seems unlikely. Given the political quiescence of evangelicals, it can be argued that they count for less than their large numbers suggest. "The irrelevance of Protestantism became so great that, if the Rapture occurred today," Robinson Cavalcanti has written scornfully, "Brazilian society would take a week to notice that the believers were no longer there."[14]

Pentecostalism, which accounts for three-quarters of the Protestants in Brazil and an even greater proportion in Chile, has received particularly poor reviews. When Lalive d'Epinay studied Chilean pentecostals in the late 1960s, he noted the determination of the largest denomination, the Pentecostal Methodist Church, to build a cathedral "bigger than the Catholic one." Despite his assessment of pentecostalism as a reactionary force, many believers seem to have voted for the Allende government and its attempt to build socialism. Whatever this rapprochement might have led to, it was cut short by the September 1973 military coup led by General Augusto Pinochet.

Little more than a year after Pinochet seized power, an act that included murdering his constitutionally elected predecessor, he helped inaugurate the new Pentecostal Methodist "cathedral," the huge Jotabeche Church in the capital. Offended by the Catholic hierarchy's condemnation of his human rights violations, Pinochet designated the Jotabeche Church as the site of the nation's annual thanksgiving service. Subsequently he asked Jotabeche pastor Javier Vásquez to serve as his minister of religion.[15] Although Vásquez refused the honor, he and other evangelical chieftans did consent to administer an official carnet system, to regulate the access of pastors to government institutions[16]—the kind of system many evangelicals accuse communist regimes of using to persecute the church. No matter, this was a marriage made in heaven. Even as Pinochet's seizure of power enabled reactionary older leaders to "reaffirm . . . their hold over the faithful," Lalive d'Epinay writes, they provided the new dictator with the stamp of divine approval he could not obtain from the Catholic Church.[17]

When Lalive surveyed pentecostal pastors in Buenos Aires, Argentina, he found that 50 percent prohibited membership in trade unions; 64 percent rejected the proposition that the Protestant Church should be concerned with the country's social and political problems; 85 percent said they forbade their members from taking part in politics.[18] Based on such attitudes, Lalive d'Epinay was not alone in concluding that pentecostalism represented a profound and mystical accommodation to the status quo. Over the last two decades, many a critic has reiterated that pentecostal churches provide their members with false, unrealistic solutions to their problems rather than expressing their real interests.[19]

Alienation and false consciousness do not sound like the road to social reformation. Jean Pierre Bastian feels that Protestantism in Latin America missed its historical mission. The state in Latin America was too patrimonial and authoritarian to permit the kind of social reformation that occurred in Europe, he argues. Instead of secularizing or "disenchanting" Latin American society, Protestantism has been "reenchanted" by Latin America, in the form of a mainly reactionary pentecostalism which mystifies the interests of the poor.[20]

Liberation theology is the salutary contrast we are supposed to draw because it seems to express the interests of the poor so clearly. Yet there are reasons to be wary, among them the capacity of politicized religion for losing touch with the people it claims to represent. As Frederick Turner pointed out in 1970, partisans of liberation theology assume that churches can thrive only by fighting for broad social reforms. Yet pentecostal churches have reached mammoth proportions without supporting such causes.[21] Their success in improving the situation of many members suggests that no relation may exist between the perspicacity of their social analysis and their survival value to the poor. The people attracted to pentecostal churches evidently define their needs differently than liberation theology does.

It is easy to dismiss such believers as misguided, for failing to conform to some model of the class conscious mind. But if pentecostals are so effective at reaching the poor, their rivals might try to learn from them. One possible lesson is the ability of pentecostal churches to speak to people in terms of magical power. Lalive d'Epinay pointed out that, whereas Marxism tends to spread from the place of work, pentecostalism tends to spread from the family and home.[22] That is, pentecostalism comes out of the heart of the struggle for personal survival, from core issues of health and reproduction hedged about with beliefs in the supernatural.

The left has tended to assume that the intercourse of the poor with supernatural forces is diversionary, as if such beliefs inevitably prevent people from understanding their situation and acting to change it. But if the masses feel the need to protect themselves against evil spirits, then doing so is not "escapist," as Guillermo Cook has pointed out.[23] Rather, it is necessary, leaving the question of how it will be done and with what implications. Evangelical Protestantism is not necessarily the strongest competitor, it is important to remember. As we saw in Chapter 5, even evangelicals fear they are being outmatched by the various forms of spiritism which appeal to so many Brazilians and other Latin Americans. Yet if we are looking for a religious movement that promotes the kind of rationalization associated with bourgeois and socialist revolutions, then pentecostalism is an interesting beast. Like spiritism, it appeals to the magical proclivities of the population. But unlike spiritism, which encourages amoral clientalistic relations with a plethora of deities, pentecostalism places authority in a single godhead, creates universal ethical standards, and promotes individual responsibility.[24]

A second way in which pentecostals may be able to serve as a model is their ability to organize relatively stable, expanding structures, with a definite capacity for adapting to changing conditions. Again, the secret may be the foundation of pentecostal churches in homes and families rather than workplaces. Where a proletariat is not brought together in large factories, where the poor instead are forced to become shrewd petty traders in order to survive, the household could be considered the basic unit of social struggle.

Just this easy-to-ignore nucleus of evangelical conversion has been studied recently by Elizabeth Brusco in Colombia. Her unpublished doctoral dissertation poses quite a challenge to most writing on the subject. Like the work in hand, most studies focus on the male-dominated apparatus of evangelism and church life— the missions, the denominations, the revivalists. Yet as Brusco reminds us, the supreme expression of male evangelism, the great crusades in public stadiums, have often failed to produce many new church members, in Colombia and other countries as well. The embarrassing results of so many of these brash male displays—waves of enthusiasm which then evaporate—suggest that the basis of evangelical conversion is elsewhere. Still other phenomena—the success of home Bible studies and house churches, their importance to many of the most rapidly growing groups, and the numerical preponderance of women in Latin American Protestantism— also point to the household as the key to evangelical expansion.

Women do not always take the first step in converting to Protestantism: one common exception is among indigenous populations with strong male-headed households. Yet in poor urban neighborhoods, women do tend to take that leading role, which Brusco attributes to disappointed expectations of economic and emotional support from males. Some men then become willing accomplices in conversion: they, too, wish to escape the destructive implications of *machismo*. Their reward is confirmation as "head" of the household, now buttressed by biblical authority. But Protestantism redefines their goals to coincide with the child- and subsistence-centered aspirations of their women. Such aspirations are not so different from the "spirit of asceticism" in Calvinism, Brusco suggests, even if their cultural basis is rather different.

This is not the first time that born-again fervor has been analyzed as a feminist strategy to domesticate men. Although revolutionary assaults on gender inequality have failed to make much of an impression on male and female behavior, Brusco points out, evangelical religion addresses some of the most intimate and conservative areas of life, as expressed in courtship and marital roles.[25] Where the debt crisis has made it impossible for many women to feed their children adequately and revolutionary expectations have often been disappointed, the impact of born-again religion on gender roles could have implications for the socialization of children, patterns of authority in the household, conceivably even for public morality and the political culture.

Brusco's analysis is quite a twist on the usual interpretation of evangelical gender, whose paternalism has troubled many observers. In *Haven of the Masses*, Lalive d'Epinay argued that pentecostal churches reproduce the tributary social organization of the hacienda. Now the patrón is the pastor, who uses the Bible to revitalize a traditional form of authority.[26] But while Chilean pentecostalism reproduces an authoritarian form of social organization, Lalive went on to say, it also breaks with that tradition. Pentecostal churches may be full of different ranks, yet these ranks are not based on social class like the old hacienda. Such churches represent a new egalitarianism, a theoretical society of equals before God, and a new form of mobility for lower-class people into positions of leadership.[27]

A third way in which pentecostals provide an interesting model is their relation to an oppressive social order. Despite the flagrant romances between pentecostal patriarchs and right-wing regimes, congregations tend to retain considerable autonomy in their dealings with state and society. They conform to outer constraints yet maintain a degree of independence, in a paradoxical way that critics have not quite captured when they accuse pentecostals of isolating themselves from society.

That rejecting "the world" does not have to mean social isolation is suggested by *Brasil para Cristo* (BPC), the fifth largest Protestant denomination in Brazil with 450,000 members.[28] Brazil for Christ is, to be sure, unusually broad-minded for a pentecostal body: in 1969, it horrified brethren by joining the World Council of Churches.[29] It was founded by a rebel spirit in the Assemblies of God, Manoel de Melo, whose skill as a tent revivalist, then as a faith healer over the radio waves, was accompanied by a proclivity for unorthodox ideas, including some of a progressive nature. Although criticized for one-man rule, Melo used his charismatic powers to campaign for democracy and social justice as well as religious freedom. Before electoral possibilities were cut off by the 1964 military coup, he was thought to command a large bloc of votes and swing elections. Although anticommunist in that period, he was very critical of the Brazilian power structure and, like the well-known mentor of liberation theology, Paolo Freire, preached the importance of raising consciousness.[30]

As to whether pentecostals really isolate themselves from society, a North American anthropologist who studied several BPC congregations in Rio de Janeiro concluded that they do not. At least in Brazil for Christ, John Page found, the personal networks of converts were not contracting dramatically after joining. Even after converts spent eight or more years in the church, Page discovered, their nonpentecostal social networks had declined only about 25 percent, much of which could be explained on the basis of age and life cycle. The metaphors of withdrawal in BPC discourse simply did not reflect the complexities of members' interactions with nonmembers.[31] If pentecostals really isolated themselves to the extent suggested by their rhetoric, Regina Novaes has observed, they would not be able to proselytize their kin and neighbors so effectively. While pentecostal congregations represent a new social circuit, it does not necessarily replace the old one.[32]

Brazil for Christ is, admittedly, a rare find for academics searching for pentecostal social conscience. But even the most conservative churches may share significant features with it. First, as Ronald Frase has pointed out, pentecostal churches provide a stable setting in which heterogeneous populations of urban migrants become aware of themselves as a group. Second, despite frequent denunciation of politics, pentecostal churches often become what Manoel de Melo has called "marshalling grounds for the entry of these new persons into political life."[33] Third, these groups are attempting to build new moral communities. The result may seem conformist and alienating, but paternalistic ideologies have often been the means by which subordinate groups set up moral reciprocities with dominant groups, reciprocities they subsequently attempt to turn into rights.[34]

If evangelicals are to be believed, this process of building a new moral community is already well under way in Central America. Particularly interesting is the way in which pentecostals are managing to reach beyond the poor into the middle and upper classes, often through groups calling themselves charismatic. As evangelicals recognize, reaching elites is crucial to any claim to moralize the present social order, hence their interest in evangelizing Central American businessmen, politicians, military officers, and dictators. Even if descents of the Holy Spirit upon colonels and landlords have less than miraculous results, as the case of Ríos Montt suggests, they could have a certain impact. However threatening "kingdom" or "dominion" teaching appears to nonbelievers, it could conceivably encourage a new sense of moral responsibility among Central American elites, perhaps reforms of the enlightened self-interest variety.

This is only to speculate about possibilities. But when one attends the worship of a large pentecostal congregation, it is hard to avoid a sense of the immense social power in those praying masses of believers. "There was a spontaneous audible prayer by the whole congregation which made one feel as though a volcano had erupted," William Read reported of a six-thousand-person service. "It continued for a while and then suddenly ended as if by prearranged signal. With this, the Monday service of Missionary Manoel de Melo was over."[35]

Evangelism and Oliver North

Recent events have not been kind to the religious right. One embarrassment is the fall and crash of television evangelists, or at least their reputations. Pat Robertson has yet to crash, it is true. But the 1988 campaign for president failed to reach beyond his charismatic following to the wider evangelical population, let alone to nonreligious conservatives. Jim Bakker, the baby-faced founder and star of PTL Ministries, is finished as an evangelical leader. His demise is due less to the original charge of hotel sex with a church secretary than to a subsequently revealed history of homosexuality. This is not to mention his abuse of supporters, such as diverting their mission contributions to other purposes including his Christian amusement park. North American evangelicals got the message: their donations to television ministries have dropped across the board.

For evangelicals in Central America, the most serious blow was probably the fall of Jimmy Swaggart and his separation from one of the largest and fastest growing denominations in the region, the Assemblies of God. As the most active evangelist in Central America for several years, Swaggart had attracted hundreds of thousands of Salvadorans, Hondurans, and Costa Ricans to his rallies. His subsidies to the Assemblies in the region were major. In churches whose conception of the deity has been shaped by images from the United States, Jimmy Swaggart was close to God. For believers, it was therefore a shock to learn that, in the course of bringing so many to Christ, he had regularly compromised himself with a prostitute.

It is not clear how the scandal will affect the standing of Swaggart and other North American evangelists—perhaps very little, owing to the powerful need for images of redemption, so powerful that an evangelist can use transgressions and remorse to revalidate his appeal. But there probably will be at least two other effects. First, the disarray in North American religious broadcasting will affect the flow of dollars into Central American churches. In the case of Swaggart, he is said to have supplied 40 percent of the funding and materials for Assemblies of God medical and educational programs in Honduras.[36] To the Assemblies of El Salvador he reportedly had provided $6 million.[37] But following announcement of his sin and departure from the airwaves, many North American contributors stopped giving: the income of his $3-million-a-week operation dropped to $1.1 million a week.[38] To save his cash-starved operation Swaggart had to get back on the air as soon as possible, and to do that he was forced to violate the disciplinary sanctions imposed by his denomination. Owing to his major contributions to the Assemblies mission budget, the pain was not his alone. But U.S. headquarters in Springfield, Missouri, cut all ties and commitments with its most famous evangelist.

This raises a second probable effect of Swaggart's fall: to bring out differences within the Assemblies of God over their heretofore joint operations in Central America. Because of their dependence on Jimmy Swaggart's money and image, Springfield's daughter denominations to the south were not necessarily of the same mind on defrocking him. In eight or nine Latin American countries, his program reportedly continued to air despite Springfield's wish to shut it down. Were he to mount new crusades in the region, they could turn into loyalty contests for Assemblies churches forced to choose between their denominational structure and their most dynamic figure.

Another embarrassment for the religious right is the peace process in Nicaragua and the decomposition of the Reagan administration's contra war. The war was probably never very popular with Central American brethren to begin with. In Nicaragua, most evangelicals would have preferred to sit it out. Next door in Honduras, evangelicals scarcely shared the enthusiasm of North American missionaries for coming to the rescue of Nicaraguan refugees and contras.[39] Aside from diverting money and supplies away from Hondurans, North American visions of Christian freedom fighters meant going along with preparations for a war no Hondurans seemed to want. As contra troops reached a state of open rebellion against their corrupt leadership, one defection to the Sandinista amnesty was a Commander Alfa Lima, an evangelical preacher who had led a particularly effective contra unit in Chontales.[40] The disintegration of the contra left North American war enthusiasts isolated, with few for company except puzzled supporters back home.

Consider the dilemma of Christian Emergency Relief Teams (CERT), a paramilitary style enterprise headquartered next to Camp Pendleton, the major Marine base on the West Coast. To raise money for its medical expeditions to the contras, CERT was accustomed to make the crudest appeals. One began with a supposed statement by Sandinista Interior Minister Tomás Borge from the steps of the U.S. Capitol: that he was going to send millions of Mexicans across the border to kill ten Americans each.[41] Now

CERT's founder David Courson was soliciting contributions for a "secret mission" to install a water pump in a Nicaraguan village. Accompanied by a doctor to set up a clinic, a CERT team would secretly cross the border into Nicaragua, dig a well, and install the pump in less than a day. Before leaving they would weld a plaque to the pump, so that villagers would know that their Christian friends in the United States were responsible for giving it to them. A few months earlier, a Sandinista commander had allowed the same North American sending out this appeal to distribute Bibles to Sandinista troops.[42]

Because the war of sabotage and terror for which the religious right volunteered was secret, it is not clear exactly who and what was involved. But two things are clear. First, recruiting evangelists into the contra war was Lieutenant Colonel Oliver North. Second, the stigma will be shared by evangelicals who were quite innocent. Since Oliver North will be used to explain evangelism elsewhere, it is important to form an idea of how his scheme worked and how typical it might be.

To justify attacking Nicaragua, let us recall, the Reagan administration engaged in a systematic effort to place the Sandinista revolution in the worst possible light. From 1983 on, the flow of information, much of it false or distorted, was channeled through two new entities, the Office of Public Diplomacy in the State Department and the Outreach Working Group on Central America in the White House. Among the key constituencies at which they aimed were evangelicals, whose leaders were invited to regular briefings in Washington.

Serving occasionally as briefers were representatives of the Institute on Religion and Democracy (IRD), which conceived its most important duty to indict the Sandinistas for religious persecution. Also involved was a staffer of the National Security Council, a Marine officer named Oliver North, who was soon de facto coordinator of the Reagan administration's psychological warfare against the Sandinistas. North's target consisted of North Americans as well as Nicaraguans. "The idea is to slowly demonize the Sandinista government in order to turn it into a real enemy in the minds of the American people," an official opposed to his efforts explained.[43] Particularly open to North's message was a wing of the evangelical movement that takes demons very seriously, the pentecostals and charismatics of the religious right.

At a time when public support for counterinsurgency was low, the Reagan administration and the religious right succeeded in demonizing revolutionary movements in Central America which, ironically, happened to be supported by large numbers of Christians. In Nicaragua, overthrowing a government whose record compared favorably with U.S. allies in the region became a crusade. Given the general unpopularity of the war, the religious right in the United States became probably its largest constituency, and perhaps the Reagan administration's only conquest on the Nicaraguan front. Strangely, those who professed their Christianity most strenuously were the most indifferent to the methods involved: destroying clinics, raping women, cutting the throats of prisoners, blowing up truckloads of civilians. It was quite a testimony.

After the U.S. Congress cut off aid to the contras in 1984, North began recruiting sympathetic evangelists into a "private support network" authorized by the White House in violation of many laws. Phil Derstine of Gospel Crusade has acknowledged that his ministry to the contras in Honduras grew out of an invitation from Oliver North, who "opened some doors for us."[44] John Olson of Trans World Missions was also very impressed by White House briefings, from North as well as others, and started a ministry to contra refugees in Costa Rica.[45] Other groups participating in North's contra support network, judging from their activities, include Operation Blessing, the relief arm of Pat Robertson's Christian Broadcasting Network; the Christian Emergency Relief Teams mentioned above; Friends of the Americas of Baton Rouge, Louisiana; and Freedom's Friends of Addison, Texas, the latter organized by the born-again son of crusading atheist Madelyn Murray O'Hare. One reason North was successful at recruiting these mainly charismatic groups into the contra war was that he was a charismatic himself, a member of the Church of the Apostles in Fairfax, Virginia.[46] "I study the Good Book," he apparently said of liberation theology at one White House meeting, "and Jesus Christ never advised anyone to pick up a rifle."[47]

This, then, is what stood behind the buzzing activity of North American evangelists in Honduras. Behind all the coming and going—into restricted areas through connections with the U.S. embassy, on military aircraft, bringing relief supplies to refugees and ministering to contras—was a lieutenant colonel in the White House, orchestrating evangelists into sensitive areas to hand out gifts and ideology. Nor was that all. To the anti-Sandinista wing of the Catholic Church in Nicaragua, Oliver North and the CIA provided money, apparently concealing the source from recipients.[48] When Monsignor Federico Argüello inquired about the source of $31,000 anonymously deposited in his bank account, North told him that it was from a private foundation.[49] It is quite a picture, exactly what alarmists have been warning about for some time.

There are similar scenes of evangelical activity in El Salvador and Guatemala. A regular industry of groups are attending to the physical and spiritual needs of Central Americans. Frequently charismatic, their style is an effective bridge, not just to the poor, but to many middle- and upper-class Central Americans who occupy positions in the power structure and have been converting to charismatic churches.[50] While a few agencies are well-known, others are so small and new that they are not listed in the standard reference, the *Mission Handbook*.[51] Some seem little more than an inspired individual with hometown backers and a plane to fly in relief supplies. What is behind all the activity? Perhaps it merely reflects the entrepreneurialism of Sunbelt evangelicals, up-and-coming provincial North Americans who have discovered the world and are trying to save it, just as eastern and midwestern Protestants took their gospel around the world in the nineteenth century.

This is the explanation I would prefer, a simple sociological one. Unfortunately, the contra war forces us to ask whether Oliver North or men like him could be orchestrating evangelism elsewhere, too. Lately there has been no shortage of volunteers for God and country. Often the new groups in Central America seem to have working relations with U.S. embassies, through such mechanisms as USAID funding for private voluntary organizations. In this respect, the figure of Oliver North and the evangelists he oriented may be simply a dramatic version of a common relationship: the foreign evangelist, often an inexperienced small-timer, working with the spook contingents at U.S. embassies which have been refurbished and bolstered under Reaganism. Eventually we will get the memoirs of some of these embassy warriors, a few of them disillusioned, others defending their service as honorable men. No doubt we will read how naive and useful the charismatic ministries were: first handouts to win over people, then lively pentecostal meetings to get their minds off the revolution and into line with the next U.S. move.

To those who distrust and fear evangelical growth, Oliver North and his friends have confirmed the view that it is the result of strategic U.S. planning. That evangelism is a spiritual con game, of attracting Latin Americans with dollars, working closely with the local power structure, and following orders from Washington. This is the conspiracy explanation for evangelical growth in Latin America, an explanation widely accepted in the Catholic Church, on the left, and wherever sectarianism divides the poor against each other. It is not the picture I wanted to draw when I started this book; it is the folk mythology I wanted to refute, not affirm. Yet Oliver North and his evangelists have done this great disservice to their brethren: they have shown that it is true.

Despite encouraging changes in part of the mission movement, Oliver North and the religious right have shown that some things stay the same. Evangelism continues to be used as an instrument not just of U.S. foreign policy but of covert and immoral "dirty wars." Vietnam attracted the same kind of evangelist, and so will the next American counterinsurgency war. From southern Africa to the Philippines and back to Central America, evangelists of the religious right will continue to project their demons into struggles for elementary human rights. Should the next U.S. administration continue to rely on the religious right as a core constituency, this wing of the mission movement will continue to have the kind of outsize impact it had on Nicaragua—lobbying for militaristic policies, publicizing and helping implement them in coordination with U.S. embassies.[52]

If experience in Central America is a guide, the more established evangelical missions will have their doubts. But little will be said in public. Least of all will anything be said at home, lest supporters get the idea that their missionaries are suspiciously liberal. As for these supporters, whose voting behavior has so much impact on the rest of the world, they will continue to have little conception of who is responsible for so much of the terror and impoverishment on the mission field. And so they will continue to vote for politicians who prefer to send in air strikes. To the extent that the religious right's visions of holy war continue to infuse American foreign policy, the activities of all evangelicals will be identified with it. Missionaries will continue to face accusations of working for the U.S. government, and they will have mainly themselves to blame, by failing to take a stand against the perversion of their message.

This could be the sorry result of all the effort to evangelize the world by the year 2000. But even though men like Oliver North are turning evangelism into a Pentagon strategy, I continue to believe that they are not the whole story. Even if the CIA has an academy for turning out preachers, I believe that they and their converts will go in directions not originally envisioned. Just like U.S.-sponsored labor unions and aid programs, religious groups are not bound by the objectives of their founders. The most important issue, I continue to believe, is not that North American missionaries continue to succumb to the temptations of militarism. Evangelical religion in Latin America runs deeper than that. The most important story is what is going on at the popular level.

Reaping the Harvest

"Since 1979 the church has grown from 200,000 to 1,200,000 people in El Salvador," a missionary of the religious right claimed in 1986. "Now think of it: what has been the catalyst? . . . [It is] the social unrest, the war. . . . Now let's look at it cold logically. If our primary purpose is to win souls for Jesus Christ, and since we evangelical churches have been the primary beneficiaries of the war in El Salvador, folks, don't you think we should do everything possible to keep the war going? . . . That's pure logic, isn't it?" The speaker, Ted Ward of Paralife Ministries in Fort Worth, Texas, quickly added that he was not advocating that kind of logic. But it certainly came to mind as he went about his ministry to refugees, in cooperation with the pacification programs of the Salvadoran army.

"[Subversion] is made just on promises," Ward continued. "Just the promise to these poor people of participating in the wealth of the nation, of having a house, of having education provided for the children, of having medical care provided for your family, just the promise of these things produced such a strong reaction within the people.

"Now I ask you, what would happen if evangelical churches, manifesting an honest to God love for the neighbor, would begin to move into these countries and provide the promises that the Marxists made? . . . What would happen to the Marxist threat in Latin America if evangelical churches, missions and humanitarian church-related groups would go in using the right principles of sharing life with these people?"[53]

Missionaries like Ward realized that, to compete with the revolutionary left, they had to respond to the needs of ever more impoverished people. Preaching about the peace within, the end of the world, and the great haven in the sky would only go so far. If conservatives wished to remain at the head of their converts' march into godliness, they had to help them in their day-to-day struggle for survival. New churches would not endure unless they halted the slide into misery.

Simply prohibiting alcohol, cigarettes, and the like helped the poor tighten up their household economies. But that was only a respite as their purchasing power plummeted. Even in Chile, a declining economy appeared to disillusion the Pinochet regime's pentecostal supporters and encourage opposition, in a return to the politically divided churches of the early 1970s.[54]

Developmentalism claimed to offer long-term solutions. But here evangelicals seemed to be reviving the illusions of previous generations of developers and missionaries. According to Guillermo Cook, a member of the Latin America Mission, economic crisis has neutralized the ability of the Protestant ethic to "redeem and lift" converts. Under less hostile conditions, Protestantism helped converts move upward in the social scale. Now, Cook believes, the dynamism unleashed by Protestantism will have to go in another direction.[55]

The history of social movements is replete with shifts from a redemptive (saving one's soul) to a transformative (changing the world) emphasis, or vice versa, often after the first generation.[56] Such a shift might provide an opportunity for elements of liberation theology to come into play on a far wider basis than at present. As for pentecostal beliefs in ultimate deliverance, in Brazil at least they clearly descend from that country's tradition of messianic movements. The sense of urgency pentecostals generate, their adversarial attitude toward "the world," and their opinion of themselves as "the poor of the earth" add up to what Carlos Brandão has called "the feeling of a holy war . . . together with the hope of a final struggle that will re-create a social order." Could the dualist, Manichean emphasis on purity, on the radical distinction between this sinful world and the blessed otherworld, become a driving political force?[57]

Various scenarios can be envisioned. One is a direct confrontation with the Latin American state, implying that a shift from a redemptive to a transformative focus will have to take place. Yet except to insist on religious freedom, evangelicals in Latin America have rarely challenged the state. Observers like Jean Pierre Bastian and Rubem Alves believe that Protestantism has failed, coopted by Latin America's authoritarian tradition. But perhaps we need to be patient: in Europe the social process associated with the Reformation unfolded over centuries.

Giving moral reformers the benefit of the doubt, the second scenario has the diverse sects extending from the lower into the middle classes, coalescing into an evangelical establishment—a process already under way—and then impressing their standards on national life—a process which has far to go, judging from the rise and fall of Ríos Montt. By gradually renegotiating their position with the dominant classes, according to this scenario, a rising middle sector could conceivably produce a more democratic, open system without overthrowing the old power structure.

Even if this is a utopian vision, evangelical missions and churches are at least producing new leaders for popular movements. One example is the Summer Institute of Linguistics in Peru. Although SIL can be criticized on many scores, much of the leadership of current native rights organizations in the Peruvian Amazon comes out of its bilingual schools. Like liberation theology in more obvious ways, the new organizations and institutions that result from evangelism could place new pressures on elites and conceivably redefine the political culture.

"You have to take a long perspective," Presbyterian missionary and anthropologist David Scotchmer told me, "because in the short term, yes, evangelical religion is reactionary. But a lot of the second and third generation lose their spiritualism and start asking different questions of the Bible."[58] As long as evangelical churches grow rapidly, these effects are masked by the continuous influx of new members. But growth has its limits. Subsequent generations usually fail to maintain the fervor of the first but do find themselves in new and challenging situations, in which they use their Protestant inheritance in new ways.

There is, of course, a third scenario: that evangelical Protestants will fail to be a major force for social change. The bitter sectarianism of so many evangelicals, their avoidance of a political agenda, and the isolation of "reformers within the reformation" make this the most defensible scenario at present. "Let me do my thing and, if a social revolution results, that's up to God, . . . not me," is the prevailing attitude.[59] The apparent exhaustion of Protestantism in the English- and Dutch-speaking Caribbean—Jamaica, the Bahamas, Belize, Barbados, Guyana, and Suriname—suggests that even the emergence of Protestant majorities could have little effect on the social structures encouraging poverty and violence in Latin American life. Under such conditions, evangelicals might well continue their conservative political stance, as the most conducive to survival in deteriorating economies without genuine political alternatives.

Still, evangelical Protestants are giving Latin Americans a new form of social organization and a new way to express their hopes. The extent to which they can provide converts with the terrestrial corollaries of grace—freedom from hunger, a measure of personal security and advancement—is probably very limited. But for millions of Latin Americans struggling to survive capitalist development and botched social experiments, evangelical churches have become what Richard N. Adams calls survival vehicles.[60] Where traditional social organization is breaking up, evangelical churches constitute new, more flexible groups in which participation is voluntary, where leadership is charismatic, and which are therefore more adaptable to rapidly changing conditions. What that holds for the future is an open question.

Appendix 1

Estimates of Protestant Representation
in Latin America and the Caribbean

	Protestants as Percentage of Total National Population				
	Johnstone 1986		Holland 1981	Barrett 1982	
Country	Protestants	Marginal Groups	Protestants	Professing	Affiliated
Argentina	5.5	1.1	—	3.4	4.7
Bahamas	56.4	1.1	83.0	69.7	62.3
Barbados	59.3	2.5	79.0	88.0	56.5
Belize	25.8	2.0	54.4	27.7	18.7
Bolivia	7.6	0.7	—	2.3	4.8
Brazil	17.4	0.5	—	6.1	15.1
Chile	22.5	2.0	—	9.9	18.9
Colombia	3.1	1.1	—	0.9	2.2
Costa Rica	7.7	2.2	7.9 + 0.9 marg.	7.3	4.2
Cuba	2.4	—	2.0	0.9	2.4
Dominican R.	6.4	0.6	2.0	1.6	3.0
Ecuador	3.4	0.9	—	1.9	3.6
El Salvador	14.0	1.2	7.0	2.9	5.9
French Guiana	6.5	1.7	—	3.9	6.6
Guatemala	20.4	0.7	21.0	4.9	7.9
Guyana	28.0	1.8	—	34.0	26.7
Haiti	17.2	0.6	10–20	15.8	14.7

Protestants as Percentage of Total National Population

Country	Johnstone 1986 Protestants	Johnstone 1986 Marginal Groups	Holland 1981 Protestants	Barrett 1982 Professing	Barrett 1982 Affiliated
Honduras	9.9	0.7	8.0	2.6	3.4
Jamaica	38.6	5.0	75.0	80.1	38.6
Mexico	4.0	1.0	—	2.2	4.5
Nicaragua	9.3	2.1	12 + 2 marg.	4.6	9.8
Panama	11.8	1.0	12.0	6.7	11.8
Paraguay	4.0	0.3	—	2.1	2.2
Peru	3.6	0.9	—	3.0	3.3
Puerto Rica	27.2	2.7	8.0	6.6	12.8
Suriname	19.9	1.0	—	37.0	30.2
Uruguay	3.1	2.2	—	1.9	2.9
Venezuela	2.6	0.7	—	1.3	2.9

Sources. Johnstone's (1986:26, 498–99) figures are based on church growth projections to June 1985. His "Protestant" category includes ecumenical as well as evangelical Protestants. But it excludes the "Marginal" category, for unorthodox groups such as the Mormons and Jehovah's Witnesses. Holland's (1981:12) figures are the work of the Central America Socio-Religous Studies Project (PROCADES) of the Institute of In-Depth Evangelization (INDEPTH) in San José, Costa Rica. They include ecumenical as well as evangelical Protestants. Barrett's (1982: by country entry) figures represent church growth projections to June 1980 based on 1970 figures. The numbers given here are the sum of his figures for various categories including Anglicans, Protestants, marginal Protestants, and indigenous denominations. "Professing" (to a government census or in some public manner) and "affiliated" (to a church) represent two different estimates of the same quantity; they are not to be added together.

Appendix 2

Estimate of Evangelical Population
in Latin America and the Caribbean

Country	National Population	Evangelical Population
Argentina	30,600,000	1,438,000
Bahamas	256,000	77,000
Barbados	300,000	56,000
Belize	184,000	22,000
Bolivia	6,200,000	403,000
Brazil	138,400,000	22,144,000
Chile	12,000,000	2,592,000
Colombia	29,400,000	706,000
Costa Rica	2,600,000	169,000
Cuba	10,100,000	212,000
Dominican Republic	6,200,000	291,000
Ecuador	9,400,000	301,000
El Salvador	5,500,000	704,000
French Guiana	68,000	3,000
Guatemala	8,403,000	1,597,000
Guyana	979,000	85,000
Haiti	5,800,000	713,000
Honduras	4,372,000	385,000
Jamaica	2,358,000	330,000
Mexico	80,484,000	2,495,000
Nicaragua	3,218,000	203,000
Panama	2,140,000	210,000
Paraguay	3,600,000	90,000

Appendix 2 (continued)

Country	National Population	Evangelical Population
Peru	19,500,000	585,000
Puerto Rico	3,350,00	697,000
Suriname	393,000	12,000
Uruguay	3,036,000	58,000
Venezuela	17,300,000	363,000

Source: Johnstone 1986:55, 62.
Note: "Evangelical population" here refers only to theologically conservative Protestants, not all Protestants.

Appendix 3

Estimate of Evangelical Growth Factors in Latin America from 1960 to 1985, with Extrapolation to 2010

Country	Evangelical Percentage of Total Population		Growth Factor from 1960 to 1985	Evangelical Percentage of Population Extrapolated to 2010[a]
	1960	1985	(in number of times)	(in percentages)
Argentina	1.63	4.69	2.9	13.6
Bolivia	1.27	6.51	5.1	33.2
Brazil	4.40	15.95	3.6	57.4
Chile	11.71	21.57	1.8	38.8
Colombia	0.39	2.43	6.2	15.1
Costa Rica	1.30	6.48	5.0	32.4
Cuba	2.41	2.11	0.9	1.9
Dominican Republic	1.73	5.17	3.0	15.5
Ecuador	0.48	2.75	5.7	15.7
El Salvador	2.45	12.78	5.2	66.5
Guatemala	2.81	18.92	6.7	126.8
Haiti	6.09	14.18	2.3	32.6
Honduras	1.51	8.75	5.8	50.8
Mexico	2.21	3.08	1.4	4.3
Nicaragua	2.26	6.32	2.8	17.7
Panama	4.40	9.72	2.2	21.4
Paraguay	1.05	2.47	2.4	5.9
Peru	0.63	2.98	4.7	14.0

Appendix 3 (continued)

Country	Evangelical Percentage of Total Population 1960	Evangelical Percentage of Total Population 1985	Growth Factor from 1960 to 1985 (in number of times)	Evangelical Percentage of Population Extrapolated to 2010[a] (in percentages)
Puerto Rico	5.87	20.85	3.6	75.1
Uruguay	1.19	1.91	1.6	3.1
Venezuela	0.82	1.95	2.4	4.7

Sources: The statistics in the first two columns are from Mr. and Mrs. P. J. Johnstone, International Research Office, WEC (Worldwide Evangelization Crusade) International, Gerrards Cross, England, January 15, 1988. These figures are based on denominational membership totals from the World Christian Encyclopedia (Barrett 1982) and other sources but include "extrapolatory estimates" where information is lacking. The member totals for each denomination have been multiplied by a factor, generally between two and three depending on the social composition of the group, to account for children, neophytes, and other unbaptized persons participating in church life. For further caveats, see Johnstone 1986: 498–99.

Note: "Evangelical" refers to theologically conservative Protestants, not all Protestants.

[a]Based on 1960–1985 growth rate.

Notes

Preface

1. James Montgomery, quoted in "DAWN is About to Break on Guatemala," *Global Church Growth* (Milpitas, Calif.: O.C. Ministries), March–April 1984, p. 351.

2. Conor Cruise O'Brien, "God and Man in Nicaragua," *Atlantic Monthly*, August 1986, p. 56.

3. Msgr. Boaventura Kloppenburg at 1984 bishops' conference in Bogotá, cited by Thomas Stahel, "The Sects in Paraguay," *America*, September 27, 1986, pp. 139–41.

4. Bastian 1986:16.

5. To find out about an organization, start with Barrett 1982, S. Wilson and Siewert 1986, and Johnstone 1986; for Central America and the Caribbean, see Holland 1981 or Resource Center 1988a, 1988b, 1988c. Most groups are eager to put potential contributors on their mailing list. In Latin America, evangelicals at the nearest Bible institute or seminary will know if a national church directory has been published and are often willing to explain a visiting revivalist's background.

1. The Invasion of the Sects in Latin America

1. Bamat 1986:25–26. Author's translation.

2. With the parade ground little more than half full, I doubted there were more than 250,000 in attendance.

3. "Denuncias de la FIDH," *Enfoprensa* (Mexico City: Agencia Guatemalteca de Noticias), November 12, 1983, p. 7.

4. Author's notes, November 28, 1982. "Mass Palau Rally Caps Guatemala Centennial Year," *Christianity Today*, January 7, 1983, p. 48.

5. "Luis Palau: Evangelist to Three Worlds," *Christianity Today*, May 20, 1983, pp. 30–31. Luis Palau, "The Gospel's Social Impact," *Briefing* (Portland, Ore.: Luis Palau Evangelistic Team), Summer 1984, pp. 14–16.

6. Richard N. Ostling, "Into a Perilous Volcano," *Time*, March 7, 1983, p. 10.

7. As quoted in Montgomery 1979:91–92.

8. For a systematic definition of sects, see B. Wilson 1970:13–35.

9. Johnstone (1986:56, 65) represents conventional wisdom. Kenneth Woodward and Penny Lernoux suggest a figure of 12.5 percent (*Newsweek*, September 1, 1986, pp. 63–64).

10. Faith Sand Pidcoke, "Dateline: Brazil . . . a Protestant Nation?" *Latin America Pulse* (Wheaton, Ill.: Evangelical Missions Information Service), November 1973, pp. 1–4.

11. Based on country and regional evaluations in Johnstone 1986:55, 62, 112, 135; see also Appendixes 1 and 2.

12. See data in Appendix 3.

13. Taylor (1984:5–6), who is a member of the Central American Mission.

14. For more detailed although less recent assessments by country, see Read et al. 1969 and, for Central America and the Caribbean, Holland 1981. For the many analyses of national, regional, denominational, and ethnic growth trends produced by the church growth movement, consult D. M. Wagner 1984. For a list of other analyses of church growth, consult the William Carey Library, P.O. Box 40129, Pasadena, Calif. 91104.

15. Costas 1982:108–9, S. Wilson and Siewert 1986:584. Wilson and Siewert's figures do not include Mormon missionaries (see Chapter 5), who numbered 8,136 in 1985.

16. Al Hatch, "What's Coming in the Light of Current Money Squeeze," *Pulse* (Wheaton, Ill.: Evangelical Missions Information Service), April 1983, pp. 2–4.

17. Donald Zook, "Nicaraguan Pastors Tell Reasons for Growth," *Pulse*, November 1983, pp. 7–8.

18. James Montgomery, quoted by Sharon E. Mumper, "Where in the World Is the Church Growing?" *Christianity Today*, July 11, 1986, pp. 17–21.

19. Annis 1988.

20. Núñez C. et al. 1983:67, 76.

21. Willems 1967:248 and Lalive 1969:36.

22. Willems 1967:169 and Brusco 1986.

23. Curry 1968:251, 255–57.

24. Bamat 1986:26.

25. *Christianity Today,* October 10, 1975, pp. 62–64.

26. Ibid.

27. Barry et al. 1986:21, 48–49.

28. Clawson 1976:136–39.

29. Fernandes 1980:131.

30. "Is Wycliffe Biggest?" *Mission Frontiers* (Pasadena, Calif.: U.S. Center for World Mission), January–February 1984, p. 7.

31. "Muerta en Lomalinda maestra del ILV," *El Tiempo* (Bogotá, Colombia), May 6, 1986, p. 2A.

32. *Washington Report on the Hemisphere* (Council on Hemispheric Affairs), June 11, 1986, p. 6.

33. Hundley 1983:40.

34. "Los protestantes denuncian discriminación" and "Afirman los protestantes: 'Somos ciudadanos de tercera,'" *El Tiempo,* June 27 and 28, 1985.

35. "Impossible . . . Difficult . . . Done!" *Latin America Evangelist* (Coral Gables, Fla.: Latin America Mission), January–March 1986, p. 13. "Mexicans Criticize Activities of Sects," *Latinamerica Press,* June 13, 1985, pp. 1–2.

36. *Noticiero Milamex* (Mexico City: Latin America Mission), July 1985.

37. Willems 1967:117.

38. D. A. Smith 1985.

39. Wilde 1986:14–16.

40. Guillermo Cook to author, September 24, 1986.

41. Author's interview with Plutarco Bonilla, Centro Evangélico Latinoamericano de Estudios Pastorales, San José, Costa Rica, July 12, 1985.

42. Hundley 1983:32–33.

43. McLoughlin 1978:10–11.

2. Reformation and Counter-Reformation in the Catholic Church

1. Wood 1900.

2. Recently the argument has been revived by Catholic neoconservative Michael Novak (1986) in his critique of liberation theology.

3. Costas 1982:58–70.

4. S. Wilson and Siewert 1986:59–60.

5. Curry 1968:161.

6. Goff 1968:chap. 1, p. 2.

7. Pablo Richard quoted by Deborah Huntington, "Visions of the Kingdom: the Latin American Church in Conflict," *NACLA Report on the Americas,* September–October 1985, pp. 22–23.

8. Cited by John Shannon, "Catholicism's Coat of Many Colors," *Latin America Pulse*, November 1983, pp. 2–5.

9. Author's interview with Arnoldo Mora, San José, Costa Rica, July 18, 1985.

10. Thomas Bamat, "Ecuador: Controversy Surrounds Growing Evangelical Presence," *Latinamerica Press*, November 29, 1984, pp. 5–6.

11. For a description of Catholic charismaticism, see Thomas Chordas, "Catholic Pentecostalism," in Glazier 1980:143–75.

12. Erich Bridges, "Catholicism in Brazil: Problems and Promise," *Commission* (SBC), February–March 1982, pp. 26–29.

13. Read et al. 1969:267.

14. Ibid., p. 268.

15. Author's interview with Msgr. Vicente R. Cisneros Durán, Ambato, Ecuador, June 17, 1985.

16. "DAWN is About to Break on Guatemala," *Global Church Growth*, March–April 1984, p. 351.

17. Bamat 1986:34.

18. Elisabeth Isais, "Apostolic Delegate in Mexico Urges Governments to 'Counteract' and 'Nullify' Protestant Groups," *Missionary News Service*, December 15, 1984, pp. 2–3.

19. *El Nuevo Diario* (Managua, Nicaragua), January 28, February 14, and February 16, 1985.

20. "Los protestantes denuncian discriminación," *El Tiempo*, June 27, 1985, and "Afirman los protestantes: 'Somos ciudadanos de tercera,'" *El Tiempo*, June 28, 1985.

21. Author's interview with Fernando Ramírez, Alianza Evangélica Costaricense, San José, Costa Rica, July 11, 1985.

22. Associated Press, "El CELAM decide contrarrestar influencia de sectas protestantes," *La Razón* (Guatemala City), March 16, 1983, p. 11. "Latin America: Counter-Evangelism," *Evangelical Missions Quarterly*, July 1983, pp. 259–60. Taylor 1984:5.

23. "Study Says Cults Reflect Church's Pastoral Failure," *National Catholic Reporter*, May 16, 1986. Holy See 1986.

24. Simons 1982:116.

25. Rockefeller Commission 1969:31.

26. Allan Figueroa Deck, "Fundamentalism and the Hispanic Catholic," *America*, January 26, 1985, pp. 64–66.

27. William Dinges, "The Vatican Report on Sects, Cults and New Religious Movements," *America*, September 27, 1986, pp. 145–47, 154.

28. Author's interview, Jesuit Residence, Quito, Ecuador, May 24, 1985.

29. For a critique of the radical Catholic left in Peru and its reproduction of clericalism, see Pásara 1986.

30. Ruiz Navas 1984:10.

31. Hollenweger 1986:9.

32. Author's interview, San José, Costa Rica, July 9, 1985.

33. Nelson 1983:334.

34. Deck, "Fundamentalism and the Hispanic Catholic."

35. Arturo Chacón and Humberto Lagos, *La religión en las fuerzas armadas y de orden,* sponsored by Lutheran World Relief and Church World Service, cited in *Latinamerica Press,* March 6, 1986, p. 7.

36. Simons 1982:47.

37. W. Dayton Roberts, "Latin America in the 1980s," *Latin America Evangelist,* January–February 1981, pp. 4–5, and March–April 1981, pp. 6–8, and "What Latins Are Saying About Pope John Paul II," *Latin American Evangelist,* May–June 1982, pp. 10–11.

38. *Latin America Evangelist,* October–December 1985, p. 20.

39. Taylor 1984:5.

40. C. René Padilla, "Liberation Theology Is Remarkably Protestant," *Christianity Today,* May 15, 1987, p. 12.

41. Thomas Scheetz to author, November 2, 1986. For case studies of conflicts over authority in the Catholic Church, see the essays in Levine 1986.

3. From Doomsday to Dominion in North American Evangelicalism

1. Bromley and Shupe 1984:148.

2. This sketch of Pat Robertson is indebted to 700 Club–watchers Sara Diamond and Richard Hatch; Dick Dabney, "God's Own Network," *Harper's Magazine,* August 1980, pp. 33–52; and John Fialka and Ellen Hume, "Pulpit and Politics," *Wall Street Journal,* October 17, 1985, pp. 1, 25.

3. On premillennialism, see William Martin, "Waiting for the End," *Atlantic Monthly,* June 1982, pp. 31–37, and Weber 1983.

4. Quoted by John Dart, "Churches Try to Reverse Decline," *Sacramento Bee,* April 20, 1985, p. B7.

5. William Willimon, "A Crisis of Identity," *Sojourners,* May 1986, pp. 24–28.

6. Tom Sine, "Shifting Christian Mission into the Future Tense," *Missiology,* January 1987, p. 16.

7. "The Christianity Today Gallup Poll: An Overview," *Christianity To-*

day, December 21, 1979, pp. 14–17. For a detailed analysis of the figures, see Hunter 1983.

8. Richard Ostling, "Evangelical Publishing and Broadcasting," in Marsden 1984:55.

9. Marsden 1980:194.

10. Nathan Hatch, "Evangelicalism as a Democratic Movement," in Marsden 1984:71–82.

11. Hutcheson 1981:32–35; and James Speer, "The New Christian Right and Its Parent Company," in Bromley and Shupe 1984:31–32.

12. Barr 1978:193.

13. "Main Street in Evangelicalville" and "What Is the Moody-Dallas Agenda?" *Eternity*, November 1981, pp. 19–22, and December 1981, pp. 26–29.

14. Menzies 1971:339.

15. Steve Scott, "True Confessions: The Miracle in Your Mouth" [pamphlet] (Sacramento, Calif.: Apologetics Resource Center), 1985. Stafford 1986.

16. My distinction between neo-evangelicals, fundamentalists, and more separationist fundamentalists follows Quebedeaux 1974:18–32.

17. Carl F. H. Henry, cited in Hill and Owen 1982:89.

18. Carl F. H. Henry, *Christianity Today*, January 4, 1980.

19. Mark Noll, "Evangelicals and the Study of the Bible," in Marsden 1984:109.

20. Ralph Chandler, "The Fundamentalist Heritage of the New Christian Right," in Bromley and Shupe 1984:56; "Billy Graham: Evangelists Go Too Far," *Sacramento Bee*, January 4, 1985, p. A2.

21. Quebedeaux 1978:84–96.

22. Grant Wacker, "Uneasy in Zion," in Marsden 1984:18.

23. For a description of the recruitment of conservative evangelicals by the religious right, see Wallis 1986.

24. Kenneth L. Woodward, "The Split-Up Evangelicals," *Newsweek*, April 26, 1982, pp. 88–91.

25. "Billy Graham," *Sacramento Bee*.

26. Marvin Antonio Guevara García, "Cristianos revolucionarios únanse," *El Nuevo Diario*, May 25, 1984.

27. For supportive editorials, see *Christianity Today*, March 21, 1986, pp. 14–15, and April 4, 1986, pp. 34–35.

28. Kenneth A. Briggs, "Evangelicals Debate Their Role in Battling Secularism," *New York Times*, January 27, 1981, p. 6.

29. Maureen Wells, "A Dash of Latin Verve," *Religious Broadcasting* (Morristown, N.J.: National Religious Broadcasters), March 1983, pp. 34–35.

30. "Jesse Jackson Spoke, But Not Many Listened," *Christianity Today,* March 7, 1986, p. 47.

31. For a debate between a moderate and a fundamentalist Southern Baptist, see "Patterson vs. McCall on the Southern Baptist Controversy," *Fundamentalist Journal,* May 1985, pp. 10–21.

32. "1985: The World in View," *Commission,* May 1986, pp. 31–42.

33. R. Keith Parks, *Commission,* September 1982, pp. 2, 80.

34. Quoted by Thomas Byrne Edsall, "Republican America," *New York Review of Books,* April 24, 1986, pp. 3–6.

35. *Washington Insight* (NAE), June 1986.

36. Barbara and Michael Ledeen, "The Temple Mount Plot," *The New Republic,* June 18, 1984, pp. 20–23.

37. Tom Sine, "Bringing Down the Final Curtain," *Sojourners,* June–July 1984, pp. 10–14.

38. Ibid.

39. "Critics Fear That Reagan Is Swayed by . . . a 'Nuclear Armageddon,'" *Christianity Today,* December 14, 1984, pp. 50–51.

40. Dennis Peacocke, California Alliance, Capitol Christian Center, Sacramento, September 21, 1985.

41. Monte Wilson of Fishers and Builders, Tallahassee, Florida, "The Nations of the World Are His!" *Forerunner* (Gainesville, Fla.: Maranatha Campus Ministries), August 1986, pp. 20–21.

42. *Christianity Today,* September 5, 1986, pp. 30–31.

43. David Rausch and Douglas Chismar, "The New Puritans and Their Theonomic Paradise," *Christian Century,* August 3, 1983, pp. 712–15.

44. Gary North, quoted by Rodney Clapp, "Democracy as Heresy," *Christianity Today,* February 20, 1987, pp. 17–23.

45. Darrand and Shupe 1983:33–59; see also Holdcroft 1980.

46. "The Manifest Sons of God," 1985, and "Satan Unmasked," n.d. [pamphlets] (Sacramento, Calif.: Apologetics Resource Center).

47. Edward E. Plowman, "The Deepening Rift in the Charismatic Movement," *Christianity Today,* October 10, 1975, pp. 52–54; John Maust, "Charismatic Leaders Seeking Faith for Their Own Healing," *Christianity Today,* April 4, 1980, pp. 44–46; Berberian 1983:40–41, 82–109.

48. For a portrait of a related movement in Britain, see Walker 1985.

49. Larry Tomczak, "God's Solution to the Current Crisis," *People of Destiny* (Wheaton, Md.), September–October 1983, pp. 4–9.

50. Diane Divoky, "UCD Ministry: Evangelism or Mind Control?" *Sacramento Bee,* June 4, 1984, pp. B1–2.

51. Randy Frame, "A Team of Cult Watchers Challenges a Growing Campus Ministry," *Christianity Today,* August 10, 1984, pp. 38–43.

52. John Fialka, "Fervent Faction," *Wall Street Journal*, August 16, 1985, pp. 1, 15.

53. *Freedom Fighter* (Washington, D.C: Coalition for Democracy in Central America), January 1985, p. 12.

54. Lee Grady, "Communist Aggression in Nicaragua," *Forerunner*, December 1984, pp. 17–19, 24.

55. Author's interviews, Coalition on Revival, Washington, D.C., July 2–4, 1986. For an exposition of pre-, post-, and amillennial positions, see Clouse 1977.

56. For Robertson's views, see his *The Secret Kingdom* (Nashville, Tenn.: Thomas Nelson, 1982); and Andy Lang and Fred Clarkson, "What Makes Pat Robertson Run?" *Convergence* (Washington, D.C: Christic Institute), Spring 1988, pp. 17–23.

57. Lee Grady, "A Declaration of Christian Dominion," *Forerunner*, October 1984, pp. 15–17.

58. Charles Mahaney, "From Fatalism to Victory," *People of Destiny*, January–February 1985, p. 29.

59. Dennis Peacocke, California Alliance, Capitol Christian Center, Sacramento, September 21, 1985.

60. Mariano Sotelo, "Moonies Bid for Power Throughout Latin America," *Latinamerica Press*, September 29, 1983, pp. 5–6.

61. Fred Landis, *Media Line* (San Francisco), September 1984.

62. Ellen Hume, "The Right Stuff," *Wall Street Journal*, December 17, 1985, pp. 1, 18.

63. Carolyn Weaver, "Unholy Alliance," *Mother Jones*, January 1986. *Christianity Today*, October 19, 1984, pp. 42–43; June 14, 1985, pp. 55–58; January 17, 1986, pp. 40–41; and November 7, 1986, pp. 46–48.

64. Townsend 1940; Stam 1981.

65. Bill Bright, quoted by YWAM-Washington director Ron Boehme, "Why Is God Being Merciful to America?" [tape cassette] (Severna Park, Md.: Maranatha Tape Ministry, 1986).

66. Colonel Doner of Christian Voice, interviewed in *Christian Life*, October 1984, pp. 36–42.

67. Jerry Falwell, quoted in Conway and Siegelman 1984:247.

4. The Evangelical Mission Movement

1. *Fishers and Builders* (Tallahassee, Fla.), November 1986.
2. Stafford 1984:16.
3. Sandeen 1970:188–91.
4. *Santa Ana Register*, December 24, 1984.

5. Don Bjork, "Foreign Missions: Next Door and Down the Street," *Christianity Today,* July 12, 1985, pp. 17–21.

6. Johnstone 1982:40–47.

7. Joel A. Carpenter, "From Fundamentalism to the New Evangelical Coalition," in Marsden 1984:15, and "The Parachurch Vision," *Christianity Today,* November 8, 1985, pp. 44–47.

8. One example is the early career of the founder of the Summer Institute of Linguistics, William Cameron Townsend (Stoll 1982:69–70). Another is the Presbyterian pioneer in Guatemala, Edward Haymaker (Scotchmer 1985), as well as a subsequent Presbyterian missionary to the same country, Paul Burgess, whose career has been described by his granddaughter (Dahlquist 1985).

9. Barrett 1982:17.

10. Cf. Hatch 1981.

11. Peter Wagner, "The Greatest Church Growth Is Beyond Our Own Shores," *Christianity Today,* May 18, 1984, pp. 25–31.

12. Quebedeaux 1978:83.

13. "Urbana '84: Biggest and Best Yet," *Mission Frontiers,* January–March 1985, p. 19.

14. Dayton 1981:120. Of the 4,349 missionaries affiliated with the NCC's Division of Missions in 1985, nearly one-fourth—1,052—belonged to one of the NCC's most conservative and atypical members, the Seventh Day Adventist Church (S. Wilson and Siewert 1986:38, 177).

15. The official proceedings were published in Douglas 1975.

16. C. P. Wagner 1981:115.

17. Kenneth S. Kantzer, "Revitalizing World Evangelism: The Lausanne Congress Ten Years Later," *Christianity Today,* June 15, 1984, pp. 10–12; C. René Padilla, "El Congreso de Lausana: Diez años después," *Misión* (Buenos Aires, Argentina: Latin American Theological Fraternity), September 1984, pp. 110–11.

18. Lindsell 1976; Quebedeaux 1978:84–90.

19. Stafford 1984:17.

20. Tucker 1983:477–79. Tim Stafford, "The Father of Church Growth," *Christianity Today,* February 21, 1986, pp. 19–23. McGavran 1955 and 1970.

21. Hutcheson 1981:120.

22. Ralph H. Elliott, "Dangers of the Church Growth Movement," *Christian Century,* August 12, 1981, pp. 799–801; Costas 1984a.

23. C. P. Wagner 1981:196.

24. C. P. Wagner 1973:36.

25. Wimber 1984. "Signs and Wonders Today," *Christian Life,* October 1982, pp. 18–76.

26. Barrett 1982:3.

27. Winter 1980:39.

28. Johnstone 1982:34–35.

29. Ibid., p. 89.

30. Tapp 1986.

31. Tom Goosman and Edward Plowman, "Visitors See Signs of Strong Evangelical Faith in China," *Christianity Today*, September 6, 1985, pp. 46, 48.

32. Ralph Covell, "The Church in China: Another View," *Christianity Today*, February 1, 1985, pp. 62–64.

33. Chastain 1984:86–87.

34. Sharon E. Mumper, "New Strategies to Evangelize Muslims Gain Effectiveness," *Christianity Today*, May 17, 1985, pp. 75–76.

35. Johnstone 1982:162–65.

36. Roberta Winter, "The Great Re-Commission," *Moody Monthly*, November 1982, p. 11.

37. Linda Howard, "The Mission Field Isn't What It Used to Be," *Charisma*, June 1984, p. 31.

38. Keyes 1983:62. Interview with O.C. Ministries president Lawrence Keyes, "Getting the Whole Story," *Mission Frontiers*, February 1983, pp. 8–11.

39. "COWE: 200,000 by the Year 2,000," *Christianity Today*, August 8, 1980, pp. 10–11.

40. Dayton and Wilson 1984:175.

41. Stafford 1984.

42. Ibid.

43. S. Wilson and Siewert 1986:39–41, 63, 573.

44. Mrs. Milton A. Gabler, *Practical Anthropology* 2(2):43–44, 1955, in a review of the influential Nida 1954.

45. Reyburn and Reyburn 1955:73, 123.

46. Nida 1981:5.

47. Aulie 1979:72–73; Cardiel Coronel 1983:47–51.

48. Aulie 1979:155; Juan Schuster to author, November 16, 1983.

49. Quoted in Weerstra 1972:252.

50. Aulie 1979:140, 156–57, 165–67.

51. Schuster to author; Cardiel Coronel 1983:105 and Fretwell 1983:23.

52. Fretwell 1983:14.

53. Aulie 1979:185–88.

54. Quoted in Kaleli 1984:75.

55. Shaw 1981. Joseph P. Grimes, "To Reach Certainty," *In Other Words* (Huntington Beach, Calif.: WBT), September 1981, pp. 1–2.

56. David F. Wells, "An American Evangelical Theology," in Marsden 1984:88.

57. Lara-Braud 1983:3.

58. Nida 1981.

59. Concerning YWAM: Bruce Joffe, "Man with a Mission," *Charisma,* November 1985, pp. 21–26; Bryan Bishop, "YWAM Steps Out," *World Christian* (Pasadena, Calif.: U.S. Center for World Mission), January–February 1986, pp. 18–23; John Holzmann, "Youth with a Mission," *Mission Frontiers,* October–December 1985, pp. 9–17. The figures for the other organizations are from their annual reports.

60. Bruce Shelley, "The Parachurch Vision," *Christianity Today,* November 8, 1985, pp. 41–43.

61. Bright 1985.

62. Quebedeaux 1979:54, 107, 181, 184.

63. John Capon, "Video Conference Links Christians in 54 Countries," *Christianity Today,* February 7, 1986, pp.46–47.

64. Quebedeaux 1978:58.

65. "Alfa y omega: Ya la encontramos!" *Alternativa* (Bogotá, Colombia), January 29, 1979, pp. 12–13.

66. Jeleta Fryman, "The Movement," *World Christian,* January–February 1986, pp. 25–28.

67. Sharon E. Mumper, "Are Short-Term Volunteers the Way of the Future?" *Christianity Today,* April 4, 1986, p. 41.

68. Bishop, "YWAM Steps Out."

69. Deborah D. Cole, *Charisma,* November 1984, pp. 22–25.

70. Holzmann, "Youth with a Mission."

71. Interviews with Loren Cunningham: Joffe, "Man with a Mission," and "Taking the Gospel into All the World . . . with Signs Following," *People of Destiny,* July–August 1985, pp. 25–29. For an account of the formation of YWAM, see Cunningham 1984.

72. Author's interview, Quito, Ecuador, May 15, 1985.

73. Al Hatch, "What's Coming in the Light of Current Money Squeeze," *Pulse,* April 1983, pp. 2–4.

74. Samuel and Sugden 1983.

75. Reapsome 1984.

76. The January 1985 issue of *Missiology* is devoted to this question.

77. Alan Neely, review of C. P. Wagner 1983, *International Bulletin of Missionary Research,* July 1985, pp. 133–34.

78. C. P. Wagner and Dayton 1981:27; Dayton and Wilson 1983:33.

79. Quoted by Samuel and Sugden 1983:152.

80. C. P. Wagner 1973:97, 114 backtranslated from a Spanish translation of the original English.

81. William R. Burrows, in Samuel and Sugden 1983:156.
82. George Pixley, quoted in Mondragón 1983:158–62.

5. The Evangelical Awakening in Latin America

1. "Revolution and Religion in Nicaragua," *Guardian* (New York), September 15, 1982, p. 21.
2. Author's interviews, Matagalpa, Nicaragua, August 14, 1985.
3. Read et al. 1969:58; Bastian 1986:14.
4. Willems 1967:104. For a historical survey of Latin American Protestantism, see Bastian 1986.
5. Bastian 1984:50–51, 63–64.
6. Johnstone 1982.
7. George Colvin, "Adventists Balance Gains, Challenges," *Christian Century*, August 14, 1985, pp. 738–39.
8. Read et al. 1969:58–60, 109–11.
9. Read et al. 1969:114 and K. D. Scott 1985.
10. Joan Craven, "The Wall of Adventism," *Christianity Today*, October 19, 1984, pp. 20–25.
11. Molina Saborío 1984:12, 16.
12. Nelson 1963:129.
13. David Brion Davis, "Secrets of the Mormons," *New York Review of Books*, August 15, 1985, pp. 15–20.
14. Ralph C. Chandler, "The Fundamentalist Heritage of the New Christian Right," in Bromley and Shupe 1984:52–53.
15. Kenneth L. Woodward, "Bible-Belt Confrontation," *Newsweek*, March 4, 1985, pp. 65–66.
16. *Frontline Report* (Eureka, Calif.: International Love Lift) 10(2), 1985.
17. Beekman 1972:3, 5, 7.
18. Albrecht and Rogers 1987:9.
19. James C. Hefley, "In Bogotá, a Banquet of Hope," *Christianity Today*, November 18, 1977, pp. 44–46.
20. Number of Mormon missionaries provided by Don Le Fevre, Latter Day Saints Public Communications, Salt Lake City, May 1986. Number of non-Mormon Protestant missionaries from S. Wilson and Siewert 1986:584.
21. Heinerman and Shupe 1985:162–68.
22. *El Nuevo Diario*, August 2, 1985, p. 3.
23. "Guatemalan Journalists in Exile," *Guatemala* (Oakland, Calif.: Guatemala News and Information Bureau), May–June 1984, p. 3.

24. Religious News Service, "Do Jehovah's Witnesses Still Hold to Their 1984 Doomsday Deadline?" *Christianity Today,* September 21, 1984, pp. 66–67; Marvin Millis, "Watchtower World View," *Christianity Today,* November 22, 1985, pp. 43–44; Arthur Jones, "Michael's 'Victory Tour' Spawns Cult," *National Catholic Reporter,* December 14, 1984, p. 4.

25. Statistics from Mike Creswell, "Jehovah's Witnesses: Challenge on the Mission Field," *Commission,* January 1984, pp. 45–55; Ruth Tucker, "Foreign Missionaries with a False Message," *Evangelical Missions Quarterly,* October 1984, pp. 332–34.

26. Statistics from Assemblies of God Division of Foreign Missions, *1984 Annual Report* and *1985 Annual Report.*

27. Read 1965:121; C. P. Wagner 1973:23–24.

28. Read 1965:121, 126.

29. Curry 1970:435–38.

30. Paul Pretiz, Latin America Mission, San José, Costa Rica, July 9, 1985.

31. Menzies 1971:252–53.

32. Read 1965:130–42.

33. Assemblies of God Division of Foreign Missions, *1985 Annual Report,* p. 23.

34. Huntington and Domínguez 1984:18.

35. Judith Chambliss Hoffnagel, "Pentecostalism: A Revolutionary or Conservative Movement?" in Glazier 1980:111–23.

36. David Brackenridge, quoted in C. P. Wagner 1973:101 and back-translated from a Spanish translation.

37. Wolf 1982:83.

38. Hoffnagel, in Glazier 1980:121.

39. Author's telephone interview with Ronald Iwasko, Assemblies of God, Springfield, Mo., October 28, 1986.

40. Willems 1967:113–17; Read 1965:170–71, 212.

41. Curry 1968:1–2; Lalive d'Epinay 1969:130.

42. Hoffnagel, in Glazier 1980:118–20. For detailed sociologies of pentecostal churches in Chile and Brazil, see Willems 1967 and Lalive d'Epinay 1969. For an evangelical explanation of why pentecostal churches were growing faster than nonpentecostal ones, see C. P. Wagner 1973.

43. Read et al. 1969:102.

44. Willems 1967:228.

45. For a summary of the political alternatives available to Chilean pentecostalism, see Lalive d'Epinay 1983.

46. Hefley and Hefley 1981:554–57; Barrett 1982:228.

47. "Chile's Junta Courts the Once-Spurned Protestants," *Christianity Today*, September 4, 1981, p. 59.

48. Wimber 1984: section 7, p. 7.

49. Garry Parker, "Evangelicals Bloom Brightly amid El Salvador's Wasteland of Violence," *Christianity Today*, May 8, 1981, p. 34–35.

50. Thomas Chordas, "Catholic Pentecostalism," in Glazier 1980:166. The January 1985 issue of *Missiology* is devoted to such phenomena.

51. Westmeier 1986:22.

52. Bastian 1984:64.

53. Frederick Conway, "Pentecostalism in Haiti," in Glazier 1980:7–25.

54. Glasser 1986:413–15; Stafford 1986:19–20.

55. John Maust, "By the Light of the Ominous Moon," *Latin America Evangelist*, October–December 1985, pp. 4–9.

56. K. D. Scott 1985:46. Estimate of number of Protestants from Vittorio Bacchetta, "Brazil's Diverse Protestant Groups United in Conservative Social Role," *Latinamerica Press*, December 5, 1985, pp. 5–6.

57. Gary Nigel Howe, "Capitalism and Religion at the Periphery," in Glazier 1980:125–41. See also Fry 1978.

58. B. R. Roberts 1968.

59. Anderson 1979:221–22,239–40.

60. Flora 1976:226–27,231–35. For a summary, see Flora, "Pentecostalism and Development," in Glazier 1980:81–93.

61. Garma Navarro 1983 and 1984. For a parallel case not included here for reasons of space, see Rappaport 1984.

62. Costas 1984a:9.

63. Read et al. 1969:119, 147, 300–336.

64. C. P. Wagner 1973:136–37.

65. Read et al. 1969:58.

66. Ibid., p. 312.

67. Author's interview with John Kessler, Institute for In-Depth Evangelization, San José, Costa Rica, July 13, 1985.

68. Huntington and Domínguez 1984:15.

69. W. D. Roberts 1971:94.

70. Huntington and Domínguez 1984:17. *Christianity Today* as quoted in Rosales 1968:chap. 4, p. 12.

71. Fernandes 1981:31–40.

72. Author's interview with John Kessler.

73. Huntington and Domínguez 1984:14, 17.

74. Palau 1983:169.

75. Tucker 1983:452.

76. Ibid., p. 449.

77. "Bolivian Government Puts New Emphasis on Teaching Morality,"

Briefing (Luis Palau Evangelistic Team), January–March 1981. Luis Palau, "The Lord's Chessboard," *In Other Words*, Summer 1981, pp. 15–17.

78. Luis Palau Evangelistic Team, "Audited Financial Statements," September 30, 1984, and December 31, 1985.

79. "Easter Gospel Messages Shake Hispanic World," *Briefing*, no. 2, 1985, pp. 2–5.

80. "Palau Power in Latin America," *Time*, November 7, 1977, p. 123.

81. Randy Frame, "NAE: Trying to Avoid a Midlife Crisis," *Christianity Today*, April 4, 1986, pp. 34–35.

82. For the transcript of a Palau press conference in Argentina in 1986, see Silletta 1987:39–46.

83. Fundraising letter, November 1, 1984.

84. Palau 1983:179.

85. Interview with O.C. President Lawrence Keyes, "Getting the Whole Story," *Mission Frontiers*, February 1983, pp. 8–11.

86. Núñez C. et al. 1983 was published for a 1984 conference of this nature.

87. Núñez C. et al. 1983:128–34.

88. W. D. Smith 1978:114.

89. Piedra S. 1984:7.

90. Martha Skelton, "Guatemala City: Wide Open for Witness," *Commission*, January 1984, p. 28–44.

91. Kinsler 1978:182.

92. C. P. Wagner 1973:94.

93. Clyde W. Taylor, "An Upper-Class People Movement," *Global Church Growth*, March–April 1980, pp. 22–23.

94. Skelton, "Guatemala City," pp. 31–32, 36.

95. Godwin 1984:37, 119.

96. "Starting City Churches" [pamphlet] RBMU International (Philadelphia), 1982.

97. Read et al. 1969:349–50.

98. Fernandes 1981:32–33.

99. Ramos 1984:92.

100. Bastian 1979:13–15.

101. Ibid., p. 68.

102. Miguez Bonino as quoted in Montgomery 1979:91–92.

103. C. P. Wagner 1970:17–20.

104. Hundley 1983:2.

105. Bastian 1984:53–55, 58–61 and 1986:158–61.

106. Savage 1981:11; Huntington and Domínguez 1984:20.

107. Samuel Escobar, "Heredero de la reforma radical," in Padilla 1984:64.

108. C. P. Wagner 1970; Huntington and Domínguez 1984:20–21.

109. Author's interview with Robert Allen Hatch, Quito, Ecuador, May 25, 1985.

110. Fernandes 1981:44; J. Andrew Kirk, "Theology in Latin America: Where Is It Today?" *Latin America Evangelist,* May–June 1978, pp. 6–7, 14; interview with René Padilla, *Latin America Evangelist,* May–June 1982, p. 7.

111. Montgomery 1979:87–107.

112. Savage 1981:8–9.

113. Costas 1982:150–51; Savage 1981:13–15; "Literature Named Priority of Theological Fraternity," *Entre Nos* (Quito, Ecuador: Puente), June 1984, p. 6.

114. "CONELA to Focus on Biblical Answers to Continent's Problems," *Briefing,* December–February 1982, p. 17.

115. Bill Conard, "Should Latin American Churches Stay Away from Social Problems?" *Christianity Today,* October 21, 1983, p. 38.

116. "CONELA Celebrates Its First Four Years," *Entre Nos,* May 1986, pp. 1–2.

117. Al Hatch, "The Significance of CONELA," *Latin America Pulse,* July 1982, pp. 1–7.

118. Roger Velásquez, "Reuniones de CONELA," undated memo for World Vision International Regional Office, San José, Costa Rica, pp. 5–6. For another critical analysis of CONELA, see Santos 1984.

6. The Religious Right Comes to Latin America

1. Advertisement, *World Christian,* January–February 1987, p. 9.

2. Open Doors 1984b. A few years before, Dean Jones played an American military adviser in a feature-length film produced by the Sandinista government, the award-winning *Alcino the Condor.*

3. Open Doors 1984a.

4. Hundley 1981 and 1986.

5. Hundley 1983:9.

6. As represented by Bill Conard, "Latin America's Revolution Theology," *Briefing,* December 1981–February 1982, pp. 10–13; Luis Palau, "Evangelist to Three Worlds," *Christianity Today,* May 20, 1983, pp. 30–31.

7. W. Dayton Roberts, "Liberation Theologies," *Christianity Today,* May 17, 1985, pp. 14–16.

8. J. Andrew Kirk, "Theology in Latin America: Where Is It Today?" *Latin America Evangelist,* May–June 1978, pp. 6–7, 14.

9. Hundley 1986.

10. Huntington and Domínguez 1984:25.

11. For an analysis of the contra support movement as a network set up by the CIA, the National Security Council, and the White House, see Barry et al. 1986:14–30.

12. Berryman 1984:29.

13. Peter Kemmerle, "Liberation Theology, from the Inside," *Guardian*, October 24, 1984, p. 20. Alan Riding, "The Sword and the Cross," *New York Review of Books*, May 28, 1981, pp. 3–8.

14. Barry et al. 1986:9, 35.

15. Cf. Costas 1982:66.

16. Subcommittee on Security and Terrorism 1984.

17. Barrett 1982:254; Dan Pawley, "Cuban Believers Walk the Tightrope Under Castro," *Pulse*, October 11, 1985, pp. 2–4; Rosemary Radford Ruether, "Christians and Cubans," *Christianity and Crisis*, August 26, 1985, pp. 329–33.

18. Ramos 1984:93–94. For a lengthier treatment of the post-1959 Protestant churches in Cuba, see the appendixes of Ramos 1986.

19. Crahan 1979:243–46.

20. Adolfo Ham, "Historical Background," in Hageman and Wheaton 1971:148.

21. Harry Genet, "The Church Finds Its Role in a Socialist State," *Christianity Today*, December 21, 1979, pp. 40–41.

22. Hageman and Wheaton 1971:210.

23. Crahan 1979:247, 259.

24. White 1981:72, 129, 168.

25. Major Keith Roberts, "Analysis of the Church in Grenada," Ministry of Interior, July 12, 1983, distributed in conjunction with Institute on Religion and Democracy 1984a.

26. Dan Wooding, "Christians on Island Were Praying for Marxist Rule to End," *Forerunner*, March 1984, p. 7.

27. Dan Wooding, "Freedom in Grenada," *Open Doors* (Orange, Calif.), November–December 1985, pp. 4–5.

28. "Prohibiting Federal Intelligence Agency Involvement with the Clergy," *Congressional Record*, Senate, 121 (185), December 15, 1975.

29. "No CIA Involvement," *Christian Century*, January 6, 1982, p. 9; Anita Bowden, "CIA Assures It Won't Use Missionaries," *Commission*, August 1982, pp. 68–69.

30. Hesselgrave 1979:26–27; Ralph Covell, "Evangelicals and Totalitarian Governments," in Hesselgrave 1979:69–72. Romans 13:1, King James Version.

31. Charles Troutman and Lois Troutman, "We Don't Believe in Violence But . . . ," *His* (Madison, Wis.: Inter-Varsity Christian Fellowship), December 1983, pp. 16–17.

32. Bill Sampson, "El Salvador Again," *Christian Crusade* (Tulsa,

Okla.: Christian Crusade), May 1984, p. 2. Billy James Hargis, "Are We Facing Victory or Defeat in El Salvador, Central America?" *Christian Crusade*, June 1984, p. 14.

33. Edward E. Plowman, "The Rise and Fall of Billy James," *Christianity Today*, February 27, 1976, pp. 42–43.

34. W. Steuart McBirnie, "What You Should Know About the Growing Communist Threat in Central America" [pamphlet] United Community Churches of America (Glendale, Calif.) 1983, pp. 3–5.

35. Barry et al. 1986:16, 19–20, 51.

36. *Christian Anti-Communism Crusade* (Long Beach, Calif.: Christian Anti-Communism Crusade), December 1, 1983, p. 3; April 1, 1984, pp. 6–8; August 15, 1984, p. 1; March 15, 1985, p. 3; and May 15, 1986, p. 3.

37. Conn 1977:40.

38. Sherrill and Sherrill 1967:14, 19.

39. Brother Andrew 1981:82–83.

40. *Open Doors*, May–June 1978, p. 23.

41. Dennis Smith, typescript review of Peter Horsfield, *Religious Television: The American Experience* (New York: Longman, 1984).

42. Estimate of 70 percent from Resource Center 1988c:38.

43. Assemblies of God Division of Foreign Missions, *1985 Annual Report*, p. 3. "Swaggart Says He Sinned, Will Stop Preaching," *San Francisco Chronicle*, February 21, 1988, p. 1ff.

44. Statistics from "Jimmy Swaggart Ministries" [pamphlet] (Baton Rouge, La., 1986).

45. Smith and Ruiz 1987:143, 145, 155.

46. Plutarco Bonilla, "Comunicación y evangelio," *Pastoralia* (San José, Costa Rica: CELEP), July 1987, pp. 8–9, author's translation from Spanish. For more on broadcast evangelism, especially in Brazil, see Assman 1987.

47. Author's interview with Wade Coggins, executive director of EFMA, October 27, 1986.

48. Eric E. Wiggin, "Sandinistas Assailed by Comrade-Turned-Christian," *Mission Frontiers*, September–October 1986, p. 12.

49. Chamorro 1987:50–52.

50. Open Doors with Brother Andrew, Inc. (North America), "Financial Statements and Schedule," December 31, 1983, and December 31, 1985.

51. Fundraising letter, August 23, 1985.

52. "All of Poland to Be Reached with Christian Literature," *Forerunner*, December 1985, p. 8.

53. "Do These Communist Rulers *Like* the Bible?" [fundraising letter], May 5, 1986.

54. Winebrenner 1985:108–13, 140–46.

55. Dick Hillis's letter on Chile, quoted in Edwards 1972:9.

56. "Boletín extra, Congreso Hispano de Evangelización," October 1985.

57. "Mottesi Claims Latin America for Christ in Historic Conference," *Forerunner,* June 1986, p. 4.

58. Brian O'Connell, "Evangelicals and the War/Peace Debate," *Evangelical Newsletter,* February 1, 1985, p. 4.

59. Hitchens 1986.

60. "Religious Liberty Conference Spawns Controversy," *Religion & Democracy* (Institute on Religion and Democracy), May–June 1985, pp. 1, 3–4. "U.S. Underwrites IRD Conference," *The Other Side* (Philadelphia), August–September 1985, p. 4.

61. Author's telephone interview with Brian O'Connell, NAE, March 13, 1986. "Guidelines: Peace, Freedom and Security Studies," NAE, October 1986.

62. "Nelson Hunt Loses a Bundle But Raises a Billion," *Christianity Today,* May 2, 1980, p. 54; Conway and Siegelman 1984:176; Barry et al. 1986:27, 63.

63. Wallis and Michaelson 1976; Quebedeaux 1979:186–89.

64. Bright was on the steering committee of the Coalition on Revival (*Forerunner,* December 1985, p. 7); on the board of the Reverend Tim La Haye's American Coalition for Traditional Values (La Haye, "Should Ministers Be Involved in Politics?" [pamphlet], n.d.); and was a member of the (pro–Star Wars) Religious Coalition for a Moral Defense Policy (*Christianity Today,* April 4, 1986, pp. 43–44).

65. Interview with Christian Voice cofounder Colonel Doner, "We Must Take Action," *Christian Life,* October 1984, pp. 36–42.

66. Wallis 1986:22.

67. "Marxist Students Can't Stop Chile's 'Revolution,'" *Open Doors,* September–October 1985, pp. 8–9.

68. Author's interview with Sergio García Romo, Mexico City, September 2, 1985.

69. "Alfa y omega: Ya la encontramos!" *Alternativa,* January 29, 1979, pp. 12–13. *El Tiempo,* December 3, 1978, pp. 11, 13–14.

70. Author's interview with García Romo.

71. Peter Wagner, "What Happens When You See Jesus," *Christian Life,* April 1986, p. 73.

72. For El Salvador, see Simons 1986 and Resource Center 1988b:17.

73. Conferencia Episcopal Panameña 1984:50.

74. "Lector denuncia," *Unidad Indígena* (Bogotá), May 1982, p. 5. "Los agapes," *Unidad Indígena,* December 1982, p. 3.

75. Institute on Religion and Democracy 1986:1.

76. Author's interview with Pablo Martínez, Quito, Ecuador, June 18, 1985.

77. Huntington and Domínguez 1984:31.

78. Simons 1986.

79. Author's interview with Sergio García Romo.

80. "El Salvador: A Special Report," *CAM Bulletin* (Dallas, Tex.: Central American Mission), no. 2., 1984, pp. 2–12.

81. Garry Parker, "Evangelicals Blossom Brightly amid El Salvador's Wasteland of Violence," *Christianity Today*, May 8, 1981, p. 34.

82. Author's telephone interview with Ronald Iwasko, Assemblies of God, Springfield, Mo., May 31, 1988.

83. Simons 1986. Erich Bridges, "El Salvador: Hanging in There," *Commission*, October–November 1984, pp. 17–22. For background on Salvadoran evangelicals, see Holland 1981:53–68.

84. Dan Wooding, "I Saw El Salvador in Crisis," *Moody Monthly*, May 1982, pp. 97–99.

85. Stephen Sywulka, "Romero's Death Undermines Evangelical Neutrality," *Christianity Today*, May 2, 1980, p. 61. Parker, "Evangelicals Blossom."

86. Rob Cogswell, "El Salvador Still Suffers," *Christian Century*, November 27, 1985, pp. 1094–98.

87. Ivan Santiago G., "Salvadoran Protestants Succor War Victims, Risk Reprisals," *Latinamerica Press*, January 16, 1986, pp. 1–2.

88. Bridges, "El Salvador: Hanging in There."

89. Ibid.; "El Salvador: A Special Report," *CAM Bulletin;* Ward 1986.

90. Simons 1986; Barry et al. 1986:24; and Resource Center 1988c.

91. Meredith Puff, "Central America: Strategic in God's Kingdom," *Frontlines* (Youth with A Mission), Winter 1985, pp. 13, 15. Also *Frontlines*, Spring 1985, p. 4.

92. Judy Ford, "Battle for an Anguished Land," *Worldwide Challenge* (San Bernardino, Calif.: Campus Crusade for Christ), January 1983, p. 57.

93. *EHC World News* (Studio City, Calif.: World Literature Crusade), February 1986, p. 1. WLC is also known as Every Home Crusade.

94. Kietzman 1986:3, 49–50; see also Kietzman 1985.

95. Open Doors 1984b.

96. Kietzman 1986:49.

97. John Maust, "Seminary Crisis a Case Study in Political, Doctrinal Tensions," *Christianity Today*, May 8, 1981, pp. 40–43.

98. Kietzman 1985:83.

99. D. A. Smith 1985. For a commentary from the Latin America Biblical Seminary on these events, see Piedra S. 1984.

100. Author's interview, San José, Costa Rica, July 16, 1985.

101. Amnesty International, "A Government Program of Political Murder," *New York Review of Books,* March 19, 1981, pp. 40–43.

102. Stam 1985. Order of paragraphs rearranged.

103. Author's interview with John Stam, Guatemala City, August 24, 1985.

104. William Taylor, "Contextualization: What Does It Really Mean?" *CAM Bulletin,* no. 3, 1983, pp. 3, 12–13.

105. Stephen Sywulka, Radio TGN, Guatemala City, August 28, 1985.

106. Author's interview, Mexico City, September 2, 1985.

107. Bastian 1984:61.

108. "Heredero de la Reforma Radical," in Padilla 1984:64–70.

109. Harry Genet, "Latin Evangelicals Chart Their Own Course," *Christianity Today,* December 7, 1979, pp. 44–46.

110. David Scotchmer to author, November 30, 1986.

111. Kinsler 1978:183, 186–87.

112. Costas 1984b.

113. Maust, "Seminary Crisis."

114. Author's interview with John Stam.

115. Miguez Bonino 1985. For a denunciation of sects in Argentina, see Silletta 1987.

7. The New Jerusalem of the Americas

1. Lynda Schuster, "Latin Revival," *Wall Street Journal,* December 7, 1982, pp. 1, 21.

2. Holland 1981:71; "DAWN is About to Break on Guatemala," *Global Church Growth,* March–April 1984, p. 351.

3. Melville and Melville 1977.

4. William Cameron Townsend, "Tolo, the Volcano's Son," *Revelation* (Philadelphia), serial, April through October 1936.

5. Julian Lloret, "Forces Shaping the Church in Central America," *CAM Bulletin,* Summer 1982, pp. 2–3, 13.

6. Interview with Bob Means, *Radiance* (Eureka, Calif.: Gospel Outreach), September 1982. International Love Lift fundraising circular, September 15, 1982, signed Bob Means and Carlos Ramírez. ILL circular, June 30, 1983, signed Carlos Ramírez.

7. Anfuso and Sczepanski 1983:ix–x, 154.

8. Paul Goepfert, "The Lord and Jim Durkin," *California,* February 1983, pp. 53–54.

9. This portrait of Durkin's theology is based on tapes of his sermons mailed to the author by Gospel Outreach's cassette library.

10. "Why Not the Whole World?" *Global Church Growth*, May–June 1983, p. 270.

11. Zapata A. 1982.

12. Author's interviews, July–August 1985.

13. Anfuso and Sczepanski 1983:79–100.

14. Ibid., pp. 93–96.

15. Ibid., pp. 104–9.

16. Ibid., pp. xiv, 119.

17. Author's interview, Guatemala City, August 27, 1985.

18. Juan M. Vásquez, "Prophecy Comes True for New Leader in Guatemala," *Los Angeles Times*, March 28, 1982, pp. 1, 8. Carlos Ramírez, "Prophecy Comes True," *Frontline* (Eureka, Calif.: International Love Lift) 9(7):6.

19. Joseph Anfuso, "The Coup in Guatemala," *Radiance*, May 1982, pp. 3, 6–8.

20. Davis and Hodson 1982.

21. Shelton H. Davis, "The Evangelical Holy War in El Quiche," *Global Reporter* (Boston: Anthropology Resource Center), March 1983, pp. 7–10.

22. David Scotchmer to author, personal communication.

23. Guatemalan Church in Exile, "Sebastián Guzmán: Principal de Principales" [ten-page typescript], n.d., pp. 2, 5. Guatemalan Church in Exile 1984.

24. Guatemalan Church in Exile 1984:16.

25. Arias 1984:156.

26. Author's interview, October 2, 1983.

27. Payeras 1984:15, 90.

28. Thomas R. Melville, "The Catholic Church in Guatemala, 1944–82," *Cultural Survival Quarterly* (Cambridge, Mass.: Cultural Survival), Spring 1983, p. 25.

29. Guatemalan Church in Exile, *Iglesia Guatemalteca en el Exilio*, special edition, "Martirio y lucha en Guatemala," December 1982, p. 44.

30. Subcommittee on Security and Terrorism 1984:233–34.

31. Guatemalan Church in Exile 1984:19.

32. Anfuso and Sczepanski 1983:125.

33. Contrary to an earlier version of this chapter, Pastor Nicolás belonged to the Full Gospel Church of God, a pentecostal denomination affiliated with the Church of God (Cleveland, Tenn.).

34. Author's interview, Cotzal, Guatemala, December 20, 1982.

35. Form letter from Sharon Townsend, Guatemala City, May 14, 1982.

36. Author's interview, Cotzal, Guatemala, December 20, 1982.

37. "Guatemalidad y autodefensa civil" and "Apreciación de asuntos civiles para el área Ixil," *Revista Militar* (Guatemala City: Centro de Estudios Militares), September–December 1982, pp. 4–14, 24–72.

38. Ray Elliot, memorandum on visit to Nebaj, July 5–9, 1982.

39. Ray Elliot, "Translation of interview in Ixil" [typescript memo], August 20, 1982.

40. Author's interviews, Campamento Nueva Vida, November 21–22 and December 20, 1982.

41. Reports to this effect include "Guatemala's Conversion," *NACLA Report on the Americas,* September—October 1982, pp. 42–43; Allan Nairn, *New Republic,* April 11, 1983, pp. 17–21; Americas Watch 1984:93–94; Guatemalan Church in Exile 1984:22; Vincent Flynn, "Model Villages in the Ixil Region," *Cultural Survival Quarterly,* December 1984, pp. 83–85.

42. Piero Gleijeses, "The Guatemalan Silence," *New Republic,* June 10, 1985, pp. 20–23.

43. Americas Watch 1983:15–19.

44. Edgar Nuñez, "From Embittered War Atrocities to the Love of Jesus Through FUNDAPI," *Frontline Report* 9(6):4–5.

45. Annis 1988.

46. "Diagnóstico integral de salud," Health Centers of Cotzal (December 1983), Chajul (October 1984), and Nebaj (November 1984).

47. Fajardo 1987:2, 72–74.

48. See Arturo Arias, "The Guatemalan Revolution: A Reassessment," *Guardian,* May 23, 1984, p. 19.

49. Anfuso and Sczepanski 1983:137.

50. Falla 1983.

51. Author's interview with adviser, March 24, 1983.

52. Philip Taubman, "Slaying Case in Guatemala Angers U.S. Aides," *New York Times,* September 11, 1983, pp. 1, 10; Americas Watch 1984:136–39.

53. Amnesty International 1987:96.

54. Word elder Alfred Kaltschmidt to author, August 1985.

55. Richard Ben Cramer, "Dictator of Divine Right," *Philadelphia Inquirer,* Sunday magazine, August 28, 1983, pp. 15–31.

56. "World Scene," *Christianity Today,* April 22, 1983, p. 43; Anfuso and Sczepanski 1983:138.

57. Anfuso and Sczepanski 1983:23, 128, 131–36.

58. Anfuso and Sczepanski 1983:23–24, 135. "Luis Palau: Evangelist to Three Worlds," *Christianity Today,* May 20, 1983, p. 30. Bill Conard, "Central America: Is There a Political Solution?" *Briefing,* Spring 1984, pp. 10–11.

23. "The Full Gospel Business Men's Fellowship International," *Covert Action Information Bulletin* (Washington, D.C.: Covert Action), Spring 1987, pp. 15–17.

24. Author's interviews, San José, Costa Rica, July 1985.

25. Author's interview with refugee pastor in Costa Rica, July 1985. While I was unable to corroborate this account, the press ("Denuncian a sectas que conspiran aquí," *Nuevo Diario*, April 21, 1981) did publish a complaint that evangelicals were using "Nicaragua '81" to provoke incidents that could be used to accuse the government of religious persecution.

26. Institute on Religion and Democracy 1983:5–6.

27. Author's interview, Managua, August 1985. See also Dodson and Montgomery 1982:175.

28. Author's interview with National Council of Evangelical Pastors of Nicaragua (CNPEN), Managua, August 1985.

29. Patricia Lee Hulsey, "Mass Crusades, National Training, Penetrate Central American Countries for Jesus Christ," *Deeper Life* (San Diego, Calif.: Morris Cerrullo World Evangelism), July–August 1981, pp. 4–6, 10–11. Wimber 1984: section 8, p. 14.

30. Author's interview, San José, Costa Rica, July 1985.

31. Author's telephone conversation with Paul Stubbs, Compassion International, March 6, 1985.

32. "Nicaragua: Blood and Hope," *Commission*, October–November 1984, p. 35; "Nicaragua: A Church in Transition," *CAM Bulletin*, no. 1, 1984, pp. 4–5.

33. Paul Goepfert, "Nicaraguan Emergency Isn't Obvious, but 'War' Over the Churches Is Bitter," *Baltimore Sun*, December 12, 1985.

34. "Cristianos proponen un frente ecuménico," *Barricada* (Managua), June 12, 1982; Casco 1982:21–22; Centro Ecuménico Antonio Valdivieso 1982.

35. Margaret Randall, quoted in Belli 1984:194.

36. "Atlantic Coast Disturbances Ring Alarm Bells in Managua," *Latin America Weekly Review*, October 17, 1980, pp. 7–8; "Security Jitters as Bluefields Sees Red," *Regional Reports: Mexico and Central America*, October 24, 1980, pp. 2–3.

37. Bourgois 1981:32–36; Adams 1981a:25, 55.

38. Interview with Armstrong Wiggins, "Colonialism and Revolution," *Akwesasne Notes* (Rooseveltown, N.Y.: Mohawk Nation) 13(4), Late Autumn 1981, pp. 4–15.

39. Interview with Brooklyn Rivera, "Miskito Nation: Some Further Words," *Akwesasne Notes* 14(3), Early Summer 1982, pp. 18–20; Ohland and Schneider 1983:18, 92–93, 171.

40. Georgie Anne Geyer, quoted by Roxanne Dunbar Ortiz, "The Miskitu Case," *Covert Action Information Bulletin*, Winter 1983, p. 23.

41. Author's interview, Managua, July–August 1985.

42. Saul Landau and Craig Nelson, "The CIA Rides Again," *Nation* (New York), March 6, 1982, pp. 274–75.

43. Jack Epstein and J. H. Evans, "Nicaragua's Miskito Move Based on False Allegations," *National Catholic Reporter* (Kansas City, Mo.), December 24, 1982, pp. 1, 22.

44. Alberto Reyes, "La invasión de las sectas," *Barricada*, March 3–5, 1982.

45. *Barricada*, August 11 and 12, 1982.

46. Xavier Reyes, "Las sectas y la contra," *Barricada*, July 16, 1982.

47. "Persecution of Protestant Groups," *White House Digest* (Washington, D.C.: White House Office of Media Relations and Planning), February 29, 1984, pp. 10–11.

48. "Cmdte. Borge destapa: 99 sectas operan," *Barricada*, July 16, 1982; "Ocupan tres reductos de sectas en Ciudad Sandino," *Barricada*, July 22, 1982.

49. "Entregan a CEPAD templos evangélicos," *Barricada*, July 24, 1982.

50. "Investigan a fondo atentado frustrado de 'pastor' contra," *Barricada*, July 24, 1982; "Presentan a 'pastor' metido a terrorista," *El Nuevo Diario*, August 4, 1982.

51. "Protesta popular contra las sectas," *Barricada*, August 11, 1982; "Evangélicos en diálogo con el gobierno," *La Prensa* (Managua), August 16, 1982; "Grabación prueba que es verdad lo que dijo La Prensa," *La Prensa*, August 20, 1982.

52. Author's interviews, Managua, July and August 1985.

53. Author's interview, Sheila Heneise, Managua, July 29, 1985.

54. "Pastores evangélicos dialogan con gobierno," *Amanecer* (Managua: Centro Ecuménico Antonio Valdivieso), October 1982, p. 6.

55. October 7, 1982, communique from *Coordinator de la Comisión Política de la Dirección Nacional FSLN* to CDS coordinators, Bayardo Arce Castaño letterhead.

56. Author's interviews, Managua, July and August 1985.

57. Randall 1983:165–66.

58. For the range of positions, see the interviews of revolutionary Christians by Margaret Randall (1983) and Teófilo Cabestrero (1986).

59. Dodson 1986:47–48.

60. Berryman 1984:231, 265–66.

61. "Evangélicos denuncian un plan diversionista de CIA," *Barricada*, July 2, 1983.

62. See the newsletter *Christian Anti-Communism Crusade*, December 1983 through 1985.

63. May 20, 1981, fundraising circular, Open Doors with Brother Andrew, plus Huntington and Domínguez 1984:30. See also Pit 1981:65–76; Gonzalez 1983:180–81; and Kietzman 1985:56–57.

64. Author's interview with John Kessler, San José, Costa Rica, July 9, 1985.

65. Huntington and Domínguez 1984:29–30.

66. Author's interviews with Carlos Escorcia and Miguel Ángel Casco, Antonio Valdivieso Ecumenical Center, Managua, July–August 1985.

67. Beth Spring, "Tensions Between Church and State in Nicaragua Pose Dilemmas for U.S. Christians," *Christianity Today*, September 6, 1985, p. 54–57.

68. Author's interview, Managua, August 1985.

69. Author's interviews, Managua, July–August 1985.

70. Carr 1963:127, 209.

71. "Mediation Resolves Conflicts over Draft," *Newsletter* (CEPAD), January 1986, pp. 3–4. Pablo Vander Harst, "Los evangélicos nicaraguenses: Ser cristiano entre cuatro paredes" [typed ms.], Antonio Valdivieso Ecumenical Center, June 20, 1985.

72. Subcommittee on Security and Terrorism 1984:151–52; author's interview, Managua, August 1985.

73. "Expulsados diez 'testigos' diversionistas," *Barricada*, March 22, 1982.

74. Author's interview, Managua, July 29, 1985.

75. Author's interviews, Managua, August 1985.

76. Centro Ecuménico Antonio Valdivieso 1982; Torres 1981:43–46.

77. Axis fund appeal quoted in Institute on Religion and Democracy 1984b:8. See also "Nicaragua: Different Perspectives on Church and State," *Pulse*, November 1982, pp. 5–7.

78. "Comunicado del eje ecuménico: Sectas deben legalizarse!" *El Nuevo Diario*, July 30, 1982.

79. Centro Ecuménico Antonio Valdivieso 1984. Comisión Evangélica de la Responsibilidad Social (CEPRES), "Cada oveja con su pareja," *El Nuevo Diario*, September 29, 1983; "Sospechosa la 'cruzada' evangélica," *El Nuevo Diario*, February 4, 1984, p. 1. See also Marvin Antonio Guevara G., "Coincidencias de las Asambleas de Dios y la administración Reagan," *El Nuevo Diario*, June 18, 1984.

80. "Declaración de CEPRES ante el juicio iniciado a uno de sus miembros," *El Nuevo Diario*, March 6, 1984; Miguel Angel Casco G., "Las Asambleas de Dios en Nicaragua," *El Nuevo Diario*, June 29, 1984.

81. Author's interviews, Managua, August 1985.

82. For a portrait of grass-roots evangelicals who generally favor the revolution, see Roger Lancaster's (1986:177–216) comparative study of popular religiosity, liberation theology, and evangelical Protestantism in several barrios of Managua.

83. Colburn 1984.

84. Belli 1985:177.

85. Author's notes, CEPAD assembly, Managua, August 15, 1985.

86. "Señala evangelista Alberto Montessi [sic]: El mayor compromiso del cristiano es con Cristo," *La Prensa*, January 24, 1984.

87. "Sospechosa la 'cruzada' evangélica," *El Nuevo Diario*, February 4, 1984, p. 1.

88. Rafferty 1984.

89. Author's interview with Sixto Ulloa, Managua, August 5, 1985.

90. Rafferty 1984.

91. Huntington and Domínguez 1984, translated excerpts from which were published in *El Nuevo Diario*, March 26–29, 1984; Kate Rafferty, "A Cry for Prayer," *Open Doors*, September–October 1984, pp. 14–15. Author's interviews in Costa Rica and Nicaragua, July–August 1985.

92. Institute on Religion and Democracy 1985.

93. Author's interview, Managua, August 1985.

94. Author's interviews, Managua, July and August 1985.

95. "Presionan para que CEPAD retorne al camino original," *La Prensa*, June 6, 1985; "CEPAD aclara un mar de calumnias," *El Nuevo Diario*, June 12, 1985.

96. "Para grupos de trabajo y deliberación en asamblea" [seven-page typescript], Hermanos Bautistas de Reflexión Cristiana, July 30, 1985.

97. Author's interviews with Pedro Antonio Aguirre of CEPAD and Anastasio Martínez, Pentecostal Mission of Christian Churches, Matagalpa, Nicaragua, August 14, 1985.

98. Philip Beisswenger, "A Christian Presence," *The Other Side*, April–May 1985, pp. 17–19.

99. Institute on Religion and Democracy 1983 and 1984b.

100. Steve Askin, "Institute Says It Reveals Threat . . . ," *National Catholic Reporter*, February 4, 1983, pp. 1, 7, 18–19; Hitchens 1986.

101. Askin, "Institute Says It Reveals Threat. . . ." Karen Rothmeyer, "Citizen Scaife," *Columbia Journalism Review*, July–August 1981, pp. 41–50.

102. "Novak, Simon Head New Contra Fund," *National Catholic Register*, May 26, 1985.

103. Institute on Religion and Democracy 1985.

104. "Protestan calumnias a CEPAD!" *El Nuevo Diario*, March 19, 1985; "La respuesta de CEPAD," *La Prensa*, April 11, 1985; "NCC Official

Urges Nicaraguans to Repudiate IRD Report," *Religion and Democracy,* May–June 1985, pp. 1–2. Author's interviews, Managua, July and August 1985.

105. Author's interview with Pedro Antonio Aguirre, CEPAD–Matagalpa, August 14, 1985.

106. Author's interview, CEPAD–Managua, August 1985.

107. *Noticiero Milamex* (Mexico City: CLAME), August 31, 1984.

108. Author's interview, Managua, August 1985.

109. Hefley and Hefley 1981:528–30.

110. Fundraising circular, Trans World Missions (Glendale, Calif.), May 1985.

111. John G. Olson, transcript of telephone interview with Brother Bob, Trans World Missions, May 1986.

112. Fundraising circular, Trans World Missions, May 1985.

113. Author's interview, Managua, August 1, 1985.

114. "Los Moskitos y la Costa Atlántica," *Envío* (Managua: Central American Historical Institute), June 1984, p. 13.

115. *Survival International Review* (London), Autumn–Winter 1982, pp. 89–90; Jack Epstein and J. L. Evans, "Honduras: Miskito Refugees Enjoy Privileged Status," *Latinamerica Press,* October 7, 1982, pp. 3–4, 8. Letter from Tom Hawk to Roxanne Dunbar Ortiz, January 29, 1985.

116. "The Contras, Miskito Indians, and the U.S.A.," *Resource Center Bulletin* (Albuquerque, N. Mex.: The Resource Center), Winter 1986, pp. 1–4.

117. Guillermo Espinoza, "Terror somocista en campamentos," *Barricada,* August 6, 1985, p. 9; James LeMoyne, "U.S. Program in Honduras Helps Families of Nicaraguan Guerrillas," *New York Times,* April 19, 1985, pp. A1, 8. Author's telephone interview with Tom Hawk, September 28, 1985.

118. "Miskito Indians Flee Sandinista Terror; Children Dying of Malnutrition and Disease," *Friends Report* (Baton Rouge, La.: Friends of the Americas), Fall 1984, p. 1; "Refugees Still Pouring out of Nicaragua; Children Suffering in Remote Jungle Area," *Friends Report,* Summer 1985, p. 9.

119. Quoted by Robert Matthews, "Sowing Dragon's Teeth," *NACLA Report on the Americas,* July–August 1986, p. 31.

120. Bob Armstrong, "Mission Field on the Front Lines," *Blessings* (Bradenton, Fla.: Gospel Crusade), Summer 1986, pp. 20–22.

121. Invitation: Phil Derstine to Bill Moyers in "God and Politics: The Kingdom Divided," 1987, public affairs television. Briefing: "The Truth . . . Nicaragua," Gospel Crusade, handout at February 1986 convention of National Religious Broadcasters, p. 8.

122. Kenneth L. Woodward, "A Pentecostal for President," *Newsweek*, October 14, 1985, p. 77.

123. Vicki Kemper, "In the Name of Relief," *Sojourners*, October 1985, pp. 4–5, 12–20.

124. Joel Brinkley, New York Times News Service, "CIA Manual Brings out Reports of Rebel Abuse," *Arizona Daily Star* (Tucson) December 27, 1984.

125. Tayacán 1984:3, 31–34.

126. Author's interview, San José, July 1985.

127. White House press release, April 16, 1985, p. 3. *Newsweek*, April 29, 1985, p. 10.

128. "¡Al descubierto infame mentira de Reagan!" *El Nuevo Diario*, June 16, 1985, pp. 1, 7.

129. Pedro Fiallos's denunciation, "Nicaragua hoy" supplement to *La Nación* (San José, Costa Rica), April 27, 1985.

130. Prudencio Baltodano, March 14, 1984, declaration in possession of the Permanent Commission on Human Rights, Managua.

131. Dickey 1985:94–95, 138–42, 190–94. For an analysis of the contradictions in the Sandinista agrarian reform, see Colburn 1986.

132. "Nueva Guinea," *Barricada*, June 5, 1982.

133. Author's interview, Costa Rica, July 1985.

134. "Development Means Progress and Survival for People of Nueva Guinea," *Newsletter* (CEPAD), June 1986, pp. 5–9.

135. Author's interview, Managua, August 1985.

136. Dodson and Montgomery 1982:172.

137. "The Challenge to Democracy in Central America," Departments of State and Defense, June 1986, p. 39.

138. Johnstone 1982:288.

139. National Council of Churches 1984:7.

140. Sources for these figures include a 1985 interview with a Moravian pastor who requested anonymity; Americas Watch 1985:14, 53; *Envío*, June 1984, p. 48; and the National Council of Churches 1984:8–9, although the latter's figures differ somewhat from the Moravian pastor's.

141. Linde Rivera, interview with John Wilson, "La Iglesia Morava y los Misquitos," *Amanecer*, November–December 1984, pp. 29–33.

142. Margaret D. Wilde, "Moravian-Sandinista Dialogue," *Christian Century*, May 11, 1983, pp. 458–59.

143. Anthony Quainton, quoted by Tom Minnery, "Why the Gospel Grows in Socialist Nicaragua," *Christianity Today*, April 8, 1983, pp. 34–42.

144. Stephen Sywulka, "Latin American Evangelicals Gear up for Overseas Missions," *Christianity Today*, October 5, 1984, pp. 94, 96.

145. "Prison Ministry Celebrated," *Newsletter* (CEPAD), April–May 1986, p. 4; and "Pardoned Prisoners Go Free to Construct New Lives," *Newsletter*, July 1986, pp. 3–5.

146. Holland 1981:121; "National Leaders, Churches Adjust to Political Change," *Pulse*, November 1982, pp. 8–9; Evangelical Press, "Instability in Nicaragua Not Hurting Church of God," *Charisma*, November 1984, p. 114.

147. Spring, "Tensions Between Church and State."

148. Ronald Sider, "Why Me Lord?" *The Other Side*, April–May 1985, pp. 20–25.

149. National Council of Churches 1984:4.

150. Author's interview, Managua, August 1985.

151. "Pese a grupos manipuladores, en Ciudad Sandino se han inscrito 1,650 en el SMP," *El Nuevo Diario*, October 28, 1983; author's interviews, August 1985.

152. Author's interviews, Managua, July and August 1985.

153. Alaníz Pinell 1985:77–78.

154. Author's telephone conversation with Roy Beck, *United Methodist Reporter*, Dallas, December 4, 1985.

155. Author's interview, Managua, August 2, 1985.

156. See also "Interrogados y vejados: Pastores evangélicos llevados a Chipote," *La Prensa*, November 5, 1985.

157. Sam Dillon, "People's Courts Take on Contras," *Miami Herald*, December 27, 1985, pp. 1, 4.

158. Tayacán 1984:30, 34.

159. Ambrose Evans-Pritchard, "How the Poorest Feel the Most Betrayed by the Sandinistas," *Sacramento Bee*, February 23, 1986, p. C6.

160. Radio Sandino (Managua), November 28, 1985, translated and published by *Foreign Broadcast Information Service*, December 6, 1985, pp. P9–15; "Pastors Implicated in Illegal Acts," *Barricada Internacional*, December 5, 1985, p. 3; Roy Howard Beck, "Nicaraguan Pastors Accused of U.S. Connections," *National Christian Reporter* (Dallas), December 13, 1985, p. 1; Goepfert, "Nicaraguan Emergency Isn't Obvious."

161. Mistaken analogy: *Foreign Broadcast Information Service*, December 6, 1985, pp. P14–15, quoting *Barricada*, December 1, 1985, p. 5. CIA subsidies: "Nicaraguan Internal Opposition Receives U.S. Funds," *Washington Report on the Hemisphere* (Council on Hemispheric Affairs), March 16, 1988, p. 5.

162. Eric Alterman, "For the Contras, After a Fashion," *Harper's Magazine*, August 1986, pp. 66–67; Barry et al. 1986:58; Joel Brinkley, "Iran Sales Linked to Wide Program of Covert Policies," *New York Times*, February 15, 1987, pp. 1, 8.

163. "Campus Crusade Runs into Nicaraguan Opposition," Missionary News Service, August 1, 1984; Permanent Commission on Human Rights (Managua), cases 84-11-080 and 84-12-029.

164. Institute on Religion and Democracy 1986.

165. *The Standard* (Virginia Beach, Va.: CBN University), special reprint edition for the February 1986 National Religious Broadcasters convention.

166. Roy Howard Beck, "Bishops Voice 'Strong Objections' to Reported Nicaraguan Repression," *National Christian Reporter,* November 22, 1985, p. 3. For a critique of the Sandinista security system, see Amnesty International 1986.

167. Radio Sandino, November 28, 1985.

168. Author's interview with John Kessler, San José, Costa Rica, July 13, 1985.

9. World Vision in Ecuador

1. Author's interview, Centro Indígena de Atocha, Ambato, Ecuador, May 27, 1985.

2. Author's interviews, Pallaloma, Ecuador, June 9, 1985.

3. Author's interview, Mulanleo, Ecuador, June 9, 1985.

4. Author's interview, Centro Indígena de Atocha, Ambato, May 27, 1985.

5. "Human Rights Reports of the Mission: Honduras, Salvadorian Refugees," Pax Christi International, October 1981.

6. Frank Viviano, Pacific News Service, "CIA Church Group in Honduras," *Guardian,* August 26, 1981, p. 13.

7. Mike Creswell, "Some Haitian 'Ministries' Don't Exist," *Commission,* August 1982, pp. 24–27, 30, 64.

8. Frederick Conway, "Pentecostalism in Haiti," in Glazier 1980:20–21.

9. Author's interviews, Managua, Nicaragua, July–August 1985; *Boletín de Noticias* (U.S. Embassy, Managua) May 21, 1985; and *Charisma,* November 1985, p. 94.

10. For accusations that World Vision in Honduras and Guatemala has continued to condition aid on submission to evangelical instruction, see Resource Center 1988a:55–56 and 1988b:49.

11. Resource Center 1988c:40.

12. Cf. Resource Center 1988a:7.

13. Jeff Stein, "CIA's 'Secret Army' Moves from Thailand to Bolivia," *Latinamerica Press,* December 21, 1978, pp. 7–8.

14. Bolling and Smith 1982:189–91.

15. George Cotter, "Spies, Strings and Missionaries," *Christian Century*, March 25, 1981, pp. 321–24.

16. For analysis of this issue in Central America, see Resource Center 1988a, 1988b, and 1988c.

17. Elisabeth Elliot's novel *No Graven Image* (1966) is set around Colta, Chimborazo, and poses this question.

18. J. Klassen 1975:106.

19. Penny Lernoux, "The Revolutionary Bishops," *Atlantic Monthly*, July 1980, pp. 6–14.

20. H. Klassen 1976:13.

21. "La intervención imperialista y la respuesta de los pueblos," Coordinadora Popular de Chimborazo, Riobamba, 1984, p. 18. WV directory, quoted in Bamat 1986:109.

22. Santana 1983:168.

23. Maynard et al. 1965:82.

24. Dilworth 1967:48.

25. Maynard et al. 1965:65–72, 77, 90.

26. Gellner 1982:129–42.

27. Dilworth 1967:48.

28. Muratorio 1980:42; Santana 1983:168.

29. The best overall description of the Chimborazo movement is Muratorio 1980. For missiological analyses, see J. Klassen 1975 and H. Klassen 1976.

30. "Informe de la Diócesis de Riobamba, 1979–1984."

31. Proaño Villalba 1983:4–6, 10.

32. Author's interview, Hogar Santa Cruz, Riobamba, May 26, 1985. For a detailed analysis of the difficulties facing sacramental reform, the formation of lay leadership, and liberation theology in another Andean milieu, around Lake Titicaca in Bolivia, see S. Nelson 1984.

33. Casagrande 1978:110–11.

34. Cf. Dilworth 1967:58.

35. A six-page memo, headed "Cicalpa, 9 de julio de 1973," to "Señores y Autoridades del Cantón," signed Manuel Barba, Graciela Gallegos, and Delfín Tenesaca, describes evangelical seizures of two Catholic chapels and the destruction of two in 1972–1973. A January 7, 1982, denunciation by the Federation of Licto, "Atropello a lideres de la Federación de Licto . . . ," describes the destruction of another Catholic chapel by evangelicals, in May 1980 in Pungalbug-Licto, and two evangelical assaults on Catholics organizing against the Summer Institute of Linguistics.

36. Author's interviews with Henry Klassen, Majipamba, Colta, Chimborazo, June 13, 1985, and Ben Cummings, Radio HCJB, Quito, Ecuador, June 18, 1985.

37. Santana 1983:173.

38. Author's interview, Latacunga, Ecuador, June 8, 1985.

39. Tucker 1983:470.

40. Ted W. Engstrom, "The Year the World Cared," *World Vision* (Monrovia, Calif.), February–March 1986, pp. 14–15.

41. World Vision, *1984 Annual Report*, pp. 6–12.

42. Geoff Renner, regional director, "Visión Mundial y la misión integral de la iglesia en América Latina," November 1983, p. 5.

43. World Vision, *1985 Annual Report*, p. 10. Some of the largest such agencies were not evangelical, including the Christian Children's Fund, Foster Parents Plan, and Save the Children.

44. Randy Frame, "Relief Agencies Confront a Major Crisis of Their Own," *Christianity Today*, September 19, 1986, p. 36–37.

45. But adopting a community may have played better in the United States than in World Vision's other donor countries. According to the *1984 Annual Report* (pp. 1–2), donors in the United States provided two-thirds of World Vision's $187 million income that year but sponsored only 46 percent of the children.

46. Youngren 1982:38–40.

47. Michael Lee, "World Vision, Go Home!" *Christian Century*, May 16, 1979, pp. 542–44; July 4, 1979, pp. 707–8; August 1, 1979, p. 772. Steve Askin, "Hostility, Conflict Engulf World Vision," *National Catholic Reporter*, April 23, 1982, pp. 9ff.

48. Askin, "Hostility." According to World Vision's *1984 Annual Report* (pp. 1, 12), 68.9 percent of its $127.4 million income from the United States that year came from individuals and families, 4.2 percent from churches, 19.5 percent from gifts-in-kind (apparently from the U.S. government, largely for Poland), 4.5 percent from corporations and foundations, and 2.9 percent from planned giving and investments.

49. World Vision International 1981:20.

50. "Press-Time Report: Inside Lebanon," *World Vision*, August, 1982, pp. 12–13, 18. W. Stanley Mooneyham, "Shattered Buildings, Broken Lives," *World Vision*, September 1982, pp. 3–11.

51. Lee Huhn, "Dateline Nicaragua," *World Vision*, October 1979, pp. 18–19.

52. Oscar A. Romero, "Taking Risks for the Poor," *World Vision*, June 1982, pp. 6–7. The April–June 1985 issue of World Vision's journal *Together* was devoted to liberation theology.

53. Faith Sand, "An Unpredictable Volcano," *World Vision*, October 1982, pp. 2–7, 10–11.

54. Author's interviews, October 1982 through February 1983.

55. Lissner 1977.

56. Renner, "Visión Mundial y la misión integral de la iglesia," pp. 7–9.

57. August 28, 1981 reply by James Jewell, World Vision–Monrovia, to Frank Viviano, Pacific News Service.

58. World Vision International 1981:3, 6, 22.

59. Kenneth Woodward, "Missionaries on the Line," *Time*, March 8, 1982, pp. 69–70.

60. World Vision International 1981:10, 16, 19.

61. Harrell 1983.

62. María Rodríguez Araya, "U.S. Relief Agency Accused of Complicity with Honduran Military," *Latinamerica Press*, February 25, 1982, pp. 7–8; "Salvadorean Refugees Face New Threats," *Regional Reports: Mexico and Central America*, February 12, 1982, pp. 4–5.

63. Letter from Eugene L. Stockwell of the National Council of Churches to W. Stanley Mooneyham, March 5, 1982. Reply from Mooneyham to Stockwell, March 18, 1982.

64. Huntington and Domínguez 1984:21.

65. Mooneyham to Stockwell, p. 8.

66. Interview with Ted Engstrom, World Vision president, *World Vision*, November 1982, p. 4.

67. WV–Ecuador director Frank Boshold, quoted in Centro de Planificación y Estudios Sociales 1984:25–26.

68. "Una visión de lo que hace VM en el Ecuador," *Nueva* (Quito), October 1985, pp. 40–42.

69. Miriam Ernst, "Otra transnacional de la caridad," *Nueva*, January–February 1983, pp. 17–20.

70. Author's interview, Christian Aponte and José Aráuz, World Vision–Quito, February 28, 1984.

71. "Plata, libertad y Salvación . . . ," *Nueva*, January 1984, pp. 39–41. Centro de Planificación y Estudios Sociales 1984:75–102.

72. Author's interview with Aponte and Aráuz, February 28, 1984. Centro de Planificación y Estudios Sociales 1984:29, 51.

73. Centro de Planificación y Estudios Sociales 1984:176–77. According to World Vision, every year about fifty new communities were soliciting its services nationwide, of which twenty to thirty were being accepted.

74. Santana 1983:158–62; Barry Lyons, personal communication.

75. Diego Iturralde to author, June 11, 1985.

76. Cf. Centro de Planificación y Estudios Sociales 1984:74–75, 103

and "Penetración Cultural: Visión Mundial en el Cantón Otavalo" [fifty-four-page unsigned typescript], 1983.

77. "Somos la esperanza de mi pueblo" [pamphlet] Movimiento Indígena de Chimborazo, 1984. Proaño Villalba 1984:221–23.

78. Lentz 1985.

79. Author's interview, Riobamba, May 18, 1985.

80. Author's interview with AIECH president Jorge Veñán, AIECH executive committee, and Henry Klassen, Majipamba, Colta, June 4, 1985.

81. Author's interview with Henry Klassen, Majipamba, Colta, February 23, 1984.

82. Author's interviews, Majipamba, Colta, February 23, 1984; May 16, 1985; and June 4, 1985. For similar complaints from Honduras about an unnamed child-care agency, see Harrell 1983.

83. Author's interviews, World Vision–Quito office, May 15 and June 11, 1985.

84. Colegio de Antropólogos y Lingüistas de Pichincha 1983:21, 26–30.

85. Comité Ecuménico de Proyectos 1982:28.

86. Author's interview, Quito, May 14, 1985.

87. Author's interview with Frank Boshold, June 11, 1985.

88. Centro de Planificación y Estudios Sociales 1984:178–79.

89. "Visión Mundial: Otro lobo vestido de oveja," *Amanecer Indio* (Quito: Confederación de Nacionalidades Indígenas de la Amazonía Ecuatoriana), August 1983, p. 9.

90. Casagrande 1978; Muratorio 1981.

91. Degregori 1978:168.

92. Santana 1983:167–74.

93. Dilworth 1967:40, 76–77, 87, 93–94.

94. Muratorio 1980:52 and 1981:526, 529–30.

95. Diego Iturralde to author, Quito, June 11, 1985.

96. Brandi et al. 1976:33–39.

97. Muratorio 1980:52, 56. For a brief description of evangelical mobilization against a hacienda owner, see Lentz 1985.

98. Santiago Tribout, Diocese of Riobamba, to author, May 1985.

99. Muratorio 1981; Santana 1983:167–74.

100. Author's interview with Ben Cummings, executive vice-president of Radio HCJB, Quito, June 18, 1985.

101. Paredes A. 1979:45.

102. Author's interviews with Alfredo Viteri, Confederación de Nacionalidades Indígenas de la Amazonía Ecuatoriana, Quito, February 28, 1984, and Manuel Naula, FEINE, Quito, February 28, 1984.

103. Lucía Salamea, Centro de Planificación y Estudios Sociales, Quito, to author, February 22, 1984.

104. Author's interview with Pedro Castañeda, La Compañía, June 16, 1985.

105. Santana 1981:33.

106. Author's interviews, Pilahuín and Ambato, May and June 1985.

10. Reinterpreting the Invasion of the Sects as an Evangelical Awakening

1. Quoted in Simons 1982:117.

2. Author's interview, January 24, 1985, Monrovia, Calif.

3. Assemblies officials denied there was any connection between the two events.

4. Tom Jelton, report from Managua, Nicaragua, for "All Things Considered," National Public Radio, early February 1988. Richard Boudreaux, "U.S. Evangelist Preaches to 25,000 in Managua," *Los Angeles Times,* February 15, 1988, pp. 1, 18. Author's telephone interview with Newman Peyton, Jr., March 23, 1988. For Swaggart's account, see "From Me to You," *The Evangelist* (Baton Rouge, La.: Jimmy Swaggart Ministries), April 1988, pp. 24–26.

5. Among those who have recently drawn comparisons with the Reformation in Europe are Cook 1985, Levine 1985, and Bastian 1986.

6. For such interpretations, see Lernoux 1980, Berryman 1984, Frank and Wheaton 1984, Dodson and Montgomery 1982, Randall 1983, Cabestrero 1986, and the publications of Orbis Books (Maryknoll, N.Y.).

7. Wilde 1986:15.

8. Lionel Groulx, International Conference on Liberation Theology, Simon Fraser University, Vancouver, British Columbia, February 7, 1986.

9. Susan Rosales Nelson (1984), to whom I am indebted for this point, provides an example from the Lake Titicaca region of Bolivia.

10. J. C. Scott 1987:xv–xvii.

11. Johnstone 1986:55–56,62–65.

12. Hoffnagel 1979:258–59.

13. Alves 1985; Bastian 1986; and Deiros 1986.

14. In Deiros 1986:203.

15. "Chile's Junta Courts the Once-Spurned Protestants," *Christianity Today,* September 4, 1981, p. 59.

16. Sidney Rooy to author, June 25, 1987.

17. Lalive d'Epinay 1983:250–51.

18. Lalive d'Epinay 1969:108, 122.

19. Page 1984:49–50.

20. Bastian 1986:173–78.
21. Turner 1970.
22. Lalive d'Epinay 1983:44.
23. Cook 1985:227.
24. Gary Nigel Howe, "Capitalism and Religion at the Periphery," in Glazier 1980:127.
25. Brusco 1986:199–201, 209, 215–16, 223–25.
26. Lalive d'Epinay 1969:83.
27. Lalive d'Epinay 1983:45.
28. Johnstone 1986:112.
29. Frase 1975:566.
30. Frase 1975:562–66; Read 1965:144–58.
31. Page 1984:359, 367–68, 383, 390.
32. Cited in Page 1984:366–68.
33. Frase 1975:567.
34. J. C. Scott 1977:14–15.
35. Read 1965:144–50.
36. Resource Center 1988a:15.
37. Ibid., p. 38.
38. Fundraising letter, May 1988, Jimmy Swaggart Ministries (Baton Rouge, La.).
39. Resource Center 1988a:7, 50.
40. Associated Press, *San Francisco Chronicle*, May 28, 1988, p. A10.
41. Victor Miller, "Becks Says Contra Revolution Began as a Spiritual Battle," *Chattanooga News–Free Press*, January 31, 1988.
42. Fundraising circular, CERT (Carlsbad, Calif.), received May 1988.
43. Barry et al. 1986:15.
44. Bill Moyers, "God and Politics: The Kingdom Divided," 1987, public affairs television.
45. Trans World Missions fundraising letter, May 1985.
46. Alessandra Stanley, "Faith in a True Believer," *Newsweek*, February 16, 1987, p. 23.
47. *Washington Post*, September 24, 1983, p. A5.
48. Robert Parry and Tamar Jacoby, "Covert Aid and the Church," *Newsweek*, June 15, 1987, p. 27. For further details, see "Nicaraguan Internal Opposition Receives U.S. Funds," *Washington Report on the Hemisphere*, March 16, 1988, p. 5.
49. Joseph E. Davis, "Covert Aid and the Church," *Nicaragua in Focus*, July–August 1987, pp. 4–8, a publication of Humberto Belli's Puebla Institute, which seeks to refute the *Newsweek* report.
50. "The Rise of the Religious Right in Central America," *Resource Center Bulletin*, Summer–Fall 1987, pp. 1–4.

51. S. Wilson and Siewert 1986. For directories to these groups, particularly in Honduras, see Resource Center 1988a, 1988b, and 1988c.

52. Robert Matthews, "Sowing Dragon's Teeth," *NACLA Report on the Americas* July–August 1986, pp. 16–18.

53. C. Edward Ward, Coalition on Revival, July 2–4, 1986, Washington, D.C.

54. Chacón Herrera and Lagos Schuffeneger 1986:48–49, 59.

55. Cook 1985:280–81.

56. Aberle 1966:315–33.

57. Carlos Rodrigues Brandão, as quoted in review of his *Os Deuses do Povo* (Rio de Janeiro: Editorial Brasilense, 1980) by Guillermo Cook, *Missiology*, April 1982, pp. 245–56. Also Endruveit 1975:150–51.

58. David Scotchmer to author, October 4, 1986.

59. David Scotchmer to author, March 4, 1987.

60. Adams 1981b.

Bibliography

Aberle, David F.

1966   *The Peyote Religion Among the Navaho.* New York: Wenner Gren Foundation.

Adams, Richard N.

1981a   "The Sandinistas and the Indians." *Caribbean Review* 10(1):23–25, 55–56.

1981b   "The Dynamics of Societal Diversity: Notes from Nicaragua for a Sociology of Survival." *American Ethnologist* 8(1):1–20.

Alaníz Pinell, Jorge

1985   *Nicaragua: Una revolución reaccionaria.* Panama City, Panama: Kosmos Editorial.

Albán Estrada, María, and Juan Pablo Muñoz

1987   *Con Dios todo se puede: La invasión de las sectas al Ecuador.* Quito, Ecuador: Editorial Planeta.

Albrecht, Mark and Paul Rogers

1987   "Hidden in Plain Sight: Uncovering Mormon Mission and Evangelism Strategies." Seattle: Issachar Frontier Mission Strategies.

Alves, Rubem

1985   *Protestantism and Repression: A Brazilian Case Study.* Maryknoll, N.Y.: Orbis Books.

Americas Watch

1983   *Creating a Desolation and Calling It Peace.* New York: Americas Watch.

1984   *Guatemala: A Nation of Prisoners.* New York: Americas Watch.

1985   *Human Rights in Nicaragua: Reagan, Rhetoric and Reality.*
            New York: Americas Watch.

Amnesty International
    1986   *Nicaragua: The Human Rights Record.* London: Amnesty
            International Publications.
    1987   *Guatemala: The Human Rights Record.* London: Amnesty
            International Publications.

Anderson, Robert Mapes
    1979   *Vision of the Disinherited: The Making of Modern Pentecos-
            talism.* New York: Oxford University Press.

Anfuso, Joseph, and David Sczepanski
    1983   *He Gives, He Takes Away: The True Story of Guatemala's
            Controversial Former President Efraín Ríos Montt.* Eu-
            reka, Calif.: Radiance Publications. [Reissued as *Servant or
            Dictator?*]

Annis, Sheldon
    1988   *God and Production in a Guatemalan Town.* Austin: Uni-
            versity of Texas Press.

Arias, Arturo
    1984   "Cultura popular, culturas indígenas, genocidio y etnocidio
            en Guatemala." In *La cuestión étnico-nacional en América
            Latina,* pp. 141–61. Mexico City: Instituto Panamericano
            de Geografía e Historia.

Assman, Hugo
    1987   *La iglesia electrónica y su impacto en América Latina.* San
            José, Costa Rica: Editorial Departamento Ecuménico de
            Investigaciones.

Aulie, Wilbur
    1979   "The Christian Movement Among the Chols of Mexico with
            Special Reference to Problems of Second-Generation
            Christianity." Dissertation, School of World Mission, Fuller
            Theological Seminary.

Bamat, Tomás
    1986   *Salvación o dominación? Las sectas religiosas en el Ecua-
            dor.* Quito, Ecuador: Editorial El Conejo.

Barr, James
    1978   *Fundamentalism.* Philadelphia: Westminster Press.

Barrett, David B., ed.
    1982   *World Christian Encyclopedia.* New York: Oxford Univer-
            sity Press.

Barry, Tom, Deb Preusch, and Beth Sims
    1986   *The New Right Humanitarians.* Albuquerque, N. Mex.:
            The Resource Center.

Bastian, Jean Pierre

1979   "Protestantismo y política en Mexico." *Taller de Teología* (Mexico City), no. 5, pp. 7–23.

1981   "Guerra fría, crisis del proyecto liberal y atomización de los protestantismos latinoamericanos, 1949–59." *Cristianismo y Sociedad*, no. 68, pp. 7–11.

1984   "Protestantismos latinoamericanos entre la resistencia y la sumisión: 1961–1983." *Cristianismo y Sociedad*, no. 82, pp. 49–68.

1986   *Breve historia del protestantismo en América Latina.* Mexico City: Casa Unida de Publicaciones (CUPSA).

Beekman, R.

1972   "The Mormon Mini-Empire." *NACLA's Latin America and Empire Report* 6(5):2–10, 31.

Belli, Humberto

1984   *Christians Under Fire.* Garden City, Mich.: Puebla Institute.

1985   *Breaking Faith.* Westchester, Ill.: Crossway Books.

Berberian, Samuel

1983   *Two Decades of Renewal: A Study of the Charismatic Renewal in Latin America, 1960–1980.* Guatemala City: Ediciones Sa-ber.

Berryman, Phillip

1984   *The Religious Roots of Rebellion: Christians in Central American Revolutions.* Maryknoll, N.Y.: Orbis Books.

Bolling, Landrum R., and Craig Smith

1982   *Private Foreign Aid: U.S. Philanthropy for Relief and Development.* Boulder, Colo.: Westview Press.

Bourgois, Philippe

1981   "Class, Ethnicity and the State Among the Miskito Amerindians of Northeastern Nicaragua." *Latin American Perspectives* 8(2):22–39.

Brandi, John, Michael Scott, and Mal Warwick

1976   *Chimborazo.* Rooseveltown, N.Y.: Akwesasne Notes.

Bright, Bill

1985   *Come Help Change Our World.* San Bernardino, Calif.: Campus Crusade for Christ.

Bromley, David G.

1985   "Financing the Millennium: The Economic Structure of the Unificationist Movement." *Journal for the Scientific Study of Religion* 24(3):253–74.

Bromley, David G., and Anson Shupe, eds.
1984   *New Christian Politics*. Macon, Ga.: Mercer University Press.

Brother Andrew
1981   *Building in a Broken World*. Wheaton, Ill.: Tyndale House.

Brusco, Elizabeth
1986   "The Household Basis of Evangelical Religion and the Reformation of Machismo in Colombia." Ph.D. dissertation, City University of New York.

Burnett, Virginia Garrard
1986   "A History of Protestantism in Guatemala." Ph.D. dissertation, Tulane University.

Cabestrero, Teófilo
1986   *Revolutionaries for the Gospel: Testimonies of Fifteen Christians in the Nicaraguan Government*. Maryknoll, N.Y.: Orbis Books.

Cardiel Coronel, José Cuauhtémoc
1983   "Cambio social y dominación ideológica: 43 años de evangelización del ILV en la Zona Chol de Tumbalá." Thesis for Licenciado in Social Anthropology, Universidad Autónoma Metropolitana–Iztapalapa, Mexico.

Carr, Albert Z.
1963   *The World and William Walker*. New York: Harper & Row.

Casagrande, Joseph B.
1978   "Religious Conversion and Social Change in an Indian Community of Highland Ecuador." In *Amerikanistiche Studien*, ed. Roswith Hartmann and Udo Oberem, pp. 105–11. St. Agustin, West Germany: Haus Volker und Kulturem, Anthropos-Institut.

Casco, Miguel Ángel
1982   "Las sectas en Nicaragua." Congreso Nicaragüense de Ciencias Sociales, October 29–31, 1982, Asociación Nicaragüense de Científicos Sociales.

Centro de Planificación y Estudios Sociales
1984   *Visión Mundial: Evaluación y seguimiento en algunas comunidades de la sierra ecuatoriana*. Report for the Oficina Nacional de Asuntos Indígenas, Ministerio de Bienestar Social. Quito, Ecuador: Ediciones Abya Yala.

Centro Ecuménico Antonio Valdivieso
1982   "Los evangélicos en los tres años de revolución." *Amanecer*, June–July, pp. 24–25.

1984   "Conflicto en las Asambleas de Dios." *Amanecer*, March–April, pp. 9–10.

Chacón Herrera, Arturo, and Humberto Lagos Schuffeneger

1986   *Religión y proyecto político autoritario.* Concepción, Chile: Programa Evangélico de Estudios Socio-Religiosos.

Chamorro, Edgar

1987   *Packaging the Contras: A Case of CIA Disinformation.* New York: Institute for Media Analysis.

Chastain, Warren

1984   "Islam Gears Up for Action." *International Journal of Frontier Missions* (Pasadena, Calif.: U.S. Center for World Mission) 1(1):83–87.

Clawson, David Leslie

1976   "Religion and Change in a Mexican Village." Ph.D. dissertation, University of Florida.

1984   "Religious Allegiance and Economic Development in Rural Latin America." *Journal of Interamerican Studies and World Affairs* 26(4):499–524.

Clouse, Robert G.

1977   *The Meaning of the Millennium.* Madison, Wis.: Inter-Varsity Christian Fellowship.

Colburn, Forrest

1984   "Rural Labor and the State in Postrevolutionary Nicaragua." *Latin American Research Review*, no. 3, pp. 103–17.

1986   *Post-Revolutionary Nicaragua.* Berkeley: University of California Press.

Colegio de Antropólogos y Lingüistas de Pichincha

1983   "Estudios de pre-factibilidad para desarrollar proyectos . . . en comunidades indígenas." Quito, Ecuador.

Comité Ecuménico de Proyectos

1982   "Visión Mundial en el Ecuador." Quito, Ecuador.

Conferencia Episcopal Panameña

1984   "El ecumenismo: Objectivos, logros y fallas en Panamá." Pastoral letter, October 18, Panama City.

Conn, Charles Paul

1977   *Battle for Africa.* Old Tappan, N.J.: Fleming H. Revell Company.

Consejo Episcopal Latinoamericano (CELAM)

1982   *Sectas en América Latina.* Guatemala City: Imprenta Gutenberg.

Conway, Flo, and Jim Siegelman
  1984   *Holy Terror: The Fundamentalist War on America's Free-
            doms.* New York: Dell.
Cook, Guillermo
  1985   *The Expectation of the Poor: Latin American Basic Ecclesial
            Communities in Protestant Perspective.* Maryknoll, N.Y.:
            Orbis Books.
Costas, Orlando E.
  1982   *Christ Outside the Gate.* Maryknoll, N.Y.: Orbis Books.
  1984a   "Origen y desarrollo del movimiento de crecimiento de la
            Iglesia." *Misión* (Buenos Aires: Fraternidad Teológica Lati-
            noamericana) 3(1):7–13, and 3(2):56–60.
  1984b   "El CELEP y la Pastoral." *Pastoralia* (San José, Costa Rica:
            CELEP), July–December, pp. 81–90.
Crahan, Margaret
  1979   "Salvation Through Christ or Marx: Religion in Revolution-
            ary Cuba." In *Churches and Politics in Latin America,* ed.
            Daniel H. Levine, pp. 238–66. Beverly Hills, Calif.: Sage
            Publications.
Cunningham, Loren
  1984   *Is That Really You, God?* Lincoln, Va.: Chosen Books.
Curry, Donald Edward
  1968   "Lusíada: An Anthropological Study of the Growth of Prot-
            estantism in Brazil." Ph.D. dissertation, Columbia Univer-
            sity.
  1970   "Messianism and Protestantism in Brazil's Sertão." *Journal
            of Inter-American Studies and World Affairs* 13(3):416–38.
Dahlquist, Anna Marie
  1985   *Burgess of Guatemala.* Langley, British Colombia: Cedar
            Books.
Darrand, Tom Craig, and Anson Shupe
  1983   *Metaphors of Social Control in a Pentecostal Sect.* Lewis-
            ton, N.Y.: Edwin Mellen Press.
Davis, Shelton H., and Julie Hodson
  1982   *Witnesses to Political Violence in Guatemala: The Suppres-
            sion of a Rural Development Movement.* Boston: Oxfam
            America.
Dayton, Edward R., ed.
  1981   *Mission Handbook: North American Protestant Ministries
            Overseas,* 12th ed. Monrovia, Calif.: Missions Advanced
            Research Center, World Vision.

Dayton, Edward R., and Samuel Wilson, eds.
1983   *Unreached Peoples '83.* Monrovia, Calif.: Missions Advanced Research Center.
1984   *The Future of World Evangelization: Unreached Peoples '84.* Monrovia, Calif.: Missions Advanced Research Center.

Degregori, Carlos Ivan
1978   *Indigenismo, clases sociales y problema nacional.* Lima, Peru. Centro Latinoamericano de Trabajo Social.

Deiros, Pablo Alberto, ed.
1986   *Los evangélicos y el poder político en América Latina.* Grand Rapids, Mich.: Eerdman's.

Dickey, Christopher
1985   *With the Contras.* New York: Simon and Schuster.

Dilworth, Donald R.
1967   "The Evangelization of the Quichuas of Ecuador." Master's thesis, School of Mission and Institute of Church Growth, Fuller Theological Seminary.

Dodson, Michael
1986   "The Politics of Religion in Revolutionary Nicaragua." *Annals of the American Academy,* January, pp. 36–49.

Dodson, Michael, and Tommie Sue Montgomery
1982   "The Churches in the Nicaraguan Revolution." In *Nicaragua in Revolution,* ed. Thomas W. Walker, pp. 161–80. New York: Praeger.

Douglas, J. D., ed.
1975   *Let the Earth Hear His Voice.* Minneapolis, Minn.: World Wide Publications.

Edwards, Rick
1972   "Protestant Ethic and Imperial Mission: The Latin American Case." *NACLA's Latin America and Empire Report* 6(2):2–15.

Eich, Dieter, and Carlos Rincón
1985   *The Contras: Interviews with Anti-Sandinistas.* San Francisco: Synthesis Publications.

Elliot, Elisabeth
1966   *No Graven Image.* New York: Harper & Row.

Endruveit, Wilson H.
1975   "Pentecostalism in Brazil." Ph.D. dissertation, Northwestern University.

Escobar, Samuel, and John Driver
1978   *Christian Mission and Social Justice.* Scottsdale, Pa.: Herald Press.

Ezcurra, Ana María
1982   *La ofensiva neoconservadora.* Madrid: Instituto de Estudios Políticos para América Latina y África.

Fajardo, Andrés
1987   "From the Volcano: Protestant Conversion Among the Ixil Maya of Highland Guatemala." Bachelor of Arts honors essay, Harvard College.

Falla, Ricardo
1983   "Masacre de la Finca San Francisco, Huehuetenango, Guatemala." Copenhagen: International Work Group for Indigenous Affairs.

Fernandes, Rubem César
1980   "Um exército de anjos: As razões da missão novas tribos." *Religiao e Sociedade* (Rio de Janeiro), no. 6, pp. 129–66.
1981   "Fundamentalismo a la derecha y a la izquierda: Misiones evangélicas y tensiones ideológicas." *Cristianismo y Sociedad,* nos. 69–70, pp. 21–50.

Flora, Cornelia Butler
1976   *Protestantism in Colombia: Baptism by Fire and Spirit.* London: Associated University Press.

Frank, Luisa, and Philip Wheaton
1984   *Indian Guatemala: Path to Liberation.* Washington, D.C.: EPICA Task Force.

Frase, Ronald Glen
1975   "A Sociological Analysis of the Development of Brazilian Protestantism." Ph.D. dissertation, Princeton Theological Seminary.

Fretwell, Martha Rees
1983   "Reporte de evaluación social del impacto del ILV en Yaxoquintelá, Chiapas." National Indigenist Institute, Mexico City.

Fry, Peter
1978   "Two Religious Movements: Protestantism and Umbanda." In *Manchester and Sao Paulo,* ed. J. D. Wirth and R. L. Jones, pp. 177–202. Stanford, Calif.: Stanford University Press.

Garma Navarro, Carlos
1983   "Poder, conflicto y reelaboración simbólica: Protestantismo en una comunidad totonac." Licenciado thesis, Escuela Nacional de Antropología e Historia, Mexico City.
1984   "Liderazgo protestante en una lucha campesina en México." *América Indígena* 44(1):127–41.

Gellner, Bernhard John
    1982   "Colta Entrepreneurship in Ecuador." Ph.D. dissertation, University of Wisconsin.
Glasser, Arthur
    1986   "Church Growth at Fuller." *Missiology* 14(4):401–20.
Glazier, Stephen D., ed.
    1980   *Perspectives on Pentecostalism: Case Studies from the Caribbean and Latin America.* Washington, D.C.: University Press of America.
Godwin, David E.
    1984   *Church Planting Methods.* DeSoto, Tex.: Lifeshare Communications.
Goff, James E.
    1968   *The Persecution of Protestant Christians in Colombia, 1948–58.* Cuernavaca, Mexico: Centro Intercultural de Documentación.
Gonzales, Peter Asael, with Dan Wooding
    1983   *Prophets of Revolution.* London: Hodder and Stoughton.
Guatemalan Church in Exile
    1984   "Un nuevo estilo de vida: Los polos de desarrollo." *Iglesia Guatemalteca en el Exilio* (Managua, Nicaragua) 4(5).
Hageman, Alice L., and Philip E. Wheaton, eds.
    1971   *Religion in Cuba Today.* New York: Association Press.
Harrell, Billy
    1983   "Evangelical Relief and Development: Making Sure the Cup of Cold Water is Given in the Name of Jesus." *Pulse* (Wheaton, Ill.: Evangelical Missions Information Service), August, pp. 4–6.
Hatch, R. Allen
    1981   "Church-Mission Relations: Case Studies from Latin America." Thesis presented to the Wheaton Graduate School, Wheaton, Ill.
Hefley, James, and Marti Hefley
    1981   *By Their Blood: Christian Martyrs of the Twentieth Century.* Milford, Mich.: Mott Media.
Heinerman, John, and Anson Shupe
    1985   *The Mormon Corporate Empire.* Boston: Beacon Press.
Hesselgrave, David J.
    1979   *New Horizons in World Mission.* Grand Rapids, Mich.: Baker Book House.

Hill, Samuel S., and Dennis E. Owen
1982   *The New Religious-Political Right in America*. Nashville, Tenn.: Abingdon Press.

Hitchens, Christopher
1986   "A Modern Medieval Family." *Mother Jones*, July–August.

Hoffnagel, Judith Chambliss
1979   "The Believers: Pentecostalism in a Brazilian City," Ph.D. dissertation, University of California at Berkeley.

Holdcroft, L. Thomas
1980   "The New Order of the Latter Rain." *Pneuma* 2(2):46–60.

Holland, Clifton
1981   *World Christianity: Central America and the Caribbean*. Monrovia, Calif.: Missions Advanced Research Center, World Vision.

Hollenweger, Walter J.
1986   "After Twenty Years' Research on Pentecostalism." *International Review of Mission*, January, pp. 3–12.

Holy See
1986   "Sects or New Religious Movements: Pastoral Challenge." Vatican City, Rome: Press Office of the Holy See.

Hundley, Ray
1981   "The Dangers of Liberation Theology," *Global Church Growth Bulletin* 18(6):149–50.
1983   *A Primer on Liberation Theology*. Greenwood, Ind.: OMS International.
1986   "The Impact of Liberation Theology on Latin American Evangelicals." *United Evangelical Action* (National Association of Evangelicals), March–April, pp. 7–8.

Hunter, James Davison
1983   *American Evangelicalism*. New Brunswick, N.J.: Rutgers University Press.

Huntington, Deborah, and Enrique Domínguez
1984   "The Salvation Brokers: Conservative Evangelicals in Central America." *NACLA Report on the Americas* 18(1). [Response, 18(3):17–18.]

Hutcheson, Richard G., Jr.
1981   *Mainline Churches and the Evangelicals*. Atlanta: John Knox Press.

Institute on Religion and Democracy
1983   "The Subversion of the Church in Nicaragua: An Interview with Miguel Bolaños Hunter." Briefing Paper no. 1, Washington, D.C.

1984a   "The Grenada Documents: Archive of Church Subversion.
         An Interview with Dr. Michael A. Ledeen." Briefing Paper
         no. 3, Washington, D.C.

1984b   "IRD Report: Church Support for Pro-Sandinista Net-
         work." Washington, D.C.

1985   "Who Speaks for Nicaragua's Protestants? An Interview
         with Kate Rafferty of Open Doors." *Religion and Democ-
         racy,* January; reprinted in *The Presbyterian Layman,*
         March–April, pp. 8–9.

1986   "State of Siege: Nicaragua's Protestants. A Press Confer-
         ence with Jimmy Hassan." Briefing Paper no. 7, Washing-
         ton, D.C.

Johnstone, P. J.

1982   *Operation World,* 3d ed. Bromley, Kent, England: Send
         the Light Books.

1986   *Operation World,* 4th ed. Bromley, Kent, England: STL
         Books and WEC International.

Kaleli, Joseph

1984   "Missionary Communication." *International Journal of
         Frontier Missions* 1(1):75–82.

Keyes, Lawrence

1983   *The Last Age of Missions: A Study of Third World Mission-
         ary Societies.* Pasadena, Calif.: William Carey Library.

Kietzman, Dale W.

1985   *Central America: Into the Crossfire.* Basingstoke, Hamp-
         shire, England: Marshall, Morgan and Scott.

1986   *The Strategic Triangle.* Canoga Park, Calif.: World Litera-
         ture Crusade.

Kinsler, F. Ross

1978   "Theological Education by Extension: Service or Subver-
         sion?" *Missiology* 6(2):181–96.

Klassen, Henry

1976   "An Accurate Picture of the Quichua Church of the Chim-
         borazo Province of Ecuador." Paper for the School of World
         Mission, Fuller Theological Seminary.

Klassen, Jacob Peter

1975   "Fire on the Páramo." Master's thesis, School of World Mis-
         sion and Institute of Church Growth, Fuller Theological
         Seminary.

Lalive d'Epinay, Christian

1969   *Haven of the Masses.* London: Lutterworth Press.

1983 "Political Regimes and Millenarianism in a Dependent Society: Reflections on Pentecostalism in Chile." *Concilium* (New York), no. 161, pp. 42–54.

Lancaster, Roger Nelson
1986 "Thanks to God and the Revolution: Class Consciousness in the New Nicaragua." Ph.D. dissertation, University of California at Berkeley.

Lara-Braud, Jorge
1983 "The Role of North Americans in the Future of the Missionary Enterprise." *International Bulletin of Missionary Research,* January, pp. 2–5.

Lentz, Carola
1985 "Protestantismo y Migración." In *Aportes Básicos para la Comprensión de las Sectas en el Ecuador,* pp. 84–89. Subcomisión "Hermanos Separados" de la Diócesis de Riobamba, Riobamba, Ecuador.

Lernoux, Penny
1980 *Cry of the People.* New York: Doubleday.

Levine, Daniel H.
1985 "Religion and Politics: Drawing Lines, Understanding Change." *Latin American Research Review* 20(1):185–201.

Levine, Daniel H., ed.
1979 *Churches and Politics in Latin America.* Beverly Hills, Calif.: Sage Publications.
1986 *Religion and Political Conflict in Latin America.* Chapel Hill: University of North Carolina Press.

Liebman, Robert C., and Robert Wuthnow, eds.
1983 *The New Christian Right.* New York: Aldine.

Lindsell, Harold
1976 *The Battle for the Bible.* Grand Rapids, Mich.: Zondervan.

Lissner, Jörgen
1977 *The Politics of Altruism.* Geneva: Lutheran World Federation.

McGavran, Donald
1955 *The Bridges of God.* London: World Dominion Press
1970 *Understanding Church Growth.* Grand Rapids, Mich.: Eerdman's.

McLoughlin, William G.
1978 *Revivals, Awakenings and Reform: An Essay on Religion and Social Change in America, 1607–1977.* Chicago: University of Chicago Press.

Mainwaring, Scott
    1986   *The Catholic Church and Politics in Brazil, 1916–1985.* Stanford, Calif.: Stanford University Press.

Marsden, George
    1980   *Fundamentalism and American Culture.* New York: Oxford University Press.

Marsden, George, ed.
    1984   *Evangelicalism and Modern America.* Grand Rapids, Mich.: Eerdman's.

Maynard, Eileen et al.
    1965   "Indians in Misery: A Preliminary Report on the Colta Lake Zone, Chimborazo, Ecuador." Ithaca, N.Y.: Department of Anthropology, Cornell University.
    1966   *The Indians of Colta.* Ithaca, N.Y.: Department of Anthropology, Cornell University.

Melville, Thomas, and Margarita Bradford Melville
    1977   "Oppression by Any Other Name." In *Ideology and Social Change in Latin America,* ed. June Nash et al., pp. 267–94. New York: Gordon and Breach.

Menzies, William W.
    1971   *Anointed to Serve: The Story of the Assemblies of God.* Springfield, Mo.: Gospel Publishing House.

Miguez Bonino, José
    1985   "Presencia y ausencia protestante en la Argentina del proceso militar, 1976–1983." *Cristianismo y Sociedad,* no. 83, pp. 81–85.

Millett, Richard
    1979   *Guardianes de la Dinastia.* Ciudad Universitaria Rodrigo Facio, Costa Rica: Editorial Universitaria Centroamericana.

Molina Saborío, Arturo
    1984   "Imagen del Protestantismo en Costa Rica 1983." San José, Costa Rica: Publicaciones IINDEF.

Mondragón, Rafael
    1983   *De indios y cristianos en Guatemala.* Mexico City: COPEC/CECOPE.

Montgomery, T. S.
    1979   "Latin American Evangelicals: Oaxtepec and Beyond." In *Churches and Politics in Latin America,* ed. Daniel H. Levine, pp. 87–107. Beverly Hills, Calif.: Sage Publications.

Muñoz, Mardoqueo
  1984   "Un estudio del ministerio pastoral y del iglecrecimiento
            entre los presbiterianos en Guatemala." Dissertation,
            School of World Mission, Fuller Theological Seminary.
Muratorio, Blanca
  1980   "Protestantism and Capitalism Revisted in the Rural High-
            lands of Ecuador." *The Journal of Peasant Studies* 8:37–61.
  1981   "Protestantism, Ethnicity, and Class in Chimborazo." In
            *Cultural Transformations and Ethnicity in Modern Ecua-
            dor,* ed. Norman E. Whitten, Jr., pp. 506–34. Urbana: Uni-
            versity of Illinois Press.
National Council of Churches
  1984   "Report of Delegation to Investigate 'Religious Persecution'
            in Nicaragua." New York.
Nelson, Susan Rosales
  1984   "The Kingdom at Hand: Religion and Politics in Highland
            Bolivia." Ph.D. dissertation, University of Michigan.
Nelson, Wilton M.
  1963   *A History of Protestantism in Costa Rica.* Lucknow, India:
            Lucknow Publishing House.
  1982   *El protestantismo en Centro América.* San José, Costa Rica:
            Editorial Caribe.
  1983   *Historia del protestantismo en Costa Rica.* San José, Costa
            Rica: Publicaciones IINDEF.
Nida, Eugene A.
  1954   *Customs and Cultures: Anthropology for Christian Mis-
            sions.* New York: Harper and Brothers.
  1981   "Why Are Foreigners So Queer? A Socioanthropological
            Approach to Cultural Pluralism." *International Bulletin of
            Missionary Research,* July, pp. 102–6.
Novak, Michael
  1982   "Why Latin America Is Poor." *Atlantic Monthly,* March, pp.
            66–75.
  1984   "The Case Against Liberation Theology." *New York Times
            Magazine,* October 21.
  1986   *Will It Liberate?* Mahwah, N.J.: Paulist Press.
Núñez C., Emilio Antonio, Jim Montgomery and Galo E. Vásquez
  1983   *La hora de Dios para Guatemala.* Guatemala City: Editores
            SEPAL.
Ohland, Klaudine and Robin Schneider
  1983   *National Revolution and Indigenous Identity.* Copenhagen:
            International Work Group for Indigenous Affairs.

Subcommittee on Security and Terrorism
1984   *Marxism and Christianity in Revolutionary Central America.* Hearings, October 18–19, 1983, Judiciary Committee, U.S. Senate. Washington, D.C.: U.S. Government Printing Office.

Tapp, Nicolas
1986   "Christianity in China Today." *Anthropology Today* 2(2):10–12.

Tayacán
1984   "Psychological Operations in Guerrilla Warfare." Translated by Congressional Research Service, Language Services, October 15.

Taylor, William D.
1984   "Central America: Can We Cap the Cauldron?" *Pulse* (Wheaton, Ill.: Evangelical Missions Information Service), April 18, pp. 1–8.

Torres, José Miguel
1981   "El cristianismo protestante en la revolución sandinista." *Nicaráuac*, April–June, pp. 38–47.

Townsend, William Cameron
1940   *The Truth About Mexico's Oil.* Los Angeles: Inter-American Fellowship.

Tucker, Ruth A.
1983   *From Jerusalem to Irian Jaya.* Grand Rapids, Mich.: Zondervan.

Tulio Cajas, Marco
1985   "La tarea política de los evangélicos" [pamphlet]. Guatemala City: Ediciones MAS.

Turner, Frederick C.
1970   "Protestantism and Politics in Chile and Brazil." *Comparative Studies in Society and History* 12(2):213–29.

U.S. Department of State
1985   "Inside the Sandinista Regime: A Special Investigator's Perspective" [testimony of Alvaro José Baldizon Áviles]. Office of Public Diplomacy for Latin America and the Caribbean, Washington, D.C.

Wagner, C. Peter
1970   *Latin American Theology, Radical or Evangelical?* Grand Rapids, Mich.: Eerdman's.
1973   *Cuidado! Ahí vienen los Pentecostales.* Miami: Editorial Vida.

1981   *Church Growth and the Whole Gospel.* San Francisco: Harper & Row.
1983   *On the Crest of the Wave.* Ventura, Calif.: Regal Books.
Wagner, C. Peter, and Edward R. Dayton, eds.
1981   *Unreached Peoples '81.* Elgin, Ill.: David C. Cook Company.
Wagner, Doris M.
1984   *Missiological Abstracts: The School of World Mission, Fuller Theological Seminary, 1966–84.* Pasadena, Calif.: Fuller Theological Seminary.
Walker, Andrew
1985   *Restoring the Kingdom.* London: Hodder and Stoughton.
Wallis, Jim
1986   "A Wolf in Sheep's Clothing: The Political Right Invades the Evangelical Fold." *Sojourners*, May, pp. 20–23.
Wallis, Jim, and Wes Michaelson
1976   "The Plan to Save America." *Sojourners*, April, pp. 4–12.
Ward, C. Edward
1986   "The Laws of the Kingdom and God's Redemptive Purposes in Central America" [tape cassette]. Severna Park, Md.: Maranatha Tape Ministry.
Weber, Timothy P.
1983   *Living in the Shadow of the Second Coming,* enlarged ed. Grand Rapids, Mich.: Zondervan.
Weerstra, Hans
1972   "Maya Peasant Evangelism." Dissertation, School of World Mission, Fuller Theological Seminary.
Westmeier, Karl-Wilhelm
1986   "The Enthusiastic Protestants of Bogotá, Colombia." *International Review of Mission* (Geneva: World Council of Churches), January, pp. 13–24.
White, Tom
1981   *Missiles over Cuba.* Upland, Calif.: Faith Messenger Publications.
Wilde, Margaret D.
1986   "Liberation Theology and U.S. Security Policy in Latin America." Unpublished paper presented at the Annual Meeting, Midwest Association for Latin American Studies, St. Louis, September 25–27.
Willems, Emilio
1967   *Followers of the New Faith.* Nashville, Tenn.: Vanderbilt University Press.

Wilson, Bryan
　　1970　　*Religious Sects*. London: Weidenfeld and Nicolson.
Wilson, J. Christy, Jr.
　　1979　　*Today's Tentmakers*. Wheaton, Ill.: Tyndale House.
Wilson, Samuel, and John Siewert
　　1986　　*Mission Handbook*. 13th ed. Monrovia, Calif.: Missions Advanced Research and Communication Center, World Vision.
Wimber, John
　　1984　　*Signs and Wonders and Church Growth*. Placentia, Calif.: Vineyard Ministries International.
Winebrenner, Jan
　　1985　　*Steel in His Soul: The Dick Hillis Story*. Milpitas, Calif.: Overseas Crusades.
Winter, Ralph D.
　　1980　　*The Twenty-Five Unbelievable Years, 1945–1969*. 8th ed. Pasadena, Calif.: William Carey Library.
Wolf, Eric R.
　　1982　　*Europe and the People Without History*. Berkeley: University of California Press.
Wood, Thomas P.
　　1900　　"South America as a Mission Field." In *Protestant Missions in South America*, ed. Harlan P. Beach, pp. 197–215. Chicago: Student Volunteer Movement for Foreign Missions.
World Vision International
　　1981　　"A Report on the Refugee Relief Program of World Vision in Honduras." Monrovia, Calif. December 17.
Youngren, J. Alan
　　1982　　"The Shell Game Donors Love to Lose." *Christianity Today*, June 18, pp. 39–41.
Zapata A., Virgilio
　　1982　　*Historia de la obra evangélica en Guatemala*. Guatemala City: Génesis Publicidad.

INDEX

Abortion, 53
Activism: Catholic, xviii–xix, 37–39, 116–17, 140–41, 142, 311; "evangelical left," 52; military coups and, 315; pentecostal, 116–17; premillennialist, 43; vs. relief and development, 270. *See also* Liberation theology; Radicals
Acts, Book of, 49
Adams, Richard N., 331
Adveniat, 35
Adventist Development and Relief Agency, 271n
Adventists. *See* Seventh Day Adventists
"Afghan Institute of Technology," 79n–80n
Afghanistan, 79n–80n, 250
Africa: famine in, 90, 150n; after Libya bombing, 154; as mission field, 78, 97, 154, 155; relief for, 283, 284; Seventh Day Adventists in, 103; Umbanda from, 114
"Agape" organization, 165
Age: in mainline denominations, 45–46. *See also* Youth
Aid. *See* Finances; Relief and development
"Airmail from God," 249
Alcino the Condor, 354n2
Alcohol addiction, 13, 183, 273–74
Alfonsín, Raul, 179
Allende, Salvador, 111–12, 160, 315, 316
Alliance for Progress, 117–18, 119
Alpha and Omega Movement, 164
Álvarez, Gustavo, 15n
Alves, Rubem, 315, 330
Amazon Jungle, 16
American Bible Society (ABS), 84–85
American Coalition for Traditional Values, 54, 357n64

Amerindians, 15–17, 85–90, 104, 105, 318; civil rights movements of, 165, 230–31, 273, 276, 303, 330; in Ecuador, xviii–xix, 266–82, 289–304; in Guatemala, 20, 136, 144, 181, 182, 190–204 passim, 212–14, 215–16; in Mexico, 15–16, 85–87, 88, 113, 116–17; in Nicaragua, 17, 230–33, 250, 251, 256–57, 261; U.S., 231
"Amillennialism," 64
Amnesty International, 171, 205, 208n
Anastasis, 70, 92–94
Andean Evangelical Mission, 118
Anderson, Jack, 250n
Anderson, Robert Mapes, 115
Andes, xx, 7, 8, 16. *See also* Bolivia; Colombia; Ecuador; Peru
Andrew. *See* Brother Andrew
Anglicans/Episcopalians, 4–5, 46n, 168
Angola, 250
Annis, Sheldon, 11–12, 201–2
Anthropology, 84–90, 278, 281, 300
Antibiotics, Maya and, 87
Anticlericalism, 25, 85, 129
Antonio Valdivieso Ecumenical Center, 235
Apathy, spiritual, 7
"Apolitical" evangelicals, 5, 19–20, 111, 141, 301–2; in Nicaragua, 228, 240, 260–61; and religious right, 5, 154–55, 157
Arabs, 79. *See also* Middle East
Arbenz administration, 129, 193
Arcadia, California, 92
Arce, Bayardo, 234
Archbishops, Catholic, 32
Argentina: dictatorship in, 178–79; Jehovah's Witnesses in, 107; Mormons in,

El Salvador, 157, 166–69, 326; anticommunist crusades in, 149–50; Catholic activists in, 39, 142; growth of church in, 9, 166–67, 328; Reagan election and, 53; student ministry in, 163n, 165; and Swaggart, 153, 322; World Vision and, 268, 270, 285, 286–88

Emotional capture: by evangelicals, 314. *See also* Personal improvement; Personal relation, with Christ

Episcopalians/Anglicans, 4–5, 46n, 168

Equal Rights Amendment, 53

Escobar, Samuel, 132, 175

Ethiopia, 150n, 284

Ethnic groups, 16–17, 72; Nicaraguan, 230–31, 261. *See also* Amerindians; Blacks

Ethnotheology, 88–90

Eureka, California, 183

Europe: Catholic subsidies from, 35; church attendance drop in, 77; Eastern, 150, 151, 159–60; and Lausanne Committee, 73; missionaries funded by, 70; as mission field, 77; Protestant immigrants from, 5; Reformation in, xiii–xiv, 4–5, 22, 40, 309, 330; relief and development funds from, 245, 283; social reformation in, 317

Evangelical Alliance of Guatemala (AEG), 214–15

"Evangelical alliances"/"councils," 155

Evangelical Commission for the Promotion of Social Responsibility (CEPRES), 235

Evangelical Committee for Aid to Development (CEPAD), 224–25, 233–34, 241–48 passim, 257, 264, 265; CNPEN vs., 242–47 passim, 262; and pastoral traininig, 178n; and relief and development, 178n, 224, 225, 242, 245, 255, 285

Evangelical Council of Venezuela (CEV), 134

Evangelical Foreign Missions Association (EFMA), 154–55, 156

Evangelical Indian Association of Chimborazo (AIECH), 278, 280, 290, 294–96, 300–302

Evangelical Indian Association of Imbabura, 302

Evangelical Indian Association of Tungurahua (AIET), 301, 303–4

Evangelical Missions Quarterly, 97

Evangelical Protestantism, xiii–xv, xvi, xvii–xix, 99–134; authority in, 36–37, 46–47 (*see also* Authoritarianism;

Leadership); Catholics imitating, 27, 29–30, 33–34, 40; defined, 3, 51; and ecumenism with Catholics, 30–33; growth of, *see* Growth; Latin American meaning of, 4 (*see also individual countries*); vs. liberation theology, xviii–xix, 20–22, 23, 137–47, 170–71; mission movement of, 68–98, 118–19 (*see also* North American evangelical missionaries); in Nicaragua, 218–65; North American, 42–67 (*see also* North American evangelical missionaries; Religious right, U.S.); pentecostal, *see* Pentecostals; persecution of, *see* Persecution; polarization within, xvi, 9–10, 19–23, 43–44, 128–34; politics of, *see* Politics; of poor (general), xiv–xv, xvi, xvii, xix, 13, 21–22, 26, 115, 314; as popular movement, xv, 10, 13–14, 29–30, 311, 328–31; as sects, 5–6, 40, 176; U.S. meaning of, 4. *See also* Neoevangelicals

Evangelicals for Social Action, 52, 161

Evangelism: Catholic, 30, 33–34; in depth, 117–21, 125, 170, 177, 275; disaster, 10–13; "frontier," 83; media, 68–69 (*see also* Radio; Television evangelists); "waves" of, 101. *See also* Evangelical Protestantism; Missionaries

Evangelism in Depth campaigns, 119–20, 177, 275

Evangelism to Communist Lands, 150n

Evolutionism, 42, 48, 52–53

"Explo 85," 92

Fagoth, Steadman, 232, 233, 252, 257

Faith America Foundation, 54

"Faith confession" movement, 50, 60

Faith healing, 13, 33; Catholic charismatics and, 29–30, 37; pentecostal, 49–50, 59, 87, 113, 114, 118

"Faith missions," 5, 47, 101, 118, 154–55

Fajardo, Andrés, 202

Falwell, Jerry, 43, 49, 53–54, 192

Family, conversion affecting, 13, 114, 318–19

Family of Love, 14n

Fanaticism, 5–6, 61

Far East, 14, 155, 160. *See also individual countries*

Fascism, 71

FDN (Nicaraguan Democratic Force), 222–65. *See also* Contras, Nicaraguan

Febres Cordero, León, 301

Federation of Ecuadorian Indians (FEI), 300

González, Jonas, 171
Good Samaritan, 70
Gospel Crusade, 252, 325
Gospel Missionary Union (GMU), 101, 155n, 272–75, 280, 281, 293–300 passim
Gospel Outreach, 105, 182–85, 186, 192, 206, 261
Government: and evangelicals helping refugees, 168; human rights violations of, *see* Human rights violations; Sandinista idea of, 220–21. *See also* Dictatorships; Electoral politics; Militarism; Revolution; Theocracy; *individual countries*
Graham, Billy: on Barbados, 118–19; and CONELA, 133, 134; and Lausanne Congress, 73; Mooneyham with, 282; Palau and, 121, 122; and religious right, 53–54, 67; Savage with, 132; and social concern, 48, 52; sponsorships by, 155, 160; from Youth for Christ, 71. *See also* Billy Graham Evangelistic Association
Great Britain, 7, 179
Great Commission, 3, 64, 67, 77, 82–83, 92, 96
Great Salt Lake, 104
Grenada, religious right and, 145–48
Grimstead, Jay, 54
Growth, 327, 331; FTL and, 174–75; Guatemalan evangelical, 9, 12, 180, 202–3; of Jehovah's Witnesses, 107; Latin American evangelical (overall), xiv, xv, xvi–xvii, 6–9, 101, 337–38; Mormon, 105; Nicaraguan evangelical, 8, 118, 257, 258, 265; pentecostal, 76–77, 101, 107–8, 179; Salvadoran evangelical, 9, 166–67, 328; Seventh Day Adventist, 103. *See also* Churchgrowth movement
Guacho, Ana Maria, 293
Guatemala, xix–xx, 114–15, 180–217, 261, 326; Amerindians in, 20, 136, 144, 181, 182, 190–204 passim, 212–14, 215–16; anticommunist crusades in, 149–50; Arbenz administration in, 129, 193; Catholics and, xviii, 3, 39, 142, 144, 180, 181, 182, 185, 193–95, 208, 211, 212, 311; DAWN in, 32; earthquake in, 11–12, 184; Evangelism in Depth in, 120; Gospel Outreach and, 184–85; growth of evangelicalism in, 9, 12, 180, 202–3; hundredth anniversary of Protestantism in, 1–3, 189–90; and liberation theology, 39, 142,

144, 181, 190, 311; Mormons in, 105, 106; Palau and, 1–3, 122, 206; pastoral training in, 126; population of Protestants in, 9, 125, 180; Presbyterians in, 347n8; Reagan election and, 53; religious right and, 136, 157, 158, 159, 182, 185, 206, 211–12; SEPAL in, 124; SIL in, 156, 182, 191, 197–99, 202; Stam in, 171–72; Texan businessmen visiting, 306; Unification Church in, 15n; U.S. overthrow of government in, 141; YWAM in, 93–94. *See also* Ríos Montt, Efraín
Guatemalan Church in Exile, 194–95
Guerrilla Army of the Poor (EGP), Guatemalan, 144, 193–203 passim
Guerrillas: government violence blamed on, 158–59, 192, 213n; Guatemalan, 144, 181, 185–205 passim, 212, 213, 214, 215; during Nicaraguan Somoza regime, 224–25; religious right and, 158–59, 160, 179; Salvadoran, 167, 168, 169n, 288. *See also* Revolutionaries
Guevara, Aníbal, 186
Gulf Coast Bible College, 146
Guth, James, 56
Gutiérrez, Jaime, 167
Guyana: businessmen visiting, 226n, 305; decline of Protestants in, 8, 331; Jonestown in, 14n, 92, 226n, 306

Hacienda regime, 13; in Ecuador, 272–76 passim, 291–92, 299–300; pentecostals and, 319. *See also* Patronage/Paternalism
Haddad, Saad, 69, 250
Hagin, Kenneth, 50
Haiti, 8, 113, 269
Hare Krishna, 14
Hargis, Billy James, 149
Hasbrouck, John, 250
Hassan, Jimmy, 263–64
Hatch, Al, 96
Haven of the Masses (Lalive d'Epinay), 319
Hawk, Tom, 251, 252, 253
Haymaker, Edward, 347n8
Healing: by magic, 112, 113. *See also* Faith healing; Medicine
Heneise, Sheila, 239
Heng Samrin, 284
"Heresy trial," 171
Hermeneutics, 88–89
Herrera, Leticia, 234

Son Sann, 250
Sorcery, 77, 117
Sosa Ávila family, 188, 214
South America, xx. *See also* Andes;
  Southern Cone; *individual countries*
South American Mission, 155n
Southeast Asia, 271, 283. *See also individual countries*
Southern Baptist Convention (SBC), 55–56
Southern Baptists, 53–56, 157; and CIA,
  148; in El Salvador, 168; growth strategies of, 126, 127; in Nicaragua, 229;
  population of, 46–47
Southern California, 38, 68–69, 90, 91,
  155, 215
Southern Cone, 8, 15n, 130, 315. *See also individual countries*
Soviet Union, 145, 149
Spain, xiii, 25, 129
Speaking in tongues, 29–30, 49, 100
Spiritism, 114, 317–18. *See also* Magic
Stam, John, 171–73, 177
State. *See* Government; Politics
State Department, U.S., 80n, 162, 271,
  324
State of emergency, Nicaraguan, 261–65
Stendal, Russell, 17n-18n
Stewart, Lyman, 68
Stewart, Milton, 68
Strachan, Harry, 118
Strachan, Kenneth, 119
Strachan, Susan, 118
"Strategic triangle," 169
Strike: in Ecuador, 300; "social," 129
Stroessner, Alfredo, 122, 305–6
Students: in El Salvador, 167; ministry
  with, 62–63, 163–66; Sandinistas led
  by, 219–20. *See also* Campus Crusade
  for Christ; Seminaries
Sugden, Chris, 95–97
Suicide, Jonestown, 14n, 226n
Summer Institute of Linguistics (SIL), 17;
  in Bolivia, 122; in Colombia, 17–18; in
  Ecuador, 281–82, 289, 301, 372n35;
  founder of, 347n8; in Guatemala, 156,
  182, 191, 197–99, 202; in Mexico, 18,
  85–86, 116; in Nicaragua, 17; in Peru,
  330; USAID funds for, 272n; Vatican
  and, 32
"Super churches," 69
Supreme Court, U.S., 52–53
Suriname, 8, 331
Survivalism, 184, 317, 331. *See also*
  World, end of
Survival of the fittest, 58

Swaggart, Jimmy, 43, 123, 152–54, 163,
  305–7, 308, 322–23

Tabasco, Mexico, 7
Taiwan, 71, 160
"Taking dominion," xvii, 58–60, 63–66
Tamayo, Jesús, 266–67, 303–4
Taxes: Guatemalan, 208, 210; Protestant
  exemptions, 33, 49
Taylor, William, 40
TEE (Theological Education by Extension), 126, 176–78, 275
Television: Nicaraguan pastor's criticism
  of, 237; World Vision fundraising with,
  283. *See also* Television evangelists
Television evangelists, 43, 49–50, 60, 98;
  Palau as, 122–24; religious right, xix,
  53, 139, 151–53, 321–22. *See also* Robertson, Pat; Swaggart, Jimmy
Tellez, Dora María, 244, 247
Tenesaca, Delfín, 372n35
"Tent-makers," 79–80, 83
Texan businessmen: and Campus Crusade, 162; in Full Gospel Businessmen's Fellowship, 226n, 227, 306; and
  Swaggart, 305–7
Theocracy, xvii, 58–59, 207
Theologians: vs. church growthers, 76;
  vs. conservative church leaders, 175–78. *See also* Latin American Theological Fraternity
Theological Education by Extension
  (TEE), 126, 176–78, 275
Theology: evangelical, 47–51. *See also*
  Dominion theology; Liberation theology; Theologians
"Third way," 132
Third World: Bible smugglers and, 151;
  and Lausanne Congress, 73; missionaries from, 80–81, 124–25; nationalism
  of, 16–17, 71, 90, 98, 107, 221; Stam
  on, 172. *See also* Africa; Asia; Latin
  America; *individual countries*
Three-Self Patriotic Movement, 78–79
Toleration: religious, 280. *See also* Ecumenism
Tomá, Nicolás (Pastor Nicolás), 196–98,
  200, 202
Torture: in Argentina, 179; in El Salvador, 168; in Guatemala, 204, 208n,
  213, 214, 261; in Nicaragua, 250n, 256,
  261, 264
"Total mobilization," 119, 177
Totonacs, 116–17
Townsend, William Cameron, 347n8

Vatican II (1962–1965), 27, 28, 31, 41, 118, 130, 277
Vekemans, Roger, 14
Venezuela, 7, 8
"Verticalism," 38
Vicente Menchú Revolutionary Christians, 186
"Victory Seminars," 236
Vietnam: relief in, 284; War, xv, 52, 66, 71, 148, 255, 327
Violence, 137, 141–42, 148–49, 165, 314, 331; Christian, 279–82; in Colombia, 17–18, 26; in Ecuador, 274; in El Salvador, 142, 166–67; in Guatemala, 20, 142, 188–205 passim, 213–15; in Mexico, 26; against Mormons, 106; in Nicaragua, 218, 221, 227, 231, 232, 233–35, 239, 250–65 passim. *See also* Armies; Human rights violations; Murders; Persecution; Rape; War
Violencia, 26
Virgin Mary cults, 40
Visa restrictions, for missionaries, 32–33, 105
Vision of the Disinherited (Anderson), 115
Visions, 208
"Voice of Americanism" radio, 149
"Voice of the Andes," 80
Volkswagen factory, Mexico, 116–17
Voodoo, 113

Wages: in Ecuador, 276, 300. *See also* Salaries
Wagner, Peter, 76, 97, 131
Walker, William, 238
War, 327; Cold, 150, 161, 282, 284; just, 142; Korean, 268, 282; Malvinas, 7, 179; nuclear (predicted), 42, 57; spiritual, 61; Vietnam, xv, 52, 71, 148, 255, 327; World War II, 71, 101. *See also* Civil wars; Peace movement; Revolution
Ward, Ted, 328–29
War of the End of the World (Vargas Llosa), 108
Washington Times, 66, 206
Watchtower Bible and Tract Society, 106
Watergate scandal, 52, 66
WEF (World Evangelical Fellowship), 155–56, 163n
Weiner, Bob, 62
Westmeier, Karl-Wilhelm, 113
Wheaton College, 52, 84, 171
Whitbeck, Harris, 191
White, Ellen G., 103

Willems, Emilio, 13, 101, 110, 111, 315
Willimon, William, 45
Wilson, Bryan, 6
Wilson, Monte, 68
Winter, Ralph, 82–83, 97
Witches, 113, 117
Woellner, David, 15
Women: and conversion, 13, 318–19; Guatemalan army treatment of, 199, 204; rape of, 193, 199, 203–4, 213n, 325
Wood, Thomas, 24
Word Church, 37n, 181–93, 198–211 passim
"Word power," 59–60
World, end of, 43, 56–57, 103, 215. *See also* Christ: return of; Millennialism
World Anti-Communist League, 162
World Christian Encyclopedia, 77
World Concern, 70, 155n, 270, 272n
World Council of Churches (WCC), 4, 45, 102, 129; CEDEN breaking with, 288; Ecumenical Axis and, 240; ISAL affiliated with, 130; Latin American Council of Churches dependent on, 132; Moravians in, 256; pentecostals in, 320
World Evangelical Fellowship (WEF), 155–56, 163n
World Literature Crusade (WLC), 135, 155n, 159, 168–69
World Neighbors, 70, 272n
World Radio Missionary Fellowship, 155n
World Relief Corporation (WRC), 70, 270, 272n; in El Salvador, 168; in Nicaragua, 250–52; and religious right, 157, 171, 251–52
World Vision, 70, 90, 91, 134, 266–73, 282–304, 305; development of, 282–86; in Ecuador, xviii–xix, 266–73, 282, 289–304; in EFMA, 155n; finances of, 266–68, 270, 272, 282–90 passim, 294–304 passim, 373nn45, 48; in Honduras, 272, 286–89; Missions Advanced Research Center of, 69, 82, 97–98; and religious right, 157, 160, 171; USAID funds for, 272n, 282–83, 284
World War II, 71, 101
Worldwide Evangelization Crusade, 7, 8
WRC. *See* World Relief Corporation
Wurmbrand, Richard, 69, 150n, 159
Wycliffe Bible Translators, xix, 68, 83–91 passim, 156, 169; field arm of, *see* Summer Institute of Linguistics

Compositor:	Graphic Composition, Inc.
Text:	11/13 Caledonia
Display:	Caledonia
Printer:	Edwards Brothers, Inc.
Binder:	Edwards Brothers, Inc.